COVIDOCRACY

COVIDOCRACY

Do Pandemics Defend Dictatorships and Challenge Democracies?

Nicolai Due-Gundersen

BLOOMSBURY ACADEMIC
LONDON • NEW YORK • OXFORD • NEW DELHI • SYDNEY

BLOOMSBURY ACADEMIC
Bloomsbury Publishing Plc, 50 Bedford Square, London, WC1B 3DP, UK
Bloomsbury Publishing Inc, 1359 Broadway, New York, NY 10018, USA
Bloomsbury Publishing Ireland, 29 Earlsfort Terrace, Dublin 2, D02 AY28, Ireland

BLOOMSBURY, BLOOMSBURY ACADEMIC and the Diana logo are
trademarks of Bloomsbury Publishing Plc

First published in Great Britain 2026

Copyright © Nicolai Due-Gundersen, 2026

Nicolai Due-Gundersen has asserted his right under the Copyright, Designs and
Patents Act, 1988, to be identified as Author of this work.

Cover image © Inna/Adobe Stock

All rights reserved. No part of this publication may be: i) reproduced or transmitted in
any form, electronic or mechanical, including photocopying, recording or by means of
any information storage or retrieval system without prior permission in writing from the
publishers; or ii) used or reproduced in any way for the training, development or operation
of artificial intelligence (AI) technologies, including generative AI technologies. The rights
holders expressly reserve this publication from the text and data mining exception as per
Article 4(3) of the Digital Single Market Directive (EU) 2019/790.

Bloomsbury Publishing Plc does not have any control over, or responsibility for, any
third-party websites referred to or in this book. All internet addresses given in this
book were correct at the time of going to press. The author and publisher regret
any inconvenience caused if addresses have changed or sites have ceased
to exist, but can accept no responsibility for any such changes.

A catalogue record for this book is available from the British Library.

Library of Congress Cataloging-in-Publication Data available

ISBN:	HB:	978-1-3505-8124-1
	PB:	978-1-3505-8125-8
	ePDF:	978-1-3505-8127-2
	eBook:	978-1-3505-8126-5

Typeset by Integra Software Services Pvt. Ltd.
Printed and bound in Great Britain

For product safety related questions contact productsafety@bloomsbury.com.

To find out more about our authors and books visit www.bloomsbury.com
and sign up for our newsletters.

For my wife, Arwa. Thank you for taking this journey with me and for your constant support for the past eleven years. You taught me that dreams can come true.

CONTENTS

List of Figures ix

Chapter 1
WE ARE NOT PREPARED 1
Analyzing the Politics of Pandemics 1
Vaccines as Nationalism or Diplomacy? 6
Social Movements, Public Spaces 8

Chapter 2
A HISTORY OF PANDEMICS 19
This Is Not the Flu 19
Legitimizing State Control under Covid 20
What Is a Coronavirus? 24
A Historical Context of Pandemics 26
    The 1918–20 H1N1 Spanish Flu 26
    The 2003 SARS Outbreak 35
    The 2009 H1N1 Pandemic 43
    The 2012 MERS Virus 54
Social Movements, Anxieties, and Pandemics 60
Vaccine Nationalism, Viral Sovereignty, Vaccine Diplomacy, and International Legitimacy 78
Pandemics Require International and Domestic Cooperation 86

Chapter 3
CASE STUDIES 87
Maintaining Government Power 87
China, Wuhan, and Power 88
Saudi Arabia and Reform 92
The UK and Brexit 99
Trump: Making America Great Again 103
Understanding Isolationism in Brexit Britain and Trump's America 109
Pandemic Profiteers 110
Power and Exploitation 121

Chapter 4
COVID SPREADS: THE SPEECHES OF PANDEMIC POLITICS 123
Citizens Turn to the State 123
Speeches of Legitimacy during Covid 123
    China's Premier Li Keqiang 123

    Saudi Arabia's King Salman   132
    Britain's Prime Minister Boris Johnson   134
    America's President Trump   138
  Economic Performance, Nationalism, and Isolationism   146

Chapter 5
PUBLIC DISCOURSE OF THE VACCINE RACE   147
  Vaccine Nationalism or Vaccine Diplomacy?   147
  Vaccines, Nationalism, and Diplomacy   147
    China's President Xi Jinping   147
    Saudi Arabia's Crown Prince Mohammed bin Salman   151
    Britain's Prime Minister Boris Johnson   153
    America's President Trump   155
  International Cooperation against Pandemics   157

Chapter 6
WILL THERE BE AN INTERNATIONAL PANDEMIC TREATY?   159

Chapter 7
CONCLUSION   169

Appendices   174
References   215
Index   244

FIGURES

1.1	A map of mutual aid groups across the UK during Covid in 2020	11
2.1	Global trajectories of the Spanish Flu	26
2.2	Map of the 2009 H1N1 spread by August 2010	44
2.3	Map of MERS spread	54
2.4	Protests and riots during 2020	60
3.1	World leaders meet virtually during the G20 summit held between November 21 and 22, 2020	88
3.2	Worldwide vaccine sales in 2021 by volume	112
3.3	Pandemic wealth increase versus pandemic pay increase	118
4.1	Trust in government during Covid	124

Chapter 1

WE ARE NOT PREPARED

Analyzing the Politics of Pandemics

The popular (and perhaps prescient) Netflix documentary *Pandemic: How to Prevent an Outbreak* was filmed across the 2018–19 flu season but burst upon our screens in early 2020, just as Covid-19 "was beginning its rampage" (Blake, April 1, 2020). "It's very strange," admitted codirector Doug Shultz, "to look back and see that we sort of took this trip through exactly what is happening right now" (ibid.). Dr. Dennis Carroll's warning ended the series' final episode, emphasizing that "[a] virus will emerge and will spread around the world," joining the voices of many experts in the documentary, like New York City Health Director Dr. Syra Madad, "pleading with politicians about resources for pandemic preparedness" and ominously envisioning "a hypothetical scenario in which a single traveler, arriving by plane in New York City could trigger an overwhelming outbreak that would, within weeks, incapacitate the city" (Netflix, 2020; Blake, 2020).

Within weeks after the documentary aired, the world would go into lockdown. In February of 2020, I returned to London from Saudi Arabia, narrowly avoiding canceled flights as the kingdom announced the suspension of all international travel (Due-Gundersen, June 15, 2020). My first trip to Riyadh showed a city far less complacent than the crowded streets of England. Saudi authorities were on the alert, and so were citizens. As our plane descended into Riyadh, health forms were issued demanding answers as to whether we had transited through Covid-infected countries or exhibited related symptoms. Upon arrival, staff wore surgical masks that would become all too familiar in the next two years. My temperature was taken by an infrared monitor (ibid.).

By the time I'd arrived in Riyadh, social spaces were already being shut. On my second evening, I visited a mall that displayed large posters on the importance of social distancing. As I entered a taxi, my driver voluntarily wore a mask. "Is there anywhere you'd recommend for *argileh*?" I asked him, craving the Middle Eastern water pipe my Palestinian wife had introduced me to in Jordan. He shook his head. "They're all closed. They're popular, always crowded. Another way for coronavirus to spread" (ibid.). As Covid continued, and as this book will discuss, many other social spaces would shut down, including newly opened cinemas, a staple of Mohammed bin Salman's Vision 2030 that is attempting to provide social (rather than political) reforms as a new avenue of the crown prince's political legitimacy (MEED Editorial, April 14, 2020).

I returned to London in March. Gone was talk of "that incident in China," replaced with news flashes as infection rates began in Europe. Then, the lockdowns were announced. For us in the UK, the day came on March 23, 2020, in a statement by then-Prime Minister Boris Johnson. "Without a huge national effort to halt the growth of this virus, there will come a moment when no health service in the world could possibly cope," he emphasized. "And as we have seen elsewhere, in other countries that also have fantastic health care systems, that is the moment of real danger." And then it came: "From this evening, I must give the British people a very simple instruction—you must stay at home. Because the critical thing we must do is stop the disease spreading between households. That is why people will only be allowed to leave their home for the following very limited purposes:

- Shopping for basic necessities, as infrequently as possible
- One form of exercise a day
- Any medical need, to provide care or to help a vulnerable person; and
- Travelling to and from work, but only where this is absolutely necessary and cannot be done from home.

That's all—these are the only reasons you should leave your home" (Johnson, March 23, 2020).

Riyadh announced a nationwide curfew the same day, after only 511 confirmed cases by March 22 (Crisis24, March 23, 2020). By that time, the UK had over 4,000 deaths (Scott, March 5, 2021). China, on the other hand, announced the lockdown of Wuhan, the city where Covid first presented, as early as January 23, 2020. What has been described as one of the harshest restrictions in response to a pandemic would eventually extend to the rest of China's Hubei province, effectively confining 56 million people to their homes (AP, January 22, 2021). In March 2020, Covid was declared a national emergency in President Trump's America. As explained by Trump himself, these "two very big words" allowed the mobilization of billions in emergency relief funds and, among other things, were intended to accelerate the pace of Covid testing at a time when the United States had experienced almost 2,000 confirmed cases and 40 deaths amid criticism of the administration's failure to provide widespread access to coronavirus testing. Individual US states also enacted measures to curb the virus, including the shutdown of sporting events, schools, and the banning of large gatherings. Trump also announced a travel ban on almost thirty European countries (BBC, March 13, 2020).

As various governments announced curfews, lockdowns, and national emergencies to counter Covid's attack, another concern was spreading. To what extent was Covid empowering authoritarianism? Within days of the British lockdown, *The Guardian* journalist Shaun Walker warned from Hungary's capital, Budapest, that "[a]uthoritarian leaders may use Covid-19 to tighten their grip" (March 31, 2020). Walker pointed out that Hungary's Prime Minister Viktor Orbán had enacted emergency measures in response to Covid that criminalized the spreading of misinformation while allowing him to "rule by decree for an indefinite period" (ibid.). In the UK, after almost a year of Covid restrictions, Boris Johnson and his ministers faced their own accusations of "appalling authoritarianism" after enacting tiered lockdowns, which saw different regions face diverse restrictions according to infection rates. Tier Three was reserved for the highest infection rates and hence the toughest restrictions, while Tier One saw the fewest restrictions. The criteria for each tier were not meant to be arbitrary but "included case detection rates in all age groups, the rate at which cases were rising or falling, the number of positive cases detected as a percentage of tests taken and the pressure on the [National Health Service (NHS)]" (Settle, November 26, 2020). Former Brexit Minister Steve Baker, "whose Buckinghamshire constituency was placed in to Tier 2, was aghast at the UK Government announcement." His blunt tweet insisted that "[the] authoritarianism at work today is truly appalling. But is it necessary and proportionate to the threat from this disease? The Government must publish their analysis" (ibid.).

Indeed, 2020 saw many new emergency laws and the mobilization of restrictions akin to wartime. *The Guardian*'s Shaun Walker expressed his fear that such restrictions created a

> terrifying situation in which anyone, anywhere, can be a potential threat [and] is a perfect mobilizing force for authoritarians, and many have explicitly compared the current situation to a state of war, applying military terminology to civilian life, and implying that the kind of restrictions applicable in wartime, when questioning the government could be seen as unpatriotic or even traitorous, should now apply. (March 31, 2020)

By 2022, some argued that "lockdowns, travel restrictions and fines are now the norm all around the world" (Ailoaiei, December 15, 2024). However, 2022 saw a wave of protests in China, where the virus seemed to have started (Sky News, December 1, 2022). This is a far cry from 2020 when the World Health Organization (WHO) praised China's restrictions (Bloomberg News, February 24, 2020). Nonetheless, experts in 2022 still ask if authoritarianism itself spread under the pretext of protection against Covid and if "excessive government powers" were accepted by "compliant publics" (Vowles, May 18, 2022, p. 1). Such concerns build on related literature from 2020 questioning how Covid would influence democracies and dictatorships. "As Covid-19 has swept through one country after another," claimed one Yale blog,

> it has given rise, in many states, to the increased assertion of authority by political executives—an assertion that, however understandable, given the magnitude of the human, social, and economic impact of the pandemic, nevertheless has, in some states, resulted in an erosion and weakening of democratic forms and practices while, in others, it has reinforced and strengthened their reliance on authoritarian politics. (De La O et al., April 24, 2020)

Related to the fear of increased authoritarianism challenging democracies and defending dictatorships is understanding the instruments of enforcing pandemic-related restrictions. Such instruments include not only punishments such as fines or even imprisonment but also the manipulation of citizens' emotions (Mironova, April 1, 2020; Travers, May 1, 2020). London School of Economics Professor Tony Travers argues that the UK's elite caused fear in citizens by constantly "stressing the cost to their lives and the NHS. [The] message has been internalised" because "the government decided to modify people's feelings and emotions" (ibid.). Indeed, "political language used during the Covid-19 pandemic in Britain has featured many references to people being 'called up' to the 'front line' and being provided with the 'equipment to fight' an 'invisible enemy'" (ibid.).

Such language when politicians address Covid restrictions is a reminder that "rhetoric [and discourse] has proven to be a powerful ally in efforts to gain public confidence and influence behavioural change" (Di-Miceli, February 7, 2021). Analyst Augusto Di-Miceli explains that prolonged crises that provoke "governments around the world to enact extraordinary and unprecedented policy measures" force elites to "find alternative tools to public compliance with their stringent policies, [including] [the] art of [political] persuasion," a "powerful method, specifically designed to persuade the public to follow a set of behavioural patterns" (ibid.).

How did leaders of democracies and dictatorships address the threat of Covid? How were speeches used to present Covid as a reason for restrictive measures, and what political factors (especially nondemocratic) were drawn on to justify restrictions and lockdowns in speeches to nations and the world? In addition, how did the eventual introduction of vaccines influence nationalism or global cooperation by leaderships? To answer these questions, this book uses critical discourse analysis to examine speeches and public discourse given in response to Covid by democratic and nondemocratic governments, including China's President Xi Jinping and Premier Li Keqiang, Saudi Arabia's King Salman and Crown Prince Mohammed bin Salman, the UK's Prime Minister Boris Johnson, and US President Donald Trump between 2020 and 2021.

The art of political persuasion was well understood by linguist John Searle. For Searle, any act of speaking or communicating through discourse (known as a Speech Act) by a leader was an intentional political act, intended to construct messages and to issue instructions to citizens (called essential conditions) (1965, pp. 1–2). Searle also argues that many political speeches can be filtered through the issuing of promises and threats, both linked to persuading listeners to obey instructions or accept messages from the speaker (ibid., pp. 3, 10–11).

Instructions were certainly issued and justified during the first year of Covid. "The strength, steadfastness, determination that you have demonstrated during the honorable defiance of this difficult phase, and your full cooperation with relevant government agencies, are the most important contributing factors and pillars of the success of the state's efforts, which has prioritized safeguarding health and made it the state's top concern," insisted Saudi Arabia's King Salman, indirectly instructing citizens to obey government restrictions while reminding Saudis that the House of Saud repaid obedience with a promise to ensure "the necessary medication, food and living necessities for citizens and residents of this blessed land" (Khalid, May 20, 2020b). On the other hand, the novel nature of Covid-19 was also used to issue indirect threats. Even democratic leaders like the UK's Boris Johnson reminded citizens that the NHS would not be available to them if they did not protect it by isolating and obeying restrictions.

> Without a huge national effort to halt the growth of the virus, there will come a moment when no health service in the world could possibly cope; because there won't be enough ventilators, enough intensive care beds, enough doctors and nurses. And as we have seen elsewhere, in other countries that also have fantastic health care systems, that is the moment of real danger. To put it simply, if too many people become seriously unwell at one time, the NHS will be unable to handle it-so we [must] protect the NHS's ability to cope[.] And that's why we have been asking people to stay home during this pandemic. (March 23, 2020b)

Searle's Speech Acts is a framework that provides a structured analytical understanding of political persuasion in discourse. Hence, each analyzed speech is filtered through Searle's Speech Acts to understand the strength of instructions issued, promises given, and threats made under preparatory conditions or the specific political context of each leadership when the speech was given (Searle, p. 15). Such analysis is then measured against the reaction of citizens and public discourse to restrictions across 2020 to 2021. Were restrictions accepted or met with resistance? In the case of so-called democratic countries, were restrictions met with language descriptive of images traditionally associated with authoritarian systems? Examining speeches through this understanding of political persuasion will ultimately address the book's central question: Do pandemics defend dictatorships while challenging democracies?

In addition to analyzing speeches to understand political legitimacy during Covid-19, this book complements its discussion of government responses to Covid and previous pandemics with an overview of social movements that emerged during the pandemic. This approach considers the threat of authoritarianism within the context of to what extent social movements emerged or spread to engage in resistance to any ostensible reduction in civil liberties. The notion of a tug-of-war between authoritarianism and civil liberties during pandemics is highlighted by Donatella della Porta. Porta refers to this clash as "Pandemics as Emergency Junctures," meaning that a sudden global (health) crisis branches out into "economic, social and political crises" that create periods of "crisis or strain that existing policies and institutions are ill-suited to resolve" (2022, p. 5). These events assemble to provoke "careful assessment of the trade-off between different rights and liberties," with governments imposing restrictions ostensibly aimed at curbing infections that require "a suspension of some rights and a centralization of decision-making in the national government," on the one hand, while social movements may act as a counterbalance, on the other, by adapting to, for example, social distancing but "play[ing] an important role during a pandemic, mobilizing for an expansion of civic, political and social rights" (ibid., pp. 7, 6).

Finally, this book also considers the role of corporate actors during the pandemic, including online retailers and pharmaceutical companies, due to their profits from Covid, to better elucidate the relationship between states and private actors during a health crisis. This discussion returns us to Porta's consideration of how a pandemic can provoke not only political but also economic crises and empower actors in the international system at the expense of ordinary citizens (ibid., p. 5). However, it also connects with a key argument of this book, which is that, during Covid, economic performance became a core concern for state political legitimacy and was echoed by the activities of corporate actors who profited from the pandemic. This does not mean that there was no civic resistance during Covid or protests aimed at restoring civic rights or demanding social justice. However, as the book will show, the economic damage of the pandemic became a focal point for many governments, and even social movements that emerged during the pandemic were, in some cases, focused on economic welfare rather than civic rights (Christakis, 2020, p. 207).

While the issue of increased authoritarianism during pandemics is not new, Covid represents the first major global health crisis of the twenty-first century, with Covid's genetic makeup facilitating a faster and more deadly spread than previous related viruses (Pitlik, 2020, p. 2). In addition, Covid provides an interesting case study to understand the intersectionality between health, fear, and control, in addition to science versus politics and collectivism versus individualism. This intersectionality under a major pandemic also came during the age of social media, disinformation and misinformation, and the rise of populism and the far right in the United States, along with isolationism through Trump's America First approach and isolationism in the UK under Brexit (Barber et al., 2022, p. 1).

Vaccines as Nationalism or Diplomacy?

My wife's mother in Jordan had finally received her appointment for the Covid vaccine. However, upon learning that the offered jab was AstraZeneca, she refused, choosing instead to wait it out for the Pfizer shot. She wasn't the only one. When my wife attended her second appointment, she was relieved that it would again be Pfizer. "I was worried," she later confided in me. "If it was AstraZeneca or Moderna, how would I react? Better if they're all Pfizer shots." When my own vaccine appointment came, I found myself secretly hoping for Pfizer as well and was equally relieved when my second and booster shots were Pfizer. I had read about blood clots from the AstraZeneca vaccine, and despite knowing that these were rare, I had likely internalized the fear of clots from AstraZeneca specifically after exposure to exaggerated media reports, some from dubious sources (France24, October 27, 2022).

As different countries (and pharmaceutical companies) raced to bring a Covid vaccine to market, there did seem to be a point of national pride in being the first state to do so and of having a homemade vaccine. Russia was the first to announce the development of a vaccine for Covid-19 in August 2020, which was followed by "a relentless publicity blitz [to] promote the attributes of the Sputnik vaccine," the efficacy of which was questioned "inside Russia, let alone in other countries where it is marketed" (Stronski, November 15, 2021). For Trump, "American companies were the first to produce a verifiably safe and effective vaccine," and he made it clear that "American citizens have first priority to receive American vaccines" (December 8, 2020).

What was apparent in such pride (and priorities regarding who would receive American vaccines first) was what some analysts have termed vaccine nationalism. For global health academics, national pride in producing a "homebrewed" vaccine is "a secondary symbolic meaning [of vaccine nationalism] by attaching a national 'character' to vaccines, often expressed through nationalist metaphors of winning and achievement" (Douglas et al., 2021, p. 3). However, such patriotism is superseded by the central definition of vaccine nationalism: "national control and ownership of vaccines" (ibid.). The concept of vaccine nationalism as an almost competitive form of vaccine control for one's nation was explored in thorough detail by Bollyky and Bown in the last months of 2020. Writing for the US-based international relations magazine *Foreign Affairs*, the pair outlined the dangers of vaccine nationalism as a "my country first" strategy for vaccine stockpiling that would transform into vaccine hoarding (2020, pp. 96–7).

Bollyky and Bown link vaccine nationalism to Western nations especially, pointing to Trump administration officials comparing "the global allocation of vaccines against the coronavirus that causes Covid-19 to oxygen masks dropping inside a depressurizing airplane" and quoting Trump officials insisting that "'[y]ou put on your own first, and then we want to help others as quickly as possible'" (ibid., p. 96). While Covid-19 vaccines were not yet available, concerns were still raised regarding eventual vaccine availability and the gross inequality in medical care and assistance between the West and so-called developing nations. Again, Bollyky and Bown point out that traditional vaccine manufacturers are often linked to pharmaceutical firms in Europe, the UK, and the United States. With no global coordination, countries may compete and bid against one another, risking an increase in vaccine and related material prices that poorer nations may struggle to afford (ibid., p. 98). Such rivalry and medical resource inequality were already forming in the early days of Covid regarding personal protection equipment and related medical supplies. This "decided shift in the wrong direction" saw "first China; then France, Germany, and the European Union; and finally the United States hoard supplies of respirators, surgical masks, and gloves for their own hospital workers' use" (ibid., p. 100).

As will be discussed in Chapter 2, such a lack of global cooperation during a pandemic

> is not new. A vaccine was developed in just seven months for the 2009 pandemic of the influenza A virus H1N1, also known as swine flu, which killed as many as 284,000 people globally. But wealthy countries bought up virtually all the supplies

of the vaccine. After the World Health Organization appealed for donations, Australia, Canada, the United States and six other countries agreed to share 10 [percent] of their vaccines with poorer nations, but only after determining that their remaining supplies would be sufficient to meet domestic needs. (ibid., pp. 100–2)

In contrast to this trend of vaccine and medical nationalism from mainly Western countries, some world leaders approached the production and distribution of any Covid vaccines "as global public goods—a resource to be made available to all, with the use of a vaccine in one country not interfering with its use in another" (ibid., p. 98).

Such a global approach to vaccines has been regarded by some as the opposite of vaccine nationalism and a form of what has been termed vaccine diplomacy, typically harnessed by "vaccine-producing countries" and presented as "a desire to help other developing countries fight Covid-19" by distributing domestically produced vaccines globally (Kirgizov-Barskii, Morozov, 2022, pp. 165, 170). However, vaccine diplomacy is not borne of a moral desire to offer a global public good but from the strategic realization that "these life-saving inoculations [can] secure favor and influence" as a soft power "foreign policy tool [to] improve one's image worldwide, even in places where it seemed to be irreversibly damaged, as well as achieve economic profit and capitalize on new opportunities" (ibid., p. 165). The concepts of vaccine nationalism and vaccine diplomacy will be further explored in Chapter 2 section "Vaccine Nationalism, Viral Sovereignty, Vaccine Diplomacy, and International Legitimacy," and analysis of chosen public discourse will also consider this politicization of vaccines to discuss to what extent Covid has seen an increase of isolationism or global cooperation.

Social Movements, Public Spaces

Although this book seeks to examine how pandemics may bolster authoritarianism and challenge democracy, it is worth considering the social movements that occurred during Covid (and perhaps in previous pandemics). The examination of social movements versus authoritarianism during Covid is heightened by the fact that the Covid pandemic represents the first truly global pandemic of the twenty-first century and the first pandemic during this time to change how people protest amid various (initial) restrictions (Kim, Sangubotla, 2021, p. 287; Bill of Health, n.d.). In addition, it is interesting to note that economic performance and gaps seemed to play a role in the galvanizing of many social movements to address vulnerable groups that governments did not seem to immediately respond to as the pandemic accelerated.

In the UK and elsewhere, there was certainly a disconnect between the national unity demanded of governments during Covid versus the sometimes-strong reaction by activists and social groups that are more than aware of the socioeconomic inequalities the pandemic widened. As explained by Porta, Covid has brutally emphasized social inequalities and hierarchies previously ignored by elites. This is why government demands for compliance with restrictions have not always been passively accepted, but instead "we have seen heterogenous forms of riots in jails, mass abstention to work, strikes, solidarity actions, forms of protest, that make visible how, even within a pandemic, inequalities and injustices still play a crucial role in forming our contemporary societies" (2022, p. 44).

While states called for national unity and claimed we're all in this together, some social movements emerged with a parallel narrative of "social justice that was certainly resonant with emerging knowledge about the unequal impact of the virus" (ibid.). The nature of social justice movements during Covid will be elaborated on in Chapter 2 section "Social Movements, Anxieties, and Pandemics." However, one immediate result of the pandemic was widespread anxiety, or what physician Nicholas A. Christakis calls "parallel epidemics of a psychological or existential nature—less tangible but equally virulent. Grief, anger, fear, denial, despair, and even anomie are not unexpected emotional reactions ... in a serious outbreak of infectious disease" (p. 139).

To a degree, social movements tapped into these anxieties as the pandemic unfolded, bearing in mind that Covid heightened preexisting anxieties over socioeconomic inequality rather than solely Covid-related worries that only emerged as lockdowns spread. It is therefore understandable that some social movements emerged not directed at Covid restrictions as such but at the false image of equality and stability that had hidden ongoing inequalities. Political action is often linked to spikes in anxiety because

> [p]olitical structures such as communities or states cannot exist with the ever present experience of danger and insecurity. They create fantasies to ensure relative safety and security for the majority of citizens. However, the global pandemic which revealed the intersecting vulnerabilities of life, the growing inequalities between different communities and deepening racial, class, [and] gender divides, dismantled these fantasies. It exposed the incompetence and failure of governance, in particular in relation to the management of life. (Zevnik, 2023, p. 167)

On the other hand, anxiety could also encourage compliance with government restrictions. In Saudi Arabia, fear of exposure to Covid influenced many citizens to adhere to government orders and to be frustrated at family members refusing to comply (Alkhaldi, 2024, p. 5). As will be later discussed in Chapter 2 section "Social Movements, Anxieties, and Pandemics," anxieties in Saudi Arabia also included "cultural stereotyping when a few participants [from a 2024 study] talked about the possibility of the spread of Covid-19 among ethnic groups within the community due to their limited knowledge and understanding of the pandemic and their limited rights to access free healthcare" (ibid., p. 8). The blaming and othering of certain social groups will be expanded upon; however, it acts as a reminder that the pandemic provoked social responses to preexisting anxieties that included discrimination of minorities and, in some cases, frustration with government reactions to Covid. In particular, rather than solely being focused on democratic or political rights, the UK and the United States saw the creation of mutual aid groups, social movements aimed at plugging economic gaps during Covid that governments had not responded to.

In the UK, Covid-19 saw a post-Brexit Britain struggle to adequately respond to rising infection rates. Some authors refer to this incident and subsequent localized social movements as a "pandemic shock," under which Covid came atop previous sociopolitical events (financial crises, climate change) as a more "extreme event that has challenged the center-local relationship, just at the point when the political right, in Britain, was preparing to capitalize on its newly found support in England's 'left-behind' communities" (Bradley et al., 2021, p. 148). At the same time, the shortcomings of government responses can be linked to the wider concern that, amid "the rise of pandemics and epidemics, public health and disaster preparedness experts long have questioned global, national, and more localized capacity to prevent, detect and respond to outbreaks of infectious disease," exacerbated by the WHO's opinion that "more often than not, emergency preparedness plans have been developed, assuming that public health crises would be short-term and fairly localized in scope" (Santiago, Smith, 2020, p. 90).

Indeed, as concerns over state responses to Covid grew, reactions from social movements weren't simply focused on democratic or individual rights but on whether the state had the capacity to meet basic welfare needs for its citizens during an unprecedented long-term crisis. This concern transformed discussions of governance from assuming change through centralized administration to ensuring progressive justice and basic needs "by increasing the participation of citizens," including meeting basic welfare needs through "a revival of the claim of rights to commons, defined as being so fundamental that they need to be managed through the direct participation of the citizens," because when "the state, market, or monarchy fail to provide for basic needs, commoners themselves usually step up to devise their own mutual aid systems" (Porta, p. 57).

In Britain, locals and neighborhoods began organizing to create mutual aid groups, acting less as charities and more as an ecosystem of "collective, reciprocal care and egalitarian social relations" (Christakis, p. 207). By November 2020, there were over 4,000 such groups in the UK alone

> formed by neighbours coming together to help those self-isolating in their area due to Covid-19. Neighbours run errands for those who cannot leave their homes, including dog walking, picking up shopping and prescriptions, posting mail or paying bills at the post office. They also make friendly phone calls to those who may be feeling lonely and anxious in self- isolation. (Kavada, 2022, p. 147)

Such groups could certainly be seen as apolitical and addressing the socioeconomic challenges (and anxiety) wrought by Covid, returning us to the notion that economic performance by the state during a pandemic becomes a key issue of political legitimacy during a crisis. However, the nonhierarchical nature of mutual aid groups and their success in plugging socioeconomic gaps meant to be filled by the state can be politicized when citizens illustrate solidarity and resilience independent of and despite state activities and failure. Such citizen action "has the potential to transform social relations and lead to deep shifts in political culture," as mutual aid by definition exists and interacts "outside of the formal frameworks of charities, NGOs and government. It is, by definition, a horizontal mode of organising, in which all individuals are equally powerful. There are no 'leaders' or unelected 'steering committees' in mutual aid projects; there is only a group of people who work together as equals" (ibid., p. 148).

The UK government seemed to take heed of such groups, as it prompted them to launch the NHS Volunteer Responders Service, which "help[ed] those registered as vulnerable by facilitating volunteers to undertake similar activities to those assumed by mutual aid groups" while ensuring complementary rather than duplicate or rivaling assistance (ibid., p. 150).

Figure 1.1 A map of mutual aid groups across the UK during Covid in 2020. Users can click on their area from the map to find groups close to them to assist with running errands or to connect with others online or by phone to combat loneliness. Source: Together TV (n.d.) "Together for good – mutual aid Covid-19." https://www.togethertv.com/together-good-mutual-aid-Covid19 (last accessed May 22, 2025).

"Together TV played its part during the Covid-19 pandemic," explains Head of Marketing Francesca Aita from Together TV, a community benefit TV channel.

> During these times of mass anxiety and months of lockdown isolation the UK's public relied on television to connect with the news, get local support and watch comforting programming. Ahead of the first lockdown in March 2020 we launched our You Are Not Alone campaign to support vulnerable viewers in self-isolation by brokering individual introductions to local mutual aid groups. We launched a Help Line as our viewers prefer to contact us by the phone and then SMS, then email, WhatsApp and Facebook. Through these we spoke to and matched hundreds of self-isolating people to their local Mutual Aid group coordinators—largely for food and medical support. Alongside this we built the first searchable map of the growing UK Mutual Aid movement, with the map becoming the top Google search for mutual aids with over 20,000 unique users. (Aita, email to author, May 22, 2025)

Did all mutual aid groups appear overnight in response to Covid? While it may seem that the UK saw thousands of such social movements rapidly organize, some critics argue that many such groups that illustrated the most resilience and response to Covid occurred in towns and areas with preexisting "activist local (state) councils, key pillar institutions, business community leadership, strong interconnecting organizational networks and communication" (Bradley et al., p. 153). Ultimately, however, the existence of protest groups already concerned with lack of government intervention to address interrelated issues such as environmentalism allowed such groups to form cohesive social movements to address the socioeconomic impact of Covid more so than local state councils, which were "relatively impotent in anticipating crises and mounting early responsiveness to create the conditions for societal resilience" (ibid., p. 168).

In America, mutual aid groups were localized and even broader. On the one hand, larger groups like Covid-19 Mutual Aid USA "compiled resources for those who wanted to help and those in need by curating detailed lists of all mutual aid networks in every state and town," while others like Mutual Aid NYC "compiled organizations in multiple categories, including elder care, delivery and transport, internet and technology, mental health, safety and pet care," and on the other hand, individual Americans "volunteered to help their neighbors and their communities in other ways by supporting or staffing food banks and helping with shopping" (Christakis, p. 207). In Michigan, community leaders preempted increased water needs for the vulnerable, and "the People's Water Board, a coalition of community, environmental, faith-based and labor organizations, including the Michigan Welfare Rights Organization (MWRO), sent a letter to Governor Gretchen Whitmer in February 2020 asking her to restore water services to the approximately 3000 to 9000 households that experienced shut offs in Detroit" (Santiago, Smith, 2020, p. 94). While Governor Gretchen seemed initially hesitant, "on March 10, 2020—the day Michigan announced its first confirmed Covid-19 cases—she issued an order to restore water service and found the resources to pay for it" (ibid.).

In Detroit, low-income families found that school closures severely disrupted the ability of children to receive two meals a day. In response, community centers across Detroit "agreed to host meal distribution services," and access to food for the vulnerable was transformed from a physical, congregational activity to contactless delivery or takeaway options (ibid., p. 95).

These examples of mutual aid groups as social movements in the UK and the United States emphasize the need during Covid to plug socioeconomic gaps and the immediacy of this need rather than a sole focus on political or democratic rights. At the same time, these movements represent the transformation of social and public space during the pandemic. While these movements did not attack their respective governments or protest restrictions, the existence of such groups emphasized the basic human right of access to food and water in localized contexts. Ultimately, such bottom-up approaches illustrate the symbolic significance of controlling social spaces and "potential options for reimagining the relationships between institutions, the community, work, and home" (ibid.).

While this book discusses the political legitimacy of governments during Covid (and previous pandemics), social movements are worth considering during Covid, especially as such movements can provide alternatives to the state during a pandemic. Many such groups promptly (re)organized themselves during the arrival of Covid to respond to gaps that governments left and "deal with the social costs of this pandemic and to cope with the needs that the most underprivileged communities are experiencing" (Gravante, Poma, 2022, p. 157). Further, such groups represent actors that are independent of the state. At a time when some states attempted to engage in centralized leadership to respond to a crisis, the success of such movements in plugging welfare gaps represents a

> grassroots activism ... born of autonomous, self-organized groups that carry out direct action not only at protest events but also in everyday practices. In this case, direct action is aimed at producing improvements in the human condition within a certain oppressed community, and is able to develop self-organization methods to weaken the links of dependence and blackmail relationships existing between the state and communities, such as, for example, illegal immigrant communities, homeless people, nomadic communities, prisoners and the many different marginalized communities in cities. (ibid.)

The distrust between state and citizen and minority groups will be expanded upon later in this book. In any case, it is clear that while social movements can be regarded as plugging gaps during the pandemic, their activities and existence also raise questions regarding state-citizen relations and the equally significant element of how social space may be controlled by state and non-state actors during emergencies.

In China, a highly centralized government is wary of the emergence of any independent social movement and "promotes social transformations through the process of State Campaign-Style Governance (CSG). State Campaign-Style Governance is a top-down campaign initiated and organized by the state to achieve a specific political, economic, or social task, often requiring the state to mobilize significant human and financial resources" and sees centralized authority meet localized adaptation, with cities like Shanghai subjected to "downward acceleration of implementation pressures from the center to the grassroot level" that seeks to control, inter alia, social spaces through localized government intervention (Wang, 2023, pp. 3–4).

Within the context of competing for social space, there are "four preconditions for spontaneous [social] movements: the absence of hierarchical organisation, uncertainty, emotional framing, and spatial contexts" (ibid., p. 7). Critics argue that (public) space for social movements is important as a resource that can be politicized. Within this context, a public space that is influenced by social actors also creates a community within which there are "contingent interactions of diverse actors [that] helps to enhance the flow of dissident ideas" (ibid.). For this reason, social spaces can be transformed into territories by social movements or state actors, defined as "a politicised place sustained by power" through being controlled by either the state or social movements themselves (ibid.).

You-Tien Hsing expands on this concept through discussion of how local state resources are directed toward urban development projects and other projects in public spaces that, "through access to and control over land, resources and population in a jurisdiction" creates a "territorialization of state power" through local state actors (2011, p. 3). This process of "Territorialization, De-territorialization, and Re-territorialization (TDR)" sees "the occupation of places for survival or struggle, next it reconstructs the social relation with new territory-based identities and networks, and then new values and encounters are formed in territorial mobilisation" (Wang, 2023, p. 9).

The ability of local government to control social space during Covid through the process of TDR is illustrated by the case of Shanghai. With a population of almost 25 million, Shanghai is an international megacity directly controlled by the central Chinese government. As China's largest aviation hub, there was great pressure to avoid importing cases from Wuhan and beyond. While Covid waves across 2020 and 2021 were relatively contained in Shanghai, the emergence of the Omicron variant in 2022 saw an explosion in cases, reaching 1,000 on a daily basis (ibid., pp. 10–11).

With the failure of its zero-Covid policy through lockdowns targeting only affected areas, Shanghai turned to mass testing and complete lockdown. This all-out response presented "an intense exertion of state power, both despotic and infrastructural, [which] penetrated and controlled society through comprehensive mobilisation from central, regional to grassroots through territorial pandemic control strategies" (ibid., p. 11). The intervention of Shanghai authorities emphasized the control of social and community spaces through total lockdown that included mobilizing local and municipal actors. Due to the centralized nature of China's governance model, such local actors were often members of the Chinese Communist Party and "task-oriented pressure and incentives were accelerated downward, and administrators, district governments, subdistrict offices, neighbourhood committees (NCs), property management companies and resident representatives ... were quickly mobilised to implement ... territorial policies" (ibid., p. 12). As one resident reported, such mobilization allowed for an almost overnight lockdown. "The lockdown started at midnight, and by the time we were informed it was early morning. By the time you see it, the gate is locked. We can't go out" (ibid., p. 12).

The efficacy of total lockdown by authorities was aided by Shanghai's grid governance system, the highly centralized structure of governance that mobilized obedient party members down to an almost grassroots level, and the plethora of gated communities, which could easily be locked to prevent residents from leaving. These elements allowed Shanghai authorities to "occupy the neighbourhood communities" and ensure territorial control (ibid., p. 14). However, as with the UK and the United States, the emphasis on welfare could not be overlooked. The ability of the state to provide for welfare needs was part of the larger regime of containment and mass testing that, if successfully run by the state, allowed the lockdown to carry "dual political legitimacy, both ideological and performance-based on public health—making it a political project that highlighted the superiority of [a] political system" that "emphasised that collective and individual interests overlapped during the pandemic, so it was legitimate for the state to implement strict lockdown policies, and it was necessary for residents to comply with them. In summary, the process of community territorialisation and territorial mobilisation was completely dominated by state power in the primary stage" (ibid., p. 16).

While local party leaders could coordinate some food provision, the central government's attempts to provide through them "was challenged by inequality, corruption, and technological issues" and the inability of residents to leave even when out of food or medicine "posed threats to the livelihoods of vulnerable groups and the elderly with underlying medical conditions" (ibid., p. 18).

In this instance, as with the UK and the United States, we can see that economic performance and welfare were key gaps that concerned citizens. Shanghai authorities were able to territorialize social spaces, including neighborhoods, gated communities, and other public spaces that may typically be used by social movements (ibid., p. 18). However, with gaps in food provision and the inability of residents to leave for essentials, resistance was expressed through limited physical spaces and online (ibid.).

In direct response to lacking food and related provisions, residents in Shanghai "agreed to stand on their balconies at the same time and bang kitchen utensils and iron basins to make loud noises to protest the government and the [neighborhood committee's] muddling through logistics," which was complemented by "[r]esidents [who] went out at night and avoided the guards for exercise and damaged the lockdown gates. This resistance was pragmatic, responded to the primitive desire for outdoor activities, and challenged the strategic power of the state in the territory with irregularity and mobility" that emphasized that if the state failed to provide basic necessities, its total control over (physical) social space could be challenged even under lockdown. As with the United States and the UK, Shanghai in this instance saw social movements challenge the state and municipal authorities over welfare gaps rather than democratic rights (ibid., pp. 18–19).

Mirroring mutual aid groups in the United States and the UK, Shanghai residents also took to online platforms such as WeChat to plug welfare gaps, "posting their needs for exchanging, including antipyretic medicine, food, alcohol, and baby products" (ibid., p. 19). The use of social media and chat for mutual aid was a reminder that governments attempting to control physical territory and its symbolic importance as social space during crises did not always have full control of digital space. While in this instance, the digital domain was used to coordinate mutual aid (itself proof that the government could not ensure economic performance during the pandemic), as we will see in Chapter 2 section "Social Movements, Anxieties, and Pandemics" online space could also be used by Chinese citizens to engage in limited civil disobedience that circumvented censorship norms to pressure the government into acknowledging specific failures during Covid.

An overview of social movements during Covid helps to contextualize the socioeconomic aspect of the pandemic and the fact that many such movements rose to plug welfare gaps, a key failure in terms of each government's economic performance, which itself can be regarded as a measure of its political legitimacy during a crisis. In addition, social movements may tap into preexisting anxiety that is exacerbated by crises, and many such groups that mobilized quickly to plug welfare gaps in, for example, the UK built on preexisting networks and social issues. Finally, the case study of Shanghai shows us the importance of capturing social space during emergencies. The attempt by competing actors (e.g., the state versus local social actors) to control social space as politicized territory can be regarded as hinging on the state's economic performance and its ability to meet essential needs distribution. As the example of Shanghai shows, the immediate concern of citizens during a pandemic may be socioeconomic, including job loss, access to essentials, and access to outside space during lockdown. The failure of the state to steadily provide access to such welfare needs can provoke resistance and (online) organization that not only plugs welfare gaps through mutual aid but also challenges the state's centralized authority by illustrating its incompetence to meet basic needs through top-down measures and the importance of grassroots activities that are formally outside of state control.

In understanding the importance of political legitimacy for the state and the risk of a turn to authoritarianism during a pandemic, it is worth reiterating the fact that, for many social movements, democratic rights were not necessarily the immediate concern but rather the ability of the state to meet socioeconomic needs at a time of sudden change that included restrictions with significant economic impact for many citizens. That said, the basic human right of access to food and water would certainly be considered under threat during Covid and feeds into a broader discussion of not only socioeconomics but also social inequality and injustice that Covid widened, including in terms of individual and collective rights. This discussion will be considered in Chapter 2 section "Social Movements,

Anxieties, and Pandemics." Nonetheless, as discussed by Porta, the socioeconomic and social injustices highlighted by Covid form part of a wider issue that a sudden global health crisis highlights, including political crises "that existing policies and institutions are ill-suited to resolve" (p. 5). The trade-offs created by governments as they impose certain restrictions over others (or an all-out lockdown) may not only be protested by citizens but also by (emerging) social groups that highlight the reduction of and mobilize for "an expansion of civic, political and social rights" (ibid., pp. 7, 6).

The arrival of Covid prompted a variety of restrictions across China, Saudi Arabia, the UK, and the United States. We have touched upon what some of these restrictions were, how leaderships presented them in public discourse and how such discourse, as understood by Searle, can be used as a form of political persuasion for issued instructions to be followed. The arrival of Covid also prompted debate over vaccine hoarding and what has been termed vaccine nationalism, or a "my country first" approach to the purchase and distribution of vaccines that will be considered in Chapter 2 section "Vaccine Nationalism, Viral Sovereignty, Vaccine Diplomacy, and International Legitimacy." Finally, the key argument of this book, that Covid prompted an emphasis on economic performance, has also allowed us to introduce discussion of social movements that arose during Covid in response to welfare gaps while also considering how social space can become politicized by state and non-state actors and how such movements tapped into preexisting anxieties widened by the pandemic. The existence of these movements and the focus of such transnational movements on social justice and tackling inequality (especially for minorities) will be expanded upon in Chapter 2 section "Social Movements, Anxieties, and Pandemics."

Chapter 2

A HISTORY OF PANDEMICS

This Is Not the Flu

We have discussed the arrival of Covid and how it prompted fears of vaccine nationalism, debate over restrictions, and the rise of anxiety, while also prompting social movements that aimed to tackle social welfare gaps that centralized governments did not immediately address. However, to better discuss the intersectionality of health politics, control, fear, and economic performance, it is worth discussing previous pandemics, how governments reacted to them, and how citizens responded to government intervention during such health crises. Chapter 2 therefore examines how some governments initially framed Covid, the genetic traits of Covid that helped it to spread, and considers theoretical approaches to political legitimacy. From there, we trace key pandemics, from the 1918 Spanish Flu to the 2012 Middle East respiratory syndrome (MERS) virus. We also discuss the relationship between social movements and pandemics to better contextualize the role such movements play during a health crisis and to discuss how some movements saw the need to address preexisting issues of social justice and inequality that Covid widened. This discussion considers socioeconomic inequality in often minority communities before broadening to consider how health inequality between nations influenced vaccine nationalism and the desire of some states to use viral samples as bargaining chips to gain better terms of vaccine equity before and during Covid, ultimately highlighting the need for better global cooperation to address pandemics.

"This is a flu," Trump insisted in late 2020. "This is like a flu. It's a little like a regular flu that we have flu shots for" (Phillips, September 9, 2020). For me, it started with a runny nose and cough that lasted for two days. After four days, I felt I was struggling to breathe. My veins and lungs ached, as if I'd inhaled mold or toxic fumes that were spread across the inside of my body. I cleaned our home meticulously, most likely in denial of the fact that the time had come to be tested. When I awoke one day later with fatigue and body aches, I finally gave in.

My wife swabbed my throat and nostrils. Alexa announced the start of a fifteen-minute timer. We sat at the dining table and waited. Then came the two red lines no one wants to see. My body aches deepened even with generous amounts of over-the-counter medication. This was worse than the side effects I'd had from my first Pfizer shot. This was most certainly not the flu.

Chapter 2 discusses the theoretical framework of Fabienne Peter's Political Legitimacy as applied to understanding both democratic and nondemocratic legitimacy during the pandemic and how these two forms of political legitimacy can tie into a wider debate on isolationism and nationalism versus globalization, before explaining what a coronavirus is and why Covid-19 (known as the novel coronavirus) is not our first encounter with a coronavirus. In addition, this chapter traces the history of four pandemics: the 1918 Spanish Flu, the 2003 severe acute respiratory syndrome (SARS) outbreak, the 2009 H1N1 pandemic (also known as swine flu), and the 2012 MERS virus that gripped the Middle East and parts of Asia, examining how states like China, Saudi Arabia, the UK, and the United States reacted to each pandemic that affected them. Finally, an expanded discussion of vaccine nationalism and vaccine diplomacy is outlined to understand how Covid-19 has contributed to isolationism and globalization and to what extent vaccine production became a tool of soft power for some and a source of national pride and security for others.

Legitimizing State Control under Covid

Fabienne Peter's Political Legitimacy is a framework that considers democratic and nondemocratic elements of rule. Such a consideration of democratic and utilitarian modes of governance allows the democratic and nondemocratic case studies of this book to be analyzed within the context of Covid-19 as a global pandemic that has influenced authoritarian and democratic styles of leadership. To reiterate, the examined case studies are:

- The People's Republic of China, where Covid-19 first emerged in the city of Wuhan (Maxmen, February 27, 2022).
- The Kingdom of Saudi Arabia, where Crown Prince Mohammed bin Salman's (MBS) Vision 2030 reforms were threatened by Covid (MEED Editorial).
- The UK, which had recently left the European Union through Brexit (Fieschi, December 2, 2022).
- The United States of America, which saw Trump's America First policy create an exclusionary nationalism and isolationism as Trump withdrew the United States from international agreements (McTague, Nicholas, October 29, 2020).

When debating the democratic and nondemocratic sources of Political Legitimacy, Peter admits that in "contemporary political philosophy, many, but by no means all, hold that democracy is necessary for political legitimacy" (Peter, April 29, 2010). For this reason, "democratic forms of political organization [such as elections and referendums] are necessary for political legitimacy" (ibid.). When considering the relationship between democracy and political legitimacy, Peter addresses the importance of political decision-making and to what extent such decision-making can include popular participation, separating democratic decision-making procedures across three categories:

- Democratic Instrumentalism or the belief that "democratic decision-making procedures are best able to produce legitimate outcomes" (ibid.).
- Pure Proceduralist Conceptions of Democratic Legitimacy or the notion that "democratic decisions are legitimate as long as they are the result of an appropriately constrained process of democratic decision-making" (ibid.).
- Mixed Conceptions of Democratic Legitimacy or the belief that the "legitimacy of democratic decisions depends on both procedural values and on the substantive quality of the outcomes that these deliberative decision-making procedures generate" (ibid.).

A summary of Peter's considerations of democratic decision-making and political legitimacy reveals not only an emphasis on popular participation in political decisions but also considers the quality of the outcomes created by such popular participation. We can consider how these sources can be applicable to, for example, elections, which can be regarded as a "constrained process of democratic decision-making" but one that may not always guarantee "substantive quality of outcomes" (ibid.). It is certainly worth mentioning that both democratic and nondemocratic regimes engage in what may be termed political participation procedures like elections and referendums such as Brexit, which may be hard to classify, as for some such a referendum did represent a *de facto* democratic decision-making procedure that was thus legitimate; yet for others, this democratic procedure has yet to produce "substantive quality of outcomes," though evaluating the positive or negative outcomes of Brexit in detail is beyond the scope of this book (ibid., Zhai, November 10, 2016). Let us now consider sources of political legitimacy that, according to Peter, governments may use to validate their rule.

Peter's framework outlines three sources of political legitimacy:

- Consent to be ruled by a specific leadership.
- Beneficial Consequences or acceptance of a ruler in exchange for utilitarian benefits.
- Public Reason/Democratic Approval, the notion that any political decision was reached through a decision-making process (Peter, April 29, 2010).

Peter admits that consent remains the most difficult even in the most ideal form of political legitimacy, as "those governed [can] consent [only] under certain ideal conditions," which explains why objections to the feasibility of consent "are about as old as consent theory itself" (ibid.). Considering "that actual states have almost always arisen from acts of violence," consent as a measure of legitimacy remains "at best, wishful thinking" (ibid.). By contrast, Beneficial Consequences provides a very utilitarian source of political legitimacy. Peter argues that governments can avoid justifying their right to rule so long as they present positive results of that rule to citizens. Hence, "legitimacy based on beneficial consequences is compatible with everyone having reasons to obey the directives of a legitimate authority" (ibid.). In other words, the state creates a social contract between itself and its citizens, whereby the state provides material benefits rather than popular participation in exchange for citizens recognizing the state's right to rule, allowing political legitimacy to be based on the state's economic performance (ibid.). Such a social contract is certainly relevant to oil states like Saudi Arabia that are known for a ruling bargain, funded by oil, under which welfare and other material benefits are provided to citizens in exchange for their loyalty or political acquiescence (Brumberg, July 3, 2018). Even the Chinese Communist Party (CCP) has historically provided a social contract "between Party and public of economic opportunity for acceptance of constricted social space" (Feigenbaum, November 27, 2017). Under Xi Jinping, the CCP has redefined this social contract with a focus on tackling corruption, plugging social service gaps, and being responsive to public demands, all moves that should ensure material benefits without opening any political space for popular participation (ibid.). Xi Jinping's rule of China will be further elaborated upon in Chapter 3.

Public Reason/Democratic Approval is Peter's final source of political legitimacy and interestingly relevant to democratic and nondemocratic rule. According to Peter, Democratic Approval does not guarantee a pure democracy but can be focused on proceduralism, as discussed earlier when outlining Peter's considerations of democratic decision-making processes (Peter, April 29, 2010). If Democratic Approval is linked to a publicly approved constitution, citizens should "accept a democratic decision even if they disagree substantially with it" (ibid.). In other words, government actions and policies do not necessarily need public approval if they are filtered through a supposedly democratic procedure, as discussed earlier when considering Pure Proceduralist Conceptions of Democratic Legitimacy and Democratic Instrumentalism.

A proceduralist approach can certainly be linked to a variety of our case studies. For example, Trump's Muslim (Travel) Ban was initially rejected in 2017, but after revision was accepted by the US Supreme Court in 2018, despite widespread belief of "Trump's anti-Muslim statements and the [Islamophobic] intent behind the controversial policy" because, according to the majority of Supreme Court justices the revised "Proclamation is expressly premised on legitimate purposes: preventing entry of nationals who cannot be adequately vetted and inducing other nations to improve their practices" (Gerstein, Hesson, June 26, 2018). In other words, the ban was approved as it could formally conform to procedural rules and benefitted from recent procedural revisions that "allowed Republicans to bypass a Democratic blockade" and appoint one Justice Neil Gorsuch, who represented the majority of justices approving the ban (ibid.). Saudi Arabia, as another example, has also seen proceduralism used as part of King Salman's elevation of MBS to the role of crown prince. As a formality in securing his son's new position, it was expected that the Saudi Allegiance Council would vote for MBS's new status. The council "is made up of 34 royal family members who are sons or represent the families of sons of Saudi Arabia's founding King Abdulaziz" (Human Rights Watch, 2019, pp. 15–16). Out of the council's thirty-four members, "all but 3 votes" were in his favor amid the arrest and marginalization of potential rivals (ibid.).

Relevant to this book's further discussion of vaccine nationalism and vaccine diplomacy and their impact on isolationism and nationalism versus globalization is Peter's Political Nationalism and Political Cosmopolitanism. Political Nationalism considers the state the highest authority in the international system, arguing that "it is the [common] view that only the political institutions of nation states can overcome the legitimacy problem and hence be a source of political legitimacy" as Political Nationalism ensures that "obligations of justice are tied to nation states" (Peter, April 29, 2010). On the other hand, Political Cosmopolitanism argues that states are part of a system of "both international and global legitimacy" and that such an international system means states coexist through "international [stability], and the rules that regulate their behavior are supposed to preserve a peaceful order of sovereign states" (ibid.). The notion of states appealing to a form of global legitimacy and global institutes (perhaps the World Health Organization [WHO] during a pandemic) can further be linked to what Ahram and Lust may call international legitimacy. In their article "The Decline and Fall of the Arab State," the pair argue that sovereignty is an artificial construct, requiring the legitimation of the international system (Ahram, Lust, 2016, p. 8). Hence, Chapter 5's analysis of discourse given by leaderships as vaccines became available will consider to what extent each leadership promoted vaccine nationalism (and hence isolationism and perhaps an exclusionary nationalism, linked to Peter's Political Nationalism) or vaccine diplomacy (linked to Peter's Political Cosmopolitanism and an attempt to gain international legitimacy). In addition, we will discuss vaccine nationalism and diplomacy as they relate to our case studies in more detail in this chapter's section "Vaccine Nationalism, Viral Sovereignty, Vaccine Diplomacy, and International Legitimacy."

An overview of Peter's Political Legitimacy illustrates democratic and nondemocratic elements of political legitimacy while also discussing how proceduralism can be applied by democratic and nondemocratic leaderships to pursue desired policies and political changes. Chapter 3 will expand on such use of proceduralism across our case studies. Further, Peter's Political Nationalism and Political Cosmopolitanism provide relevant structure to understand the roots of vaccine nationalism and vaccine diplomacy, respectively, and how the former may be linked to isolationism and exclusionary nationalism while the latter may be linked to international legitimacy, as understood by Ahram and Lust. As Chapter 3 will also later discuss, the years leading up to Covid-19 saw proceduralism and Beneficial Consequences such as economic growth or benefits utilized by democratic and nondemocratic leaders to centralize their power base and ultimately strengthen their ability to rule through chosen narratives, including pluralism (Brexit, Trump) and social reform (MBS's Saudi Arabia).

Further, it is worth noting that while Peter's Political Legitimacy provides an expedient framework to understand utilitarianism, it does not discuss how religion can be politicized and considered utilitarian, as will be discussed regarding Saudi Arabia in Chapter 3 onward. Hence, analysis of religion in this book will treat it as a Beneficial Consequence to discuss how, for example, Islam is drawn on as a utilitarian benefit (Due-Gundersen, 2022, pp. 13–14). This extension of understanding religion as a Beneficial Consequence will help answer this book's central question: do pandemics defend dictatorships while challenging democracies?

What Is a Coronavirus?

As sudden and widespread as Covid-19 has become, it is not the first time we have been infected by a coronavirus. Coronaviruses are so-dubbed due to the presence of a "spike-protein" that determines "viral transmission capacity" and "also gives these viruses their distinctive crown-like (corona) appearance under electron microscopy" (Abousaleh et al., 2021, p. 969). In 1965, we saw the identification of "the first strain of coronavirus as a significant cause of the common cold," and in total, "seven human-infecting strains have been discovered of which four generally cause mild symptoms and three cause potentially severe disease" (ibid., p. 968). The three potentially fatal strains are the 2002 SARS, also known as SARS-CoV-1; the 2012 MERS; and 2019's Covid-19, also known as SARS-CoV-2 (ibid.). Unsurprisingly, much literature was published in 2020 on the differences between Covid-19 and other coronaviruses. What made Covid-19 so scary and possibly deadly? Did it spread faster than other coronaviruses we have encountered? An early 2020 article by UK Research and Innovation explained that "reports suggest the new virus is more contagious than the one causing SARS but less likely to cause severe symptoms" while still cautioning that there was "much we need to learn about the new (or novel) coronavirus (Covid-19)" (UK Research and Innovation, March 25, 2020).

Coronaviruses infect humans and animals; however, it is when a coronavirus jumps from animals (such as bats) to humans that "a new type of coronavirus is formed, or a 'novel' coronavirus" (Pondo, April 23, 2020). In addition, when a coronavirus transmits from animals to humans for the first time, "it can cause severe disease," and experts noticed "that the Covid-19 strain is a lot more infectious, or contagious, than other novel coronaviruses" (ibid.). As Covid-19 continued to spread, health experts compared it to SARS and MERS. Both these outbreaks saw "two highly pathogenic coronaviruses with [animal] origin" that caused "fatal respiratory illnesses," and Covid-19 was thus the latest "public health concern in the twenty-first century" (Guo et al., October 6, 2020, p. 141).

Indeed, as Covid-19 spread in late December 2019 across Wuhan, China, patients presented with symptoms similar to SARS and MERS, such as "viral pneumonia, including fever, cough and chest discomfort, and in severe cases dyspnea (shortness of breath) and lung infiltration" (ibid.). The majority of initial cases were linked to a Wuhan wet market, "which sells not only seafood but also live animals, including poultry and wildlife" (ibid.). Unfortunately, "the outbreak coincided with the approach of the lunar New Year [and] travel between cities before the festival facilitated viral transmission in China" (ibid.). Covid-19 would soon spread across the world thanks to global air travel. By the time Chinese authorities locked down Wuhan and blocked travel to and from the city in late January, it was too late. The novel coronavirus was spreading worldwide (ibid.).

For many health experts, the threat of Covid-19 did not come as a surprise. A 2007 report on SARS warned that "the large reservoir of SARS-[Covid] like viruses in bats, coupled with the trade of wild animals in China [was] a 'time bomb'" (Abousaleh et al., p. 968). Further, the MERS outbreak saw international scientists "reiterate the potential risk of [further coronavirus outbreaks]" (ibid.). And as health authorities began to analyze Covid-19, it was clear that the current pandemic was not a mirror of SARS. Most glaringly, Covid-19 "spreads faster and further than the 2003 SARS CoV-1 virus" due to "how easily it is transmitted from person to person, even from asymptomatic carriers" (John Hopkins Medicine, n.d.).

Another key feature of Covid-19 has been its rapid mutation. While mutation is a common trait of all viruses, Covid-19 has seen variants that increasingly "enable [it] to continue its spread in the face of rising population immunity while maintaining or increasing its replication fitness" (Fera et al., September 17, 2021). By 2021, Covid-19 was spreading through "four variants of concern (Alpha, Beta, Gamma and Delta) associated with increased transmissibility, increased risk of infection and/or reduced vaccine efficacy" (ibid.). By 2022, we faced a further mutation: Omicron. Along with a new variant came the hope that Covid was getting milder. As hospitals across South Africa, the UK, and the United States began examining patient data, many discovered that "the risk of a patient with Omicron being admitted to a hospital is about half that observed with the Delta variant," and that if "you are admitted to the hospital, the risk of being put on a ventilator has dropped by about 75 [percent]" (Doucleff, January 14, 2022). The milder symptoms of Omicron compared to Delta were put down to Omicron spreading less deeply into the lungs (ibid.). However, scientists warned that pinning hope on Covid evolving into progressively milder variants ignores the fact that it is "a virus that's gotten progressively more severe over time" and that "future variants will likely continue to improve their ability to infect and continue to be more immune evasive" (ibid.).

Comparisons between SARS and Covid-19 emphasized less their similarity in symptoms and more how dangerous coronaviruses must be contained. Disturbingly, SARS and Covid thrived in hospital settings, illustrating the urgent need for personal protective equipment (PPE), along with strict disinfection protocols for health workers, visitors, and patients. Further, not only Covid and SARS but previous outbreaks demonstrated the need to regulate and monitor wet markets, implement early warning mechanisms, and ensure that healthcare systems are well-funded to maintain adequate PPE and medical equipment, along with clinical laboratory testing before pandemics rather than during. In addition, modern technology can be incorporated as part of public health measures (such as the use of Android apps for contact tracing). Finally, there must be international support for (and coordination with) "communicable disease prevention and control programs and agencies even when global outbreaks are not in the headlines" (Abousaleh et al., p. 973). As we shall now see through a history of pandemics, global cooperation and even domestic coordination for protective and preventive measures have not always been prioritized, and as with Covid-19, previous pandemics have provoked protests against restrictive measures.

A Historical Context of Pandemics

The 1918–20 H1N1 Spanish Flu

As Covid's death toll increased, many outlets began comparing the novel coronavirus (and containment measures taken) to the Spanish Flu pandemic of 1918–20. However, it is important to note that the Spanish Flu did not get its name from where this influenza virus (an H1N1 virus of avian origin) began (Centers for Disease Control and Prevention, March 20, 2019). Rather, the name stuck because Spain, as a neutral nation in the First World War, allowed extensive media coverage of the pandemic at a time when many governments sought to suppress news of the viral outbreak as soldiers returned home (Centers for Disease Control and Prevention, August 10, 2018). To this day, the exact geographical start of the Spanish Flu remains unclear. However, what is clear is that the virus thrived among soldiers in trenches and combat, many of whom returned home to spread it further. As explained by author Maya Prabhu, "it's clear that the war created ideal conditions for the mutation and spread of such an animal virus," with "soldiers huddled in a line of trenches" as strong winds "swept in a season of uncommon cold and unusually high rainfall" that ensured "the trenches were freezing and muddy," a perfect breeding ground for rats (Prabhu, July 30, 2021).

From trenches in Europe, the flu spread "through Spain, France, Great Britain and Italy, causing havoc with military operations during the First World War" (Barberis et al., March 29, 2019, p. 64). The first wave did not draw much medical attention due to mild symptoms and a duration akin to seasonal flu outbreaks. However, the second wave that began in August 1918 showed lethal outbreaks of "nasal hemorrhage, pneumonia, encephalitis (brain swelling), temperatures

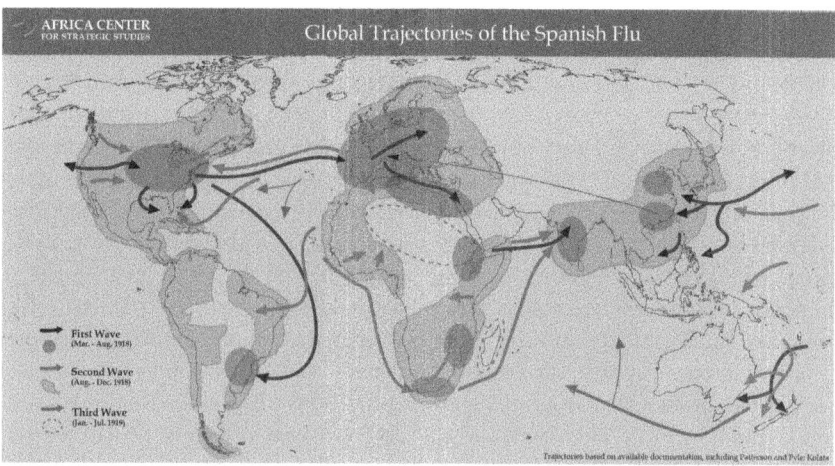

Figure 2.1 Global trajectories of the Spanish Flu. Source: Africa Center for Strategic Studies 2020. "Lessons from the 1918–1919 Spanish Flu Pandemic in Africa." May 13. https://africacenter.org/spotlight/lessons-1918-1919-spanish-flu-africa/ (last accessed May 27, 2025).

of up to 40 degrees C, blood-streaked urine and coma" (ibid.). The second wave spread "from the port-city of Plymouth in south-western England by ships bound for Freetown in Sierra Leone and Boston in the United States," and further through "the movement of armies" (ibid.). Within a span of roughly six weeks, it continued "from North America to Central and South America, from Freetown to West Africa and South Africa in September, and reaching the Horn of Africa in November." Covering Europe by September's end, the pandemic spread from Russia "throughout northern Asia, arrived in India in September" and by October re-infected China (ibid.).

A third wave began in 1919, seeing equally troubling mortality rates as the second wave. The northern hemisphere declared the pandemic over by May 1919; however, Japan was hit by the third wave between 1919 and 1920 (ibid.). It was not until 1930 that the Spanish Flu was "rightly attributed to a virus," and in 1933 the first human influenza virus was isolated (ibid.). The United States alone saw fatalities of almost 700,000, and global mortality estimates for the Spanish Flu were between 50 million and 100 million (Branswell, September 20, 2021, Metcalfe, July 15, 2022). For comparison, the WHO estimates excess mortality for Covid worldwide in 2020 at three million (WHO, May 20, 2021).

No vaccine meant that only restrictive measures could control the spread of the virus, along with "improvised remedies" (Barberis et al., p. 65). From August 1918, Europe saw a variety of restrictive measures that would return in 2020 under Covid, including "the obligatory notification of suspected cases, and the surveillance of communities such as schools," followed in October 1918 by stronger measures such as "the closure of public meeting places such as theatres, and the suspension of public meetings. In addition, long church sermons were prohibited and Sunday instruction was to last no more than five minutes" (ibid.).

Just as Covid has seen sanitation initiatives, "the disinfection of public spaces, such as churches, cinemas, theaters and workshops" were implemented along with "banning crowds outside shops and limiting the number of passengers on public transport. However, they did not prove very effective." While Covid's spread saw a rise in hand sanitizers, common interventions to address the 1918 pandemic included "distributed free soap" from health authorities who also ensured "clean water for the less wealthy; services for the removal of human waste, the regulation of toilets, and the inspection of milk and other food products were organized" (ibid.). Mortality rates saw "collection points for corpses" under simplified "mortuary police services" that "abolished all the rituals that accompanied death." Finally, management of the Spanish Flu without a vaccine saw a now familiar system of "identifying cases of illness through surveillance and/or mandatory quarantine or isolation" (ibid.).

As previously mentioned, the Spanish Flu traveled to Asia, affecting India and Japan. However, scarce records exist of how the 1918 pandemic affected China. Compared to other parts of Asia, such as India, China "was not fully colonized by European powers, leaving much of its agrarian population isolated from disease-spreading colonials" (Farley, March 25, 2020). Nonetheless, this did not mean that China was immune to the 1918 virus. Some accounts do exist of China's brush with sickness, recorded mainly by foreign missionaries on hygiene measures in relation to spreading illness in the early twentieth century. Such accounts were published in early English-language medical journals edited by foreign experts within China (Cheng, Leung, 2007, p. 360).

The summer of 1918 saw initial outbreaks of influenza in Canton (now modern-day Guangzhou, close to Hong Kong). These initially affected young males between eleven and twenty years of age and continued into October of that year but with fairly mild symptoms (ibid.). However, from September to November, there was a marked shift in symptom intensity. Around September there was an increase in patients presenting with pneumonia, though mortality rates remained low. However, rural areas seemed to experience a higher death rate than urban spaces. One report detailed how a village of roughly two hundred saw forty members dead within a month, while other nearby villages hosted daily funerals to the extent that coffin supplies could not meet demand as death rates soared to 10 percent (ibid.). In larger cities such as Shanghai and Hong Kong, however, death rates remained lower than in the UK and the United States. Nonetheless, Spanish Flu in China saw the introduction of restrictive and hygiene measures (ibid.).

During Covid, China's Hebei province saw lockdowns that affected millions (AFP, August 30, 2022). Hebei also became the site of restrictive measures during the Spanish Flu. "The local government took a series of measures to control the pandemic, and instructions such as 'houses should be sprayed with limewater or lime powder, and rhubarb and [traditional herbs] should be burned to disinfect the air'" were given. For prevention, "villagers were advised to drink more soup prepared with powdered mung bean and rock sugar, several times a day." For those who had been infected, "more than 5000 doses of herbal formula were distributed to the families." According "to the statistics available for the period between October 15, 1918, and November 15, 1922, in the areas governed by the Rehe Police Office, the total number of male patients reached 3573, of which 3490 recovered and 67 died" (Cheng, Leung, pp. 361–2).

Such accounts are a reminder that China was not spared the Spanish Flu, which seemed to spread "from the south (Shanghai, Guangzhou) to the north as far as Harbin, even to remote regions like Gejiu Yunnan province" (ibid., p. 362). As in the United States and Europe, the Spanish Flu seemed to come in waves. The second wave saw up to 20 percent of influenza cases complicated by pneumonia, and although the pandemic subsided by October's end (1918) in some areas, Beijing's morbidity rates were as high as 50 percent (ibid.). While sparse records on the Spanish Flu imply moderate rather than large-scale impact in China, records from the port city of Guangdong (also close to Hong Kong) "were plentiful. The records show that influenza first occurred in schools, post offices and hospitals in June of that year. In October, influenza cases were also found in mental hospitals. Three weeks later, schools for the blind and theological seminaries were struck" (ibid.).

Another often overlooked region affected by the Spanish Flu from 1918 was the Arabian Peninsula, including what is now modern-day Saudi Arabia. The Arabian Peninsula itself was and remains a geostrategic location for trade, religious pilgrimage, and politics, attracting in 1918 what was to be known as the "year of mercy" and "year of fever" as the flu spread and within a few months began to "wipe out towns and villages and dramatically decrease the populations in the Arabian Peninsula" (Ben Gassem, March 29, 2020). In what some would describe as a twist of fate, the Spanish Flu also claimed one Sir Mark Sykes, co-architect of the Middle East's controversial division under the Sykes-Picot Agreement. He "would have had an agonising death as his body convulsed and contorted from the ravages of the Spanish Flu" and killed him at the age of thirty-nine. As with China and the rest of the world, the Spanish Flu attacked the Arabian Peninsula in three waves, with the second wave "a deathly grip on the likes of the Ottoman province of Greater Syria (encompassing the modern-day states of Syria, Lebanon, Jordan and Palestine) around September 1918" (Soussi, February 10, 2018).

With many of the infected dead after forty-eight hours, volunteers began to wash and bury the deceased almost relentlessly, "except during prayer times, which was considered their break" (Ben Gassem). Within the Najd region of what became modern-day Saudi Arabia, the response to the outbreak, as with China, was isolation of patients in homes or even outside city limits. Author Rahman Al-Suwayda claims that the Spanish Flu in the Arabian Peninsula also saw early attempts at vaccination and inoculation, whereby officials took "pus from patients and vaccinate[d] the rest of the people in primitive ways, thereby limiting the spread of the disease. Herbs and medicinal formulations were some of the methods used in fighting diseases" (ibid.). In addition, a special broth was prepared as part of a recovering patient's diet. This mix of camel, lamb, and goat meat was called *Al-Qiru* and was intended to prevent complications and relapse (ibid.).

Eventual Saudi Arabia founder King Abdulaziz personally called upon medical experts to address the spread of flu. After the loss of his son Turki and wife Jawhara bint Musaed, Abdulaziz summoned Dr. Paul Harrison "to visit Riyadh with urgency." Upon his arrival, Abdulaziz received the good doctor "in a small, modest room" and with "a warm handshake" before explaining that "he had requested a doctor not to take care of his health or that of his family, but for the need of his people, and that he had allocated a house nearby to be a hospital, and he wanted his people to be treated for free" (ibid.).

However, as noble as saving his people sounded, an ulterior motive of Abdulaziz may have been the very real threat of revolt against his emerging power. The Spanish Flu came atop drought and the erosion of trade after the First World War, which affected tribes and fed into "the first revolts of the famous *Ikhwan* against Emir Abdulaziz Ibn Saud at a time when he was setting about some difficult conquests in northern Najd (an emirate of the Al Rashid of Hail) and in the Hejaz (the Hashemite Kingdom of Mecca)" (Petriat, May 21, 2020). In addition, as helpful as Dr. Paul Harrison may have been, his connections to the American Protestant Mission in Bahrain seemed to affect Abdulaziz's religious credentials and weaken support of his rule from the conservative militant *Ikhwan* group (ibid.).

Discussing the arrival of Spanish Flu in China and the Arabian Peninsula reveals some shared use of restrictions also found during Covid, and especially before vaccine availability, including patient isolation. However, it is clear that the

1918 pandemic hit harder in the Middle East, and for the then-Emir Abdulaziz, compounded threats to his political authority that was still being established. Indeed, once Abdulaziz conquered Jeddah and the holy cities of Mecca and Medina, he "ordered the creation of [the] first public health agency at Mecca, with branches in the rest of the future kingdom" (ibid.). While the domestic population did not yet have a significant pool of medically educated citizens, Abdulaziz had learned his lesson of relying on Western health figures and subsequently "surrounded himself with Syrian, Lebanese and Egyptian doctors" (ibid.). Hence, while the Spanish Flu did not scar Arabia in the same way as it did Europe and America, the three months of its spread across the Middle East "confronted the Saudi state in the throes of its establishment under the constraints of globalisation, the fragility of its own ecosystem, and the risks inherent in resorting to foreign expertise at a critical moment in its territorial expansion and institutional formation" (ibid.).

As this book examines, the Spanish Flu in Arabia illustrated how pandemics and politics can be dangerously intertwined and affect not only the political power-building of nascent states but also their mode of political legitimacy. Indeed, when Saudi Arabia suffered from the spread of MERS in 2012, "the Spanish Flu of 1919 was rapidly resurrected in the Saudi press, alongside Health Ministry bulletins" as a reminder of the triumph of the Saudi state over previous pandemics, ignoring the fact that outside observers pointed out that "[f]rom one epidemic to the next, the crisis symptoms displayed by the Saudi state recur with astonishing regularity: the broadening scope of state intervention, medical and security control of the holy places, and a nervous relationship with the outside world" (ibid.). The response of the Saudi state to MERS, especially, and the importance of Mecca during outbreaks will be discussed in more detail in this chapter.

The relationship of the Spanish Flu (and other influenza outbreaks) to the UK and to the British is an interesting one to examine. As with other case studies, the arrival of Covid prompted comparisons between the novel coronavirus pandemic and the Spanish Flu's effects on society, with Professor Martin Bayly considering to what extent fatalism on the back of the Great War's casualties induced a certain "absence of public grief" (Bayly, October 28, 2020). As with other countries, the UK was hit with three waves, "[t]he first in the spring of 1918; the second, and most deadly, in the winter of 1918; and the third wave in the early spring of 1919" (ibid.). As with the early days of Covid-19, "public and political response to the pandemic" was partly influenced by "the sheer uncertainty over what the disease was" and some health workers at the time made comparisons to the earlier Russian Flu (1889–92), the symptoms of which included breathing problems and a loss of taste and smell that would later be key traits of Covid (ibid., Prater, April 23, 2022).

In addition to press censorship imposed by all European countries barring neutral Spain, the UK prioritized resources for the war rather than tackling the pandemic, despite the fact that the "Spanish Flu pandemic killed an estimated 228,000 in the UK, making 1918 the first year on record in which deaths exceeded births" (Bayly). There were some organizations like the British Red Cross that "distributed large numbers of medical supplies to hospitals across the country as well as overseas" (British Red Cross, January 27, 2021). On the whole, however, the war in Europe diverted medical practitioners away from the UK. Furthermore, the horrifying scale of fatalities as a result of the war had normalised death in such a way as to induce a degree of fatalism in the crisis narrative. Added to this, in the absence of comparative or time-series data, the public were given few tools to anticipate the future course of the outbreak, nor were policy elites willing to regularly narrate the chronology of deaths. The difference to today's slick PowerPoint-led data-heavy government briefings is stark. Certain newspapers and public figures, including those within the medical profession, encouraged the idea that worrying about the disease would increase one's susceptibility to illness and even weaken the nation's resolve in the war effort. In the words of Sir Arthur Newsholme, the Chief Medical Officer of the Local Government Board (LGB), the national circumstances compelled an individual duty to "carry on." (Bayly)

Indeed, the Spanish Flu's arrival, amid what was once dubbed "the war to end all wars," seemed to affect the UK's response to mortality rates due to sickness being second to the battlefront's casualties. Some analysts have even argued that the trauma of the First World War overshadowed the spread of the Spanish Flu within the UK to the extent that it was dubbed "the forgotten pandemic." Civilian responses to the pandemic were regulated by the fog of war and the fear that "war-weariness" could be exacerbated by a second battle with a pandemic, leading some critics at the time to consider "the flu something of a joke" and that critics' "wry remarks, though clearly calculated to amuse, were typical of British attitudes to the 'Spanish Flu'" before the later deadlier waves, which themselves still revealed a certain British stiffness. "'Never since the Black Death has such a plague swept over the face of the world,' commented *The Times* in December 1918, '[and] never, perhaps, has a plague been more stoically accepted'" (Honigsbaum, April, 2013, p. 166). As we will see later in this chapter, the British attitude toward more than one influenza pandemic has shown a laissez-faire attitude of dismissing some pandemics as "just a flu." Such an approach was discussed by some critics in the initial months of Covid-19's arrival in Europe and eventually the UK, with some observers pointing out that a so-called bad flu season may take "about a quarter of the life years lost among those older than 75 from Covid-19" (Krelle, Tallack, March 23, 2021).

Nonetheless, a detached attitude toward the Spanish Flu did not mean a complete lack of response attempts. Indeed, when compared to Covid, it would seem that "the actions taken by [the] government and individuals have a familiar ring to them" (BBC, May 10, 2020). That said, advice provided to the government by the Royal Society of Medicine's Sir Arthur Newsholme "was buried by the government" after outlining the need for people "to stay at home if they were sick and to avoid large gatherings" (ibid.). The war effort took precedence, and Newsholme himself conceded that "[t]here are national circumstances in which the major duty is to 'carry on', even when risk to life and health is involved" (ibid.).

During Covid, Boris Johnson warned that "if too many people become seriously unwell at one time, the NHS will be unable to handle it-so we [must] protect the

NHS's ability to cope" (Johnson, March 23, 2020). Under the sickness of 1918 influenza, hospitals quickly overflowed with patients, prompting "many theatres, dance halls, cinemas and churches [to] close, in some cases for months," though a centralized lockdown was not imposed (BBC, May 10, 2020). Disinfection of streets began "in some towns and cities and some people wore anti-germ masks as they went about their daily lives"; however, pubs "mostly stayed open" and sports matches that had not already been canceled due to the war "attracted large crowds, continuing throughout the pandemic" (ibid.).

The issue of sports and crowds would also be paralleled during the Covid-19 pandemic. Although pubs and restaurants were issued with a 10:00 p.m. curfew in October 2020, the response to early eviction of some sports fans in the British capital was to stage "an impromptu cricket match on a high street in South London after venues were forced to close at 10 pm in line with the government's coronavirus restrictions" (Batchelor, October 11, 2020). A video recorded by documentary maker James Jones shows "[t]he atmosphere was very sweet and exuberant. I'll leave it to other people to debate the rights and wrongs but it was a joyful moment at a time when we all need a bit of joy in our lives" (ibid.)! Jones admitted that the spontaneous match "coincided with everyone being kicked out of the pubs and bars at 10 pm so it grew into a larger crowd." It is not known if anyone was keeping score, though some would argue that the true winner of the crowded match was the novel coronavirus (ibid.).

Haphazard containment measures during the Spanish Flu came amid a flurry of confused public health messages, and, as with Covid-19, "fake news and conspiracy theories abounded, although the general level of ignorance about healthy lifestyles did not help" (BBC, May 10, 2020). Misunderstanding of health and virology also meant mixed results for proposed health measures. Some believed tobacco smoking could prevent infection, while others in parliament wondered if three daily doses of cacao was an effective agent to prevent infection as well. Some hygiene campaigns were more aligned with today's better knowledge of well-being. Some "campaigns and leaflets warned against spreading diseases through coughs and sneezes" and a November 1918 publication by News of the World "advised its readers to: 'wash inside nose with soap and water each night and morning; force yourself to sneeze night and morning, then breathe deeply. Do not wear a muffler; take sharp walks regularly and walk home from work; eat plenty of porridge'" (ibid.).

Of note regarding Britain's response to the Spanish Flu is the fact that the government did not oversee a centralized and coordinated response to the virus. Indeed, some recommendations for hygiene measures came from private individuals or publications and hence were not enforced, with some advice even buried by the government itself amid the fatigue of war. Because the UK's response to Spanish Flu was not highly centralized with the enforcement of restrictions, and perhaps because of war fatigue, conspiracy theories and fake news were not uncommon, but protests against hygiene measures and the use of less-than-democratic policies were not a concern. In the United States, however, the Spanish Flu provoked very different public and government responses.

During the Spanish Flu in the United States, some citizens kept diaries to chronicle this time of sudden and unprecedented restrictions. Some, like 42-year-old historian Dorman B.E. Kent, resorted to diary-keeping after infection, recording "his symptoms in vivid detail" (Solly, April 13, 2020). In response to "'a high fever', 'an awful headache' and a stomach bug," he was instructed by one "Dr. Watson" to "place greased cloths and hot water bottles around his throat and chest." For fifteen-year-old Violet Harris of Seattle, her initial diary entries revealed "a childlike naivete." One entry from mid-October 1918 celebrated the announcement "'in the papers tonight that all churches, shows, and schools would be closed until further notice, to prevent Spanish influenza from spreading. Good idea? I'll say it is! So will every other school kid, I calculate. The only cloud in my sky is that the [School] Board will add the missed days onto the end of the term'" (ibid.). A brief analysis of Harris's later accounts reveals a mix of relief at lifted restrictions while also illustrating some fear toward the effects of a new illness. On the one hand, Harris rejoices on November 12 at the thought of "'[n]o more masks. Everything open too. School opens this week—Thursday! Did you ever? As if they couldn't have waited till Monday!'" On the other hand, Harris's observation of her best friend, Rena, reveals a fear of infection as she describes her friend's condition as so severe "she could hardly walk." After Rena's recovery, "Harris asked her 'what it felt like to have the influenza,' and she said, 'don't get it'" (ibid.).

Compared to much of Europe, significant effort was put into hygiene measures across the United States. This gap may have been partially influenced by the fact that Europe overall experienced one autumn wave, while many US cities suffered from two waves in the same season (Bootsma, Ferguson, 2007, p. 7588). As with the UK, however, restrictions were not nationally coordinated and at times contradictory. Philadelphia, for example, detected its first influenza case on September 17, 1918, and responded within a day with "a campaign against coughing, spitting, and sneezing in public. Yet 10 days later—despite the prospect of an epidemic at its doorstep—the city hosted a parade that 200,000 people attended" (Champine, Strochlic, March 27, 2020). Once the first case emerged in neighboring St. Louis, it took two days for that city to "shut down most public gatherings and quarantine victims in their homes" (ibid.). The result of such restrictions was that "the death rate in St. Louis was less than half of the rate in Philadelphia" (ibid.).

However, with ever-increasing restrictions comes the risk of civil disobedience. Then, as now, masks became one of the first lines of defense and therefore a symbol "in political and cultural wars" (Hauser, August 3, 2020). In San Francisco, there were 7000 cases by October 1918. In response, Mayor James Rolph signed into force "'[t]he Mask Ordinance,' [which made] San Francisco the first American city to require face coverings, which had to be four layers thick" (ibid.). Penalties were imposed on those who refused to have their individual "appearance, comfort and freedom" affected by "[m]asks that looked like 'slabs of ravioli,'" including punishment of "$5 to $10 (between $102 to $204 adjusted for inflation), or 10 days' imprisonment" (ibid.). In one case, "a San Francisco health officer shot three people, two of them innocent bystanders," for refusal of the intended target to wear a mask (Price, March 19, 2020). As outlined by *The Bellingham Herald* and according to San Francisco police at the time, "[Officer] Henry D. Miller shot in the air when [James] Wisser first refused his request. Wisser closed in on him and in the succeeding affray, Miller shot him in the leg and right hand. Wisser was taken to the central emergency hospital, where he was placed under arrest for failure to comply with Miller's order" (ibid.).

Enough opposed the wearing of masks in San Francisco to see "prisons swell to standing room only" (Hauser). However, other cities like Los Angeles invited public debate on masking. In Illinois, the wearing of masks was politicized heavily by suffragists who "rejected covering their mouths at a time when their voices were crucial" and addressed the pandemic by practicing limited gathering and social distancing at events. However, San Francisco would see masks seriously challenged by the organization of the Anti-Mask League. By the end of 1918, fatigue of and skepticism toward restrictions was collating around the city's decision to reinstate the original mask ordinance, which had been suspended until deaths began to increase, "with the new year seeing almost 2,000 infections and over 100 deaths" (ibid.). The league protested "at a Board of Supervisors meeting," questioning the scientific validity of masking and arguing that mandatory wearing of masks was "unconstitutional" (ibid.).

In a sense, the Anti-Mask League was targeting not only masks but the political legitimacy of the city's elite. As explained by history professor Bill Issel of San Francisco State University, "protests back in 1918 and 1919 were organized. That sort of distrust of experts, distrust of the government's point of view was very strong. The San Francisco of 1870 to 1920 was only gradually moving away from a city that had a huge problem raising enough money through bond issues and taxation to put sidewalks in the street" (Kane, April 29, 2020).

Hence, the nascent administrative competence of San Francisco's elected officials, tied to preexisting suspicion of government, meant that the Anti-Mask League represented not only the personal freedom to refuse the wearing of masks but also the right to question

> the legitimacy of state power, underscored by the discomfort of citizens who could not see one another's faces. Publicly concealing oneself has always been associated with lawlessness and behaviors deemed antisocial or deviant, from the bandanas worn by train robbers to the Guy Fawkes masks found on antifa street protests to the beaked plague doctor costume found at masquerades and Edwardian balls. (ibid.)

In any event, the anti-mask protests of 1918 are a reminder that similar protests during Covid are not new, and more contemporary oppositions to masks in the United States also drew on concepts of personal freedom and criticized the science behind mask usage. The death of one such "freedom fighter" from Covid is a reminder that, as in 1918, the wearing of masks when vaccines are unavailable remains one of the first weapons in the fight against a pandemic (Associated Press in San Angelo, Texas, August 29, 2021).

An overview of how the Spanish Flu affected China, the Arabian Peninsula, the UK, and the United States reveals that, although Europe and the United States were more severely affected, China did suffer from the 1918 pandemic. For the Arabian Peninsula, the Spanish Flu came at a time when Abdulaziz was attempting to consolidate his authority and relied on the militant but traditional *Ikhwan* forces for his conquests. The Spanish Flu threatened to erode his political support and risked portraying the emerging Emir as over-reliant on Western medicine and medical staff. Indeed, the Spanish Flu seemed to directly contribute to the creation of Mecca's first health agency, which was later expanded across what became Saudi Arabia and staffed initially with Arab health workers rather than Americans associated with Christian missionaries in the Gulf.

In the UK, the wounds of war left Britain and its government weary of death counts, and even when influenza began to circulate, resources were prioritized for combat in the trenches of Europe rather than the hospitals at home, some of which relied on medical equipment from the British Red Cross. Advice to the government that would be regarded as "following the science" under Covid, such as social distancing, lockdowns, and case isolations, was ignored by the government for fear of exacerbating fatigue already caused by the First World War. Finally, the flu pandemic in the United States also illustrates the lack of a centralized response but perhaps a tougher set of measures in some cities, including the enforcement of masks on threat of fines or imprisonment. As we will see across the rest of this chapter, the lack of a coordinated and timely response to pandemics remained an issue for some case studies. Pandemics that emerged in the twenty-first century had a different impact on each state but continued to provoke questions of governmental authority and the ability of world leaders to accurately assess the risk of new illnesses.

The 2003 SARS Outbreak

The SARS predated Covid-19 by almost two decades as a serious coronavirus that had a relatively low transmission rate but "a remarkably powerful and negative psychological impact on many populations worldwide. The relatively high case fatality rate, the identification of super spreaders, the newness of the disease, the speed of its global spread, and public uncertainty about the ability to control its spread may have contributed to the public's alarm" (Knobler, Lemon, Mahmoud, 2004). Typical symptoms include fever and chills, body aches, headaches, and a persistent dry cough, the latter a feature that would be one of the first signs of Covid-19 infection. Nausea, vomiting, and diarrhea were also reported, with experts pointing out that such symptoms could be mistaken for originating from the flu, risking that those infected with SARS would not seek medical help or isolate, which in turn could risk spreading infections further (Chan et al., 2004). The disease seemed to first spread from mainland China to Hong Kong via a 64-year-old doctor who traveled to Hong Kong in late February 2003 and eventually succumbed to SARS-related severe pneumonia in early March. From Hong Kong, SARS spread to Vietnam, Singapore, and as far as Canada (ibid.).

By the time of the Hong Kong outbreak, mainland China was already dealing with a novel coronavirus that had at first been mistaken for severe pneumonia as early as mid-November 2002 in the province of Guangdong, where the regional capital, Guangzhou, had been hit with the Spanish Flu almost a century earlier. By February 11, 2003, the Guangdong health authority officially announced an outbreak and by the end of March, SARS was an identifiable disease, and under WHO global travel alerts (Ahmad, Krumkamp, Reintjes, 2009, pp. 36–7). Compared to the Spanish Flu, SARS spread through an established mode of transport that also benefited Covid across 2019 to 2020: air travel (ibid., p. 37).

Within Hong Kong, SARS became concentrated and attacked in three distinct waves. The first such wave "was an explosive outbreak in a teaching hospital, affecting a large number of staff and medical students in March 2003," and was followed by a second wave characterized by hospital-to-community infection that spread to the Amoy Gardens residential estate, infecting over three hundred residents and killing thirty-three (Hung, 2003, p. 374). The third and final wave hit in early May, "with continuing recurrence of the disease in eight hospitals and more than 170 housing estates throughout the city [of Hong Kong]" (ibid.).

In response to the spread of SARS, Hong Kong countered with measures that would later be seen during the Covid pandemic. These included:

- Compulsory isolation of infected and surveillance of those that had contact with the infected through contact tracing
- Preventive education and public communication campaigns
- Closure of schools and universities
- Open information exchange on infections between Hong Kong and mainland China
- Temperature checks for arriving and departing travelers
- District-wide cleansing campaigns (Lee, 2003, p. 653)

In mainland China, similar steps were taken. However, there seemed to be a lack of coordination across all regions. Guangdong responded rapidly to the emergence of SARS, which included quickly publishing a nascent case description that was distributed across the region. This report, though initially referring to the disease as "atypical pneumonia," was eventually used by many other countries affected by SARS "in a modified version" (Ahmad, Krumkamp, Reintjes, 2009, p. 38). Following the production of this report came a system of case reporting, whereby "[a]ll hospitals [in China] had to report cases to the local centre for disease control, which in turn reported it to the provincial centre" (ibid.). While many other measures echoed efforts in Hong Kong, some cities, such as Beijing, saw a faster explosion of cases, which in turn provoked stern containment attempts. Such measures included Beijing's Treatment and Provision Law, which "instituted collective quarantine for 12,000 people by sealing off hospitals, construction sites, residential buildings and universities. In rural areas in China, entire villages were cordoned off in Hubei province" (ibid., p. 40).

As discussed throughout this book, pandemics and the response by governments to them will inevitably spread into the political sphere, and SARS indeed seemed to have such an effect on the CCP. Some analysts widely speculated that SARS would be "China's Chernobyl, leading to far-reaching political change and perhaps democratization," though other observers cautiously argued that China's "political system will simply absorb the impact and not change" (Fewsmith, 2003, p. 1). It would certainly seem, however, that "China's failure to report SARS in a timely and accurate fashion was apparently due to the desire to maintain 'stability' during a period of leadership transition as well as a deeply ingrained bureaucratic impulse to maintain secrecy (even within the political system)" (ibid.).

Added to the impulse for secrecy were the mixed messages of different political departments. On the one hand, Head of Government, Premier Wen Jiabao led meetings that seemed intended to illustrate that "the issue was being taken very seriously at the highest level" and there would be accountability, as symbolized by "the dramatic firing of Minister of Health Zhang Wenkang on April 20" (ibid., p. 2). On the other hand, there seemed to be inaccurate reports of case numbers amid an atmosphere of political tension and insubordination that culminated in the last-minute removal of Wenkang after it was revealed that he was aware of city officials' attempts to downplay the spread of SARS (ibid., p. 3).

The removal of Wenkang and Beijing Mayor Meng Xuenong was followed by a wave of "similar, but lower profile sackings around the country," which included up to 120 officials being let go for "dereliction of duty," while almost 70 other officials were disciplined in an attempt to scare other officials back into line and show citizens that SARS was being taken seriously. However, while media outlet Xinhua touted such dismissals as unprecedented, a similar move to restore government confidence was used during a flood disaster in 1998, and commentators were careful to consider such action as in any way indicative of political reform (ibid., p. 5). Complementing such dismissals was an aggressive state media campaign intended to also bolster "the leadership's decision to reverse course and report the SARS crisis honestly," which meant not only accurate numbers but "[President] Hu Jintao and Wen Jiabao in a constant blur of activity—convening meetings, visiting hospitals, meeting health workers," and an eventual theme of patriotism, under which Li Changchun of the CCP's Propaganda Department emphasized "uniting the will of the masses into a fortress, dedicating ourselves in unity, seeking truth in a scientific way, overcoming difficulties, and winning victory" (ibid., p. 7).

Ultimately, such propaganda attempted to create "the new emphasis on ordinary people sacrificing for the national struggle against SARS" and even included glorifying health workers such as "Deng Lianxian, a senior doctor in a hospital in Guangzhou who died of SARS while treating other SARS sufferers," with Hu Jintao expressing his condolences to the doctor's family and using him as an example of the "struggles and contributions of medical workers throughout the country" (ibid., p. 7).

Such praise contrasts the treatment of key medical workers in the early stages of Covid-19, during which "the authorities censored information, concealed the virus, and silenced doctors who tried to warn their colleagues" (Sparrow, March 18,

2021). Such an atmosphere also meant that hospital management leaders "refused to authorize masks or other personal protective equipment (PPE) on the grounds that it would cause panic. As patients infected health care workers and health care workers infected one another, hospital leaders insisted that spread among humans was impossible—that no staff members were infected—even altering diagnoses that suggested otherwise" (ibid.).

In any event, even though the CCP's leadership used the media as an attempt to restore their legitimacy and public confidence during the SARS crisis, Chinese media outlets themselves were critical of the government's cover-up attempts. One outlet "compared keeping the lid on such stories to engaging a societal pressure cooker: 'The final result,' it said, 'would either be the lid bursting open, harming countless people; or the lid staying on, with countless victims under the lid'" (Fewsmith, p. 9). In addition, the combination of initial lack of transparency and, in some cases, arbitrary quarantines "eroded the public's trust and contributed to the spread of rumors even after the government adopted a more open stance" (Huang, 2004).

Such an erosion was not only a significant contributing factor to civil opposition to government restrictions during SARS but also "could deplete the social capital that would be so important for future government outbreak control efforts" (ibid.). Indeed, already during SARS,

> thousands of residents of a rural town of Tianjin ransacked a building, believing it would be used to house ill patients with confirmed or suspected SARS even though officials insisted that it would be used only as a medical observation facility to accommodate people who had close contacts with SARS patients and for travelers returning from SARS hot spots. Opposition to official efforts to contain SARS was also found in a coastal Zhejiang province, where several thousand people took part in a violent protest against six people being quarantined after returning from Beijing. (ibid.)

Of course, such protests during SARS pale in comparison to 2022 protests against Covid restrictions in China. That year, China's zero-Covid policy was being challenged by severe civil resistance. Restrictions had included travel bans and so-called "quarantine camps." Such quarantine measures especially had been linked to "a deadly fire in the western Xinjiang region—critics said the victims had been unable to escape the building because of lockdown measures" and, whether true or not, this incident seemed to act as a catalyst for popular unrest that was mounting amid severe delays in emergency medical care for those in locked-down areas. The result of such protests at the end of 2022 was that China was forced to abandon the most extreme methods of countering Covid, including mass quarantine, which was downgraded to home isolation, and comprehensive travel bans. Perhaps both SARS and Covid illustrate that pandemics have challenged China's nondemocratic leadership and that perceived security from a deadly virus is not enough to maintain a regime's legitimacy for long periods (Mao, December 7, 2022).

Saudi Arabia did not share China's spread of SARS. However, just as the Spanish Flu affected the nascent politics of the Saudi kingdom and prompted the creation of a health agency in Mecca, there were concerns that SARS could explode across Saudi Arabia and beyond during the *hajj*, or religious pilgrimage season, that sees the holy cities of Mecca and Medina host millions of Muslims annually. This unique congregation in Saudi Arabia specifically presents its own risks such that "even a single case of severe acute respiratory syndrome in such an overcrowded environment could ignite a massive epidemic of the disease in these holy places and lead to a further spread of the disease internationally by the returning pilgrims" (Madani, 2004, p. 120).

It is here worth mentioning that the religious value of Mecca (and Medina), coupled with the *hajj*'s millions of annual visitors, no doubt creates the need for unique responses to pandemics in Saudi Arabia, as we shall further discuss as we continue examining how diseases affect the power politics of our case studies. Indeed, while it seems Saudi Arabia did not receive significant SARS cases (or adopt strict control measures), the government still launched several preventive measures (ibid.).

A scientific task force was composed and chaired by Ministry of Health official Tariq Madani and charged with designing "very strict strategies to prevent introduction of SARS into these holy places and into Saudi Arabia at large" (ibid.). Writing for a medical journal in 2004, Madani outlined key measures akin to what some countries would later use for Covid (and measures used by China during SARS), including comprehensive travel restrictions and quarantine. Travel bans included barring entry into Saudi Arabia of any passenger from "countries with reported local transmission of SARS (epidemic countries), whereby people from these countries are not allowed to enter Saudi Arabia unless 10 days (the maximum incubation period) have elapsed since departure" (ibid.). An exception to this rule was the return of Saudi citizens and residents who would then be "subjected to clinical assessment on entry and home quarantine for 10 days with daily follow-up by the nearest primary health care facility." Such precise measures came atop the need for returnees to "sign a form confirming that they will remain indoors, allow no visitors into their residence, fully cooperate with the health care personnel who will be contacting them on a daily basis for 10 days, and notify the nearest Ministry of Health facility of any respiratory symptoms developing during the 10 days of home quarantine" (ibid.).

The development of any such symptoms during the SARS incubation period meant immediate hospitalization and isolation "until the acute illness has completely resolved regardless of the results of the SARS confirmatory laboratory tests, which have limited sensitivity" (ibid.). As previously stated, Saudi Arabia did not seem to import any significant SARS cases. Nonetheless, these outlined restrictions, including quarantine and hospital confinement, partially echo the more brutal mass quarantines during China's own battle with SARS, and it is interesting to consider whether Saudi Arabia would have seen any civil disobedience, as in China, had significant numbers of SARS cases been discovered.

Other measures undertaken would foreshadow Saudi Arabia's response to Covid-19. Infrared thermal cameras were installed across most major airports to detect passenger temperatures (ibid.). The same technology would be used in 2020 at airports and places of worship to monitor the spread of coronavirus (Hajj Reporters, May 31, 2020, Serrieh, April 17, 2020). In addition, passengers entering Saudi Arabia during SARS could only do so "after signing a statement confirming that in the preceding 10 days they have not been to any country with locally transmitted SARS and that they will bear full responsibility if this information is proven to be incorrect" (Madani, p. 120). As discussed in Chapter 1, I observed a similar system of forms used during Covid and, upon entering Saudi airspace, had to fill out forms confirming that I had not been suffering from Covid-related symptoms, transited through a country with significant cases, or (to the best of my knowledge) been in direct contact with anyone who had tested positive for Covid-19.

Travelers who had transited through any country with locally transmitted SARS cases were allowed entry into Saudi Arabia but only after a clinical assessment, and they would then be subjected to a similar ten-day quarantine "with daily follow-up by the nearest primary health care facility" (ibid.).

SARS-testing facilities were established in Riyadh, with a focus on technology that could detect both the SARS virus genome and antibodies against SARS. However, such testing capacity suffered from technical limitations, meaning antibodies were only traceable "after the 10th day of onset of illness" and limited sensitivity of tests also meant that negative results could not guarantee there was no infection (ibid., p. 121).

Finally, a further measure would be that of public awareness and training for health workers, two elements that would also be practiced by some countries that were later facing MERS and Covid, respectively. For health workers, education on SARS included "case definition, epidemiology (or disease control), mode of transmission, clinical features, diagnostic tests, hospital infection control measures, and preventive strategies" through lectures and dissemination of educational material. An intensive public awareness campaign pervaded "using newspapers, radio, television, brochures, posters, and the Ministry of Health website. Digital screens of football stadiums were also used to display short health educational messages" (ibid.).

Saudi Arabia did not suffer from any significant SARS cases, yet there was a comprehensive response to the pandemic, including travel bans, restrictions, and quarantines. We will never know if these responses are the reason why SARS did not infect the kingdom. However, as with Saudi Arabia's later response to Covid, these measures imply that, if anything, Saudi Arabia did not wish to be complacent and also illustrate an awareness of how the holy cities of Mecca and Medina created unique opportunities for infection and had to be protected both due to their religious but also subsequent political importance for the House of Saud. It was precisely such awareness and preparedness that many health experts argued for right before Covid.

As discussed in Chapter 1, experts warned in 2019 that a new virus could emerge and become global. Such fears were presciently echoed in Madani's, 2004 article, in which he argued that "given massive international air travel, it is possible that the SARS disease will become an established disease in the world despite all efforts to eradicate it. The recent identification of various animal species as possible sources of the SARS virus makes SARS eradication even more difficult or virtually impossible" (ibid.). Both SARS and Covid-19 are believed to have emerged from bats. A key difference between the two, however, is that SARS remains without a vaccine yet did not become global. Covid-19, on the other hand, spread worldwide and remained a strain on some healthcare systems in 2022, despite the production of multiple vaccines (Cheung, Gan, Wang, December 26, 2022).

Unlike Saudi Arabia, the UK did experience SARS cases, albeit in the hundreds. Between March and July 2003, the UK experienced a total of 368 cases (compared to Beijing's collective quarantine of 12,000 people alone) and was thus classified by domestic bodies as low-risk (Delpech et al., 2006, p. 27). From mid-March, the UK began SARS tests and announced its first case in May 2003. Out of a total of eight cases in late May, three were later confirmed as influenza (Parry, May 24, 2003).

Key to the UK's response to the SARS threat was its collaboration with the WHO and health agencies representing SARS-affected countries across Asia and North America. Such cooperation included working with Hong Kong "to establish a Centre for Health Protection (CHP) in light of recommendations of the Hong Kong SARS Expert Committee Report" (Delpech et al., p. 28). In addition, the UK's then-Health Protection Agency (HPA) sent staff "abroad with WHO Geneva and WHO Western Pacific Region, which provided useful contact points for information and discussion" and also saw HPA staff as part of "the multi-national team that identified the causative agent of SARS as a coronavirus" (ibid.). The UK's emphasis on international cooperation during SARS is of note compared to what seemed to be a complete lack of cooperation among states and between states and international bodies during the initial stages of Covid-19 (Kliem, April 11, 2020).

HPA even contributed to investigating the hotel in Hong Kong "believed to have been pivotal to the initial international spread of SARS," which included tracking down almost 150 UK residents who had stayed at the said hotel. Two of them "tested positive for SARS-CoV antibodies" (Delpech et al., p. 28).

Again, for the UK, SARS seemed to trigger an emphasis on international cooperation. The need to intercept a flight from Europe to London "with a SARS patient on board led to the formation of the UK SARS Taskforce," with representatives "from the Health Departments, National Health Service (NHS), and national surveillance centres in England." Objectives for the Task Force included:

- "Oversee and coordinate the surveillance of potential SARS cases
- Provide guidance on the management of cases and contacts
- Consider and recommend broader public health control measures
- Provide timely information to professionals and the public" (ibid., p. 29)

In addition to the Task Force, other specialist groups were created to advise the Task Force and other relevant departments on strategic issues and responses to SARS. The result of such a framework was "an effective mechanism for rapid exchange of information and expertise" that streamlined "consensus on operational issues and strategic response to SARS" and even served as a model "during 2004 to address issues related to the outbreak of avian influenza in south east Asia" (ibid.). Certainly, the resources poured into a SARS response by the UK were in stark contrast to the limited measures during the Spanish Flu, as war coffers drained cash flow from healthcare and toward the front line. Furthermore, SARS foreshadowed how Covid would challenge "ensuring NHS and partner organisations maintain continuity of key services," as contingency planning under the HPA and in response to SARS "raised a number of issues regarding NHS" preparedness that would widen during Covid (ibid., pp. 30–1). These included, especially, availability and purchase of PPE and ventilators (ibid., p. 31). In a sense, then, although SARS remained a low-risk infection in the UK, the response of the Task Force and subsequent contingency planning revealed gaps that could have been addressed long before Covid-19 would sweep across the nation, foreshadowing PPE shortages and related problems during the novel coronavirus pandemic.

As will be discussed in Chapter 4, the spread of Covid-19 saw the creation of various emergency laws to issue a variety of restrictions (Council of Europe, 2022). However, during SARS, the US government gave a comprehensive legal response that saw SARS be classified as a quarantinable disease (Cetron et al., 2004, p. 353). It is worth noting that prior to SARS, the Centers for Disease Control and Prevention (CDC) already had the "legal authority to apprehend, detain, or conditionally release persons" but only under previously listed diseases. Hence, adding SARS to this list gave the CDC power to detain or conditionally release that was already a precedent for some other diseases (ibid.). However, observers note that such legal amendments did not mean that the CDC prioritized maximizing their authority. This may be especially true as, like in the UK, SARS cases in the United States were fairly low, reaching 115 in April 2003 (Roos, April 4, 2003). Of the said number, there were no fatalities and most patients recovered (ibid.).

Indeed, some argued that making SARS a quarantinable disease simply "provided U.S. federal health officials with quarantine powers comparable to those in other countries affected by SARS," and similar "to actions taken in other countries, CDC quarantine officers also began screening incoming passengers for symptoms of SARS, distributing health alerts and advisories regarding SARS, and coordinating with airport personnel in the evaluation of sick passengers" (Cetron et al., p. 354). Perhaps recognizing the risk of seeming to abuse authority, the CDC prefers to maintain collaboration with individual affected states, respecting each state's independent response, and "is likely to invoke federal quarantine power only rarely, such as at ports of entry or other time-sensitive situations" (ibid.).

There is a parallel in the lessons learned during SARS between the United States and the UK. Both states saw low cases, but SARS revealed the need for international cooperation (the UK) and cooperation across states within a federal system regarding quarantine (the United States) (ibid.). Moreover, pandemics and related crises often reveal that "legal issues are nearly always intertwined with public health responses" and hence, just as the UK's Task Force cooperated with the WHO and other national health agencies to rapidly exchange information on SARS, there is a similar need to ensure that legal information and relevant legislation can be equally exchanged across state or county lines in the same country to ensure that responses to pandemics are streamlined, efficient, and transparent (ibid., p. 355).

An overview of how SARS affected democratic and less democratic states reveals how politicized pandemics can be and to what extent restrictive measures may begin to provoke unrest, as seen to an extent in China when institutionalized quarantine was adopted. In addition, SARS prompted some countries to take comprehensive preventive measures that recognized how, for example, religious tourism risked creating the perfect environment for the virus to spread domestically and globally, as in Saudi Arabia. Such measures may have created a model for addressing future pandemics, including Covid-19. Further, the UK used SARS as an opportunity to expand international cooperation, illustrating a much-needed requirement of pandemic management. The UK's HPA also assessed gaps in the purchase and distribution of PPE and ventilators; however, rather than be used as an opportunity to close such gaps, the proposed contingency plan response simply foreshadowed a widening of such problems during Covid, identified by a UK body that would close in 2013 and be absorbed by another institute that would itself be replaced by two separate institutes sometime later (gov.uk, 2013, gov.uk, n.d.).

Cooperation was also a key lesson learned during SARS in the United States and is a theme that will be returned to across this book, especially when discussing the response to Covid by democratic and nondemocratic states.

The 2009 H1N1 Pandemic

I had just recovered from Covid-19, pushing through the body aches with plenty of aspirin. My body's return to wellness was thankfully a few days before my wife and I had planned a much-longed trip to Istanbul, our first vacation since the end of travel bans. I'd tested negative for a week and enjoyed the flight. On the third day, I began coughing but put it down to the tobacco smoke in some of the cafés we frequented. Two days later, I gave an online guest lecture, ironically about Covid in conflict zones. I'd taken an aspirin to deal with fatigue and what I now suspected was a breaking fever. I awoke in the middle of the night with a queasy stomach and chills. It seems each time we visit Turkey, I learn something new. That April in 2022, I discovered that Istanbul had excellent healthcare (though we visited a private hospital). Upon arrival, I was given an intravenous solution that eased my fever and malaise within minutes. My blood was taken for a test. The results would be available in less than an hour. "It's not Covid," confirmed our doctor. "It's influenza A." I had swine flu.

The H1N1 pandemic arrived six years after SARS as a descendant of the 1918 Spanish Flu (Kansas State University, May 1, 2009). The H1N1 virus caused what the CDC described as "the first global flu pandemic in 40 years" (CDC, August 31, 2023). H1N1 is also known as swine-origin influenza A, likely because "[s]ix of the genes are closest in sequence to those of H1N2 influenza viruses isolated from pigs

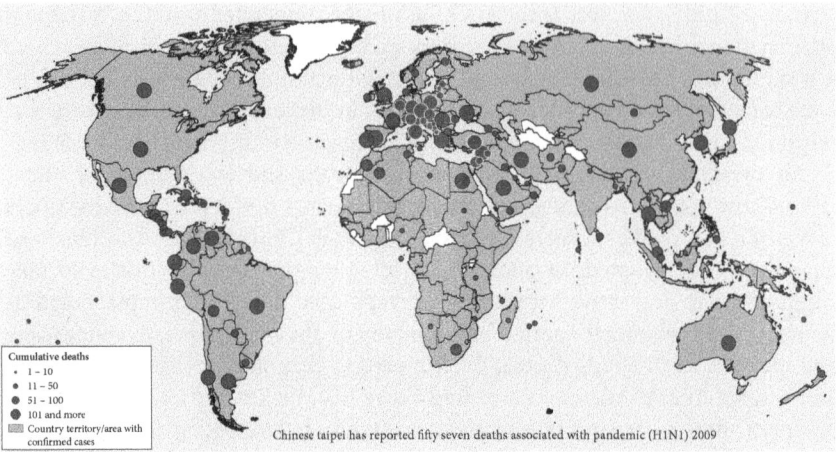

Figure 2.2 Map of the 2009 H1N1 spread by August 2010. Source: World Health Organization. 2013. *Evolution of a pandemic: A (H1N1) 2009, April 2009-August 2010* (2nd edition). Geneva, Switzerland: World Health Organization, p. 41.

in North America around 1999–2000" (Armstrong, Downie, Gibbs, 2009, p. 1). H1N1 was first found circulating in human beings in Mexico (ibid.). From there, it spread to almost two hundred countries and was subsequently classified by the WHO as a global pandemic (BBC, n.d.).

Within Mexico itself, the outbreak of H1N1 led to a response that would later seem prophetic as Covid infected the world. The H1N1 virus was first isolated for study in mid-April 2009 (Armstrong, Downie, Gibbs, p. 1). By the end of that month, Mexico would enter lockdown (Carroll, Tuckman, April 30, 2009). While short when compared to many Covid lockdowns, journalists still reported that it was "an unprecedented nationwide lockdown [under which] the government ordered most of the economy to shut and for people to stay indoors" (ibid.).

"There is no safer place than your own home to avoid being infected with the flu virus," insisted then-President Felipe Calderón in a televised address as Mexico battled what would become almost 1000 cases and, in some instances, saw a mortality rate of roughly 8 percent (BBC, n.d., Carroll, Tuckman, 2009). As with Covid lockdowns, there was the dilemma of balancing reducing the spread of the virus with economic risk. The announced lockdown weakened the Mexican peso, and tourism, which at the time represented 8 percent of gross domestic product, came to a halt. Before the announced restrictions, Mexico was "already operating on half-battery since earlier [that] week when schools, cinemas, restaurants, gyms and other services were closed or heavily restricted." Now, all public services and venues would close except for "transport, policing, supermarkets and hospitals" (ibid.). The reality of economic loss for many was acknowledged by Calderón in the same address. "I know many of you have had to suspend your activities and may have seen your earnings fall but it is worth it if we can look after the health of our loved ones and protect Mexico from this evil" (ibid.).

Mexico's comprehensive and early response was praised by some observers, who noted that Mexico as early as 2003 "had developed a National Preparedness and Response Plan for an Influenza Pandemic focused in risk communication, health promotion, healthcare, epidemiological surveillance, strategic stockpile, research and development" (Arzoz-Padrés et al., 2009, p. 1).

Although the 2003 plan faced challenges under a novel influenza virus in 2009, Mexico's highly centralized response ensured the

> rest of the world benefitted from the Mexican experience thanks to the timeliness with which the government issued the [global] sanitary alert and informed about the course of the epidemic. The knowledge shared by Mexico provided the countries who have faced the human influenza virus A (H1N1) with information about its characteristics, its clinical picture and the chance of cure if timely healthcare is provided. This, in turn, has led to mitigating the economic, sanitary and social effects. Upon donating this strain of virus to the world through WHO, Mexico has contributed to developing a specific vaccine that will make it possible to prevent and control this new variety of human influenza. Moreover, the country has given proof of solidarity and responsibility for global health even at a time of a major economic crisis. (ibid.)

Indeed, once an H1N1 vaccine was available, Mexico provided it to citizens at no cost through government vaccination centers (DeSisto et al., 2019, p. 5). Mexico's handling of H1N1 thus echoes how some countries ensured international cooperation during SARS but also were willing to impose restrictive measures to address rising case numbers. Further, a vaccine for H1N1 was quickly developed. However, in a move foreshadowing the fragmented response to Covid, "wealthy countries bought up virtually all the supplies of the vaccine" and only agreed to donate 10 percent of their supply after WHO intervention (Bollyky, Bown, pp. 100–2). A discussion of such vaccine nationalism will further explore the disconnect between wealthy and poorer nations during pandemics at the end of this chapter.

In China, Beijing once again became a hotbed of strict sanitary measures. SARS had seen controversial mass quarantine. While infected countries such as "the United States and Canada suggested that infected people should stay at home, and enforced school closures whenever necessary," in response to H1N1, China "adopted a much stricter prevention approach" (Geng et al., 2013, p. 4691).

Despite no recommendations by the WHO to do so, China enacted a "one-week mandatory quarantine for all 'close contactors' (i.e., those who had close contact with an infectious person in hospitals or hotels)" (ibid.). The quarantine lasted "from the first identified imported (from the United States) case on 9 May to July 8, 2009" and provoked retroactive debate on China's pandemic responses, with critics arguing that "either minimalist or maximalist responses may potentially be very harmful" and that "strict preventative measures might cause misunderstanding over the justification of losing one's movement freedom for a week, or even raise international conflicts" (ibid.). Any passengers entering China "with body temperature over 37.5 °C were also quarantined" (ibid., p. 4692).

By late December 2009, China had confirmed cases of 121,805 in the mainland, representing "only 0.00094 [percent] of the total population" (ibid.). However, it was Hong Kong that seemed to lead a more comprehensive research response. Attempting to learn from the SARS outbreak, Hong Kong had established the Center for Health Protection "to take a leading role in the prevention and control of diseases in Hong Kong" and in 2004 "the Hong Kong Government created the Research Fund for the Control of Infectious Diseases with an endowment of US$57 million, aiming to encourage, facilitate and support research on the prevention, treatment, and control of infectious diseases" (Cowling et al., 2013, p. 367). While mainland China enacted strict measures without waiting for WHO recommendations, Hong Kong enacted measures following the WHO's global alert related to H1N1 in April 2009. Measures "initially operated under containment efforts, including entry screening at airports, ports, and border crossings, hospital isolation of cases, tracing and quarantine of contacts, and routine antiviral [treatment]" (ibid., p. 368).

By June 11, Hong Kong's first case was identified and efforts shifted from containment to mitigation. As with Covid, closures were instigated of public spaces, especially kindergartens and schools. "All kindergartens and primary schools were closed from June 12 until summer vacation in early July, while 43 secondary schools were closed after 1 or more confirmed cases was identified" (ibid.). It was later estimated that the early closure of schools and kindergartens may have reduced infection among children by up to 75 percent, with observers also arguing that kids "appeared to be more susceptible to infection and more infectious than adults" (ibid., pp. 377, 369). Hospitalized patients with H1N1 often had pre-existing health complications but "tended to be younger and have higher mortality rates," although overall "[s]easonal influenza and H1N1 had similar patterns of viral shedding, clinical presentation, and risk of admission to an intensive care unit (ICU) and death" (ibid., p. 369).

Indeed, when the first wave of H1N1 started in Hong Kong, mild symptoms meant that "the local population generally did not perceive infection to be a threat nor estimate a high possibility of having a local outbreak." Nonetheless, "[a]voidance behaviours, such as hand washing, mask wearing, or social distance, had been taken by many since the beginning of the pandemic, while social distancing measures declined in frequency through the course of the first wave" (ibid., p. 372).

As with measures during Covid, it is worth noting that the public's willingness to engage in further preventative action was "dependent on a variety of factors, such as knowledge about the virus and the efficacy and adverse effects of protective measures, perceived risk of infection, trust in formal/informal information about H1N1, and previous experiences with avian influenza and SARS" (ibid.). During Covid, however, it would seem that public compliance with measures in Hong

Kong was due not only to these aforementioned factors but also to distrust in the Hong Kong government's initial reaction to Covid, which was "criticized for doing too little too late; as well as for failing to put local people's interests first, and acting for political motives" (Chan, 2021, p. 547). In response to the government's perceived lack of response, distrust "caused the public to take early self-protective measures and initiated societal-wide self-help campaigns" and hence compliance was ultimately "with measures that the public themselves had demanded and agreed" (ibid.).

Once a vaccine was available in Hong Kong for H1N1, 50 percent of respondents to a medical survey confirmed they would want to take it if available at no cost; however, only 15 percent of respondents would be willing to do so if the vaccine price to be paid by patients was higher than US$25. In any event, the "government subsequently ordered 3 million doses of H1N1 vaccine for the local population of 7 million, and began distribution in December 2009. However, vaccine uptake was low, with [under] 250 000 doses administered mainly to the elderly and healthcare workers" (Cowling et al., p. 372). It is possible that the mild symptoms and overall low mortality rate (comparable with seasonal influenza) affected the public's perceived need to take the vaccine (ibid., p. 378). The belief that H1N1 was "just a flu" will be explored further as we discuss the UK's response to swine flu and place such an attitude within the context of Covid's spread in the first wave.

In mainland China, H1N1 presented low morbidity and mortality rates, prompting a by-now familiar discussion both on the effectiveness of quarantine and also on the economic cost of such action. Critics emphasized the economic loss instigated by quarantines, pointing out that the "SARS outbreak caused billions of direct losses and $30–100 billion of indirect losses" (Geng et al., p. 4696). Indeed, the Beijing quarantine itself was evaluated by some as only delaying the spread of H1N1, while "the direct cost (i.e., tracking down close-contactors, accommodations and medical service) for quarantine is higher than the cost of the scenario without quarantine. The mandatory quarantine also has indirect cost, e.g., the loss of freedom of movement and the interruption of the normal life of the people under quarantine" (ibid.).

Perhaps such indirect costs could be referred to as political costs that, under the right circumstances, risk unrest, as seen during the SARS mass quarantine in Beijing a few years earlier or protests at China's strict Covid measures by the end of 2022.

Given the uneven ratio between cost and benefit regarding quarantine during H1N1, why did the Chinese government adopt such an aggressive stance? The answer may lie in the previous SARS pandemic. As explained by Geng, Lai, Li, and Tian, in "2009, China was in a post-SARS stage, and the government took a more radical strategy against the H1N1 pandemic for the first two months. Only after the recognition of massive local transmission did China terminate the mandatory quarantine policy" (ibid.).

For Saudi Arabia, H1N1 entered the kingdom through its major transit hubs. Fifty-eight percent of the first hundred cases entered through King Khaled Airport in the capital, Riyadh, with 16 percent entering through King Fahad Airport in

Dammam, eastern Saudi Arabia, and 14 percent through King Abdulaziz Airport in Jeddah (close to Mecca) (Almazroa et al., 2010, p. 12). The average age of the first hundred cases was only twenty-four, with most symptoms including fever, cough, and sore throat and, in rarer cases, breathing problems (ibid.). Young children and the elderly were more likely to suffer from fatalities, and by the end of December 2009, Saudi Arabia had experienced 124 deaths (ibid.).

As with previous pandemics in Saudi Arabia, the holy cities of Mecca and Medina became focal points for risk of infection. As previously discussed, the annual *hajj* concentrates "2 to 3 millions in a small geographical area. This puts Saudi Arabia in the front line in facing the threat of pandemic[s]." Concern thus was not only about the spread of H1N1 from, for example, Mecca to the rest of the kingdom but also "to other countries, especially those with low [resources] to stop or control the spread of the epidemic" (ibid., p. 13). The 2009 *hajj* went ahead but saw a "high case fatality despite the low disease burden" possibly due to asymptomatic cases and pilgrims not seeking medical care if they fell ill (Ahmed et al., 2010, p. 386).

Just as the UK seemed to emphasize international collaboration during SARS, for H1N1 Saudi Arabia "collaborated with the US Centers for Disease Control and Prevention, the World Health Organization Eastern Mediterranean Regional Office, and the US Naval Medical Research Unit #3 based in Cairo on H1N1 surveillance" (ibid.). Measures included clinic-based lab surveillance from *hajj*-specific clinics and similar surveillance activities at Jeddah airport's *hajj* terminal for arrival and departure of all pilgrims (ibid.).

Airport surveillance saw noncontact infrared thermometers used to detect fever in arriving or departing passengers. A medical team was stationed at the *hajj* terminal to identify symptomatic passengers and if

> a pilgrim's signs and symptoms were deemed to be compatible with influenza, the pilgrim was immediately transported to a dedicated isolation hospital where a specimen was collected and tested for H1N1 by polymerase chain reaction (PCR). [The antiviral medication] Oseltamivir was initiated and discontinued if PCR results were negative 6 hours later. If PCR tests were positive for H1N1, the pilgrim was then admitted to hospital and treated until clinically well and afebrile for at least 24 hours before being able to participate in the *hajj*. (ibid., p. 79)

In addition to the risk of many pilgrims coming from and returning to resource-limited countries that could not maintain H1N1 surveillance or detection (or provide vaccine access), a further concern was the fact that "most of the world's Muslims reside in the Northern hemisphere, which would be in the midst of influenza season at the onset of the 2009 *hajj*" (Arino et al., 2010, p. 75). As discussed earlier, H1N1 vaccines had been bought up disproportionately by wealthier states, which meant "an extremely limited supply of H1N1 vaccine at the onset of the 2009 *hajj* in late November. Consequently, only a handful of economically prosperous countries were able to vaccinate their pilgrims with sufficient lead-time for them to develop protective immunity before starting the *hajj*" (ibid., p. 76). Tunisia responded to H1N1 by banning its citizens from participating in the 2009 *hajj* and pilgrims with health complications were instructed not to attend. While it is impossible to identify a precise number of reductions in *hajj* participants for 2009 compared to previous years, "[a]necdotal information from travel agents organizing pilgrimages for [2009] suggests that there may have been a modest decline in participation" (ibid., p. 79).

As can be seen from an overview of Saudi Arabia's brush with H1N1, while caseloads were not high, there was understandable concern that the holy cities of Mecca and Medina would concentrate millions of pilgrims in confined spaces and create the ideal environment for influenza to spread. The delay of vaccine availability after wealthier nations purchased surplus stock meant that many resource-limited countries were unable to distribute vaccines and ensure their pilgrims could attend *hajj* vaccinated. Hence, even before Covid, we can see how vaccine nationalism affected poorer states during influenza pandemics.

While Saudi Arabia was on guard in places such as Mecca to the risk of H1N1, the UK saw a far different public attitude amid government attempts to prepare for a wave of influenza that did not fully arrive. By April 27, 2009, the UK had imported its first case. Amid WHO concern over another pandemic after SARS and avian flu, the UK responded with a public health campaign "to slow the potential spread of swine flu by encouraging people to adopt protective health behaviors such as hand washing and using tissues" (Hilton, Smith, 2010, p. 1).

There was an emphasis on communicating both "the scientific uncertainty which surrounded this novel virus" and "key differences between swine flu and seasonal influenza" (ibid.). Of these, UK scientists concluded that H1N1 was a greater threat to the young, who would not have experienced any similar influenza viruses and thus lacked immunity, while older people were more likely to have "natural immunity from previous exposure to a similar influenza A virus." There were fears that there would be "between 5 [percent] and 30 [percent] of the UK population contracting the virus and up to 65,000 deaths" (ibid.).

Such speculation swiftly "captured media attention" and by "the summer of 2009 UK newsprint media was at its height, coinciding with the first wave in swine flu cases" (ibid., pp. 1–2). The UK's vaccine program commenced a few months later in October, "first targeting those deemed to be at greatest risk, with the plan of rolling out the programme to the remaining population in the coming months" (ibid., p. 2). However, as the mildness of H1N1 became apparent, as in Hong Kong, there was a dip in public interest with regard to vaccine uptake. Indeed, UK surveys "found that public levels of worry about the possibility of catching swine flu were low as were uptake levels for following government recommended hygiene behaviours" (ibid.). When it came to the public's response, it seemed that images from the media and the government-run health campaign were still used by many to assess the appropriate response to swine flu. More dramatic images of swine flu such as "'chaos', 'death', 'borders and airports closing' and 'people being quarantined'" hailed from TV and newspapers, creating the fear of "something very contagious that [the government] can't confine,'' which would ironically become a reality when Covid-19 arrived (ibid., p. 3).

As H1N1 entered the UK, the perceived threat of the virus did increase but eased "during the summer wave of swine flu cases, [as] people in Britain [became] more familiar with swine flu and less fearful of it through direct experience or knowing someone who had contracted it" (ibid., p. 3, 5). As one individual summarized: "At first, it was like we're all going to die … but before long we knew we weren't and it was no big deal" (ibid., p. 5). Hence, it was the summer wave and its relative mildness of symptoms that began to spread the belief that "it's just the flu," a notion that some in the UK would later apply when Covid began to make itself known to the world (ibid.). Returning to media depictions of swine flu, some individuals who were interviewed criticized the media's presentation of H1N1, accusing outlets of "the intent to cause hysteria in people" and ultimately "covering swine flu at the expense of more serious diseases," which seemed to result in members of the public experiencing "distrust in the information provided by the media and the motives behind media coverage." As expressed by one frustrated interviewee: "One paper tells you one thing, another paper tells you a different thing altogether. So can you actually rely on the media to give you the proper information?" (ibid., pp. 6–7).

In contrast to "media fatigue" from what seemed to be hysterical coverage of H1N1, many in Britain seemed content with the government's response to swine flu, with some confirming that the government "reacted in proportion to the people's expectations" and in proportion to "the perceived threat at the time" (ibid., p. 7). Many also seemed "reassured by the government having ordered enough vaccines" (ibid.). Despite the eventual belief that H1N1 was "just a flu," some citizens responded to it by avoiding public transport and wearing gloves "when touching communal objects such as hand rails, ticket machines and toilet door handles," however, unlike in Hong Kong, few if any "spoke of using facial masks" (ibid.).

As would eventually be seen during Covid, vaccine safety seemed a concern, especially "the speed of its development and whether it had been sufficiently trialled. For instance, one [interviewee in a study] commented: '…there's not enough trials being done before it's being sent out because they're in such a rush to get it to people'" (ibid.). Such comments foreshadow the attitude of some toward Covid vaccines and fears of unknown side effects that meant "weighing up the risks and benefits of vaccination as a way of making a decision" (ibid.). It is worth mentioning that even some health workers seemed hesitant to accept the H1N1 vaccine (ibid., p. 9).

An overview of Britain's reaction to H1N1 reveals one of the first major instances of vaccine stockpiling and vaccine nationalism that was demonstrated in the UK (and the United States, as we shall see). In addition, and with some irony, the rise of Covid and eventual race to produce a vaccine saw some commentators argue that the development of H1N1 vaccines could provide a model for safety (Salmon, Sharfstein, October 29, 2020). Perhaps unknown to some who were hesitant to accept any H1N1 vaccine, the UK's Medicines and Healthcare Products Regulatory Agency (MHRA) "established enhanced safety monitoring" that involved "real-time detection of [adverse drug reactions or ADRs]" recorded through a "dedicated online reporting system." From October 2009, this framework allowed "patients and health-care professionals [to report] more than 3300 ADRs," weighed against "[n]o serious side effects being confirmed despite administration of more than 5 million doses of vaccine in the UK" (Bryan, Davies, Seabroke, 2010, p. 417). Such real-time monitoring of the H1N1 vaccine, especially, was described during Covid as a rapid and credible "process for separating real adverse reactions from coincidental events" that could be shared across multiple health databases once Covid vaccines were distributed, as was the case with the H1N1 vaccine (Salmon, Sharfstein).

A further revelation from analyzing the UK's response to swine flu was how the mildness of symptoms created public apathy and a belief that infection was almost inevitable but harmless because "it's just a flu." This attitude would later be taken up by Covid skeptics to justify not following hygiene measures (Pekosz, 2020). For some British people abroad, Covid-19 would be no excuse to stop partying during Spain's state of emergency in March 2020. As Spain saw cases soar to over 11,000, police began to issue warnings to all that they should practice social distancing and remain indoors. However, in the tourist town of Benidorm, officers who issued such warnings were told by some partiers, "It's just a flu that you need to get over. Have a beer, happy days," leading Russian-owned RT network to tweet, "Benidorm + Coronavirus = managerial mayhem" (Scroll Staff, March 18, 2020)!

In the United States, H1N1 arrived at a time when America was preparing to counter avian flu. To that end, the Obama Administration had "procured 12.2 million courses of H5N1 (bird flu) pre-pandemic influenza vaccine to help meet the first wave of a bird flu pandemic," with said vaccine having no effect on H1N1, prompting then-Obama health adviser Jeffrey Levi to comment that H1N1 "should serve as a reminder of just how unpredictable the flu virus can be. It reinforces the need to invest in research and development so that we can respond and adapt to any flu virus mutations" (Levi, May 1, 2009).

Indeed availability of vaccines and hygiene measures seemed a priority for many Americans. A 2009 survey conducted before vaccine distribution showed "a majority of Americans were quick to adopt two central health recommendations. In the pandemic's first weeks, almost two thirds of Americans (59–67 percent) said that they or someone in their family had begun to wash their hands or clean them with sanitizer more frequently, and a majority (55 percent) had made preparations to stay at home if they or a family member got sick (Bekheit et al., 2010, p. 1)." Once the vaccine was available, many adults seemed split over accepting it (though up to 70 percent of polled parents from the same study wanted their children to be vaccinated). As with the UK, there were concerns over vaccine safety and in "making their decision, some people appeared to think there was a trade-off between accepting the perceived risk associated with the illness and accepting any perceived risk associated with the vaccine" (ibid., p. 2).

Hence, as with the UK, vaccine debate spread during H1N1, foreshadowing anti-vaxxer movements that would intensify during Covid (Waldersee, April 11, 2020). Both the H1N1 and the Covid vaccines were targeted by vocal groups that expressed "considerable mistrust that a rushed vaccine would be improperly tested" (ibid.). During 2009, concern regarding vaccine safety was expressed by some, with fear of side effects or even somehow catching another serious illness. Parents who expressed refusal to vaccinate their children reflected a high concern "that they did not trust public health officials to provide correct information about the vaccine's safety" (Bekheit et al., p. 3). At the same time, partly echoing eventual public apathy in London, some avoided the vaccine due to the simple belief that the risk of H1N1 infection to themselves, family, or community members was low (but not because they thought that H1N1 would be mild) (ibid., p. 4). Indeed, some respondents to the 2009 survey admitted that they would change their mind and get the vaccine if people close to them were infected or dying of influenza A (ibid., pp. 2–3).

As with the UK, the United States' availability of the vaccine peaked as concern over infection declined. However, as with the UK, citizen impressions of government response appeared overall positive (ibid., p. 5). Federal authorities did not rely solely on vaccine development but responded when two separate cases had been identified 130 miles apart in April 2009, prompting concerns of an outbreak (Centers for Disease Control and Prevention, June 16, 2010). The CDC informed the WHO of US cases and remained in touch with the WHO and other global health agencies as they began contact tracing and coordinated with federal authorities to identify "influenza A specimens that could not be subtyped," with further cases across California identified as influenza A and such samples contributing to the creation of a candidate vaccine (ibid.). The importance of viral samples to vaccine creation and the role of samples in vaccine nationalism will be expanded on in Chapter 2 section "Vaccine Nationalism, Viral Sovereignty, Vaccine Diplomacy, and International Legitimacy."

As vaccine development began, the CDC also issued consistent communication, perhaps akin to the UK's own awareness and hygiene campaign. Messages included recommending against any travel to Mexico, for high-risk individuals to take antiviral drugs early if experiencing symptoms, and staying home from work or school if infected. In addition, the CDC coordinated with the WHO to ensure that as new updates were issued by the WHO, the CDC's communication reflected such updates (ibid.).

Before the vaccine, specific antiviral drugs such as Oseltamivir and Zanamivir were found to be effective against influenza A. On April 26, 2009, the US government declared H1N1 a national public health emergency, allowing the CDC to release up to 25 percent of its national stockpile to prevent and counter influenza. "This included 11 million regimens of antiviral drugs, and personal protective equipment including over 39 million respiratory protection devices (masks and respirators), gowns, gloves, and face shields" (ibid.). The distribution of PPE seemed smooth during the H1N1 pandemic in the United States, a contrast to Trump's Covid response, which would be heavily criticized by a 2022 House Subcommittee Report, including for allowing Trump's son-in-law Jared Kushner to lead a PPE supply chain task force "by recruiting a volunteer staff that lacked any 'significant experience in procurement or distribution', and [Kushner] privileged tips about possible PPE suppliers from political allies over medical professionals"

(Firth, December 15, 2022). In addition, Kushner's former college roommate Adam Boehler was recruited by Trump to run the International Development Finance Corporation in 2020. With a budget of $100 million, the agency was meant to, inter alia, give companies "financial backing to help increase U.S. distribution of ventilators, vaccines, medical testing supplies, Personal Protective Equipment (PPE) and other relevant products" but by November had failed to release any funds (Strickler, November 17, 2021).

While the CDC's 2009 response to H1N1 seemed more thorough than Trump's response to Covid a decade later, some health experts argued that, retrospectively, the United States' response to H1N1 had key successes and key failures. Adjunct Fellow Seth Gannon of the Global Health Policy Center wrote on January 12, 2010, that the United States' successful response rested on "sustained government efforts against [the virus]" and well-balanced but rapid decisions by federal officials were central to asserting measures without resorting to extreme options that would be considered during Covid. Such measures included especially ensuring clear and consistent communication to ease the risk of panic, debunking anti-vaxxer myths, and ultimately combating the spread of disinformation as much as the virus itself. Such sustained effort, in addition to the more moderate "virulence of the virus," also meant that antiviral drugs were released, but the CDC and other authorities "did not use the national Tamiflu stockpile as a preventive mechanism" (ibid.). Moreover, personal choice was respected in that vaccines were not mandated, and schools were not closed at the federal level. Gannon also praised authorities for not answering "Congressman Eric Massa's call to close the border with Mexico, the source of the epidemic" (ibid.).

However, of equal importance were response gaps, with criticism "of the government's response largely focused on three areas—vaccine development, surveillance systems, and treatment infrastructure" (ibid.). With regard to vaccine distribution, the available 30 million doses by October fell far short of the predicted 160 million federal officials had hoped for. Perhaps most pertinent with regard to the current Covid pandemic was the failure to cooperate with other states, including Mexico, in an international early warning system, and that the US investment in healthcare and pandemic preparedness fell short not only domestically but "in global health—that enhancing surveillance and preparedness in other countries pays dividends here. The sooner other countries can identify a disease and the better they can contain it, the more warning the U.S. has and the fewer risks it faces" (ibid.).

Gannon, like many other health experts before Covid, warned that the 2009 H1N1 pandemic should prompt the United States to reflect on the successes and failures of its response and that this "process must start well in advance of the next outbreak." "As the second wave of H1N1 starts to dissipate," [said] [Trust for America's Health] Deputy Director Richard Hamburg, "it's time to double down and provide a sustained investment in the underlying infrastructure, so we will be prepared for the next emergency and the one after that" (ibid.). Underinvestment in health systems and pandemic preparedness would come to haunt many governments as Covid arrived.

The 2012 MERS Virus

The MERS, like SARS and Covid-19, is a coronavirus. While SARS and Covid-19 have been linked to bats, camels seem to be the primary source of MERS (Ji, January 30, 2020, p. 93). The first MERS case was reported in Jeddah, Saudi Arabia, in September 2012, with patients presenting with severe pneumonia. From Jeddah, MERS spread to cause hospital outbreaks across the kingdom and other parts of the Middle East, including neighboring Jordan and Bahrain. By March 2017, almost 2000 cases had been reported to the WHO globally, with 684 deaths spread across 27 countries (Al-Qahtani et al., August 28, 2017, p. 1).

For China, MERS arrived by way of South Korea. On May 11, 2015, a 68-year-old man became South Korea's patient-zero, developing MERS symptoms. While admitted to the hospital, it was discovered that he had traveled just the month before across Bahrain, the United Arab Emirates (UAE), Qatar, and Saudi Arabia (Bi et al., June 13, 2015, p. 2349). Both his wife and a 76-year-old fellow patient also tested positive for MERS. At the end of May, a 44-year-old South Korean was admitted to the hospital in the Chinese city of Huizhou. The man was the son of the 76-year-old patient who had been infected with MERS in a South Korean hospital. Within a day, "MERS-CoV infection was confirmed, marking the first laboratory-confirmed case in China" (ibid.).

The 44-year-old patient had visited his father in the hospital in South Korea on May 16. Within a few days, he'd developed symptoms but traveled by air to Hong Kong on May 26 before entering mainland China by road via Shenzhen (ibid.). MERS did not explode in China, but the first recorded case prompted Chinese authorities to place "38 high-risk contacts under surveillance" (ibid.). In response

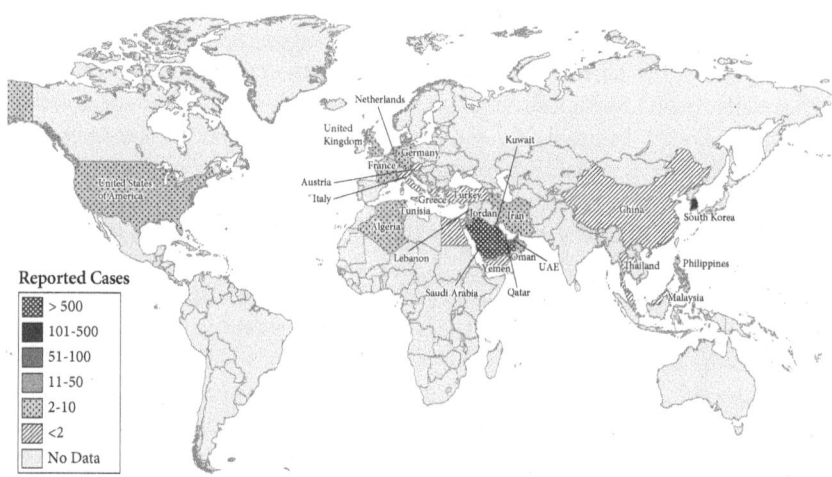

Figure 2.3 Map of MERS spread. Source: Batool, M., Durai, P., Choi, S., Shah, M. 2015. "Middle East respiratory syndrome coronavirus: Transmission, virology and therepeutic targeting to aid in outbreak control." *Experimental & Molecular Medicine*, 47 (181), pp. 1–10, p. 2.

to other MERS cases, it was also reported at the end of May 2015 that authorities had expanded their list of high-risk contacts to 193, with officials warning that MERS could spread in crowded spaces (BBC, May 29, 2015).

However, despite low numbers, the importation and spread of MERS cases came on the back of avian flu in China. Hence, as MERS spread, but even before it entered the country, it provoked reaction on a platform that would also become politicized during Covid: social media. Specifically, there was much online chatter on the Chinese microblog Weibo, described by some as the Chinese equivalent of Twitter (Chan et al., 2013, p. 1). Western media described Weibo as a novel "free-speech platform" and by the end of 2012, some Chinese Weibo service providers claimed to have up to half a billion registered users (ibid.). Like Twitter, Weibo allowed users to post word-limited messages and to share images and videos. The popularity of the platform also meant that despite "the government's control on the Internet content, Weibo still enables Chinese people to publish messages about public incidents or disseminate information during natural disasters" (ibid., pp. 1–2).

As news of MERS cases in the UK became known in China, Weibo users reacted, following a pattern of responding online "rapidly to news about infectious disease outbreaks both within and beyond China" (ibid., p. 6). That said, it is worth noting that the low cases of MERS within China meant that online activity discussing MERS was weaker than previous discussions of SARS and bird flu. Some discussions of MERS compared it to SARS; however, it was clear "that the Chinese online community reacted more strongly to an outbreak that happened in China than one outside China" (ibid., p. 9).

It would be with Covid-19, however, that Weibo would see the most aggressive activity (and censorship attempts). As Xi Jinping attempted to maintain China's zero-Covid policy, the deadly Xinjiang region fire that trapped victims in a building under lockdown provoked online outcry across Weibo and other platforms (Mullin, December 6, 2022). In addition, Chinese users employed virtual private networks to circumvent what has been called the "Great Firewall of China" and attack Xi Jinping himself. From Taipei, *The Guardian*'s journalist Helen Davidson observed how

> internet users had social media accounts suspended after they shared a song, titled "unfortunately it's not you." The word "unfortunately" in Chinese is "ke xim" while "you" translates to "ni," which is itself a banned reference to Xi Jinping. In another popular post, a book about [former leader] Jiang, titled 'He changed China' was altered to say "He changed it back," with "he" a common reference for Xi as naming him in criticism can attract swift punishment. (Davidson, December 2, 2022)

In response, authorities have cracked down on VPNs and tracked protestors for questioning (ibid.). In addition, Weibo saw the removal of many posts that "indicate residents are continuing to push back against the authorities" (Burgess, December 15, 2022). Through online tools that collect and restore deleted posts, media outlets discovered messages that stared down police attempts at intimidation as Covid protests raged. "First they're afraid of speech, then text, then white papers, now even a road sign. They're afraid of everything. So why are we afraid of them?" demanded one user. "[My text] caught the authorities' attention," confessed another post.

> They knocked my door at night and caught me for the crime of "fabricating fact and disturbing social order." They recorded my words again and again and called my compound administration office and the checkpoint I mentioned in the text. I'm not afraid because I didn't lie. But horribly, once I left my home, they took away my phone so that I couldn't contact anyone. They even forced me to say my phone's password. (ibid.)

While MERS had a limited spread across China, it did provoke online activity that connected to a pattern of Chinese users discussing pandemics and foreshadowed how Covid would see protests and resistance against Xi Jinping himself, a reminder that pandemics cannot be separated from politics.

Returning to Saudi Arabia from Jeddah, MERS spread primarily through in-hospital cases. In some cases, patients who visited one ward or hospital were moved to another ward or hospital, spreading infection to other patients and health workers (Al-Ali et al., 2016, p. 472). Recognition of in-hospital infections beyond 2012 and as late as 2015 meant the need to manage MERS patients specifically. For King Abdulaziz Hospital in Jeddah, rising MERS cases meant closure of their emergency department, cancellation of elective surgeries, and the suspension of outpatient clinic services (Al-Dorzy et al., 2016, p. 4). Within the ICU that was handling MERS cases (including infected health workers), outbreak management was modeled across:

- Leadership and communication
- Public and staff communication
- Facility management
- Staffing (ibid., p. 5)

To ensure clear leadership and communication, the hospital established a Command Center that met twice daily and ensured that patient interventions conformed to a pre-agreed Infectious Disease Epidemic Plan (IDEP). Management staff were chosen to liaise between the ICU and Command Center so that clear updates were exchanged on patient progress and management between them both (ibid.). Public and staff communication was maintained through the hospital's creation of a dedicated webpage that, akin to the Hong Kong Centre for Health Protection, provided regular updates during the pandemic and educational material on MERS, in addition to MERS management guidelines and regular updates on appropriate hygiene measures, similar to the CDC's reaction during H1N1 (ibid.). Staff received internal updates via email and were provided with direct communication channels to the Command Center for any concerns. Further, WHO guidelines were circulated among staff, and because family visits were restricted, staff ensured daily phone calls to patients' families to discuss progress and take questions (ibid.).

For facility management, a dedicated MERS unit was established, and non-MERS patients were transferred to older wards or hospitals, ensuring adequate social distancing between MERS and regular patients. Finally, staffing was addressed by ensuring a 1:1 nurse-to-patient ratio, while rotating residents on non-clinical staff were banned from the ICU to limit the risk of MERS exposure (and spread) (ibid., pp. 5–6).

Finally, it is worth mentioning that the MERS outbreak at King Abdulaziz Hospital saw attention paid to the use of PPE, especially N95 protective respiratory masks. Upon the MERS outbreak, "a clinic was emergently opened to fit test [health workers for N95 masks] and the results were documented." Such fittings were complemented by policies and procedures "for donning and doffing personal protective equipment (PPE)" and as the outbreak continued, N95 use increased by over 15 times the normal rate (ibid., p. 7). Increasing PPE measures also meant ensuring "adequate PPE supplies, such as respirators, goggles, face shields and gowns" (ibid.). Perhaps the need for a structured PPE regimen informed Saudi Arabia's response to Covid. A 2021 article on PPE shortages in Saudi Arabia during Covid admitted that in a survey "53 [percent] of the participants reported the prices of PPE in shortage had seen an increase by at least 25 [percent] during the pandemic" but although "the Covid-19 pandemic has caused a significant disruption in the global pharmaceutical supply chain, its impact was largely manageable in Saudi healthcare institutions" (Aljadeed et al., March 2021, p. 1).

As discussed across this chapter regarding Saudi Arabia, Mecca's *hajj* was also a concern during MERS. The emergence of SARS and then H1N1 showed "the potential for severe consequences of infections at *hajj*" but previous pandemics also revealed "the ability of properly organized public health plans to stop their spread" (Alhamid, Shujaa, 2015, p. 174). It is not uncommon for hospital admissions to increase in Mecca during *hajj* (remembering that many MERS cases in Saudi Arabia spread in hospitals), with respiratory ailments being the most common reason for hospital admission (ibid.). Hence, as with SARS and H1N1, the fear was that MERS "would be drawn into the *hajj* by travelling pilgrims, where it would then locally propagate before being transported back to cities and countries around the world and could amplify and accelerate the global spread of infection" (ibid.). Hence, as with previous pandemics, Saudi Arabia's Ministry of Health issued hygiene measures, recognizing the threat early and instituting "screening, monitoring port of entry and isolation for suspected cases, surveillance for infectious diseases [through] computer-based information systems, laboratory testing and [adequate and appropriate medical] treatment" (ibid.). In addition to these measures, pilgrims were recommended to wear masks and get influenza vaccinations before their *hajj* journey (ibid.).

Thankfully, no MERS cases were detected during *hajj* from 2012 to 2014. Perhaps, as before, the hygiene and screening measures implemented in Mecca prevented a MERS outbreak, coming atop preexisting measures that comprehensively consider the importance of healthcare and medical response due to Mecca's unique position as a global (and crowded) hub for local and international pilgrims. For this reason, "Emergency Medicine training in Saudi Arabia emphasizes mass gathering casualty care, disaster preparedness and ability to cope with multicultural people with no background medical knowledge. Emergency Medicine training programs include a National *Hajj* Preparation course and mandatory *Hajj* rotation during the residency program to prepare for this real-world challenge" (ibid., p. 175). In addition to specific medical training to address viral and other issues unique to *hajj*, like Hong Kong, Mecca boasts a research center to construct and assess disaster and pandemic mitigation measures, with annual recommendations submitted to the Saudi authorities to address expected challenges (ibid.).

However, such measures did not mean that Saudi Arabia's response to MERS was praised. By the summer of 2014 as MERS cases began to rise, international observers argued that the Saudi response "exposed institutional failings" linked to "poor communication and a lack of accountability in government departments, inadequate state oversight and a failure to learn from past mistakes" regarding data gathering, reporting and transparency (Kelland, McDowell, June 12, 2014). In a move that would be more common during the regional protests known as the Arab Spring, such criticism resulted in the dismissal of officials, specifically then-Deputy Health Minister Ziad Memish. By June 2014, Memish had the unpleasant honor of being "the second senior Saudi health official to lose his job in six weeks after Health Minister Abdullah al-Rabeeah was sacked when the rate of new infections started to rise rapidly in mid-April," with Memish himself dressed down for "a reluctance to collaborate with some specialist laboratories around the world offering to help investigate the possible source of MERS and explore how it spreads" (Kelland, McDowell, June 3, 2014). Refusal of international collaboration will be further explored as we discuss vaccine nationalism in Chapter 2 and the spread of Covid in Chapter 4.

Just as H1N1 did not explode in the UK, the arrival of MERS in London was even more minimal. As of 2018, six years after MERS was identified, the total number of cases in the UK had been recorded at only five (Gov.uk, October 4, 2018). Nonetheless, there was a review by experts regarding how UK health authorities responded to confirmed MERS cases transiting through London by air in 2014. In May of that year, Public Health England was alerted to two separate MERS-positive cases of passengers traveling from Saudi Arabia to the United States. As was the case in China, there was a track and trace program, with "passengers seated two seats around the cases prioritised for contact tracing," with "64 United Kingdom (UK) residents successfully contacted, 14 of whom were sat in the priority area two seats all around the case(s)" (Boddington et al., May 7, 2015, p. 1). Within fourteen days, five of the passengers reported breathing issues; however, all eventually tested negative for MERS (ibid.).

It is worth mentioning that at the time of these cases, Public Health England had no model for contact tracing of MERS but used SARS contact tracing as a model, with contacts followed up for fourteen days (the incubation period for MERS) and those with symptoms during that period self-isolated or, if deemed necessary, placed in hospital environments (ibid., pp. 1–3). Further, details of non-UK resident passengers proximate to the identified MERS cases on both flights "were passed on to relevant World Health Organization International Health Regulation focal points for follow-up, and no further cases were reported back" (ibid., p. 1). By 2015, the risk assessment of MERS for UK residents was classed as very low, travelers coming to the UK from the Middle East also being at low risk of MERS, but with testing for MERS still being recommended in some cases (Public Health England, 2015, p. 1). As can be seen in the UK's handling of MERS and previous pandemics, there was an emphasis on clear communication with international (health) bodies such as the WHO and, to an extent, international cooperation during track and trace procedures. Such cooperation and swift reaction seem to be in contrast to the initial response to Covid (by the UK and other states), with UK scientists tackling an austerity that "blunted the ambition and commitment of government to protect its people," meaning that lessons from SARS and influenza models were ignored and officials imagined "the pandemic would be much like influenza," prompting "'moderate' risk assessment of the disease to the UK population" while "China, by contrast, was scarred by its experience of SARS" and enacted mass quarantine (Horton, April 9, 2020).

Like the UK, America experienced an almost dismissible risk of MERS spread, with the CDC summarizing that "MERS represents a very low risk to the general public in this country. Only two patients in the US have ever tested positive for MERS-CoV infection—both in May 2014—while more than 1,300 have tested negative" (Centers for Disease Control and Prevention, August 2, 2019). Nonetheless, once MERS was reported as a global concern, the CDC worked closely with the WHO and other global health bodies "prior to the first case appearing in the United States in May 2014" (Bunga et al., 2015, p. 307). This involved creating an early response framework and centralizing communication on MERS through the CDC's Division of Viral Diseases, increasing CDC staff where needed and "preparing clinicians, customs and border protection agents, as well as laboratorians, for the potential importation of cases into the United States" (ibid., p. 310, 311).

Among the lessons learned from the United States' brush with MERS was, as with previous pandemics, "the importance of advanced preparation for successfully managing the response to a novel pathogen. Each new outbreak response should build on the knowledge gained from previous outbreaks, particularly if dealing with a similar pathogen, to save time and avoid the reinvention of materials that could be adapted from existing tools" (ibid., p. 313). Indeed, a 2015 briefing by Washington, DC-based health policy institute, Trust for America's Health issued a graver evaluation of gaps in US pandemic responses. Emerging viruses and subsequent

> uncertainty [regarding their behavior] means the health system must maintain vigilance at all times. Infection control practices and all-hazards public health preparedness must be routine year-round and "24/7," not only in reaction to an outbreak. Foremost in a prepared system is a well-trained public health and healthcare workforce who are well-versed in infection control, contact tracing and monitoring, prevention measures, case investigation, data/information management and communicating with the healthcare system and public.

Overstretched and under-resourced healthcare and public health systems means these capabilities vary widely from jurisdiction to jurisdiction.

Ultimately, the briefing warned "the United States to take additional steps to prepare for MERS-CoV and other emerging infections," emphasizing that "health and healthcare systems cannot afford to become complacent in preparing for infectious disease threats" (Trust for America's Health, June 2015, pp. 2, 1).

Social Movements, Anxieties, and Pandemics

After an overview of major pandemics and their effects on governance, health politics, and pandemic management, perhaps it is worth reiterating that while previous pandemics have been, at times, limited in scope, Covid-19 emerged as the first major pandemic of the twenty-first century. As previously mentioned by Porta, Covid represents an emergency juncture under which social movements will attempt to balance government-imposed restrictions by expanding economic, social, and political rights. In addition, Rohlinger and Meyer argue that Covid is "a unique moment in history, with no health emergency remotely similar in just over a century" (2024, p. 812). As with Porta, Rohlinger and Meyer explain that Covid and government responses "alter the structure of political opportunities, that is, the world around a social movement that affects the prospects for mobilization and potential influence facing activists. In addition to making some issues more salient or pressing, the pandemic—and government measures taken in response—altered the conditions under which people could organize and be mobilized" (ibid.).

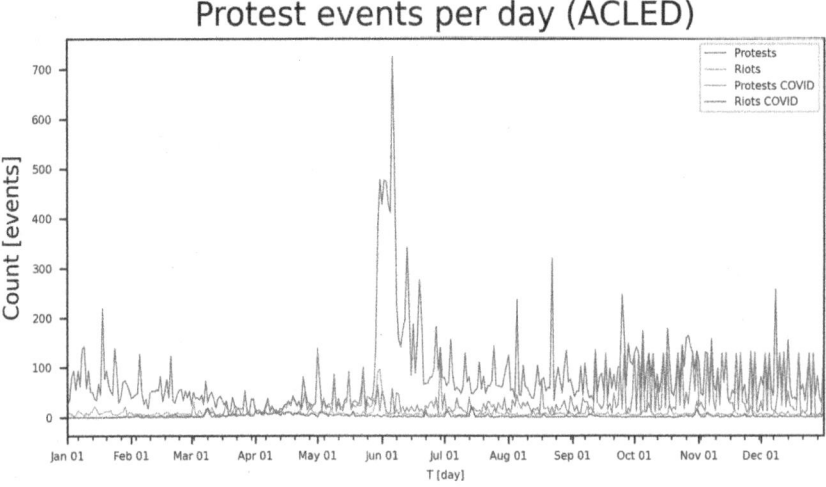

Figure 2.4 Protests and riots during 2020. Source: Barros, A.I., van Engers, T.M., Sloot, P.M., van der Zwet, K. 2022. "Emergence of protests during the Covid-19 pandemic: Quantitative models to explore the contributions of societal conditions." *Humanities and Social Sciences Communications*, 9 (68), pp. 1–11, p. 2.

The notion of Covid altering political opportunities for different actors returns us to understanding the politicized use of social space. As we discussed in Chapter 1, Shanghai saw authorities taking control of physical spaces, but their inability to meet all welfare needs led to so-called basin protests, in which residents would stand on their balconies and bang kitchen utensils and basins to create disruptive noise as a form of communicating their frustration with authorities. In Hong Kong, however, the issue of centralized versus localized power and key failures in handling the pandemic were deeper and illustrated a willingness of key sectors to protest in response to these failures during Covid.

Hong Kong's Special Administrative Region (SAR) has enjoyed relatively autonomous political administration from China since Hong Kong's formal return to China in 1997. Under the "One Country, Two Systems" principle, Hong Kong is a successful financial hub, with its "civil society movement focuse[d] on political rights of universal suffrage for the chief executive and legislative council elections, as well as the defence of the city's autonomy from the Chinese Communist Party's encroachment" (Chan, Tsui, 2022, p. 203).

As discussed in Chapter 1, stronger social movements that emerged more quickly during Covid often had roots in preexisting social networks and social movements that tackled preexisting social issues. On that note, Hong Kong had a history of social movements that targeted political and social justice. These included the 2003 resistance against national security legislation and the so-called 2014 and 2019 umbrella movement, which referred to protestors' use of umbrellas as protection from police tear gas while mobilizing against China's 2014 stipulation to allow only the election of candidates approved by Beijing and 2019 attempts to impose a law that could try Hong Kong citizens for political crimes in mainland China (BBC, September 28, 2019).

Compounding such previous social mobilization was the recent trauma of SARS. "Hong Kong's coronavirus panic buying isn't hysteria," explained journalist Ilaria Maria Sala in 2020, "it's unresolved trauma" (February 12, 2020). Hong Kong journalist Holmes Chan recalls his experience with SARS and the parallel fears as Covid spread.

> As a primary school student during Sars, I remember my face chafing under the N95 mask my parents ordered me to wear to school—that is, before classes were cancelled at the height of the epidemic. The name of Amoy Gardens, a residential estate that became the site of a major outbreak, conjured up images of a haunted house in my childhood imagination. From February to June 2003, the people of Hong Kong despaired as the economy and housing market crashed, while unemployment reached a record high. The mood in Hong Kong [in 2020] is apprehensive and people are determined not to repeat their Sars-era mistakes-the question is whether the government can say the same. (Chan, January 28, 2020)

Within the context of collective trauma from SARS, there were fears that Hong Kong's authorities were not taking the spread of Covid seriously. During the initial wave, "[w]hile towns and villages in mainland China had already enforced mandatory self-isolation for personnel entering from Hubei (the province with the most confirmed cases), by the end of January, the Hong Kong government still resorted to making nonbinding appeals to Hubei visitors to self-isolate or leave the city" and despite top scientists recommending tighter border control, "it only happened after an historical five-day strike staged by 7,000 medical workers in the city. The government was criticized for putting political reasons (not to upset Beijing) above scientific advice from experts when making decisions" (Chan, Tsui, p. 203).

Given the importance of health workers during SARS and Covid, it should come as no surprise that "public hospital workers who were on the frontline of the pandemic became the leaders on the frontline of civic resistance" (ibid.). Within this context, Hong Kong's unions are significant. Under the "One Country, Two Systems" principle, Hong Kong is the only territory under China where workers may freely join independent unions. Membership of different unions has extended into the hundreds of thousands, "union registration is not particularly difficult, and political interference has been minimal until recently" (Lin, March 8, 2022).

The strength of healthcare workers to unionize and indirectly criticize government responses to Covid (including Chief Executive of Hong Kong Carrie Lam not wearing a mask in public) no doubt was aided by the "wave of unionisation that took place in late 2019," seeing "more than 450 new unions established in less than a year, with hundreds of thousands of workers signing up for membership" (ibid.). This included the Hospital Authority Employees Alliance (HAEA), which "became the representative of over 20 percent of public medical sector employees" (Chan, Tsui, p. 203). In the HAEA, "membership skyrocketed from 300 in December 2019 to over 18,000 applications and over 10,000 successful registrations by January 30, 2020, following its public call to strike ... to protect themselves and Hong Kong citizens from a man-made disaster of government inaction" (ibid., p. 204).

The five-day strike organized by the HAEA between February 3 and February 7, 2020, came atop a January 23 demand that the Hong Kong government "ban any traveller from entering the city from the Chinese mainland border and ensure safe working conditions for all employees by providing a sufficient supply of isolation wards, stopping non-emergency services and ensuring the supply of masks" (ibid., p. 205). The strike was carefully organized to ensure emergency services remained and seemed to gain public support (ibid.). In the end, none of the HAEA's demands were formally met; however, the end of the strike was followed by enhanced border closures and quarantine measures that were

> a pattern of tactical concession from the government, aiming at dividing the strikers and sympathizers. On 28 January, after HAEA announced that they would hold an [emergency meeting] to vote on the strike plan, the government announced the closure of the Express Rail Link to mainland China and halved the flights from the mainland in two days. On 3 February, when 3,000 non-emergency service staff took part in the strike and demanded open negotiation at HA headquarters, Carrie Lam announced the closure of four more ports

connected to the mainland. On the third day of strike (5 February), when [the] number of strikers remained as high as 7,000 and several transport unions announced their intentions to call for industrial actions, Carrie Lam announced that all persons entering through mainland China would be required to self-isolate for 14 days starting from 8 February, the day when the strike was planned to end. Even though some demands of the union—that non-residents shall not enter via the mainland—were not entirely met, they won important concessions. (ibid., p. 207)

While the HAEA successfully pressured Hong Kong authorities, its existence as a social movement (or union) did not necessarily emphasize democratic rights in this instance. Strikes organized by HAEA members were done in response to a lack of restrictions and the perceived lax approach to Covid by Hong Kong authorities. While Shanghai saw some protest due to the inability of authorities to maintain food and medical provisions during lockdown, Hong Kong saw a five-day strike by 7,000 healthcare workers due to a lack of restrictions that many Hong Kong citizens demanded, remembering the trauma of SARS and afraid that infection rates would soar. From this perspective, just as social movements in the UK and the United States tackled mutual aid, the HAEA strike can be regarded as a social movement that addressed physical welfare (through safety from the virus) rather than democratic and political rights.

A further similarity between the HAEA as a social movement and UK social movements in Chapter 1 section "Social Movements, Public Spaces" is the fact that the HAEA's strength and fast mobility seemed to come from its emergence within the context of increasing support for social movements. While successful social movements in the UK built on preexisting social networks and preexisting social movements dedicated to pre-Covid social concerns, HAEA came at a time when Hong Kong citizens had supported recent social movements like the umbrella movement and the anti-extradition bill movement (AEBM). Therefore, the HAEA emerged at a time when the government's legitimacy had already been challenged by these movements, and "new unions [like the HAEA] were able to inherit the public support and mobilization capacity of the AEBM" (Chan, Tsui, p. 205). Further, the HAEA benefited from cross-sector union support. The public medical sector represented by the HAEA was one of the largest sectors in Hong Kong and in 2022 was "the second largest employer in the city (after the government itself) with nearly 80,000 employees" and the pledge to strike saw strong support from diverse ranks across the medical sector, ranging from doctors and health professionals to nurses (who formed the majority of signatories), support staff, and administrative staff (ibid.). Bolstering such sectorial unity, "[m]any unions showed active support for the HAEA strike, including Railway Power, Hong Kong Financial Industry Employees General Union and Unions for New Civil Servants," which all "formed after the AEBM" (ibid., p. 206).

While Hong Kong and Shanghai provide examples of social movements that targeted welfare and protection from the virus, this did not mean that there were no social movements focused on social justice in China. The occupation of physical social space or territorialization could be used by competing actors (including the government) to control the narrative and use of social spaces for protest to a degree. However, digital space represented an arena for protest and resistance that saw active use of social media in China that circumvented state censorship to allow criticism of the government early into the Covid pandemic.

A specific form of occupying online space (as opposed to physical social space) can be seen in how netizens engaged with the final social media post of Covid whistleblower Dr. Li Wenliang (Cao, Evans, Zeng, 2022, p. 159). As we have explored in previous chapters, social media platforms can certainly contribute to the organization and activities of social movements, being used to organize, for example, mutual aid. However, social media has also created "a heavily contested battlefield for meaning" and numerous "public discussion spaces, which are prerequisites for civil participation and for democratizing agenda building," bringing with them the potential for "political evolution in the long run" (ibid., p. 162).

At the same time, extensive censorship in China has allowed social media platforms to be used as indirect forms of government criticism that carefully circumvent taboo topics. As explained by Amnesty International, "[t]o evade the most extensive internet censorship system in the world, netizens have no option but to create their own vocabulary to discuss 'sensitive issues'. This language keeps evolving as the government constantly adds new topics and terms that are prohibited" (March 6, 2020).

The attempt of Dr. Wenliang to report Covid and his subsequent censorship by authorities was retroactively met by mourning and online protest. There is a sense of irony that Chinese social media became the vehicle for Dr. Wenliang's Covid report (that saw him questioned by authorities) and for criticism of his censorship. After sending his report to colleagues via WeChat, he was "accused by police at the Public Security Bureau in Wuhan of spreading rumours and was required to sign a letter of reprimand admitting that his action was 'wrong' and promising not to do it again or face legal punishment" (Cao, Evans, Zeng, p. 160). Within less than two months of his reprimand, Li would write in his final social media post on February 1, 2020, that he had contracted Covid-19 (ibid.).

"The test results come out positively today," he declared. "Everything is settled. It is confirmed" (Guardian reporter in Hong Kong, February 7, 2020). Within days of his passing, "[t]he death of a whistleblowing Chinese doctor who was punished for trying to raise the alarm about coronavirus sparked an explosion of anger, grief and demands for freedom of speech among ordinary Chinese" (ibid.). Posts from overseas users were blunt. "They owe you an apology, we owe you our gratitude. Take care, Dr. Li," wrote one user on microblog Weibo through "an account under the overseas edition of [the] Communist Party's People Daily" (ibid.). Domestically, the need to indirectly attack the Chinese government meant that the death of Dr. Li

> became something of a focus of popular solidarity and resistance. The reprimand that police asked him to sign was elevated to the status of a medal

in recognition of his heroism [by social media users]. Further, the official accusation against him was seen as unreasonable and an embarrassment to the Chinese government. Thousands of netizens called for an apology for the unfair allegations, an investigation into whether he was treated unfairly, and a claim to restore his reputation. In this way, netizens took the form of a cult rather than direct political resistance to avoid being suppressed by authorities, and, thereby, they gained symbolic capital for the discursive struggle. This ongoing appeal was a means to safeguard the reputation and dignity of Dr. Li and was a form of moral assistance, which netizens called "guarding": "Before his death, he devoted all his efforts to guarding us and did not even get a formal apology. Now it's our turn to guard him, and everyone is trying to justify him." Dignity is "a very private and a very public attribute" and, therefore, restoring the good name of the hero was an important symbol for netizens to uphold justice. It represented a counter-hegemonic stance and created an alternative discourse via praise of the hero instead of resorting to protest. (Cao, Evans, Zeng, p. 166)

While collective mourning was expressed through users commenting on Li's blog and final post, the insistence of an apology and elevation of Li to almost a martyr also served the purpose of using online mourning as an advocation of citizen rights,

> the right to know and the right [for citizens] to express themselves. This hidden transcript strategy was primarily transmitted through the metaphor of the whistle-blower. ... This metaphor was quickly adopted by netizens to extend the meaning of rights protection. First, whistleblower represented the power of truth and the courage to tell the truth under pressure: "You put the truth on the scales and let the world know its weight!" ... Further, netizens extended whistle blowing to include the right to free speech which became a moral force to encourage citizens to express themselves more bravely. ... Second, netizens repeatedly quoted Dr. Li with regard to the right to freedom of speech. When a journalist asked Li Wenliang how he viewed being reprimanded, he answered that "a healthy society should not have only one voice." Through persistently quoting his words, netizens sought to take advantage of the lessons of this incident to gain more space for public expression in future. (ibid., pp. 166–7)

Dr. Li's Weibo account became an online social space occupied by Chinese netizens who commented on his final post with indirect criticism of authorities and personal stories of how Covid affected them. This approach allowed disparate citizens from across China to show solidarity online, and "together they established an alternative [social and] memory space parallel to the official dominant narrative" (ibid., p. 168).

It would seem that online praise of Dr. Li and indirect demands for freer expression had an effect. By March 2020, the reprimand of Li and seven colleagues was reversed and an apology was issued to his family. The public outcry over Li's treatment led to an investigation that concluded "Dr Li hadn't disrupted public order with his actions" but rather was "a professional who fought bravely and made sacrifices" (Collier, March 20, 2020). Police officers originally involved in his reprimand were further disciplined (ibid.). The government's reaction to digital activism and subsequent reversal of Li's reprimand was a strategic compromise enacted to ensure that the political legitimacy of the ruling system would not be eroded. The CCP's ideology was incorporated into the recognition of Li as a hero by having the investigation head praise Li as a hero during the pandemic but also as a devoted communist. This approach allowed the government to regain control of the narrative surrounding Li, erasing previous labels and engaging in "a process of purification from stigma to coronation" that relabeled Li as "an advanced individual, ... awarded the title of 'Martyr'" (ibid., p. 172).

While HAEA strikes in Hong Kong emphasized the desire for government restrictions and, effectively, protection from Covid and the basin protests in Shanghai responded to welfare gaps, digital activism centered around the censorship and death of Dr. Li and, by extension, not only the government's reprimand of Li but the wider issue of freedom of speech. Returning to Porta's notion of pandemics as emergency junctures, we can certainly see how Covid created "economic, social and political crises" that not only prompted government restrictions but also saw initial state denial of Covid provoke censorship of Dr. Li that became a wider issue of freedom of speech as a social and political crisis (p. 5). In the cases of Hong Kong and online, there was a rise of social movements that acted as a counterbalance to government inaction for Hong Kong and restrictions on free expression in the case of Dr. Li's death and subsequent social media activity surrounding his demise (ibid., pp. 7, 6). As discussed by Porta, social movements mobilized online and offline to keep the government in check and question the efficacy of "a suspension of some rights [such as Dr. Li's suppression] and a centralization of decision-making" that could see, for example, Hong Kong delay restrictions to appease Beijing (ibid., p. 8). In the case of Dr. Li, we see how social media played an unprecedented role during a pandemic in resisting government restrictions on freedom of speech.

While China is a communist state, Saudi Arabia is a Muslim monarchy, with Islam at the center of daily and political life. Within the context of Covid, religion seemed to play a role in bolstering mental health during lockdown. As explained by Alkhaldi, restrictions and the subsequent

> limited opportunity for social gatherings allowed participants to focus on their religious practices in the comfort of their homes and have more time to connect with their beliefs, especially as lockdown occurred during the holy month of Ramadan for Muslims. These religious beliefs also strengthened the shared identity among many ... as a single community responsible for each other and empathetic towards their shared struggles. (p. 8)

During the initial wave of Covid, the Saudi government ran a social media campaign to emphasize the collective responsibility of citizens in obeying restrictions.

Authorities came up with the slogan "We are all responsible" to instill a sense of responsibility among all stakeholders and to increase awareness among people about the importance of their role in this fight. Since its launch on March 21 [2020] it has been one of the top trending hashtags on Twitter and, in the past few weeks, has been tweeted over 500,000 times. (Alshammari, May 11, 2020)

The use of social media by the state is a reminder of the importance attributed to online and offline social spaces. At the same time, the government's campaign emphasizing "we are all responsible" may have built on aspects of Saudi national identity. Some critics argue that Saudi national identity is one of collective responsibility and that "Saudis have a strong sense of social responsibility and solidarity, demonstrated through their active participation in initiatives and events that contribute to the development of their society" (Al-Mutairi, September 23, 2023). The influence of national identity can also tie into government legitimacy in Saudi Arabia due to the importance of religion. A collective sense of responsibility can be traced back to tribal allegiance, but this identity is second to "the use of religion by the royal family to consolidate a Saudi national identity, which in turn will constitute an additional attribute for the legitimacy of the ruling family" (Nevo, 1998, p. 34).

Due to the importance of religion, "the promotion of national identity has been an official as well as a practical policy, reflecting the regime's endeavor to enhance its position and legitimacy. This sought identity is based primarily on strict observance of Islam and, of course, on loyalty to the House of Saud" but such loyalty is part of a wider collective identity under which Saudis, like many Arabs, have a national identity that itself is collective as it "consists of traditional factors such as tribe, extended family or geographical region" (ibid.). The importance of collective identity and collectivism versus individualism within the context of Covid will be returned to later in this section.

While Saudi Arabia provides an example of religion emphasizing collective identity and a related collective sense of responsibility to obey restrictions during Covid, it is interesting to note the opposite case in the United States during the Spanish Flu. Houses of worship were typically compliant with closures, even if these were recommendations rather than enforced restrictions. However, not all clergy were happy with the fact that their churches or other places of worship were instructed to close while businesses in "poorly ventilated office buildings and shops" were allowed to continue. "Business must not be hindered, it must go on," one minister sarcastically commented in an open letter. Indeed, religious leaders seemed irked at the irony over banning religious congregations while saloons serving alcohol (during early Prohibition) went relatively unchecked, prompting the vicar general of the Diocese of Fall River in Massachusetts to ask: "Are not the motley gatherings of 'the great unwashed' assembling in these unclean places … a thousand times greater a threat than the congregations of our churches? Is German brewery power supreme in city and State House" (Markel, Navarro, 2021, pp. 418–19)?

While religion unified all in the Arab world during Covid, the United States in 1918 saw some torn between the Bible and the booze. This dilemma was a reminder that, as with Covid, restrictions and lockdowns in the United States were not centralized and at times haphazard during the Spanish Flu. On the one hand, "sheer crowding of saloons led most states and cities to order them closed" but on the other hand, "in a nod to the political, social, and economic importance of saloons, other communities allowed saloons to operate" and even saloons ordered to close challenged and defied these restrictions to serve drinks in crowded structures (ibid., pp. 419–20). Perhaps this example serves as a paragon of collective irresponsibility rather than the notion of social responsibility and its role in collective and individualistic societies.

The popularity of saloons may have reflected social anxieties in the United States at a time when Americans were dealing with a flu that infected "one third of the world's population" (Morens, Taubenberger, 2006, p. 15). Returning to the UK and the United States, we can certainly reflect further on social class and anxieties that were compounded by Covid.

It should come as no surprise that a 2019 US survey found that almost 70 percent of respondents were concerned with getting infected and even more concerned about family members becoming infected (Christakis, p. 142). With Covid came a parallel epidemic of anxiety, with worry, sadness, and anger scoring high along with loneliness (ibid.). The interaction between anxiety and illness reveals how "germs, emotions, and behaviors can act independently or they can intersect. And fear has an advantage over even the most contagious pathogens—people can contract a disease only through contact with other infected individuals, but they can contract fear through contact with either infected individuals or fearful ones" (ibid., p. 143).

The spread of anxiety also creates fragmented responses. With no vaccine in sight in 2020, increased anxiety resulted in people blaming others in an attempt to assert control over an unseen threat (ibid., p. 144). On the other hand, the implementation of restrictions or guidelines by authorities, including social distancing and mask wearing, can ease such anxiety and provide a counterbalance by reasserting a sense of control (ibid.).

The spread of anxiety and the need to assert a sense of control through either blame or compliance is a reminder that not all social groups were united, and, sadly, not all social groups were equal. In the UK, there certainly was anger that Covid impacted

> an already fragmented class structure, introducing new sources of inequality between those who work in a safe environment (or even from home) and those who are instead either occupied in essential services with limited health protection or have lost their precarious jobs due to this crisis. Even within each of these groups, there are differences in terms not only of the degree of job insecurity but also of gender discrimination in the way in which the activities of caring for young or disabled persons, which increased during the pandemic, are distributed. Among those who work in essential services, divisions have

emerged between those who have more labour rights (and can strike or threaten to strike) and the growing precariat, who do not possess stable jobs and at times are even considered to be independent workers. (Porta, p. 62)

The exploitation of contract workers by corporate actors that profited from the pandemic will be further explored in Chapter 3 section "Pandemic Profiteers." In any event, the widening of social inequality can be regarded as an economic concern, encouraging the rise of mutual aid groups as previously discussed and returning us to the argument that economic performance is a key concern for government legitimacy during a pandemic. However, in the United States especially, we saw a great emphasis on social justice through the Black Lives Matter (BLM) movement that spread to the UK and Europe after the murder of Black US citizen George Floyd on May 25, 2020 (Lavizzari, Porta, Reiter, 2022, p. 700).

Various factors came together to emphasize the institutionalized racism experienced by Black Americans. First, the murder of George Floyd came atop the murder of two other unarmed Black Americans by law enforcement, namely Ahmaud Arbery and Breonna Taylor, "and a president known for using race and racism to mobilize his conservative, white base," while Covid-19 hit the Black community at five times a higher rate than White Americans. Added to this inequality was a socioeconomic context of Black Americans being "more likely to have preexisting medical conditions, less access to health care, and work in low-wage jobs" that connected with the lived experiences of other non-White Americans, ensuring that "[u]nlike other political movements, … the causes of economic and racial inequality did not remain siloed, creating new opportunities for activists to illustrate how interlocking oppressions affect the lived realities of BIPOC (Black, Indigenous, and People of Color) Americans" (Meyer, Rohlinger, p. 816).

Indeed, Covid saw an intersectionality of global discrimination and health injustice, with activists pointing out that in the United States, Black communities saw disproportionately high infection rates, while "around the globe, indigenous communities have contracted the virus, … migrants, refugees and other marginalized folk are being stigmatized and unjustly discriminated against for supposedly spreading the virus, [yet] these populations are … disproportionately underserved or outright neglected by medical services" due to the same cause: "the systemic oppression, racism and colonial biopolitical practices that pre-figured the arrival of Covid-19. Moreover, increasing neoliberal cuts to healthcare systems as well as the constant drive towards privatization have meant that even basic healthcare is increasingly out of reach for the poor" (Porta, p. 51).

This example returns us to the notion of pandemics acting as critical emergency junctures, which will see social movements mobilize to extend civil and political rights in the face of sudden crises that have been met with highly centralized government responses and restrictions. In the case of the BLM movement, the focus was not simply institutionalized racism in America but, by extension, social justice for all communities and groups who face inequality. Through BLM, "a narrative of intersectionality emerged as the basis for a broad coalition, not only to address systemic racism (of different forms, not solely anti-black), but also ... to present various inequalities as being interlinked, due to the fact that the pandemic provided even more visibility to the deadly effects of social injustice," emphasizing how Covid "hits institutionalized, immigrant, poorer, indigenous and racialized communities harder. Neighbourhoods where there are more longstanding health problems, more crowded housing and transportation spread the virus. Shutting things down, or forcing people to separate when some people lack access to clean water or medical help or harm reduction services, means some are sacrificed for the greater good" (ibid., p. 52).

Exploitation and abuse of communities through institutionalized racism and the rise of BLM since 2013 "into the largest Black-led protest campaign since the 1960s" is a reminder that social inequalities existed long before Covid (Blackpast, 2024). However, the spread of BLM after the murder of George Floyd shows that not all concerns during Covid centered on economic performance but in some cases on social justice that was regarded as long overdue (ibid.).

As will be discussed in Chapter 3 section "Pandemic Profiteers," corporate actors exploited the pandemic for profit. In addition, the spread of BLM also saw the involvement of corporations. The BLM demand for police reform (and possibly defunding due to institutionalized racism) gained allies in corporate actors. In particular, the issue of systemic racism seemed to be acknowledged by media and sports corporations, for example. The National Football League's (NFL) then-Commissioner Roger Goodell "apologized for not listening to players about racism and pledged his support to their right to protest. This apology came nearly 4 years after 49ers quarterback Colin Kaepernick first sat and then took a knee during the national anthem to protest police brutality and racism" (Meyer, Rohlinger, p. 819).

In addition to the NFL,

> NASCAR also responded to the protests and an incident in which a noose was hung in [racing driver] Bubba Wallace's stall at the Talladega racetrack. While the FBI concluded that a federal hate crime against NASCAR's only elite Black driver had not been committed, Wallace—supported by other drivers—called on NASCAR to ban the [Confederate] flag outright, noting that fans should not be uncomfortable at races. NASCAR leapt at the opportunity to ban the flag, a measure leadership had been eager to take to diversify the audience and market for the sport, and ruled that it would no longer allow the display of the Confederate flag at its events or on its properties. The flag and by extension white supremacy are embedded in NASCAR's history; in 2015, NASCAR asked fans not to bring the flags to races after photos circulated online of the white man who killed nine Black churchgoers in Charleston, S.C., posing with it. The request was largely ignored. The protests gave NASCAR coverage to do more. (ibid.)

Further, media companies responded to BLM and the murder of George Floyd by "pulling shows that portrayed law enforcement as quintessentially good" and shows that maintained a "selective take on policing and glorifying the abuse of citizens at the hands of police officers—all in the name of preserving law and order" (ibid.).

These examples of corporate actors forced to acknowledge the existence of white supremacy and institutionalized racism illustrate how such actors, perhaps unlike some states, were not focused solely on economic performance before and after Covid but were forced to address concerns of social injustice. This shift in focus and need to accommodate (the image of) social justice can be linked to a wider spread of anti-capitalist protest during Covid directed at corporations. Just as BLM highlighted discrimination and exploitation of various groups through embedded racism, including beyond America, health workers and other precarious workers were pushing back against what they perceived to be increasing exploitation across food, agriculture, health, and logistics industries, with social movements highlighting such exploitation with such slogans as "[o]ur lives are worth more than their profits" (Porta, p. 47). The role of corporations during the pandemic and their profits at this time will be further explored in Chapter 3 section "Pandemic Profiteers."

Returning to the control of social space, there is an interesting contrast between left-wing and right-wing protests that can further feed into later discussion of collectivism versus individualism. On the one hand, left-wing social movements around the world respected hygiene measures such as mask-wearing, social distancing, and related restrictions but still "contested authoritarian measures [under governments] accused of exploiting the health crisis to centralize power and repress the opposition" and left-wing movements focused on collective social justice by denouncing "an instrumental and biased use of restrictive measures to selectively repress protests on issues such as migrants' rights or the rights of [minorities and Indigenous communities]" (ibid., p. 63). On the other hand, right-wing movements were more likely to emphasize individual rights and contest lockdowns and hygiene restrictions (ibid.).

The dichotomy between left-wing and right-wing social movements could certainly be seen in the United States during Covid and under the Trump administration. For the left, Trump's presidency was secured by "electoral campaigns which, among other things, appealed to racist resentment and anti-immigration sentiments among White Americans" and "created the conditions under which activists could coalesce around progressive issues," creating social mobilization during Covid that "tried to find ways to establish a public presence while navigating the constraints of social distance and good hygiene" (Meyer, Rohlinger, pp. 816–17).

By contrast, spring 2020 saw thousands of right-wing protestors defy stay-at-home orders and "backed by wealthy conservative groups and promoted by Donald Trump" demand "governors lift orders designed to stop the spread of the coronavirus, despite the recommendations of public health officials" (Gabbatt, April 18, 2020).

This taking of social space for individualism and to resist Covid restrictions was specific to the United States as it escalated into a later occupation of the Capitol building that seemingly had government (e.g., Trump) approval. As explained by Meyer and Rohlinger,

[o]n January 6, 2021, the day that the new Congress met to certify Electoral College votes from the states, a Trump-led rally led to an invasion and attempted occupation of the Capitol building by the defeated president's supporters. Trump spoke to a large group of disappointed supporters urging them to go to the Capitol to show their support for the incumbent and pressure members of Congress, particularly the Vice President, to reject the election's results. Trump promised to march with them, but retreated to the White House, from where he watched televised scenes of some of his supporters storming Capitol barricades, battling with police, and bustling through the building,

clearly in disregard for collective safety and social distancing (p. 815). While Trump may not have directly ordered his supporters to storm the Capitol, it "took hours for the president to tell the demonstrators to vacate the building, and for Capitol police, aided by the military, to clear the building and allow elected officials to return and certify the election results" (ibid.).

However, it must be acknowledged that "while it's clear that at least some of the Capitol invasion was planned and coordinated by far right groups, it's quite likely that some participants were just caught up in the moment" (ibid.).

As previously discussed, pandemics can provoke a parallel infection of anxiety. This can certainly be seen by social movements during Covid from both the right and left and from blame assigned to specific groups or communities in various pandemics. As discussed in Chapter 1 section "Social Movements, Public Spaces," Covid saw some nationals blame immigrants for ostensibly failing to follow hygiene measures but has also seen a rise in Sinophobia across the United States and Europe (Human Rights Watch, May 12, 2020). The attack on immigrants and minorities during Covid shows a contrast to the Spanish Flu, which "coincided with a major wave of immigration to the United States. More than 23.5 million newcomers arrived between 1880 and the 1920s, mostly from Southern and Eastern Europe, Asia, Canada and Mexico," and although "[d]uring earlier epidemics, the foreign-born were often stigmatized as disease carriers whose very presence endangered their hosts," the Spanish Flu "struck individuals of all groups and classes throughout the country, [thus] no single immigrant group was blamed, although there were many local cases of medicalized prejudice" (Kraut, 2010, p. 123).

A further difference in discrimination between the Spanish Flu and Covid in the United States was that Woodrow Wilson remained silent on restrictions during the Spanish Flu (at a time when immigration dropped due to the First World War and there were restrictive immigration laws) (Merkel, Navarro, p. 421, Kraut, p. 126). However, under Trump, there was an American president who gave public statements that "actively undermined the nation's public health response" and that blamed immigrants for importing Covid to the United States (Markel, Navarro, 2021, p. 421, De Loera-Brust, July 14, 2020).

However, further examination of the United States during Covid and the Spanish Flu showed that masks became highly politicized. Despite being almost 100 years apart, both pandemics saw the transformation of mask wearing into a question of individual choice. "They're just pieces of cloth," explains journalist

Lauren Aratani, "but a passionate portion of the US population sees an attack on individual freedom" (June 29, 2020). In 2020, polls revealed that most Americans wore masks but "whether businesses and local governments should mandate mask usage has become a divisive political issue" (ibid.). Just as protests during Covid seemed to be divided across left-wing emphasis on social justice (and respecting hygiene measures) and right-wing protests for individualism, Democrats were "more vocal about the importance of face masks" while Republicans were "more hesitant to mandate masks, even as their states [saw] surges of new cases amid reopening phases. The most obvious of these [was] Donald Trump" (ibid.).

As discussed in Chapter 2 section "The 1918-20 H1N1 Spanish Flu," during the Spanish Flu, the Anti-Mask League of San Francisco "helped turn a manageable public-health situation into a disaster" that mobilized "hostility to commonsense measures on grounds of personal liberty" (Kane, April 29, 2020). The strong organization of the Anti-Mask League and its popularity are a reminder of how anxiety during pandemics can affect state legitimacy through restrictions but, in a broader sense, as with Covid, revealed social class differences, in this case between university-educated social workers who attempted to spread information on hygiene measures but were seen as outsiders in working-class neighborhoods (ibid.). This divide also symbolized a broader fragmentation in the United States during Covid and the Spanish Flu: inconsistent responses to a pandemic.

Before Donald J. Trump's inconsistent Covid response that saw editors of medical journal *The Lancet* call for him to step down, the Spanish Flu saw a similar leadership style (Hawkins, Wagner, May 16, 2020). Newark Mayor Charles P. Gillen oversaw a city in New Jersey known for a history of politicizing health. This became apparent when Gillen reversed his initial compliance with the Department of Health's closures for public amusement venues and allowed saloons to remain open to "sell liquor by prescription out of their side doors" (Weinberg, June 11, 2020). This act contradicted "sweeping closure orders issued by state Director of Health J.G. Price" but empowered saloon operators—a significant share of his voter base—to defy such closures and effectively operate as normal (Merkel, Navarro, pp.419–20).

Just as Trump has attacked media outlets as fake news, Gillen knew how to respond when local papers condemned his actions (Marquez, Traylor, Frankel, November 3, 2024). "If the Newark Evening News attempts to interfere with any orders which I have issued or may issue for the preservation of the health of the people of Newark, I will close the paper immediately under the laws of the state, as a menace to the public health, just as I would close any place of assembly" (Merkel, Navarro, p. 420).

When another paper questioned Gillen's defiance and decision to declare the influenza pandemic over, Gillen did not hesitate in branding their articles fake news and "a vile lie from beginning to end," with that paper's reporters banned from his office "until such time as the *Newark Evening News* learns to print the truth about these affairs" (ibid.). Gillen's saloon voting base was empowered by these statements, and it gained him further support from business associations equally opposed to closures to the extent that the City Commission was hesitant to exercise their right to have him removed from power (ibid., p. 420).

Perhaps the United States during pandemics provides an interesting example of how pandemics politicize individual rights for some while also seeing social movements galvanize for social justice and collective responsibilities. This will be further elaborated upon later in this section as we turn to discussing collectivist versus individualist societies and how these opposite norms may have helped or hindered responses to Covid.

As we can see, Covid is the first truly global pandemic of the twenty-first century and has seen almost disparate protest movements addressing individual rights versus broader social justice. These polar protests show "how in times of crisis movements can harness heightened emotions of fear, anger, distrust, uncertainty, anxiety, and helplessness, and channel them into strong mobilizations," with the rise of social media creating public arenas (and social space) at a time when physical space was restricted that saw very different uses by varied social actors, from mutual aid groups to far-right groups connecting over "heightened distrust of government, misinformation, and conspiracy theories" (Daphi, Fominaya, Romanos, 2024, p. 674).

Covid's polarized protests also reflected the wider issue of us versus them identities. This split was very evident during Trump's tenure in America and, as discussed earlier, was also reflected in how some Saudis viewed immigrant residents (Madhani, June 19, 2020). In addition, a 2012 study found that during the H1N1 outbreak, the general public "focus[ed] on attributions of responsibility and blame" (Bangerter et al. 2012). Indeed, previous outbreaks such as Ebola and SARS seem to have mobilized (Western) media and collectives to engage in a process of symbolic containment and effectively othering the countries in which outbreaks occurred. One study found that "media coverage and laypersons' perceptions of Ebola … produced discourse that distanced the disease from the self by depicting far-flung countries as the primary victims of the disease [due to] … their non-occidental hygiene habits …, while it was not seen as problematic for Western countries" (ibid., p. 1014).

In the case of H1N1, it seemed that othering faraway countries gave way to othering domestic social groups as the pandemic went from being a far-flung issue to a regional and eventually domestic issue (ibid., p. 1022). In the United States, "Mexicans and other Latinos living in the US were quickly stigmatized by non-Latinos as carriers of the virus, partly because of news reports on the outbreak's alleged origin in Mexican pig farms" (McCauley et al., 2013, p. 1). Returning to Covid, collectivism and individualism seem to have influenced trust in government and assigning blame for Covid unto other social groups. Within the context of collectivist societies, a 2022 study found that collectivist social groups often had higher levels of empathy and were less likely to blame others for the pandemic, while "holding stronger individualistic values was directly related to more blaming. This might be explained by individuals with individualistic values placing more value on personal responsibility, both for themselves and for others" (Berger et al., 2022, pp. 15, 13).

The difference between collectivist and individualist countries appears to have influenced initial responses to Covid. Some critics argue that individualism fed into higher Covid infections; "[s]ince individualism values personal freedom, people in such cultures would be less likely to make the collective action of staying at home and less likely to support compulsory measures. As a reaction to the public will, governments of individualistic societies would be more hesitant to take compulsory measures, leading to the delay of necessary responses" (Jiang, Wei, Zhang, 2022, p. 791).

Building on this observation, we can examine a hierarchy of individualistic and collectivist countries. According to a 2010 study by Hofstede and Minkov,

> the USA is a highly individualistic society, which is loosely knit under the expectation that everyone look after only themselves and their immediate family members and not rely (too much) on authorities for support. Other English language countries, including the UK, Canada, and Australia are also highly individualistic societies. In contrast, China has a highly collectivistic culture, in which people act in accordance with their group interests and not necessarily their own interests. Society fosters strong relationships, where everyone takes responsibility for fellow members of their own group. "When disaster struck, help came from all sides" is the typical response to crises in China. For example, all the other provinces in China ... assisted Hubei province in the battle with Covid-19. (ibid., p. 796)

This contrast between collectivism and individualism may explain different reactions to Covid restrictions and lockdowns, at least in the early days of the pandemic. For China, the eventual acknowledgment of Covid as a pandemic meant a month-long "nationwide collective action of staying at home was formed at once. This large-scale collective action would be virtually unfeasible without a highly collectivistic cultural root" (ibid.). On the other hand, individualistic societies such as the United States would see resistance to hygiene and lockdown measures once enforced. "Several recent papers' findings support this view. For example, Bazzi et al. (2021) find that greater rugged individualism in the USA is associated with less social distancing and mask use and a weaker local government effort to control the virus. Lu et al. (2021) find that collectivism (versus individualism) positively predicts mask usage within the USA and across the world" (ibid., p. 793).

The highly individualistic structure of the United States can perhaps be linked to the notion of American exceptionalism. As explained by Choeeta Chakrabarti et al., "[i]n the US, we often see ourselves as apart from the rest of the world, but we were not spared the disease, its [e]ffects, and its deaths, and we have not been spared its long-term social ramifications" (2022, p. 2). The belief in American exceptionalism is an individualism combined with "an administration unfriendly to science and academia [that] constantly undermined those doing the work of flattening the curve and keeping U.S. residents alive" (ibid.).

Saudi Arabia, perhaps more so than China, is considered a highly collectivist society. Within Saudi communities, "social relationships [are] vertical, with clear and steep social hierarchies," and "in comparison to Western European culture, Saudi culture emphasizes social hierarchies and respect for authority. Saudi society's structure is built on families, as they form the primary source of identity, personality, values, and behavior development," with most citizens conforming to strict collective societal norms (Alqahtani, 2022, p. 2). Indeed, in a 2022 study by Alqahtani, 93 percent of the 1700 participants reported no Covid infection, which "closely replicated previously found cross-cultural differences in relation to number of Covid-19 cases. Given that Saudi Arabia is considered a collectivistic culture involving vertical social relationships with clear and steep social hierarchies and respect towards authorities, it is not surprising that the percentage of participants who reported having been infected with Covid-19 in this study was very small" (ibid., pp. 3, 5).

As previously discussed in Chapter 1 section "Social Movements, Public Spaces," a further aspect of collectivist identity in Saudi Arabia is the role of religion. The pervasion of Islam, its monopolization by the state, and its importance to social norms mean that religiosity directly influences people's subjective norms, and Covid-19 preventive behavioral intentions are indirectly influenced by subjective norms (Alhugbani, 2022, pp. 392, 397).

As Chapter 1 section "Social Movements, Public Spaces" and Chapter 2 section "Social Movements, Anxieties, and Pandemics" have discussed, social movements during pandemics can emphasize economic performance or lack thereof in state responses. We have seen that the rise of mutual aid groups in the United States, the UK, and China was due to the state's inability to meet all welfare needs for communities. At the same time, as discussed in the UK example, mutual aid groups did not always appear overnight, and those that seemed to be the strongest often built on preexisting networks that were already organized to protest ongoing social issues (such as environmentalism) before the arrival of Covid. On the other hand, we must acknowledge that not all social groups emphasized economic performance. In the United States, movements such as BLM sought to draw attention to institutionalized racism and the murder of African Americans by police officers with little to no initial consequences for the perpetrators. BLM itself predates the arrival of Covid but tapped into preexisting social anxieties that were exacerbated by the pandemic. In addition, BLM tapped into wider social issues worldwide that highlighted the growing inequality that Covid accelerated.

A further issue highlighted by social movements during Covid is the control of social spaces. As explained by You-Tien Hsing, public spaces can become politicized and sought for use by the state or by social movements during times of crisis. Public spaces can be arenas for the flow of dissident ideas or occupied by state actors to become territories sustained by power. This struggle can be referred to as Territorialization, De-territorilalization, and Re-territorialization (TDR), which can see the occupation of social space for survival or struggle between, for example, state and social actors, with the dominant or victorious actor reconstructing social relations with new "territory-based identities and networks, and then new values and encounters are formed in territorial mobilisation" (Wang, 2023, p. 9).

The battle for social space between government and social movements can be evidenced during Covid in different ways. Indeed, the start of Covid saw the concept of TDR take to cyberspace, where Chinese netizens carefully criticized state responses to Covid and emphasized the martyrdom of whistleblower Dr. Li Wenliang. This occupation of decentralized digital social space is an interesting take on the struggle for social space and the ability to politicize and control it. In the case of the social media microblog Weibo (on which Li had an account and posted his eventual infection by Covid), the occupation of Li's blog after his death as a social space saw it transform almost into a shrine that emphasized his sacrifice as a hero and a space for mourning and grief that Chinese authorities could not reoccupy. The occupation of such digital space created multiple identities, exploring how Covid had affected others and connecting Chinese netizens without face-to-face interaction. In this case, while this digital space was not controlled by a centralized social movement, it saw ordinary Chinese citizens indirectly rebuff the state-controlled narrative of Li as an agitator and eventually led to the state reversing this position, issuing an apology to his family, and rewriting their official narrative to confirm Li as a communist hero.

The control of social spaces has also been polarized between left-wing and right-wing groups, which have been split across collective versus individual rights. An emphasis on individualism was seen in the United States during the Spanish Flu; however, this refusal to comply with masks and business closures was not only attached to the politicization of masks in a culture with deeply rooted individualism but also saw social movements resist state guidelines (in some cases with the approval of, e.g., mayors) for economic reasons, as business owners feared financial loss if complying with closures, and political figures with such owners as voters shared these same concerns.

During Covid, there were echoes of the Anti-Mask League from 1918, as right-wing protestors, supported by Republicans and Trump, resisted hygiene measures such as mask-wearing on account of their individual rights. On the other hand, left-wing protestors in the UK and the United States seemed to focus on broader socioeconomic issues such as minority discrimination, exploitation of those in precarious employment, and the nexus between racism, related forms of discrimination, and poverty, including poor access to healthcare and higher infection rates during Covid.

While right-wing protests (and the storming of the US Capitol building) seemed to ignore Covid restrictions, it would seem many left-wing movements were careful to adhere to social distancing and other related hygiene measures. This contrast feeds into the wider discussion of individualism versus collectivism, with societies in China and Saudi Arabia having initially higher rates of compliance with restrictions for the greater good of the collective. Conversely, studies have shown that stronger individualism, especially in the United States, can emphasize a belief in exceptionalism that is reflected in greater disobedience of restrictions and personal beliefs that the virus may affect others but not me

(Trump certainly thought so in early 2020). When asked why he was shaking hands with infected people and not quarantining, he replied, "we have no symptoms whatsoever") (Ioffe, March 14, 2020).

Returning to Porta, the politicization of Covid, the emergence of left-wing and right-wing social movements, and the diverse focus of such movements, from addressing Covid anxiety to plugging welfare gaps, indirectly questioning government censure to protesting masks, link back to how pandemics provoke related crises across the economic, political, and health spectrum, with movements questioning government policies as state institutions struggle to resolve novel health emergencies (p. 5). In a sense, it is the centralized decision-making of states in order to respond to sudden health crises that mobilizes social movements to question how these decisions affect "civic, political [, individual] and social rights" (ibid., pp. 7, 6). Therefore, even if economic performance is a key indicator of political legitimacy during a pandemic, it is clear that social movements may not necessarily attack perceived authoritarianism or welfare gaps but the buildup of wider socioeconomic issues that have been left unaddressed or even exploited by certain actors. Within this latter context, the issue of corporate actors exploiting Covid will be addressed in Chapter 3 section "Pandemic Profiteers."

Vaccine Nationalism, Viral Sovereignty, Vaccine Diplomacy, and International Legitimacy

As discussed in previous sections, vaccine nationalism became a key reaction to Covid but was also apparent in previous pandemics. During SARS and MERS, vaccine development reached the preclinical stage, though few entered a clinical trial stage or received approval by national drug administration bodies such as America's Food and Drug Administration (FDA), with interest in SARS vaccination waning after cases lowered (Chi et al., 2020, p. 4, 1). However, the H1N1 pandemic of 2009 saw far stronger interest in vaccine development. Once H1N1 was detected, the United States and other governments wanted a vaccine to be prepared for a second wave (Nuzzo, Rambhia, December 17, 2009, p. 1). Major vaccine producers were based in the United States, Europe, China, Japan, and South Korea, with China being the first state to "approve and begin administering 2009 H1N1 influenza vaccine" (ibid., pp. 1, 3).

However, as previously discussed, despite China's lead in the vaccine race, only

> [a] month into the outbreak, several higher-income countries negotiated [agreements] that reserved most of the earlier doses of the vaccine. At the time, it was estimated that, in a best-case scenario, global capacity for short-term vaccine manufacturing was between one and two billion doses. Against this backdrop, the United States alone entered into agreements that reserved up to 600,000 doses of the first batch of vaccines to be produced targeting the novel strand of H1N1. (Halabi, Rutschman, 2022, p. 12)

As global cases rose and developed countries were pressured into donating vaccine stock, some such states seemed to prefer promising "that donations of vaccine will be supplemented with syringes and other materials needed to administer [a] vaccine" (Nuzzo, Rambhia, p. 5).

Perhaps in response to such vaccine hoarding across pandemics by richer nations, capital-strapped states have resorted to what Halabi and Rutschmann call viral sovereignty, "the term applied when a country provides access to pathogenic samples as a research input in exchange for benefits arising from the utilization of those samples to develop drugs and vaccines" (p. 17). Such a response was not only due to vaccine shortage during H1N1 but "slowly emerged over the course of vaccine nationalist episodes covering polio, smallpox, and influenza" (ibid.).

In late 2006, Indonesia asserted viral sovereignty during bird flu, withholding their samples

> from the WHO's Global Influenza Surveillance Network System. This constituted a significant measure since the H5N1 avian flu outbreak that had spiked beginning in early 2005 was not only spreading along avian flyways but threatened to become transmissible between humans; those infected experienced a terrifying fifty percent fatality rate. Indonesia asserted its decision was a response to an Australian company's patent on a vaccine derived from a virus sample Indonesia provided to the WHO's pathogen-sharing network

and that hence, the sample was akin to a natural resource like oil or gold and a biological resource from the state's territory, "protected under Articles 15 and 16 of the Convention on Biological Diversity" (ibid., p. 20).

By arguing that its provided sample was akin to a natural resource from state territory and hence a protected resource, Indonesia was able to negotiate "an interim agreement that granted it access to antivirals and vaccines and the promise to develop a broader international agreement on influenza pathogen access and benefit sharing. Indonesia's actions introduced to the scientific sharing process the theretofore unknown concept of 'viral sovereignty'" (ibid., p. 21). To an extent, viral sovereignty connects with Ahram and Lust's international legitimacy and Peter's Political Cosmopolitanism. Ahram and Lust's international legitimacy recognizes that "sovereignty is inextricable from international hierarchy" and "provides for territorial inviolability under international law" (p. 8). From this perspective of territorial integrity, poorer nations can hence invoke sovereignty to assert themselves in certain contexts and "manipulate [wealthier nations] and the international community as a whole," perhaps weaponizing their resources (be it oil or viruses) "to gain leverage in the international system by threatening to withhold [resources] from Europe and the US" (ibid., p. 11).

In other words, while sovereignty may require legitimation from the international system, states can weaponize their sovereignty in order to extract such legitimacy (ibid.). Indonesia certainly weaponized its influenza samples, linking them to territorial integrity and forcing concessions from the international community that emphasized Indonesia's sovereignty under the international system (Halabi, Rutschmann, pp. 20–1).

Returning to Peter's Political Cosmopolitanism, Peter argues that states coexist in an international system and that all states hence relinquish some "scope of legitimate authority to global governance institutions" while maintaining their sovereignty. Hence, a state may appeal to global institutes while also asserting their sovereignty (Peter, April 29, 2010). Again, this balance certainly seemed apparent in Indonesia's initial decision to withhold viral samples. Indonesia had initially sent samples to the WHO but subsequently refused after apparent use of such samples by an Australian company to produce a vaccine, violating a WHO statement that "its reference labs should not distribute biological specimens to other organizations without permission from the country that supplied them" (Roos, July 15, 2008). For its part, the WHO seemed to recognize Indonesia's sovereignty and its own balanced role as a global institute in the international system by admitting that "individual countries like Indonesia are free to try and influence other countries" (ibid.).

In addition to Indonesia asserting viral sovereignty, Saudi Arabia was also accused of delaying Erasmus researchers' access to samples during the MERS pandemic. Saudi Arabia's Ministry of Health argued that "Erasmus had obtained the virus illegally" and United States attempts to access Saudi samples "involved elaborate demands [by Saudi Arabia] for research in Saudi territory, participation by Saudi scientists" and seemed to also be an attempt to weaponize a biological resource through claims linked to territorial sovereignty (Halabi, Rutschmann, pp. 7–8). However, it is worth noting Saudi Arabia did eventually agree to send the United States animal samples by late May 2013 "as part of the hunt for the source of Middle East respiratory syndrome coronavirus" (Roos., May 24, 2013).

Given the emphasis on vaccine nationalism and viral sovereignty under the H1N1 pandemic, Covid-19 did not see the start of but a repeat of vaccine nationalism (Halabi, Rutschmann, p. 13). As with H1N1, China rushed to develop a Covid vaccine, pushing five candidate vaccines into phase three trials and promoting its eventual vaccine globally (Jamali, Zhang, 2022, p. 280). As Sinopharm entered late-stage trials for its two vaccines, the state-owned company boasted "it could produce one billion doses of vaccines in 2021" and had its trials "in 10 nations, including Argentina, the United Arab Emirates (UAE) and Morocco," with the Chinese government seeking to hasten its vaccine race to the finish line by promising "land, loans, and subsidies for vaccine companies to make vaccines along with fast-tracking approvals" (ibid., p. 281). However, rather than hoard supply, China turned to vaccine diplomacy as a soft power tool that could rehabilitate its international image through the provision of a global public good to "uplift Beijing's role as the rule-maker of international order" and stir a domestic pride in the vaccine "as a powerful [tool] to divert its public's attention from Beijing's earlier inadequate handling of the outbreak" (ibid., p. 279).

China's outward-looking policy of vaccine diplomacy seemed to come at a time when Trump's America was withdrawing from global engagements, and through its Covid vaccines, Beijing saw "an opportunity to fill some vacuums left by the United States because of the Trump administration's bad performance on combating Covid-19 and its retreat from leading the world to fight against the virus" (ibid., p. 285).

Indeed, Xi Jinping's announcement that a Chinese Covid vaccine would be "a global public good once available to ensure vaccine accessibility and affordability in developing countries" saw China reaching out to states "who are of strategic importance to shore up alliances with its neighbors before Joe Biden becomes US president" and came atop pre-Covid efforts by China to respond to Trump's isolationism by "playing an active role in international organizations, especially the United Nations (UN), supporting multilateral cooperation and peaceful resolution over conflicts, and delivering international peacekeeping to war-affected countries" (ibid., pp. 284, 283). China's track record of increasing international engagement and more recent vaccine diplomacy certainly illustrate an attempt to gain international legitimacy and be more "welcomed into the international community" (Ahram, Lust, p. 12). In addition, such global outreach increased activity and budget allocation to the UN, tapping into Peter's International Cosmopolitanism and the recognition (and manipulation of) global governance and international bodies (Lo, October 5, 2021, Peter).

For the UK, the AstraZeneca rollout was a symbol of British greatness and proof of Brexit's success, with Leavers arguing "that the reason why Covid-19 vaccination campaign[s] could run so smoothly and quickly in Britain was that the country was no longer held back by the EU's slow approval process, making the conclusion that the UK is 'better off outside the EU' look increasingly credible" (Caliendo, 2022, p. 2). Perhaps complementing making Britain great again was "a national pride in vaccines developed in the UK" under which AstraZeneca "became a national metaphor by virtue of being generated through what was seen to be British science and scientists" with pride being expressed by some British nationals as "'being better,' 'out-competing others' or 'winning' as part of a race or competition" (Douglas et al., pp. 1, 6). Interestingly enough, just as China used vaccine diplomacy to expand its soft power and rehabilitate its image, Britain's AstraZeneca was regarded by some as a national accomplishment "that would lead the UK to be perceived more favourably by the rest of the world" (ibid., p. 6).

In addition, a 2021 focus group on vaccine nationalism and AstraZeneca found that many participants expressed the need for the UK to share rather than hoard AstraZeneca, including providing countries with "technology transfer, so that other countries could have the ability to produce vaccines for themselves" (ibid., p. 7). However, some participants "admitted that they would like the UK to receive the vaccine first, so that life could return to normal," though such participants also insisted that British lives were not more important than other lives (ibid., p. 7).

Perhaps AstraZeneca represents vaccine nationalism within the context of pride in a British savior. At the same time, Britain did seem to put its citizens first by ensuring "priority in a deal agreed before the rest of Europe" that reflected how "the vaccine's approval coincided with Britain's formal separation from the EU" and in a sense reflected how AstraZeneca got caught up in Brexit tensions between the UK and Europe. Indeed, such tensions were reflected in the fact that across "Europe many saw the AZ vaccine as either unsafe or inferior—it was nicknamed the 'Aldi vaccine' in Belgium, after the supermarket, because it was seen as a budget option" (Walsh, February 7, 2022). Hence, even if AstraZeneca was billed by some as a "gift to the world" (ibid.), its connection to Brexit and tensions between the EU and Britain pull it away from vaccine diplomacy and international legitimacy or Political Cosmopolitanism. As one Oxford professor put it, the development of AstraZeneca was surrounded by "too much nationalism. It was encouraging competition between vaccine types, between countries. That's the last thing you want in trying to control the pandemic and providing vaccines for the world" (ibid.). Coupled with Britain ensuring that AstraZeneca would first go to Britain, the UK's Covid vaccine production is more closely connected to Peter's Political Nationalism or the notion that states rather than global institutes exercise the highest political power and hence coexist in a competitive international system and that global governance cannot overcome or replace the (competitive) political legitimacy of nation-states (Peter, April 29, 2010).

For the United States, there was an emphasis on Trump's America First policy, meaning "the Trump administration quickly invested US $10 billion in several pharmaceutical corporations (e.g., Sanofi, GSK, AstraZeneca, Pfizer, Novavax, Moderna and Johnson & Johnson) as vaccine candidates, either via direct financing or through vaccine procurement agreements, through its Operation Warp Speed" (Zhou, 2022, p. 454). Procurement agreements "accounted for the purchase of over one billion doses by the U.S. government, all of which were dedicated to the U.S. market" (Halabi, Rutschmann, p. 13). As during the H1N1 pandemic in 2009, the United States demonstrated strong vaccine nationalism through hoarding, like the UK connecting less with Ahram and Lust's international legitimacy and Peter's Political Cosmopolitanism and more with Peter's Political Nationalism and emphasis on state power in a competitive international system (Peter, April 29, 2010).

Returning to Peter's Political Cosmopolitanism and international legitimacy, it is worth considering to what extent the WHO, as a global health body, may be able to address viral sovereignty and vaccine nationalism. Some critics argue that the WHO are part of the problem due to the process they have of requesting (and relying on) "member states shar[ing] newly discovered viral strains with one another in order to assist in the development of vaccines" while also providing these samples to "private pharmaceutical companies to make vaccines later purchased almost exclusively by developed countries" (Carter, 2014, pp. 719–20).

In other words, if the WHO wishes for member states to follow protocol, the involvement of for-profit pharmaceutical companies must be balanced with the likelihood that nations will assert viral sovereignty if they feel they are not given equal treatment and equitable access to a vaccine based on their samples. Within the context of influenza, in 2018, the pharmaceutical industry earned $2 billion annually and in 2022, Pfizer earned $37.8 billion from its coveted Covid vaccine (McKenna, February 1, 2018; Kimball, January 31, 2023). The role of corporate actors in profiting from Covid will be further discussed in Chapter 3 section "Pandemic Profiteers." Within this context, do developed nations and big pharma have any incentive to change a profitable system of vaccine development from samples provided by states that find themselves excluded from their fair share? It is within this context that Indonesia's then-Health Minister Siti Fadilah defended her nation's decision to withhold viral samples "to create a system that would provide benefits to countries that contribute to vaccine development" (ibid., p. 720).

Indonesia did relent and continued to provide H5N1 samples after the WHO "resolved the conflict by promising Indonesian officials that the H5N1 samples would not be given to pharmaceutical companies without the Indonesian government's permission." This solution was followed in 2007 by a resolution adopted by WHO member states to agree to share viral samples, with the WHO also wanting to

> develop potential mechanisms, including Material Transfer Agreements, that could promote equitable distribution and availability of pandemic influenza vaccines developed and produced from these viruses. Through a proposed Material Transfer Agreement, Indonesia aimed to retain sovereign rights over the donated viral strains, the right to receive the seed virus at no cost, and the right to participate in research and receive acknowledgment for its valuable contributions to the WHO's viral sharing program (ibid., pp. 720–1).

However, the voluntary nature of WHO resolutions and continuing vaccine inequality appear to have encouraged Indonesia to continue expressing concern over exploitation of its natural resources. The issue of viral sovereignty for Indonesia appears to be part of a larger problem of biopiracy, under which "the Indonesian government has taken seriously allegations that foreign researchers have used all kinds of ways—including disguising themselves as tourists—to steal the nation's genetic resources" (Jong, Ompusunggu, March 20, 2017). As for Covid, in 2024 Indonesia made it clear that its participation in the WHO Pandemic Treaty, launched in response to Covid, was dependent on its ability to advocate its national interests, with a focus "on strategic issues like surveillance systems, technology transfer, and equitable access to [address] pandemic threats in the negotiations" (Prisie, June 5, 2024). The creation of a pandemic treaty in response to Covid will be further addressed in Chapter 6.

Considering possible solutions to resolve vaccine inequity and the subsequent risk of a country asserting viral sovereignty, legal scholar Jason Carter argues that there can be positive material incentives to encourage nations to provide samples of emerging infectious diseases. One such approach could be royalties from vaccine sales. This approach would minimize the financial burden on the WHO, as "[s]uch a system would directly compensate developing member states for their contributions to the international viral sharing program without placing too much of a burden on the WHO. Since the source of funding would come from the private sector rather than from the public sector, developed nations would be more likely to embrace such a proposal" (p. 737). Developing nations would be likely to agree to such an arrangement, arguing "that other industries routinely pay royalties to those who help in the development of a final product and that vaccine development should be no different" (ibid.).

However, there may be resistance from the actors who are meant to provide such royalties: pharmaceutical companies. In the case of some infectious diseases like H5N1, vaccine manufacturers were already opposed to this idea "due to the high investment costs, limited markets, and complex regulatory requirements" and may further argue that, while nations may discover and provide viral samples, it is the pharmaceutical company or vaccine manufacturer that bears "all the risks of developing a particular vaccine, and therefore, should be entitled to all of the rewards" (ibid.).

A further complication with establishing a vaccine royalty system could be the risk of incentivizing disease research based on profitable vaccines and the expectation of high payout from the private drug sector rather than nations, along with the WHO, focusing on disease trends and the long-term likelihood of a disease becoming severe and widespread, whether globally or regionally. This scenario may create a backlash that affects public trust in vaccines and in states that claim to discover emerging infectious diseases. Already in 2005, there was a parallel scandal at the US National Institutes of Health (NIH), in which patients who volunteered in clinical trials were unaware "that scientists at the institutes received $8.9 million (£4.8m; €6.8m) in royalty payments and might benefit financially for the use of their discoveries by pharmaceutical companies and device makers," with former NIH researchers receiving "annual royalty payments averaging $9700 but could receive as much as $150 000" (Tanne, 2005). While the "almost $56m in royalties" the NIH received was ostensibly rolled back into its research, it is hard to imagine that such financial generosity from drug companies does not risk influencing vaccine and related research, in addition to the risk of states frivolously reporting emerging viruses in the hopes of lucrative royalties or reporting such discoveries selectively in line with the development trends of vaccine manufacturers (ibid.).

Perhaps the most workable solution to countering viral sovereignty would be equitable vaccine access. In other words, the WHO should target the primary concern of countries that provide samples, which is ensuring that a fair number of vaccines produced from these samples is allocated for the nation that provided the required samples in the first place. Indeed, Indonesia's response to the WHO over its assertion of viral sovereignty was that it wanted to see "transparent, fair and equitable sharing of the benefits arising from the generation of information, diagnostics, medicines" and especially "increase[d] vaccine access for developing countries by providing financial support and building vaccine-manufacturing capacities" (Hong, May 1, 2018).

However, even this solution may have drawbacks. What would be equitable vaccine access and how would this be calculated or determined? The WHO "would have to choose between establishing a bright-line rule and determining what is 'equitable' on a case-by-case basis" while also contending with the fact that "often there are not enough doses of a particular vaccine to inoculate everyone who needs it" (Carter, pp. 738–9). Indeed, in the case of Covid, the WHO announced in 2021 that it set a goal of 70 percent global vaccination by mid-2022 (World Health Organization, 2024). However, by May 2022, the WHO announced that there was a huge gap between vaccination in high-income countries and low-income countries, with 80 percent of citizens in wealthy nations receiving a vaccine compared to 16 percent in poorer nations (World Health Organization, May 20, 2022). This huge disparity acts as a reminder of vaccine inequality, the very reason Indonesia's then-Health Minister Siti Fadilah was "happy" when scientists discovered Indonesia's H5N1 sample was particularly virulent—it meant stronger bargaining power for vaccine access (Elbe, 2022, p. 12).

This disparity is a reminder that, even if the WHO were to advocate a system of equitable vaccine access,

> developed countries might object to such a system if they fear that they will not be able to purchase enough vaccines to protect their citizens. However, if the WHO was able to convince developed nations that one of the best ways to stop the spread of infectious diseases that originate in developing countries is to contain them at the source, developed countries might agree to grant developing nations greater access to certain vaccines. (Carter, p. 739)

The international legitimacy of the WHO sees most states acknowledge its existence as a global health governing body, perhaps returning to Ahram and Lust's international legitimacy or the belief that states need international recognition of their sovereignty within an international system of global actors, including in the realm of global health (p. 8). However, the conflict between the WHO and viral sovereignty is a reminder of the WHO's existence as part of a global health governance system that is voluntary. In addition, we can return to Porta's discussion of pandemics as emergency junctures, with the rise of infectious diseases that become or risk becoming pandemics provoking "economic, social and political crises" that themselves bring "crisis or strain that existing policies and institutions are ill-suited to resolve" (p. 5). In the case of viral sovereignty, can the WHO promote a system of vaccine equity that would be accepted by all? In a sense, the source of viral sovereignty and its assertion by developing states mirrors the social inequality that Covid has exacerbated and that was picked up by social movements discussed in this chapter. On the other hand, as seen with the example of Indonesia, assertion of viral sovereignty has not been only due to perceived inequitable vaccine access but lack of economic acknowledgment for the role viral samples play in not only vaccine production but enriching vaccine manufacturers. Within the context of global health governance, it is difficult to say whether the WHO can mimic social movements in their ability to keep governments in check by balancing viral sovereignty and vaccine exploitation to keep (member) states cooperative. Without a universal system of vaccine equitability, developing states have little to no motivation to abandon viral sovereignty, while vaccine manufacturers may have little incentive to abandon a for-profit model that sees vaccine preorders prioritized for states that can afford it.

Pandemics Require International and Domestic Cooperation

An overview of pandemics reveals the importance of international cooperation and early response. In addition, it is clear that restrictions that provoked questions of personal freedom and choice and even the legitimacy of governing authorities are not unique to Covid but were also key features of some past pandemics, such as the Spanish Flu in the United States and SARS in China. Pandemics in the twenty-first century were also highlighted by health experts as illustrating the need for future preparedness and constant vigilance rather than states and health authorities only improving policies in response to pandemics. Further, analysis of social movements shows that some movements protested lack of restrictions during Covid due to recent memories of the effects of previous pandemics. However, while we discussed in Chapter 1 section "Social Movements, Public Spaces" how during Covid, economic performance became a core concern for state political legitimacy and a core concern of social movements that rose to address welfare gaps, social justice was also a key concern for the BLM movement and saw it connected with related transnational movements regarding minority discrimination.

An overview of certain states' relationship with vaccines during pandemics reveals that wealthier states have acted as vaccine producers and hoarders in earlier pandemics, prompting some poorer nations to exercise what has become known as viral sovereignty to gain fairer access to vaccines. In addition, during Covid, states like China have engaged in vaccine diplomacy as a form of soft power to rehabilitate their image and maintain alliances. The contrast between vaccine nationalism and vaccine diplomacy can be linked to Political Nationalism and international legitimacy and Political Cosmopolitanism, respectively, a theme that will be returned to in public discourse from state leaders during the Covid vaccine race in Chapter 5. Chapter 3 discusses the ruling style of leaderships in China, Saudi Arabia, the UK, and the United States in the years leading up to Covid, focusing on how each leadership established their legitimacy or popularity through their ruling style. This approach to understanding each leadership provides political context for the arrival of Covid and each leadership's response to it.

Chapter 3

CASE STUDIES

Maintaining Government Power

The previous chapter discussed how governments and social movements responded to pandemics during key historical periods, including to what extent social movements protested any restrictions (or even not enough restrictions), discussing to what extent such movements were linked to or affected economic performance or social justice, especially during Covid, which allowed some such movements like Black Lives Matter to connect with other transnational activists regarding racial and socioeconomic discrimination. It also considered how vaccine nationalism and hoarding affected vaccine inequality before Covid, prompting viral sovereignty from developing nations, which refused to provide viral samples without promises of vaccine access and other related benefits derived from these samples. The focus of wealthier states and pharmaceutical actors maintaining a for-profit system further emphasizes the book's argument that during a health crisis, economic performance becomes a key factor of political legitimacy, with many social movements responding to welfare gaps during Covid rather than solely protesting restrictions.

To better understand the political legitimacy of each case study's leadership leading up to Covid, this chapter will explore the political profiles of each case study's leadership that was in power when Covid arrived in their country. Before examining how public discourse from such leaders drew on democratic or nondemocratic factors of political legitimacy in response to the pandemic, an overview of each leadership's ruling style and political image will provide such discourse and the effects of Covid with a clearer context. For some leaderships, the years leading up to Covid meant getting Brexit done as proof of respecting popular will, whereas for others, these years were focused on offering social reform that ultimately would not erode autocratic rule (List, April 16, 2019, Schaer, June 27, 2021). As this chapter will show, democratic and nondemocratic regimes were engaged in sometimes similar methods to shore up support for their political agendas, and the use of democratic and nondemocratic factors of political legitimacy before Covid certainly elucidates each regime's political reaction to the pandemic.

Figure 3.1 World leaders meet virtually during the G20 summit held between November 21 and 22, 2020. Source: EU Council Newsroom, email to author, May 16, 2025.

China, Wuhan, and Power

Xi Jinping's first public address as party chief in 2012 emphasized how the CCP, or Chinese Communist Party, guided a nationalism that was to be regarded as transformative and a rebirth of China while also augmenting China's global role and eventual recognition as a world power (BBC, November 15, 2012). As the "son of a veteran revolutionary leader," Xi was a "red princeling" or the child of a communist official who had gained favor "during the communist takeover of China in 1949" (Li, September 2019, p. 3). As such, Xi's ascendence in 2012 as General Secretary of the CCP saw him portray himself "as inheritor of the legacies of both Mao Zedong and Deng Xiaoping; consolidating power based on both his communist 'red nobility' and his understanding of 'ordinary people,'" the latter gained when "his father fell out of favor with Mao and was purged from the CCP," leading to a sixteen-year-old Xi being moved "to mountainous Yan'an, where he and his compatriots lived in caves, slept on brick beds, and toiled as peasants. Xi spent over six years—his formative years—in the arduous physical environment, which gave him the unusual opportunity to develop an understanding of socioeconomically disadvantaged areas of the country" (ibid., pp. 1, 3).

As Xi Jinping rose to become China's president, he used the dual identities of "red prince" and peasant "as a political asset, enabling him to switch between one and the other when it benefits him to do so" (ibid., p. 3) and to align "with diverse constituencies and socioeconomic trends" (ibid., p. 1). However, Xi also needed to focus on centralizing his power. Officially, Xi and his cohorts argued that a centralized government would bring "government, military and industry" under a "disciplined party" and ensure "a fair and sound market economy" (Kazuko, September 2020, p. 1); however, such centralization was also part of Xi's ambition to solidify his rule of "the Chinese Communist Party (CCP) and his direct command over the People's Liberation Army," culminating in 2018's "abolishment of presidential term limits" (Li, p. 2). We can thus see that even before the arrival of a health crisis, there was a concerted effort to centralize decision-making in government, albeit to bolster Xi's political authority (Porta, p. 7).

In his first term, "Xi had no choice but to lean on [fellow] princelings to balance the power of [predecessor] Hu-Jintao's protégés who hailed from humble family backgrounds" (ibid., p. 3). The reliance on fellow princelings was necessary as members of this network that Xi was part of "are bound by their shared elite political identities and the common interest to deal with some formidable rival factions such as Hu Jintao's [protégés]" (ibid.). However, Xi's dual identities as princeling and peasant allowed him to launch an anti-corruption drive "for the people" that would serve as a purge of fellow princelings (ibid.). Indeed, by 2017, Xi's ability to centralize power around himself allowed him to emphasize his populist rather than princeling image, and "[as] soon as Xi consolidated power during his first term, he began keeping his distance from [fellow] princelings and drastically reducing their representation in the leadership" (ibid.). Under his supposed anti-corruption drive, Xi targeted low-profile and high-profile officials. By 2017, "the Central Commission for Discipline Inspection (CCDI) [had] ousted over 250 senior officials from the CPC and the military. Up to two million lower-level officials [were] also investigated" (Rahn, October 17, 2017). Such purges made it clear that Xi was above his former princelings, and to augment his populist standing with the people, Xi turned to one specific (nondemocratic) Beneficial Consequence: economic growth.

According to Li, Xi's initial political legitimacy as president could be seen as raising China's middle class and tackling poverty "in the rural inland areas where [Xi's predecessor] Hu Jintao's protégés have traditionally had the upper hand in garnering support" (ibid., p. 5). To an extent, such an economic approach to political legitimacy (or what may be termed performance legitimacy) was also apparent in 2010 before Xi's rise to power. Under Xi's predecessor Hu Jintao, international pressures and domestic factors prompted the need to re-legitimate CCP rule, with "evidence of an agile, responsive, and creative party effort to religitimate the postrevolutionary regime through economic performance, nationalism, ideology, culture, governance and democracy" (Gilley, Holbig, 2010, p. 395).

It should be noted that democracy as a source of political legitimacy does not mean Western democracy or transparency often associated with democracy but rather the use of such governance according to the regime itself, defining democracy "in ways that support its existing performance and values" (ibid., p. 396). For example, the CCP allowed "direct township elections" as a form of democracy but ensured that such practices remained a limited form "of popular sovereignty under the leadership of the party" (ibid., pp. 412, 414).

Economic growth and nationalism were already regarded as traditional sources of legitimacy, but with economic growth especially, there was the risk of extensive use of such performance-based legitimacy "generating its own problems" by "creating rising expectations; and because it [risks] fueling shifts in social values and political culture" (ibid., pp. 399–400).

Nonetheless, economic growth seemed at the core of Xi Jinping's first term. Between 2012 and 2017, Xi allocated 282.2 billion yuan ($41.7 billion) to poverty alleviation funds, "more than double the level under the Hu Jintao-Wen Jiabao administration" (Li, p. 6). As previously mentioned, such programs played into Xi's image of understanding the common individual and "endeared him to the general public," including in rural areas popular with Hu Jintao's protégés (who Xi would gradually replace) (ibid., pp. 5, 8). Amid "both a domestic economic slowdown and a trade war with the United States that have damaged the confidence of the middle class, Xi adopted tax cuts and more easily-accessible bank loans to promote private-sector development and ease the anxieties of arguably the country's most important socioeconomic constituency" (ibid., p. 2). Beyond the initial promise to eliminate poverty in China by 2020, 2021 was supposed to see "a moderately prosperous society" that built on a goal from 1997 but that Xi would accelerate and perhaps take credit for (ibid., p. 6).

Just as the Chinese media was influential during the pandemic politics of the SARS outbreak, Xi used state outlets to strengthen his image with the poor and the middle classes. "Through widely publicized media coverage of his frequent visits to poverty-stricken areas in Qinghai, Guizhou, Gansu and elsewhere, [he] effectively rebrand[ed] himself as a 'leader of the people'" in a hope to use poverty elimination as political currency "to overturn decades of Chinese political norms as a Mao-like figure and enhance China's (and his own) influence on the world stage" (ibid.).

At the same time, Xi ensured that as drivers of China's economic growth, the middle classes were acknowledged through development plans that would enhance the coastal metropolises most middle-class citizens resided in (ibid.). Hence, amid the 2008 financial crisis, then-economic adviser Liu He called for "metropolis clusters" that would continue to be "the carrier[s] of industrialization, the platforms for marketization and the stage for globalization" (ibid.). Chinese media branded "Beijing, Tianjin, Shanghai, Chongqing, Shenzhen and Guangzhou as the 'six megacities'" due to being "the main indicators of China's middle class consumption" and "the country's top cities in terms of contributions to gross domestic product (GDP)" (ibid., p. 7). Xi's control and expansion of such megacities certainly tapped into economic control as part of performance legitimacy and a Beneficial Consequence for China's growing middle class.

As Li himself explains, control of these "large socioeconomic entities" is politically significant, and "[i]t is often said that a megacity is to China what a country is to Europe. Altogether, the total aggregate GDP of these cities was 14.98 trillion yuan ($2.2 trillion) in 2018, roughly equivalent to the total GDP of Brazil in the same year" and it is no coincidence that "Xi's protégés now occupy the top positions in most of these six cities, which was often not the case during his first term (2012–17)" (ibid.).

As Xi's consolidation of power peaked with the removal of presidential term limits, it was also time for China to strengthen its role on the world stage. Former Australian Prime Minister Kevin Rudd explains that since 2014, Xi's leadership has sought to expand China's hard and soft power through an increasingly aggressive "regional military presence" in the South China Sea "with a rapid program of island reclamation" and "the New Silk Road" as a "multi-trillion dollar trade, investment, infrastructure and wider geo-political and geo-economic initiative, engaging 73 different countries across much of Eurasia, Africa and beyond" (Rudd, June 26, 2018). Ultimately, Xi's ambition regarding China's international activity is to increasingly ensure Beijing's "capability to reform the global governance system to reflect [its] priorities and values" (Council on Foreign Relations, 2025).

Hence, Xi's approach to global governance and international legitimacy may be seen to promote "long-standing Chinese aims: preventing criticism of China's human rights practices, keeping Taiwan from assuming an independent role in international institutions, and protecting Beijing from compromises to its sovereignty" (ibid.). However, policies such as increasing its contribution to the UN budget echo the deeper desire "to shape the global governance system more offensively, to advance its model of political and economic development" that emphasizes "extensive state control over politics and society, and a mix of both market-based practices and statism in core sectors of the economy" (ibid.).

For Xi Jinping, China's global role includes not only international governance but also China's increasing role in global agencies and, since Covid, a leading role in global health. As previously discussed in Chapter 2 section "Vaccine Nationalism, Viral Sovereignty, Vaccine Diplomacy, and International Legitimacy," China's rise accelerated at a time when Trump's America seemed to withdraw from global governance, and Xi's demand that his country should "lead the reform of the global governance system with the concepts of fairness and justice" has been interpreted by some as "a call for a more multipolar world, one potentially with a smaller U.S. role in setting international rules" and a greater role for a more active China (ibid.).

In addition to increasing financial contributions, China has also increased their political roles within some global institutions "traditionally dominated by Western countries." Victories have included the election of Qu Dongyu, China's 2015 vice minister of agriculture and rural affairs, as the United Nations Food and Agriculture Organization's director general in June 2019, defeating a US-backed counterpart (Zampano, June 23, 2019).

Before Covid-19, China increased its focus on emerging diseases and, akin to the soft power of the New Silk Road, increased health-related aid to developing nations in exchange for increasing political and diplomatic clout in those nations (Amusa, Monkam, Viegi, April 26, 2016), in conjunction with increasing cooperation with the WHO (Council on Foreign Relations). As China wishes to lead in global governance, it seems that taking the lead in viral combat is also being used as a way of enhancing its image abroad, with China already leading efforts to eradicate malaria in the months leading up to Covid (Kushner, July 4, 2019) but maintaining a centralized approach to health aid, requesting "potential recipients to approach it for support" and emphasizing "infrastructure, such as hospitals, yet [doing] little to promote transparency in recipient countries" (Council on Foreign Relations, 2025).

Specifically influenced by Covid-19 and the use of strict quarantine, Beijing has even "promoted its model for battling Covid-19 and offered assistance to countries including Iran, Italy and Spain" (ibid.). Connected to China's exportation of its lockdown model (perhaps itself a symbol of China's external outlook but domestic isolation during the pandemic) is how Wuhan's initial lockdown was "presented as [a] mature and costly decision made by the political leadership for the greater good" and proof of the CCP "as a responsible actor standing on the moral high ground" that "has provided assistance to over 80 countries as well as the World Health Organization" (Rolland, July 2020). China's zero-Covid strategy was praised by the State Council (or cabinet) in 2020 as providing a further Beneficial Consequence: security from the virus (Mankikar, December 19, 2022). However, by May 2022, Premier Li Keqiang "proclaimed that the challenges China had faced in recent months were 'greater' than those experienced in 2020 when the coronavirus outbreak was first reported" (ibid.). Keqiang was hinting at China's economic challenges and perhaps protests (a consequence of lockdowns faced by many other nations) (ibid.). The issue of economic performance as a Beneficial Consequence and factor of justifying nondemocratic rule will be further explored in Chapter 4 through analysis of Keqiang's speech given in May 2020 as other cities were placed under a "Wuhan-style lockdown" (Davidson, May 19, 2020).

Saudi Arabia and Reform

Crown Prince Mohammed bin Salman (MBS), during an interview with *Time* magazine in March 2018, justified autocratic rule going hand-in-hand with reform and echoed the specter of Cold War enemies and "that evil narrative of the Iranian regime" (Time, April 5, 2018). In the published interview, *Time* described the then-32-year-old as an "iron-fisted regent of his ailing, 82-year-old father, King Salman," and a "frenemy" of Washington at a time when "55 [percent] of Americans disapprove[d] of Saudi Arabia" (ibid.).

Such an ambiguous welcome by the American public was even before the murder of Saudi exiled journalist and former *Washington Post* columnist Jamal Khashoggi. Khashoggi would be assassinated by a Saudi hit squad months later in October 2018 (Al Jazeera, October 20, 2018). A 2019 US intelligence report confirmed MBS's order of the hit, arguing that this move was part of a larger pattern regarding the crown prince's "support for violent measures to silence dissidents abroad, including Khashoggi," elaborating that since "2017, the Crown Prince has had absolute control of the Kingdom's security and intelligence organizations, making it highly unlikely that Saudi officials would have carried out an operation of this nature without the Crown Prince's authorization" (Roberts, February 26, 2021).

Although prepared in 2019, the report did not smear MBS's relations with President Trump, who enthusiastically blocked "the long-awaited report despite a 2019 law passed by Congress requiring its release" (ibid.).

Trump's personal relationship with MBS (and other dictators) seemed strong, and perhaps it was a key reason why MBS's US visits under Trump were highly publicized and accessed not only Trump but also "other important politicians in Washington, including influential members of Congress" (Brimelow, April 5, 2018). In a move that seemed part of Saudi Arabia's soft power strategy, MBS's leaked itinerary also "revealed meetings with journalists, media moguls, academics, and some of the biggest players in the world's economy" (ibid.). Of important note was MBS's attempt to combat America's uncertainty over his rule through "an upcoming meeting with media mogul Oprah Winfrey in Los Angeles" (The Independent, March 28, 2018). Was Hollywood as important as Washington, DC? Nader Hashimi, director of the University of Denver's Centre for Middle East Studies, certainly thought so. "When you meet with Oprah, even if you're not going to be interviewed, you're seeking the approval of an opinion maker," he explained. "You're going into people's homes and reaching deep into American culture" (ibid.).

Indeed, just as China's Xi Jinping used domestic media to bolster his image as a man of the people, Saudi Arabia's MBS wanted to create a positive international image as a reformer next in line to the throne by tapping into US media outlets especially. Employing public relations firm Qorvis to advise on the best soft power strategy may certainly have influenced MBS's meeting with Oprah and conducting an interview with *60 Minutes* that was "the first interview with a Saudi leader in more than a decade" (ibid.). Such media engagements were intended "to cement his reputation as a bold, young reformer bringing sorely needed economic and social change to his kingdom, such as curbing the power of the notorious religious police and allowing women to drive" (ibid.).

Was this carefully curated global image a reality or a mirage? Within Saudi Arabia itself, there was also an emphasis on changing the country's image of its political rulers. However, such a focus seemed to be on nationalism over religion, what Baker fellow Simon Henderson calls "Saudi Arabia [adjusting] its [h]istory" to weaken "the role of Wahhabism," a puritanical branch of Islam by preacher Muhammad ibn Abdul-Wahhab that defined the founding of Saudi Arabia (February 11, 2022). It was commonly accepted that the first Saudi state was the result of

> tribal leader Muhammad bin Saud, who ruled the area around the town of Dariyah, in central Arabia, and Muhammad ibn Abdul Wahhab who had sought refuge in 1745 after fleeing from nearby villages for preaching an Islamic orthodoxy that criticized local practices. Together, the men became allies and hatched a plan to combine Muhammad bin Saud's tribal leadership and fighting prowess with Abdul Wahhab's religious zeal to have a jihad (campaign) to conquer and purify Arabia. The relationship was cemented by family intermarriage, including the pairing of Muhammad bin Saud with one of Abdul Wahhab's daughters. (ibid.)

However, under King Salman bin Abdulaziz Al Saud, this narrative has been changed. On January 27, 2022, King Salman issued a decree that would be "the equivalent of the United States deciding independence did not occur in 1776" (ibid.). Under the Salman administration, "the first Saudi state has been declared to have been founded in 1727, eighteen years before Abdul Wahhab fled to Dariyah." The reason for such historical readjustment is to allow "King Salman and his son and Crown Prince, Muhammad bin Salman" to "diminish the historical role of the Wahhabi clerical establishment, which until Salman became king was often described as a coalition partner of the al-Saud, albeit a junior one" (ibid.).

Indeed, during my first trip to Riyadh in 2020, it would seem that under MBS's reformist image, it was not only the role of Wahhabism but also its extremism that was being diluted. At a historical landmark in the Saudi capital, the role of Abdul Wahhab is outlined

> in a softened tone by a British narrator blaring through loudspeakers. Despite Wahhabism being described by critics as "a brutal method of religious and social control," the voice of the grandfatherly Brit assures us that Ibn Wahhab was a "religious reformer" who aided the House of Saud in ensuring religious stability. This narrative is a reminder that MBS is facing a tug of war between the conservative core of Saudi political history and creating an image of openness. (Due-Gundersen, 2020)

In addition to this tug-of-war between a conservative past and the image of an open present has been the tug-of-war between royal family factions and the very real attempt by King Salman to ensure his son MBS is at the center of power (Henderson). And at the crux of MBS's claim to fame are his promised reforms under Vision 2030. Upon the death of former King Abdullah (2005–15) in 2015, the new King Salman inherited "a deteriorating economy that was overly reliant on high oil prices and unable to meet the employment and livelihood demands of Saudi Arabia's growing youth population" (Human Rights Watch, 2019, p. 1). Hence, a strengthened economy was key to Salman's reign. However, it would also seem that addressing the economy would also be used as an opportunity to debut his son MBS as an economic savior and eventually crown prince. Salman's rule began by appointing "his then 29-year old son Mohammed as the head of the newly established Council of Economic and Development Affairs and the Minister of Defence" (ibid.).

Indeed, "Mohammed bin Salman, a relatively unknown and junior prince prior to his father's accession to the throne, quickly became the face of Saudi Arabia's efforts to reform the country's economy. In April 2016 he launched Vision 2030, an ambitious government road map for economic and developmental growth that aims to reduce the country's dependence on oil" (ibid.). By the summer of 2017, MBS was elevated to crown prince, "making him next in line to the Saudi throne and de-facto day-to-day ruler of the country" (ibid.). MBS's *de facto* rule was intended to be defined by reform under Vision 2030, including:

- "Positive changes for women and youth
- [A] major push for foreign direct investment" (ibid.)

It should be noted that such reform was explicitly social rather than political and can thus be considered under Peter's Beneficial Consequences (Peter). Like Xi Jinping's China, economic, not political, growth would be a pillar of political legitimacy, in addition to reforms that would increase social freedom "for Saudi women and youth" (Human Rights Watch, 2019, p. 1).

Due to the focus on social, not political, transformation, observers such as Madawi al-Rasheed have described such change as "[h]ollow [r]eforms" and argued that "[s]ecuring the throne for young Mohammed has been the main driver of many policies sold to the public as reforms that would transform Saudi Arabia" (December 2020, p. 331). In a sense, Vision 2030 and MBS's leadership of reforms can be seen as an attempt to manipulate the demands for reform already present under King Abdullah "and growing louder. Saudi activists, Islamists, and feminists demanded improvement of the country's human rights record, freedom for detained political prisoners, and empowerment of women. Some also pushed for transforming the absolute monarchy into a constitutional one, restricting the royal household's privileges, and establishing an elected national assembly to replace the old consultative council" (ibid., p. 333).

Of course, by promoting some reforms that did not alter the core political power of the monarchy, it is possible that MBS and King Salman hope to prevent eventual united opposition to Al-Saud rule by seeing some groups lose interest in opposition if a few of their wishes were granted, but then again, the "House of Saud survived the Arab Spring by mixing incentives with severe crackdowns and leveraging its alliances with the religious establishment" (London, July 7, 2022). Even after economic sweeteners were offered to quell protests and especially under Vision 2030, "MBS must try to balance some citizens' demands for social change with others' concerns that the kingdom is losing its identity" and may still need to be careful with how he treats the religious class (Sheline, Ulrichsen, September 19, 2019, p. 5).

Indeed, while Vision 2030 was announced in 2016 and promised to target the authority of religious institutions, there have been limits to such action. On the one hand, in 2016, "Saudi Arabia's Council of Ministers removed the powers of arrest from the country's abusive religious police" (Human Rights Watch, 2019, p. 11). However, even by 2019, "in the religious arena, Mohammed bin Salman's stated intention to implement reform [had] not been followed by significant changes in policy." Instead, social reform was used as cover to crack down on religious dissidents. Despite American portrayals of MBS challenging Wahhabism, "the Saudi government has largely ignored clerics that represent the core of the religious establishment, instead pursuing individuals who have a history of criticizing government policies" (Sheline, Ulrichsen, p. 5).

In a sense, then, the historical religious-political agreement between monarchy and religious elites (known as the *ulema*) is being maintained, making religion a further Beneficial Consequence that is both drawn on in public discourse and used to ensure religious authorities legitimize controversial royal decisions by issuing an Islamic ruling or *fatwa* that the decision is religiously correct, whether the House of Saud attempts to lead a blockade against Qatar or allows US troops to be stationed on holy land (ibid.). The importance of religion as a Beneficial Consequence in public discourse will be further discussed in Chapter 4.

If the religious elite must still be somewhat appeased, the same cannot be said for royal family members who may become rivals. Just as Xi Jinping purged fellow princelings from the CCP as he rose to power to centralize his rule, MBS has attacked those from his house he perceived as a threat, culminating in what became known as the "Riyadh Ritz-Carlton purge" of 2017 (Chulov, November 19, 2020). The Ritz-Carlton Riyadh is frequently praised by guests as exceptional in service and accommodation. "We thoroughly enjoyed all parts of our stay," claimed one reviewer on travel site Agoda. Another reviewer was more explicit. "My family will remember Ritz Carlton Riyadh because of the people and staff who welcome, assist and take care of us" (Agoda, 2022).

For "400 of Saudi Arabia's most powerful people, among them princes, tycoons and ministers," the Ritz Riyadh would be memorable for very different reasons (Chulov). Perhaps the Ritz roundup left more of a mark than Vision 2030 and "shook the foundations of Saudi society, in an instant turning untouchable establishment figures into targets for arrest." Akin to Xi Jinping's anti-corruption drive that allowed him to purge uncooperative colleagues once untouchable (NBC News, January 1, 2015), MBS ensured that "[s]tatuses were discarded, assets seized and business empires upended. A conventional pact between the state and its influential elite was shredded overnight" (Chulov).

The Ritz raid came months after MBS was promoted to crown prince and was not without some irony. Only "a year earlier [the Ritz Riyadh] had been the venue for the launch of Prince Mohammed's ambitious 'Vision 2030' plan" and was now host to "people tied to the walls, in stress positions. It went on for hours, and all of those doing the torturing were Saudis" (Al-Rasheed, p. 335, Chulov). Of course, this targeting of wealthy and influential rivals coexisted with a purge of "former security and intelligence officials," the restructuring of "intelligence and counterterrorism functions formerly held by the Interior Ministry," and the centralization of the armed forces under MBS (Human Rights, 2019, pp. 2, 17). With the prosecution and security services under MBS's purview, the crown prince held "the primary tools of Saudi repression" in the palm of his hand and "then launched a series of arrest campaigns, targeting dozens of critics and potential critics of Saudi government policies. These arrest waves targeted prominent clerics, public intellectuals, academics, and human rights activists," making it clear that Vision 2030 was not an opportunity for political demands or any shift of power away from MBS and his father (ibid., p. 2).

It is worth remembering that Vision 2030 was equally an attempt to gain international legitimacy for MBS. However, the 2018 slaying of Khashoggi threatened the ambitions of the crown prince to be "a great power" (Gause, December 12, 2018). In the same month of Khashoggi's murder, MBS held an investment conference billed as "Davos in the Desert" but found "the guest list was much reduced. A number of high-profile political leaders and CEOs backed out, including the U.S. treasury secretary, the president of the World Bank, the managing director of the International Monetary Fund (IMF), and the CEOs of JPMorgan Chase, HSBC, Credit Suisse, BNP Paribas, and the London Stock Exchange" (ibid.). However, the same conference announced "$50 billion in investment deals, over $30 billion with Saudi Aramco, the state oil company" (ibid.).

Some analysts argue that MBS risks being brought down by his own sense of entitlement and expectation that he "can act with the kind of impunity that Putin's Russia and Xi's China do on the international stage" (ibid.). It is not without note that after Khashoggi's murder, MBS seemed to tilt Saudi Arabia toward Moscow and Beijing. By the time of the G20 conference, "warm welcomes for MBS by Presidents Putin and Xi saved him from pariah status" (Storey, February 8, 2019).

In any event,

> King Salman is the key player here. He has reasserted himself in the wake of the Khashoggi killing but at the same time appointed MBS to oversee the "reform" of the intelligence services announced in the wake of the killing. He is both the crown prince's protector and the one person who can limit the crown prince's power. It is appeals to the king, from senior members of the Al Saud family, important constituencies in the country, and international actors that could lead to greater constraints on the crown prince's authority. (Gause)

The arrival of Covid-19 across Saudi Arabia certainly threatened the economic hopes of Vision 2030. According to a United Nations team that visited the kingdom during Covid, "[u]nder the Vision 2030, [Saudi Arabia] smoothly executed a slew of economic reforms aimed at reducing [Saudi] dependence on oil for economic activity and revenues, increasing the role of [the] private sector in the economy and improv[ing] the overall socioeconomic wellbeing of its citizens (health, education, housing, employment, poverty & inequality)" (United Nations Saudi Arabia, November 2020, p. 8).

However, such large structural changes in Saudi Arabia's socioeconomics provoked "a relatively higher fiscal deficit" that made Riyadh even more vulnerable to "dual shock from Covid-19 and volatility in oil prices" (ibid., p. 9). Learning from the lessons of past pandemics, the House of Saud prioritized the continued availability of essential health services. Just as MERS saw dedicated wards, under Covid additional financial resources allowed "dedicated health facilities to deal with Covid-19." *Hajj* was restricted and there was emphasis on "provision of adequate and surplus [personal protection equipment] to healthcare workers and the overall population, and running regular media campaigns to provide regular updates and information about the crisis" (ibid., p. 10).

The first case of Covid in Saudi Arabia was announced in early March 2020 by way of Iran, which had "reported the most deaths from the coronavirus outside China" (Reuters, March 2, 2020). By March 23, Saudi Arabia had decided on restrictions, announcing "a nationwide curfew from 19:00 to 06:00 for 21 days" (Crisis24, March 23, 2020). In addition to the curfew, Riyadh

> suspended all domestic transportation services for 14 days, affecting domestic flights, trains, buses, and taxis. All international travel [was] suspended for two weeks from Sunday, March 15, and most private sector business[es] [were] ordered to suspend operations for 15 days. Only businesses providing vital food, health, or utility services [remained] operational. Malls, restaurants, coffee shops, and public parks also closed. (ibid.)

While most of the country saw curfews, the eastern region of Qatif was placed under lockdown "after 11 individuals from the area tested positive for the virus" (ibid.). As mentioned across this book, pandemics and politics are often intertwined, and this was certainly the case with the Shia-minority Qatif. With Saudi Arabia Sunni-majority, the oil-rich eastern region has often "accused the Sunni-dominated government of discrimination" (Agence France-Presse, March 9, 2020). Under the lockdown, "only essential services such as pharmacies and petrol stations" would operate (ibid.).

Qatif's lockdown was eased at the end of April 2020, with entry and exit permitted (Al Shrebini, April 30, 2020). Nonetheless, even if MBS would argue that lockdowns and restrictions created necessary security from Covid (or, as Peter would phrase it, a Beneficial Consequence of rule), the treatment of Shia-Qatif especially "risk[ed] fuelling resentment" and accusations of sectarianism at a time when the eastern region of Saudi Arabia was seeing "people returning from religious pilgrimages to Shia-majority Iran" (Agence-France Presse).

In addition to security from the virus, a further Beneficial Consequence that had to be considered was countering the economic impact of Covid. This included reduced housing charges, "provision of food supplies" and financial support "to [the] private sector and SMEs, providing Saudis with unemployment insurance" and updating labor regulations to protect workers (United Nations Saudi Arabia, pp. 10–11). However, the United Nations Saudi office identified "areas of improvement or gap[s] relate[d] to protection of Saudi & non-Saudi employment, protection of women [employees], and domestic and irregular workers" (ibid., p. 11).

In total, Saudi Arabia responded to Covid-19 with a $61 billion support package during 2020 (ibid.). This amount was effectively double a promised emergency finance package announced months into the first wave of the Covid pandemic intended to mitigate the effect of the novel coronavirus and low oil prices as countries entered lockdowns (Turak, March 20, 2020). The total $61 billion spent by November 2020 was almost half what the kingdom offered in response to the Arab Spring, "spending $130 billion [in 2011] to pump up salaries, build housing and finance religious organizations" (MacFarquhar, June 8, 2011). As with China, it seemed that economic performance (or cushioning) was a key Beneficial Consequence that would come under scrutiny during Covid. The importance of economic security as a pillar of nondemocratic rule for Saudi Arabia will be further explored in the analysis of public discourse in Chapter 4.

3. Case Studies

The UK and Brexit

> I welcome the outstanding news that AstraZeneca is now rolling out a new UK made vaccine that offers the hope to millions in this country and around the world, and having taken back control of our money, our borders, our laws and our waters by leaving the European Union on January 31st, we now seize the moment to forge a fantastic new relationship with our European neighbours, based on free trade and friendly cooperation. In less than 48 hours, we will leave the EU single market and the customs union, as we promised. (Johnson, December 30, 2020)

Boris Johnson's address to parliament merged two significant events of 2020: Brexit and the arrival in Britain of Covid-19 (ibid.). As previously discussed in Chapter 2's section on vaccine nationalism, the rollout of AstraZeneca, also known as the Oxford vaccine, was portrayed as a victory for Brexit and able to achieve a faster production rate precisely because the UK was no longer beholden to European Union (EU) bureaucracy (Caliendo, p. 2). Such an argument intended to turn Brexit into a triumph at a time of an unprecedented pandemic and during which observers may argue that Brexit worsened Covid's impact by weakening, inter alia, supply chains and ease of hiring European workers (Deloitte, 2023). The latter issue seemed especially pertinent for healthcare workers, with a 2022 report confirming that Brexit could "make EU doctors less likely to register in the UK" (Dayan, McCarey, November 27, 2022). Indeed, the report's "findings suggest that stagnation in the number of EU doctors has exacerbated existing shortages in areas where the NHS has not been able to find enough qualified staff elsewhere" (ibid.).

From the aforementioned perspective, the AstraZeneca vaccine became politicized to support Brexit, which itself was used by Britain's Conservatives to centralize power (Boseley, March 26, 2021). Under the Conservative party, Richard Hayton argues that, since the era of Thatcherism, the Conservatives have sought to ensure "the conditions for Conservative hegemony," which itself requires "a restoration of central authority" that will allow for "assault on social democracy" as a form of "authoritarian populism" (2021, p. 412). Hence, Johnson's leadership saw a continuation of such attempts at hegemony by "pursuing [the Conservatives'] most far-reaching statecraft strategy since the Thatcher era" by using

> Brexit itself, which serves as a national cause around which to organise the politics of support. Leaving the EU demands a renewal of the national community, which for the Conservatives, is framed as a narrow Anglo-Britishness, centred on an essentially English understanding of the Union of the United Kingdom and of Britishness itself. This assertive politics of national identity shapes the party's approach to territorial statecraft and its ideological struggle to ensure that the dominant narratives of British politics are once again Conservative ones. (ibid.)

Indeed, examining the process of Brexit and the related referendum before Johnson seems to reveal a turn by the Conservatives toward aggressive populism to centralize power. Under Conservative Prime Minister David Cameron, the referendum on whether Britain should leave the EU was used as a form of "procedural populism" that was part of a larger pattern that tapped into popular discontent through allowing "[d]evolution and referendums [as] part of a constitutional package which was meant as a response to public frustration" (Alexandre-Collier, April 13, 2022, pp. 531, 532).

However, akin to MBS's hollow reforms, such referendums and communication intended to create the image of "direct proximity between the leader and the people proved to be cosmetic and only served to reveal continuing oligarchy as well as indicating a shift in the party's balance of powers with the leader now at the top of a huge structure codified by the party constitution" (ibid., p. 534). Under the guise of reforms that tapped into populism, Cameron introduced legislation that was sold as tapping into understanding the people but "showcased a form of governance which sidelined the party and [was] actually used to conceal the 'iron control' exercised by the leadership on the party organisation, demonstrated for example through the increased control of candidate selection and attempts to ensure that all MPs were on message" (ibid.).

Under Johnson's tenure, the use of populism narrowed further to focus on identity politics and the popular will of the people to leave the EU after Cameron's referendum (ibid., p. 535). By narrowing down the use of populism to identity politics around Brexit, Johnson was able to aggressively use Brexit as "a powerful appeal to populist sovereignty" that would "mobilise voters around a patriotic national appeal to 'one nation'" (Alexandre-Collier, p. 415). Johnson's manipulation of Brexit allowed the Conservatives to appeal to voters divided across political lines but united by the desire to gain sovereignty. Such an approach gained landslide votes as Johnson could "marshal the coalition of Leave voters into party competition, while Labour struggled to do the same with Remain voters" (ibid.).

Johnson's maneuvers and use of a hard Brexit not only delivered a party victory but were also used for shoring up his own authority. Arguing that a hard Brexit was the will of the people allowed him to attempt to weaken parliament by presenting their delays on the issue as going against popular demands and hence democracy (ibid., pp. 415–16). In addition, just as Xi Jinping purged princelings and MBS pursued royal rivals, Boris Johnson used the need to get Brexit done as the official reason to "expel 21 Conservative members of parliament, including two former chancellors and Winston Churchill's grandson," for daring to disagree with Brexit (Bienkov, September 4, 2019).

Atop their dismissal, such former Conservatives would be barred from standing for the party at the next general election (Culbertson, September 4, 2019). The purge was not only about Brexit but also payback for the twenty-one members of parliament (MPs) voting against Johnson's government and defeating another attempt to centralize power under "a Commons rule that says only the government can propose new laws" (ibid.). Johnson's purge prompted some to call the Conservatives "the Brexit Party, rebadged," but it did leave Johnson "the leader of a minority government in parliament" (Bienkov). In addition, such moves by Prime Minister Johnson are perhaps a reminder that the politics of democratic and nondemocratic regimes are not always dissimilar (Peter).

Indeed, Joseph and Bradley Ward argue that "the first 18 months of the Johnson government were characterised by a propensity to centralise power" (Ward, Ward, December 28, 2021, p. 1). While Brexit (and especially the pursuit of a hard Brexit) was the instrument for Johnson's accretion of power, "Covid-19 provided yet more fertile ground for the assertion of the executive, with Johnson accelerating extant trends in the name of crisis management" to the extent that observers "express[ed] concern over a tendency to undermine parliamentary accountability and centralise power in the hands of the executive" (ibid., pp. 2, 1).

During his pursuit of Brexit, Johnson accused parliament of rejecting the will of the people as parliament debated how best to implement Brexit (Hayton, p. 415). Johnson took things a step further in summer 2019 by delaying the opening of parliament for several weeks, testing his ability to assert executive power. Although the UK's Supreme Court ruled this move "unlawful the following month" it was a taste of things to come under Covid (Ward, Ward, pp. 1–2). While previous pandemics such as H1N1 saw a fairly swift response in the UK, the reaction to Covid was fragmented in part because of resources and power being hoarded at the center (ibid., p. 2).

For Brexit and Covid, Johnson manipulated populism through the narrative of "the people versus parliament." As already discussed, attempts by parliament to avoid a no-deal Brexit and better scrutinize best processes to deliver Brexit were portrayed as delays that rejected the will of the people. At the same time, the same "people versus parliament" narrative was used "to legitimise centralisation in the management of Covid-19" (ibid., p. 14). Lockdown measures were formally implemented through the Coronavirus Act of March 2020 "to evade [parliamentary] scrutiny of [government] strategy" and objections by any MPs "who questioned the manner in which the government side-lined parliament in the implementation of lockdown measures" (ibid., p. 14).

Covid and lockdown certainly became a part of power politics under Johnson's Britain. Going back to evading parliamentary accountability, by June of 2020, the government "decided to end remote voting and online interventions in debates," arguing that MPs must send a message by being physically present at parliament. Since early May, a "hybrid parliament" had allowed MPs to debate "proposed laws and vote in virtual divisions" (The Guardian Editorial, June 2, 2020).

However, despite claims that physically returning to Westminster would make governance "more pluralistic and representative," the true effect of this move was to ensure that "MPs who have been advised to stay home and shield can no longer take part in debates or votes," allowing votes to go ahead with fewer participants and fewer debates on Johnson's legislation. By replacing virtual democracy with socially distanced attendance, there would be "only a few MPs in the parliamentary chamber to ask questions, and those who wish to vote must queue up to cast their vote in person" in a process that took thrice as long as online voting (ibid.). In response, commentators feared that "Johnson seized an opportunity in a crisis to concentrate power rather than diffuse it" and that the "end of a virtual parliament [would] reduce the Commons to a rubber stamp for whatever Boris Johnson wants" (ibid.).

In addition to using the Coronavirus Act to push through restrictive measures and weaken parliamentary oversight, there was much emphasis on "following the science," which "played a key role in legitimising the actions of the centre and constructing a narrative of blame avoidance for the government's management of the pandemic" (Ward, Ward, p. 14). Indeed, some argue that in Britain there was

> a very clear strategy at play which has revolved around the adoption of a technocratic, science-based and evidence-led approach that has ensured that no government statement has been made without the explicit caveat about "following the advice of the experts". The sight of Boris Johnson or other senior ministers flanked at the daily press conferences by the Chief Medical Officer and Chief Scientific Advisor is without doubt a strategic performative act of blame-sharing and blame-displacement. (Flinders, June 23, 2020, pp. 10–11)

In other words, the presence of science advisers like Chris Whitty was meant to ensure that Johnson's governing decisions were seen as "driven by scientific rather than political factors" (Ward, Ward, p. 14).

The emphasis on science-informed decisions also fed into maintaining the government's lockdown strategy. By "following the science" when implementing tiered lockdowns, Johnson could counter complaints of regional discrimination on political grounds by portraying such regions as uncooperative with neutral and medically informed decisions and ultimately as "obstructing the centre's management of the pandemic" (ibid.). Indeed, those who were in the north and received Tier Three restrictions (highest risk) in December 2020 regarded the decision as "an attack by the Tories on the North of England" and "collective punishment for the refusal to go quietly into a stricter local lockdown [in March 2020]" (Greig, November 26, 2020).

Brexit and the spread of Covid-19 created a dual shock for Britain, perhaps akin to Saudi Arabia addressing the drop in oil prices as Covid entered the kingdom. However, an overview of Boris Johnson's politics leading up to Covid does seem to show that Brexit became the latest project by the Conservatives in wielding populism, with Johnson narrowing such populism down to identity politics and purging his party of disloyal comrades unwilling to accept a hard Brexit. The populist narrative of "the people versus parliament" was employed to get Brexit done and test to what extent the executive could centralize power and circumnavigate parliamentary oversight. This test, though blocked by the UK's Supreme Court, was once again used to end hybrid parliamentary sessions and online voting during Covid. However, unlike when pushing for Brexit, under Covid, Johnson could shift justification from (identity) politics to following the science and ultimately security from the virus to further centralize power in Westminster and away from regional bodies. Just as MPs unwilling to support

Brexit were disloyal, regions that had not accepted a restrictive local lockdown in early 2020 were now punished for their insolence with Tier Three restrictions.

Interestingly enough, while America's Trump had tense relations with China's Xi Jinping, Boris Johnson held a phone call with Beijing a month before the UK entered lockdown. The call came after UK donations of medical equipment to China and was described by China's Ambassador Liu as "a very good conversation. It not only set the tone but also set the new direction for China-UK relations at a critical moment between China and the UK" (Haynes, February 19, 2020). During the call, Prime Minister Johnson told President Xi that he "loves China" (ibid.). Perhaps with the purge of MPs and possible punishment of uncooperative regions, it may be more accurate to wonder if Boris Johnson loves how Xi can rule China. By 2021, some veteran MPs certainly thought so, with one Conservative warning that the UK was "dangerously close to an elected dictatorship" under Johnson's "disregard for constitutional constraints," leading a party that was "more nationalist than at any [other] time" (Merrick, November 19, 2021).

Trump: Making America Great Again

Months before his election as the United States' forty-fifth president, Donald Trump "outlined an 'America first' foreign policy approach in what was billed as a major address at the Mayflower Hotel in Washington, D.C." (Beckwith, April 27, 2016), most certainly a strong contrast to a press conference at the end of his first presidential run by former New York Mayor Rudy Giuliani from "Four Seasons Total Landscaping," that saw Trump's team trade the power corridors of America's capital for "a business situated between a crematorium and a sex shop" (Bekiempis, November 8, 2020). While the conference led by Giuliani was received as a "desperate bid to hang on to the White House [that] crossed into abject farce," to dismiss Trump as a sore loser pushing claims of voter fraud risks denying his ability to be elected "after a campaign that defied norms and commanded public attention from the moment it began" (Dimock, Gramlich, January 29, 2021).

In his "America first" address, Trump promised to put "the interests of the American people and American security above all else" and argued to "no longer surrender this country to the false song of globalism (Beckwith)." In emphasizing America first and attacking globalization, Trump would become president through the use of Boris Johnson's own tactic in Britain: populism (Baker, July 7, 2022). As discussed by Salvador Santino F. Regilme Jr., Trump's election came at a time when American hegemony and the global order were shifting, and "American decline" was seeing "decreasing economic vitality underscored by concrete detrimental effects generated through sharpening material inequality within the U.S." along with "decreasing appeal and legitimacy [of America] as a dominant actor in the international system," which may have partially influenced Trump's promise to withdraw from international agreements and the United States' role on the world stage (2019, p. 157).

Indeed, a widening wealth gap in the United States risked "pervasive internal social conflicts, and as research shows in the field of democratization studies, could lead to democratic backsliding or other forms of instability" (ibid., p. 161). Trump's targeting of globalization tapped into "backlash against increasing economic interdependence," which for some Americans "generated deep-seated feelings of exclusion" if they are "unable to reap the benefits of globalization" (ibid., p. 162). To an extent, Trump's electoral victory was bolstered by a nationalism that understood "disruptions linked to globalization" and the Brexit-related belief that "the international sphere is a space of competition" and of outsourcing needed jobs abroad (Greenwood et al., October 5, 2020). However, Trump also drew on other forms of populism and even Twitter to circumvent engagement with democratic institutions.

Trump's election was "widely interpreted as an unexpected victory for populism in the United States and a harbinger of a populist era across Western democracies" (Bonikowski, 2019, p. 110). Indeed, Trump's election was months apart from the UK's decision to "take back control" by leaving the EU, and Trump and Johnson challenged political norms through a "far-right nationalism we once preferred to call populism" (Wolffe, September 6, 2019). Trump's own populism is indeed comparable to Boris Johnson's pitting of the people's will against, for example, parliament. Ultimately, populism presents itself as "a moral opposition between the virtuous people and a fundamentally corrupt elite" (Bonikowski, p. 111).

However, vague notions of "the people" are often filtered through "widely-shared but contested conceptions of nationhood" that "activate powerful in-group and out-group dynamics" (ibid.). Such logic of inclusion and exclusion also divides elites into those loyal and disloyal to the chosen concept of nationhood. In other words, "those who have ostensibly abandoned the 'true' members of the nation in favor of minorities, immigrants, and other putative outsiders must be removed from political power and replaced with the people's legitimate representatives" (ibid.). Of course, the so-called legitimate representatives of the people will then ensure that being elected is followed by "active steps to secure extensive and lasting power for themselves" (ibid., p. 112). Under such a process, "anti-elite claims" are linked to "exclusionary nationalism" and ultimately authoritarianism, though "even though these three [phenomena] are often interconnected, they need not necessarily be so" (ibid.).

At the same time, it would seem that during "his presidential campaign, Donald Trump made frequent use of all three elements of radical-right discourse" (ibid.). First, Trump attacked "Washington elites for being out of touch with the interests of the people" to draw on "longstanding anti-statist tendencies in the American electorate, which had been further aggravated by popular discontent with legislative deadlock and failed political promises by the Republican party," while Trump also joined conservative circles and media outlets in demonizing his eventual predecessor Barack Obama in an attempt to portray his administration (and by extension the Democratic Party) as unfit to govern (ibid.). In particular, Trump's questioning of Obama's Americanism, "birthplace and religion were much more than mere lies. They were ideology" (Serwer, May 14, 2020).

In an interview with Fox News, Trump insisted that Obama "doesn't have a birth certificate. He may have one, but there is something on that birth certificate—maybe religion, maybe it says he's a Muslim; I don't know," he conceded while then rebounding with the claim that he had "people that have been studying it and they cannot believe what they're finding" (ibid.). Obama was one of the other elites attacked by Trump. The president-to-be also embodied the second element of far-right discourse by repeatedly violating "norms of political decorum and responsible democratic discourse by threatening to jail Hillary Clinton, encouraging violence at his rallies, and criticizing the autonomy of the media and the judiciary" (Bonikowski, p. 113). Finally, Trump drew on exclusionary nationalism "by representing Mexican immigrants as criminals, publicly battling the parents of a fallen American soldier of Muslim faith, questioning the impartiality of a Mexican-American judge, and fanning the flames of Islamophobic and racist conspiracy theories concerning President Obama's place of birth" (ibid.). The result of this combining of "populist, authoritarian, and nationalist political frames" was to mobilize "voters who perceived the Democratic Party as fundamentally un-American and who had no qualms about violating the niceties of democratic conduct to punish their perceived enemies" through narrow identity politics driven by "anti-elite, illiberal, and exclusionary sentiments" (ibid.).

Once Trump was elected, a platform of populism and exclusionary nationalism continued, complemented by targeting democratic values such as free speech and the electoral process through "verbal attacks on journalists, persistent disinformation concerning the allegedly widespread problem of electoral fraud, portrayals of the media as a liberal conspiracy spreading 'fake news', the framing of social protest as illegitimate and un-American, and attempts to undermine the autonomy of the judiciary and federal law enforcement" (ibid., pp. 124–5).

In particular, racist policy attempts such as building a wall with Mexico, the Muslim travel ban, defunding the Civil Rights Division and ending "the Deferred Action for Childhood Arrivals (DACA) program for undocumented migrants brought to the United States as children" continued to tap into exclusionary nationalism and populism that defended the prospective erosion of democratic practices in order for the Trump administration to "deliver on its promises to champion the interests of white Americans, which have been portrayed as mutually exclusive with interests of non-whites" (ibid., p. 125).

While Boris Johnson drew on Brexit and Covid to construct a narrative of British democratic institutions going against the will of the people, Trump resorted to a newer method to bypass American democratic bodies: social media. It is common for populist leaders to attempt to centralize power by finding ways around traditional institutions for checks and balances on the executive. For Trump and other populist figures, "social media platforms [may be used] to disseminate discourse to convince people that a certain course of action is necessary and thereafter bypass formal institutions in policy-making" (Johnson, Korkut, Sahin, 2021, p. 591).

As with Britain's Boris, Trump seems to have pursued an attempt to centralize power from inside a democratic system while understanding that the "U.S. political system is vaunted for its federalism and separation of powers" yet faces "a growth in centralisation through presidential authority over the past century" that has allowed the executive to strengthen some of the authority that institutional checks were designed to balance (ibid., p. 593).

Trump's arrival did see his more aggressive policies initially blocked by the "courts, the press, the bureaucracy, and even Congress." However, it appears that Trump was learning how to master the art of dealing in Washington, and he began to find gaps in the system of checks and balances, such as weakening rather than attempting to repeal policies he did not like or pushing racist policies through via technicalities. When the Muslim travel ban was initially blocked, Trump "recrafted the travel ban to withstand the Supreme Court scrutiny by including, tokenistically, a couple of non-Muslim countries" (ibid., 594).

By shoring up allies through agreements in the Senate, Trump ensured "the judicial branch became less effective in constraining [his] actions" (ibid.). In the reverse of Xi Jinping purging princelings, Trump leaned into key Senate figures such as then-Senate Leader Mitch McConnell, who "maintained discipline within the Senate Republican caucus, gave reassurance with donors, and showed rhetorical loyalty to Trump in exchange for Trump's appointment of conservative federal judges who were acceptable to the Republican senators" (ibid.). Once Trump had ensured a pliant judicial branch, it was time to "refashion the executive branch" (ibid.). Before Twitter was used to push for policies without checks and balances, the president took to the social media platform to purge the executive branch itself. Trump's tweets were used to repeatedly spread "messages that were contemptuous of expertise, scornful of bureaucratic and legal procedures, and dismissive of norms. Even more dramatically, Trump directly intimidated members of the executive branch through menacing tweets" (ibid.).

Social media threats created a hostile environment at the White House and had the intended effect. As planned, rather than dismissing thousands of employees, Trump's tweets provoked "a mass departure of career bureaucrats" who would not be loyal to his vision of an unconstrained presidency, allowing Trump to work either with reliable underlings or ensure that "[f]or those civil servants that remained, the imperative to support the President's personal agenda became paramount for agency survival" (ibid., pp. 594–5). In other words, bodies that should be making the president aware of constitutional restraints or improper policies were trimmed, sometimes restaffed (presumably by Trump loyalists), and "repurposed for Trump's goals," including to provide legal and political support to the president's Twitter policies (ibid., p. 595). Through the aid of social media and strategic hostility, "Trump minimised bureaucratic autonomy and drew executive branch departments more closely under his personal orbit" (ibid.).

The direct communication style of Twitter would also allow Trump to reach out to "the people" of America and maintain a dialogue unconstrained by established democratic mechanisms (ibid., p. 597). In particular, Trump used social media to attempt to make policies by using tweets not to inform the general public about his policies but rather to "generate public support for [his] policies and political aims without introducing contentious, costly and time-consuming institutional changes," with tweets garnering public support by being issued without any checks and balances, thereby creating public pressure for Trump's policy demands (ibid.).

Trump's tweets were therefore part of a strategy to target "federal bureaucracy, roll back Obama-era social and environmental regulations, and reorient US migration policy" through the creation of a hostile work environment to provoke mass resignations but also through Twitter by garnering direct public support for policies without fully engaging with democratic bodies (ibid., p. 605).

Indeed, it would seem that many of Trump's tweets "were soon followed by policy change, personnel change, or a legal rationale being produced. This is the reverse of the usual policymaking process, by which executive actions receive prior clearance by relevant stakeholders in the federal government [before any social media announcement]" (ibid.). In addition, Trump took to Twitter to shape US foreign policy and

> after taking office, used his personal Twitter account to call Mexico "not our friend" and even, "an enemy" of the US; link the Paris Climate Agreement to riots in France; criticize the Trans-Pacific Partnership, initially calling it "a bad deal" for the US only to later change his rhetoric over and over again; suggest abandoning the North American Free Trade Agreement, calling it "one of the WORST Trade Deals ever made" only to later promote the signing of the United States-Canada-Mexico Agreement (USMCA), at times even in the same tweet; threaten to go to war with Iran; and blame China for the spread of Covid-19. (Pelcastre, May 25, 2020)

Such behavior on social media for foreign policy returns to Trump's attack on globalization and attempt to continue directly appealing to those Americans who feel globalization has left them behind but can also be seen as an attempt to make foreign policy without checks and balances, leading some commentators to worry that Trump "is a skilled, well-advised social media phenomenon redefining the way in which US foreign policy is made and exercised—for better or for worse" (ibid.).

As Covid-19 spread to America, media reactions to Trump's response were mixed. Trump's illness with the virus and his response to it were targeted by *The New Yorker* in an October 2020 article. After returning from hospital treatment, "in a dramatic gesture made for the cameras, he ripped off his mask and stuffed it in his pocket, a scowl flitting across his face. He remained silent throughout the photo op, but the words he had tweeted a few hours prior set the tone: 'Feeling really good! Don't be afraid of Covid. Don't let it dominate your life …. I feel better than I did 20 years ago!'" (Ben-Ghiat, October 13, 2020). This "grand display of machismo" was part of Trump's attempt to "cultivate an appearance of omnipotence," his recovery from the virus proof that he was a strong and thus legitimate leader, even if "when the mask came off he appeared to be struggling for breath" (ibid.).

Indeed, Trump's public reaction to the arrival of Covid-19 seemed to imply a belief in eugenics. "'It is what it is,' he said in September [2020], when asked about the fact that a thousand Americans were dying each day from the virus" (ibid.). Trump had no patience for genetic weaknesses. It was survival of the fittest, though he did express appreciation of "political subjects willing to sacrifice their health, or their lives [to vote for him]," an element of the personality cult common in dictatorships, while ensuring that his own bout with Covid emphasized his own strength and "miraculous recovery" (ibid.).

Other commentators were less concerned with Trump's image manipulation and joked that Trump was "leading a characteristically American response to crisis: early fumbling followed by massive public and private mobilization" (Lowry, March 17, 2020). "What happens when the supposed dictator won't dictate?" asked *National Review's* Rich Lowry. "This is the conundrum confronted by the harshest critics of President Donald Trump, who have gone from warning that he's a budding despot to complaining he hasn't done enough to impose his will during the coronavirus crisis" (ibid.). Instead of asserting the executive branch to ensure a united response to Covid across all states, Trump became "a bystander as school superintendents, sports commissioners, college presidents, governors and business owners across the country take it upon themselves to shut down much of American life" (ibid.).

In such a context, however, it may be that Trump's view of the executive as a personification of himself fed into a delayed response. In other words, just as Trump tweeted his way through policy-making, his reaction to an international pandemic reflected a "highly personalized view of the presidency and an abiding belief that he can talk his way out of any difficulty—including, initially, a public-health crisis not susceptible to spin" (ibid.).

It is clear from an overview of Trump's America that, as with Boris's Britain, there was an attempt to centralize power away from democratic institutions and toward the center or executive. Both Trump and Boris Johnson embody the use of populism and narrow identity politics. However, Trump also made extensive use of social media to circumvent checks and balances and create direct (online) support for divisive policies that he wanted by presenting them as a fulfillment of his promises to white America. While Boris Johnson's claims of following the science have been regarded by some as a further attempt to centralize power under a health crisis after Brexit, Trump's Covid response was regarded across 2020 as slow and "marred by overlapping authority" as opposed to centralized authority (Camacho, Glicksman, May 19, 2020). Chapter 4's analysis of the arrival of Covid in the United States and Trump's speech regarding his actions will examine what he did do in more detail. Nonetheless, we can see from each case study that leaderships across China, Saudi Arabia, the UK, and the United States was focused on centralizing power and decision-making before the arrival of Covid to mold existing institutions to a more personal ruling style. In Trump's case, however, his emphasis on exclusionary nationalism atop purging White House officials to centralize his rule was met with some protest, albeit focused more on his misogyny and racist remarks rather than centralization of power (Engler, Engler, November 12, 2024). However, this latter example of Trump's populism and subsequent protest returns us to Porta's argument that centralization of government decision-making can trigger social movements that mobilize if there seems to be a risk of reduced civic, political, or social rights (pp. 7, 6).

Understanding Isolationism in Brexit Britain and Trump's America

Trump's election and the Brexit vote happened within months of each other. Indeed, "Trump hailed the Brexit vote as a harbinger to his winning the presidency" and even called his candidacy "Brexit plus, saying that just as a populist movement in Britain led to the vote to leave the E.U., so too would a similar spirit usher him into the White House" (ABC News, November 9, 2016). As previously discussed, globalization seems to have fed into US and UK voting patterns across 2016 and 2017. In addition, Brexit and Trump voters "displayed a distinct pattern that correlates with voters' level of education, income, age and ethnicity" (Zhang, May 24, 2018, p. 2). Returning to Boris Johnson's Britain, "populations with higher qualifications in Britain were significantly more likely to vote Remain" (ibid.), while older voters often voted Leave (Rosenbaum, February 6, 2017). There was also "a broad pattern in several urban areas of deprived, predominantly white, housing estates towards the urban periphery voting Leave, while inner cities with high numbers of ethnic minorities and/or students voted Remain" (ibid.).

In the United States, more educated voters often tilted away from Trump and toward Hillary Clinton (Zhang, p. 2). Clinton herself was quoted as saying, "[y]ou could put half of Trump's supporters into what I call the 'basket of deplorables.' The racist, sexist, homophobic, xenophobic, Islamophobic—you name it" (Lopez, September 12, 2016). Indeed, some polls suggested that

> a great majority of Trump supporters hold unfavorable views of Muslims and support a policy that bans Muslims from entering the US. Most of them support proposals that stifle immigration from Mexico, and they agree with Trump's comments that Mexican immigrants are criminals. And many—but not a majority—say that black people are less intelligent and more violent than their white peers. (ibid.)

As previously discussed, Trump's rise to power tapped into populism and included attacking globalization and considering withdrawing from international agreements. For Britain, Brexit was symbolic of "an inward-looking and isolationist mood of sizable segments in British society which appear to prioritize autonomy from international commitments over influence in international politics" (Oppermann, June, 2017, p. 2). It certainly seemed that for many observers, Brexit was an attempt at independence from the EU that would result in a plunge into isolationism (Shapiro, January 20, 2020). While Trump himself seemed to compare his rise to Brexit (Lopez), Boris Johnson was careful to avoid Brexit being regarded as Britain's own America First (Swaine, July 22, 2016).

"I would draw a very, very strong contrast between Brexit and any kind of isolationism," he insisted at the United Nations in New York during his first US trip. "Brexit means us being more outward looking, more engaged, more energetic, more enthusiastic on the world stage than ever before" (ibid.). However, it would seem that many commentators and Trump did not agree with Brexit Britain being more global. Some analysts criticized Brexit as

> an imperial nostalgia for a time in which Britain was the master of its own destiny. But, of course, that time is long past and, today, Britain can only have global influence if it works effectively and closely with like-minded partners. What is the strategy to form such a bond with an overbearing America, a resentful Europe, or a[n] uninterested Commonwealth (Shapiro)?

And Trump would be more than happy to take advantage of the UK's newfound isolationism. By early 2020, as Brexit was weeks away from being done, Trump demanded that Britain withdraw support for the 2015 Iran Nuclear Deal if it hoped to get its own deal. "The question for Prime Minister Johnson," said a former senior aide to the president, "is, 'As you are moving towards Brexit, as your supporters of Brexit do not like the nuclear deal … what are you going to do post-January 31 as you come to Washington to negotiate a free trade agreement with the United States'" (Bartlett, Glaze, January 15, 2020)?

Other threats or pressure hurled at the UK by Trump include US efforts to convince Britain to ban 5G equipment from China's Huawei (at a time when Trump and Xi Jinping had entered a trade war), and commentators wondered if Trump would be willing to get his way by also threatening to reduce US-UK security cooperation (Shapiro). While such threats did not fully materialize, two years after getting Brexit done, it was clear that a much-prized US-UK trade deal would be unreachable for several years (Webber, September 20, 2022).

Under the month-long tenure of Prime Minister Liz Truss, her US visit to meet President Joe Biden prioritized discussing "global security and making sure that we are able to collectively deal with Russian aggression" (ibid.). In response to questions about any trade deal, Truss admitted that there weren't "any negotiations taking place with the U.S. and I don't have an expectation that those are going to start in the short to medium term" (ibid.). Perhaps in such an example there is a key difference between Trump and Brexit. Trump may have sought to make America isolationist, but such policies could be reversed by Biden as the next president. Brexit, however, appears to have a much longer-term effect. With Trump gone and replaced by Joe Biden from 2021 to 2025, some threats from the United States may have been taken off the table, yet Global Britain in 2022 wanted a major US trade deal and instead could only gain "U.S. state-level deals, which number[ed] only two: Indiana and North Carolina" (ibid.).

Pandemic Profiteers

There is a number associated with Covid that is rarely discussed: $65,000. This is the amount per minute that Pfizer, BioNTech, and Moderna made as combined profits in 2021, or roughly $3.9 million per hour (Oxfam, November 16, 2021). Almost two years after the WHO had declared Covid a pandemic, there were calls for pharmaceutical companies to share their vaccine recipes amid vaccine inequity and the hoarding of Covid shots by wealthier nations (ibid.). Maaza Seyoum of NGOs African Alliance and the related People's Vaccine Alliance Africa agreed that it "is obscene that just a few companies are making millions of dollars in profit every single hour, while just two percent of people in low-income countries have been fully vaccinated against coronavirus" (ibid.).

As discussed previously, corporate actors in different industries were regarded as having taken advantage of the Covid pandemic, with perhaps the most conspicuously scrutinized sector being pharmaceuticals. It is certainly true that as Covid spread, governments were desperate for a vaccine and willing to pay for it if they could, which no doubt risked vaccine inequity and empowering pharma companies to dictate terms of agreement with governments. Indeed, researcher Esther de Haan explains that in

> the midst of the pandemic, governments spent billions in funding to support vaccine research and development. Seven vaccine producers received at least USD 5.8 billion in public funding, with the US government being the largest funder, providing USD 5 billion. Agreements made [with pharmaceutical companies] did, as far as could be established, not include obligations for the companies to return the funds, not even when large profits were made. (February 23, 2023)

Within the context of government grants, 2021 and 2022 were good years for big pharma, with Pfizer, BioNTech, Moderna, and Sinovac earning around $90 billion (ibid.). Across these same years, that number increased with the production of non-vaccine Covid treatment, bringing in over $100 billion in 2021 and 2022 from vaccines and Covid-related medicine (de Haan, Kate, 2023, p. 11).

Within the pharmaceutical sector, the vaccine industry has typically been a small subbranch, accounting only for 3.6 percent of sales in 2019. However, "in the last 20 years prior to the pandemic, the sector has seen remarkable growth thanks to innovative products, new vaccinated population groups (adolescents) and, in developed countries, more aggressive pricing strategies" (Lobo, July 11, 2024, p. 11). The arrival of Covid-19 accelerated these preexisting elements drastically, such that

> demand, production, sales, and, therefore, the size of the global vaccine market have grown dramatically. Approximately 16 billion doses of all vaccines were supplied in 2021, compared to 5.8 billion in 2019. In value the market amounted to USD 141 billion, compared to USD 38 billion in 2019. This represents 10 per cent of the global pharmaceutical market, compared to 4 per cent in 2019. Discounting Covid-19 vaccines the market supplied 5.3 billion doses worth USD 42 billion, representative of 4 per cent of the global pharmaceutical market. In other words, the new anti-Covid-19 vaccines caused a six-point jump in the relative size of this subsector and accounted for more than double the volume and value of all other vaccines. (ibid.)

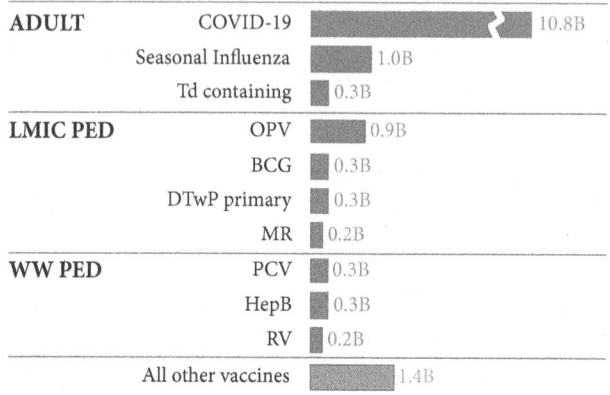

Figure 3.2 Worldwide vaccine sales in 2021 by volume. Source: World Health Organization. 2022. Global Vaccine Market Report, p. 21.

The key advantage of drug companies during Covid was not government grants (though these were substantial) but their ability to ensure profit while minimizing liability through Advanced Purchase Agreements (APAs). These agreements were made by the EU and various desperate (but wealthy) governments and gave funding to drug companies for vaccine development without knowing whether these vaccines would be successful. APAs were used

> to buy vaccines prior to vaccine approval, thereby de-risking investments in developing and producing the vaccines. Most of the APA contracts are not publicly available. Those that are have been heavily redacted or have been leaked. To be clear, the amount of money gained through vaccine sales is much higher than through APAs, as sales also involve agreements after the vaccines have been approved. APAs however greatly incentivised and accelerated vaccine development and production. They pledged unprecedented sums of public money through confidential deals. (de Haan, Kate, p. 19)

The use of APAs seemed to allow corporate actors to treat vaccines as a capitalist commodity rather than a public good and gave them key advantages over the governments that were so willing to sign such agreements. First, significant upfront payments were made that "financed development and production costs," with no repayment of such financing whether a company's vaccine succeeded or failed. Second, APAs reduced the liability of vaccine companies in the event of supply chain disruption but also in the event of injury to anyone who took the vaccine (ibid., pp. 19–20). The redaction of APAs publicly and gross lack of transparency surrounding how terms of APAs were negotiated and to what extent these APAs protect the vaccine manufacturers have led to scandals and court filings in 2024. In what has been dubbed by some as Pfizergate, the General Court of the European Union ruled in autumn 2024 that redacted terms of APAs and texts between Pfizer and EU Commission President Ursula von der Leyen should be made partially public (Chiappa, Eccles, October 8, 2024). The General Court "argued that the [EU] Commission had failed to prove how publishing more details would undermine the commercial interests of the pharmaceutical companies" and "also found fault with the Commission's refusal to provide personal details of the officials who negotiated the purchase of the vaccines over privacy concerns" (ibid.). Ultimately, such cases symbolize "a difficult balance between the right of the public ... to information, and the legal requirements emanating from the Covid-19 contracts themselves, which could result in claims for damages at the cost of taxpayers' money" (ibid.).

Connecting with the notions of viral sovereignty discussed in Chapter 2 is the common practice in pharmaceuticals of intellectual property rights (IPR). IPRs are a standard practice used to boost research and development (R&D) by theoretically protecting what will be the finished product as exclusive to its producer. IPRs "offer both light and shadow as they create a tension between incentives for innovation (long-term dynamic objective) and access to medicines, particularly for developing countries and disadvantaged social groups (short-term objective" (Lobo, 2024, p. 22). The issue of IPRs was unaddressed in APAs related to Covid (de Haan, Kate, p. 31). However, the WHO attempted to promote an IPR sharing initiative among vaccine manufacturers; this proposal did not receive widespread support (Lobo, 2024, p. 23).

While some critics argue that IPRs have limited effect, there is certainly a debate to be had on whether IPRs should be permitted during health emergencies and to what extent the ability to legally protect vaccine development and composition can feed into vaccine inequality and the assertion by poorer nations of viral sovereignty. In any event, APAs contributed heavily to vaccine inequity by effectively going to the highest bidder, allowing wealthier nations to offer far more generous funding and overbuy to the point of hoarding (de Haan, Kate, p. 31).

With such generous conditions for vaccine manufacturers and profits in the billions, what would Pfizer, BioNTech, Moderna, and Sinovac spend their riches on? Satisfying shareholders appears to be a first step, either by paying share dividends or buying back shares from shareholders. Over 2021 to 2022, Pfizer made a profit of around $35 billion, providing $9 billion in dividends to shareholders by 2022. In addition, "it returned capital to shareholders through repurchasing shares for USD 2 billion" (ibid., p. 23). BioNTech (which worked together with Pfizer to produce a Covid vaccine) offered shareholders $486 million in dividend payouts in March 2022, and by October of that year, had repurchased shares from shareholders for $1 billion. Between December 2022 and March 2023, BioNTech repurchased another half a billion dollars' worth of shares (ibid., pp. 25, 23). US manufacturer Moderna focused on the repurchase of shares to reward its shareholders. Between August 2021 and 2022, it announced plans to repurchase up to $7 billion of shares over 1.5 years. Finally, Sinovac reported a total profit of $14.7 billion in 2021, and "profit of USD 8.6 billion remained attributable to Sinovac's shareholders, but the company did not report on dividend payments or share repurchases" (ibid., p. 23).

The importance of satisfying shareholders is a reminder that vaccine manufacturers are corporate actors manufacturing what many would argue is a public good during a global health crisis. The potential profitability of a drug or a vaccine does appear to drive its selection and development. This trend is reflected in R&D, the second expense vaccine manufacturers spend profits on, as "the amount of money that pharma companies use for R&D is determined by the amount of revenue they expect to earn from a new drug, the expected cost of developing that drug, and policies that influence the supply of and demand for drugs" (Congressional Budget Office, April, 2021, p. b).

Drug companies often refer to high R&D costs to justify prices for their products. However, this façade is challenged by public financing, including through government grants and opaque APAs.

> The R&D costs are presented as exorbitant, including failed medicines and the cost of capital. At the same time pharmaceutical companies do not give transparency around the R&D costs, how much they spent on developing the medicines and how much public money went into this development. The high costs of R&D are therefore a picture gladly sketched by the industry to justify the high prices they seek for these medicines. Pharmaceutical companies' corresponding call for high prices often ignores the huge profits generally made in this industry, the lucrative yields for investors and the amount of public funding going into the development of medicines. (de Haan, Kate, p. 24)

Finally, many pharmaceutical firms devote portions of profits to mergers and acquisitions (M&A). Indeed, an increasing amount of a pharmaceutical company's budget is devoted to M&A, which can allow larger firms to buy smaller ones that have already made progress on R&D for a desired drug or medicine (ibid., p. 25). For example, in 2022 Pfizer used, inter alia, Covid profits to complete an acquisition of three separate drug companies developing treatments for migraines, sickle cell disease, and stomach- and skin-related diseases. The total amount Pfizer spent on such deals was $24.8 billion, over double its R&D spending in 2022 (ibid., pp. 24, 25).

It would seem that Covid still influenced M&As in 2024, albeit in smaller amounts. The third quarter of 2024 saw ten pharmaceutical deals announced at almost $1 billion. These included acquisitions of firms involved in the treatment of blood cancer, multiple respiratory viruses, and Covid, and firms involved in the development of painkillers. Interestingly, the second-largest acquisition at the end of 2024 was AstraZeneca's purchase of CTI BioPharma, focused on blood cancer treatment, for $1.7 billion (Global Data, December 2, 2024).

Before we turn to how vaccine manufacturers set vaccine prices, let us not forget that each company's senior management also benefitted from the pandemic. Pfizer CEO Albert Bourla was praised by the company for "exceptional performance and leadership in 2021" and "got his salary of USD 1.7 million, plus 250 percent of his target award, which amounted to USD 8 million. Adding stock and option awards to this, the total pay package was over USD 24 million. The pay package for all of Pfizer's six Named Executive Officers (NEOs) combined was USD 71 million in 2021" (de Haan, Kate, p. 26). BioNTech and Moderna CEOs became overnight billionaires due to Covid.

BioNTech's CEO, Prof Uğur Şahin was listed #400 on Forbes' real-time billionaires list on November 24, 2022, with assets worth USD 6.1 billion. Moderna's CEO Mr Stéphane Bancel was listed #429, with assets worth USD 5.8 billion. Between January 2020 and February 2022, Mr Stéphane Bancel sold some of his Moderna shares at a total value of approximately USD 408 million. (ibid., p. 26)

From this overview, it appears that vaccine manufacturers not only earn billions from their Covid vaccines (with public and government grants financing vaccine development) but also that these profits are prioritized for corporate growth, satisfying shareholders, and rewarding senior management. Barona and Mantilla argue that health should be considered "a preferred or social good, a public good and a common good, and presently as a global common good" (2022, p. 12). However, while Barona and Mantilla may consider the hope of vaccines as global public goods (GPG), they admit that

> [b]ehind the debates on considering vaccines as GPG, which would facilitate greater access at lower costs, is the tension between the private and public interests widely addressed in conventional economic analyses. The dispute goes beyond the purely economic sphere. It involves ethical aspects and shows the need for a debate on a new model of global governance, not only regarding health matters, but one that would also allow the international community to confront the multiple and interrelated crises that have a profound impact on the world-system. From this perspective, the Covid-19 pandemic made the need of considering alternatives to the current hegemonic model and global governance mechanism clear

and further highlights the tension between nationalism and globalization within the context of vaccine nationalism versus vaccine diplomacy, the latter of which considers a Covid vaccine as a public good. In other words, not only countries but also corporate actors themselves have contributed to vaccine inequity and vaccine nationalism due to their for-profit (some may say capitalist) tendencies and the limits of global governance and related bodies (such as the WHO) to ensure that vaccines are considered public goods by state, non-state, and especially corporate actors (ibid., p. 13).

The trend for Covid vaccine prices to increase over time reflects their commodification by pharmaceutical companies. In summer 2020, companies like Pfizer agreed on what they called "tiered pricing." "Wealthier nations were to pay 'about the cost of a takeaway meal' for a vaccine dose. Middle-income countries would be 'offered doses at roughly half that price', and low-income countries would be 'offered doses at cost'" (de Haan, Kate, p. 16). However, from 2020 to 2022, companies such as Pfizer and Moderna increased prices per dose, and as

> fewer vaccines will be sold in the years to come, companies want to maintain their high profits by raising prices again. In September and October 2022, Pfizer/ BioNTech and Moderna announced the commercial prices of their vaccines

for the near future. Pfizer/BioNTech have set it at between USD 110 and USD 130 per dose and Moderna at between USD 64 and USD 100. In January 2023, Moderna however stated that it also considered pricing between USD 110 and USD 130. (ibid., p. 5)

In the UK, pharmacies began offering private Covid jabs with prices being set at up to £100 ($127) per shot, with virologists concerned that this arrangement will create domestic vaccine inequity for those unable to afford the jab and ineligible for free shots. "Whilst obtaining a vaccine privately may be better than nothing, it inevitably creates two-tier access," explains University of Leeds virologist Stephen Griffin. "This is an absurd price amidst a cost of living crisis and is not how the UK should be managing such an important public health issue" (Davis, March 28, 2024).

Just as economic performance can be regarded as a measure of political legitimacy during Covid, corporate actors involved in vaccine manufacturing seem to have prioritized shareholders and economic performance as a key aspect of their own legitimacy. Those who bought shares from Pfizer, BioNTech, or Moderna appear to have done well for themselves. On the one hand, it is unsurprising that corporate actors would regard economic performance and shareholder satisfaction as essential. On the other hand, this approach may clash with the fact that vaccines can be considered a public good, allowing corporate actors to have control over a good that "in pandemic conditions has an extraordinary social value" (Lobo, 2024, p. 23). At the same time, some critics argue that the urgent need for Covid vaccines justifies public investments and funding through, for example, APAs to maximize vaccine development availability. In particular, some critics compare the public costs of financing vaccine development with the overall economic cost of maintaining lockdown.

For example,

[i]t has been estimated that the entire cost of the first vaccination campaign in Israel (one of the countries that paid the most in exchange for priority service) was equivalent to the economic losses of only two days confinement. Already the idea that governments should be "generous" in deciding such a profitable investment was forcefully defended by Nobel Prize-winning economist Michael Kremer and his collaborators in a famous article in the New York Times (Athey, Kremer, Snyder and Tabarrok 2020): 'The fact is that, from the earliest stages of development, most vaccines fail. We can't afford to fail, so we have to plan for success. To do that, we need to think and invest as ambitiously as possible' (Athey et al., 2020). And The Economist blamed the initial delays in Europe [on] vaccine availability, compared to the US: and the UK, on overly strained negotiations by the Commission (The Economist Editors 2021). In any case, it seems reasonable that these negotiations should not end in unjustifiable burdens on the public purse. (Lobo, 2024, pp. 23–4)

Building on this discussion has been consideration of how Covid impacted the vaccine industry. While it is true that vaccines can be regarded by many as a public good and a strong contributor to social welfare, vaccines are ultimately products developed and brought to market by corporate actors, and "from a business point of view, it is a complex and difficult business and that from an economics perspective it does not fit the paradigm of competitive efficiency, with notorious market failures" (Lobo, p. 40). For this reason, the role of the public sector should not be overlooked. APAs gave corporate actors key benefits in terms of pricing, liability, and selling vaccines to the highest bidder due, in large part, to the urgency for these vaccines that Covid created. Therefore, the public sector must take a greater leading role before a pandemic becomes a public health emergency by ensuring constant international cooperation on vaccine research into emerging diseases that have been flagged by, for example, the WHO (ibid.). For this reason, the call for a WHO-led international pandemic treaty is paramount (Reuters, June 1, 2024). The creation of an international pandemic treaty will be further discussed in Chapter 6.

Outside of the pharmaceutical sector, there are other corporate actors that profited from the pandemic in ways that have raised concern over worker exploitation and the ability to almost monopolize markets in manners less accepted before Covid's economic impact.

The e-commerce and digital streaming company Amazon has been praised by its former Vice President Tim Bray as "exceptionally well-managed [while demonstrating] great skill at spotting opportunities and building repeatable processes for exploiting them" (UNI Global Union, 2020, p. 3). However, what led to Bray's resignation during the pandemic was Amazon's "corresponding lack of vision about the human costs of the relentless growth and accumulation of wealth and power. If we don't like certain things Amazon is doing, we need to put legal guardrails in place to stop those things" (ibid.).

Amazon founder Jeff Bezos may be celebrated in some circles, but in others he is known as a Covid billionaire. While having reached billionaire status earlier in his career, it was during Covid that he became the richest person in the world by 2020, with lockdowns provoking a surge in online shopping that increased Amazon's market capitalization to almost $2 trillion (Business Insider, August 29, 2020). A 2020 Brookings Institution report noted that "Amazon workers will earn the equivalent of an extra $0.99 per hour (pre-tax) for each hour worked during the pandemic. Meanwhile, Jeff Bezos' wealth has risen $11.5 million an hour" (Kinder, Stateler, December 22, 2020).

The huge gap between the pandemic wealth increase for company founders and little of that profit being spent on keeping workers safe was sadly part of a larger trend in the retail sector. Amazon workers like Anna worked shifts at the peak of the pandemic and before vaccines were available, starting at 7:15 a.m. until 5:45 p.m. As orders skyrocketed during the pandemic, more and more workers were hired and put in overtime. Social distancing became impossible. "They hired a lot of people," Anna explains. "I thought there should have been fewer people in the warehouse, to have distancing. They took out some of the tables [in the canteen] because of 2-metre distancing, but it was impossible to find a free table or chair. You had to stand [for lunch]" (Harris, November 18, 2020). In addition, basic sanitary equipment was not immediately available. "The first month," Anna says, "I was asking for antibacterial gel, for wipes … basic things," and only one mask was provided for an entire shift (ibid.).

Retail analyst Natalie Berg believes "it's clear that the timing and very nature of [Covid] has been fortunate for Amazon. I think they'll be the only retailer in the UK, possibly the world, to come out stronger on the other side. If there are winners and losers of the pandemic, Amazon is hands-down the winner" (ibid.).

In the case of Amazon, pandemic wealth generation is part of a larger picture with regard to Amazon's dominance in various markets that we have become increasingly dependent on since the pandemic (UNI Global Union, p. 8).

Covid accelerated Amazon's expansionism. Since at least 2006, Amazon has begun its expansion into cloud streaming services via Amazon Web Services (AWS). Aggressively expanding this internet storage platform by offering it to existing partners and clients meant that Amazon had created a web service that could boost its revenue (Long, March 13, 2021).

Over time, AWS became "the world's biggest cloud computing business," buttressing Amazon's losses in e-commerce and other arenas. "From 2013 to 2019, its revenue increased by an average of 46 percent per year—compared to 10.3 percent

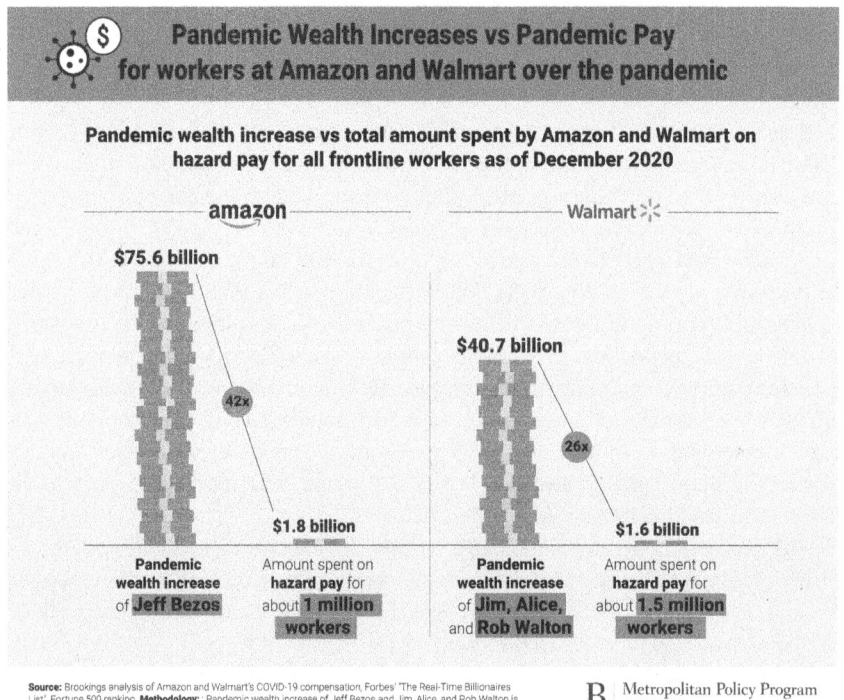

Figure 3.3 Pandemic wealth increase versus pandemic pay increase. Source: Kinder, M., Stateler, L. 2020. "Amazon and Walmart have raked in billions in additional profits during the pandemic, and shared almost none of it with their workers." *Brookings*, December 22. https://www.brookings.edu/articles/amazon-and-walmart-have-raked-in-billions-in-additional-profits-during-the-pandemic-and-shared-almost-none-of-it-with-their-workers/ (last accessed May 22, 2025).

for Microsoft or 8.7 percent for Apple" while traditional retailers like Walmart and Carrefour saw significantly weaker growth or even a drop in sales (UNI Global Union, p. 8). This strategic expansion foreshadowed the success of Prime Video as a streaming entertainment service, which would see over seven million subscribers in the UK alone by 2020 (Sweney, May 15, 2020).

Part of Amazon's expansion strategy included not only worker exploitation but

> aggressive practices towards its competition, using a range of anti-competitive techniques to acquire market share and get rid of direct competition. In its role as a retailer, Amazon acts both as a seller and as a platform provider, operating a marketplace in which two million third-party sellers are authorized to sell their products. Amazon has been accused of predatory pricing and excessive control over third-party sellers that use its platform. For the latter, Amazon has imposed contractual provisions that prohibit third-parties from selling products at lower prices through competing e-commerce platforms

making third parties (many of which are small businesses) dependent on selling through them exclusively (ibid., pp. 8–9).

With most third parties making 90 percent of their sales through Amazon, the pandemic hit them hard when Amazon announced it would suspend shipping of all nonessential third-party products. CEO of educational toys company Viahart explains that "[w]ere we to be suspended from selling on Amazon.com, it would probably take three to six months before we'd be bankrupt. We are not alone. This is typical for small to medium sized businesses which sell online today. In fact, most companies like our own, would probably go bust even faster" (ibid., p. 12).

Adding insult to injury was Amazon's practice of copying third-party products and creating their own versions. A 2021 Reuters investigation uncovered that Amazon "ran a systematic campaign of creating knockoffs and manipulating search results to boost its own product lines in India, one of the company's largest growth markets" and "studied proprietary data about other brands on Amazon.in, including detailed information about customer returns. The aim: to identify and target goods—described as 'reference' or 'benchmark' products—and 'replicate' them." These findings build on prior accusations "by employees who worked on private-brand products of exploiting proprietary data from individual sellers to launch competing products and manipulating search results to increase sales of the company's own goods" (Kalra, Stecklow, October 13, 2021).

These aforementioned practices foreshadowed Amazon's ability to engage in suspect business practices not tolerated before the pandemic. In particular, the economic damage of Covid allowed Amazon "to make anti-competitive acquisitions at rock bottom prices" (UNI Global Union, p. 6). As Covid forced millions to remain home, not only streaming but also food delivery services skyrocketed, with some delivery apps seeing a 54 percent increase in orders (Butler, March 10, 2020).

One such delivery app was Deliveroo, which had been hailed as a British tech success story by eventual British Prime Minister Rishi Sunak (Nunn, March 31,

2021). However, by the start of the pandemic, Deliveroo was facing multiple challenges, including a smaller network of restaurants than other delivery apps and significant operating losses (Bernal, February 11, 2021). Amazon's $575 million offer to buy a 16 percent stake in Deliveroo was sorely needed by the delivery firm. Nonetheless, this "bold move was blocked by the Competition and Markets Authority (CMA), the UK's competition watchdog, for almost a year. With a decision scheduled for July 2020 and an uncertain outcome, Deliveroo was strapped for cash and didn't have any backup plan. It was the perfect storm" (ibid.).

The CMA's concern seemed to stem from the pattern of Amazon's predatory practices and the fear "that Amazon's well-lined purse and logistics expertise [could] destroy the competition in the market for takeaway deliveries. It didn't matter that Amazon wasn't buying Deliveroo [outright]—it was its previous foray into the restaurant takeaway business that had caught the attention of the regulator" (ibid.). These regulatory concerns focused on the risk of Amazon's ability to use its purchased stake to assert influence over the direction of Deliveroo's business model, which was a risk exacerbated by the fact that the deal would give Amazon a seat on Deliveroo's board and by the simple fact that Amazon was considered a large tech company with substantial business influence (ibid.).

But these concerns since 2019 by the CMA were before Covid exploded and several factors came together to ensure that the deal was not only approved but expedited (UNI Global Union, p. 19). First, "Deliveroo dropped the bombshell. It told the CMA's team of around 25 case workers, lawyers and economists, led by a four-strong inquiry panel, that if it didn't approve the investment, the company would go bust" and that "[f]or Deliveroo to survive, the CMA would need to agree that the company had no alternative. More than that, the CMA had to agree that Deliveroo failing would be worse for competition than letting Amazon save it" (Bernal). Second, the UK was still reeling from Brexit and the related financial uncertainty it created for investors. Deliveroo's Amazon deal was "announced at a time when the City [was] crying out for a post-Brexit boost. The news that Deliveroo would be [completing the deal] in London rather than Amsterdam [was] greeted by segments of the Treasury with the kind of flag-waving normally reserved for [government TV appearances]" (Nunn). Finally, the arrival of Covid meant that suspicions toward the deal were being tempered by a bigger concern: how the deal would give the UK economy a much-needed cash injection. These factors combined to allow Amazon to assert corporate power in the pandemic and "make anti-competitive acquisitions that under normal circumstances would not be tolerated" (UNI Global Union, p. 19).

In a sense, Amazon's ability to see an expedited process in buying 16 percent of Deliveroo can be compared to how pharmaceutical companies oversaw APAs with strong advantages for corporate actors versus their government counterparts. With most governments desperate for a vaccine, public grants came flooding in, with no emphasis on whether vaccines would be successful or not and no government-led intervention regarding vaccine prices or equity. For Amazon, the combination of a weaker post-Brexit investment climate and further economic strain due to Covid allowed them to further diversify their platforms through Deliveroo, with the CMA willing to push the deal through once realizing that Deliveroo was on the verge of bankruptcy. As with vaccine manufacturers, another corporate actor was able to take advantage of Covid (among other factors) to finalize a deal that was seen by some as anticompetitive.

As already discussed, economic performance was emphasized by corporate actors, a criterion that also played a role in bringing some social movements together during Covid and that also seemed to be emphasized with regard to state reactions to Covid, hesitancy to enforce lockdowns, and the use of economic packages in response to restrictions (Johnson, March 23, 2020). In a sense, for corporate actors, Covid created the reverse of Porta's emergency junctures, as Covid combined, in some cases, with other building economic factors, to create economic opportunities rather than crises. However, such corporate opportunities did provoke resistance. The risk of vaccine inequity has historically encouraged states like Indonesia to assert viral sovereignty, and, during Covid, China stated that any developed vaccine should be a public good (though this assertion was within the context of vaccine diplomacy and soft power) (Wheaton, May 18, 2020). Moreover, Amazon may have succeeded in its Deliveroo deal, but its workers protested over lack of social distancing and poor hygiene provisions during Covid (BBC, March 31, 2020).

In any event, Amazon's predatory practices ended up attracting the attention of the EU, with an investigation possible in 2025 regarding breaking antitrust regulations by prioritizing its own branded goods over those of third-party sellers through its online selling platform. If found guilty, it could face a fine equating to 10 percent of its annual turnover (Chee, November 21, 2024).

Power and Exploitation

An overview of political profiles across China, Saudi Arabia, Britain, and America shows some surprising similarities in ruling styles leading up to Covid. On the one hand, dictatorships like China and Saudi Arabia saw leaders centralizing power and eliminating rivals through purges veiled under the guise of tackling corruption. For Riyadh, MBS boasted hollow reforms that were meant to boost his image while ensuring any changes were purely social and did not diminish the political clout of the House of Saud. On the other hand, the UK's Boris Johnson and America's Donald Trump did not seem afraid to engage in their own (albeit less violent) purges of disloyal party members or staff.

Like Xi Jinping, once Trump had ensured mass departures of White House and related staff, he could, in some cases, replace them with loyalists. Just as MBS restructured the prosecutor's office to be more closely connected to his wishes, Trump attempted and somewhat succeeded in eroding the judiciary and strengthening his executive abilities. Both Trump and Johnson drew on populism and "protecting the people" to circumvent checks and balances from democratic institutions. In the next chapter, we shall see how all four leaderships across Asia, the Middle East, Europe, and America responded to Covid in public discourse and to what extent democratic and nondemocratic factors of political legitimacy were drawn on to justify restrictions. However, the current chapter should make us wonder if the line between democratic and nondemocratic rule is truly distinct once leaders have access to power. In addition, it is clear that corporate actors saw economic gain during the pandemic. This is true for pharmaceutical manufacturers especially, with desperate governments willing to provide significant public funding and the development of Covid vaccines also building on previous research funded by the taxpayer. However, other corporate actors were also able to take advantage of the economic climate during Covid to push through deals that were suspect, while also seeing significant wealth. Amazon's Jeff Bezos became the world's richest person in 2020, but his good fortune did not trickle down to his workers. This chapter is a reminder that the government's relations with corporate actors must be carefully balanced with public interests, especially during a health crisis.

Chapter 4

COVID SPREADS: THE SPEECHES OF PANDEMIC POLITICS

Citizens Turn to the State

Chapter 3 addressed the rise of leaderships before Covid in China, Saudi Arabia, the UK, and the United States, comparing their ruling styles and discussing the rise of populism in the UK and the United States. We also considered the role of corporate actors during Covid and how their profiteering contributed to wealth inequality that took advantage of economic weakness during Covid and contributed to vaccine inequity, respectively, returning us to Chapter 2's discussion of vaccine nationalism and vaccine hoarding from before Covid. In this chapter, we will address how speeches were used to present Covid as a reason for restrictive measures and what political factors (especially nondemocratic) were drawn on to justify restrictions and lockdowns in speeches to nations and the world and to what extent any instructions issued, such as to stay at home, were accepted or resisted. Covid was most certainly seen as a threat by most citizens and nations, and when infections spread, many such citizens turned to the state to protect them (Kliem, April 11, 2020). Hence, all selected speeches of Chapter 4 were given in 2020 and before vaccines were widely available, although Chapter 5 will investigate vaccine nationalism and vaccine diplomacy through analysis of public discourse from the same leaderships. Analysis of speeches in this chapter also considers the economic performance of leaderships during Covid to discuss the book's argument that economic performance became a core concern for state political legitimacy during Covid.

Speeches of Legitimacy during Covid

China's Premier Li Keqiang

By mid-January 2020, China had reported its first Covid-related death. By January 23, Wuhan was put into lockdown almost overnight, with a ten-hour window from the announcement to the lockdown itself allowing "some 10,000 people to leave the city and Hubei province, which ha[d] already reported a spike in cases" (Law, December 18, 2021). Within a further month, China's borders would close, and Wuhan and other districts would find themselves in and out of lockdown as

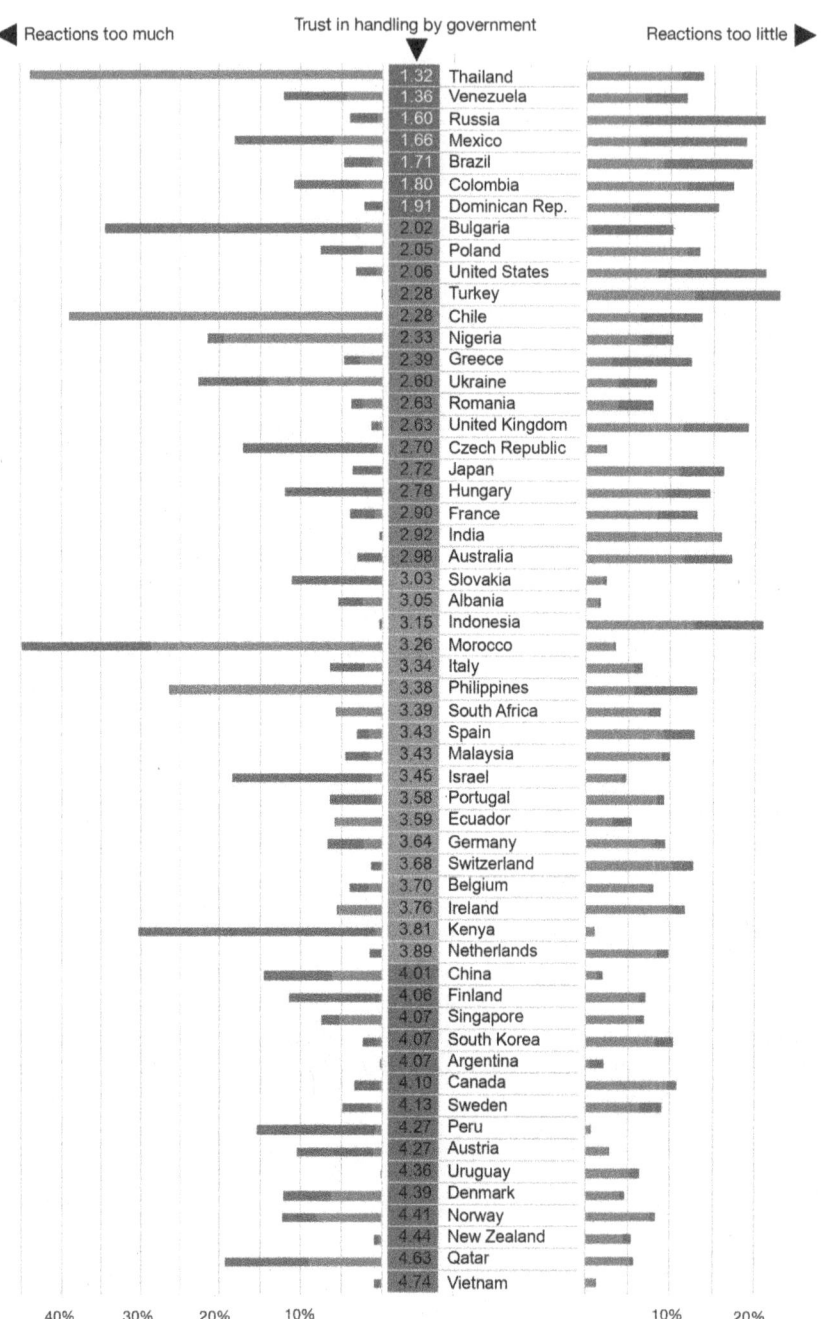

Figure 4.1 Trust in government during Covid. Source: Rieger, M.O., Wang, M. 2022. "Trust in Government actions during the Covid-19 crisis." *Social Indicators Research*, 159, pp. 967–89, p. 977.

authorities attempted to deal with soaring case clusters while also attempting to minimize economic disruption, a key element of Xi's rule, with economic growth a factor of political legitimacy (or Beneficial Consequences) he hoped to use to alleviate poverty, while expanding metropolises to also maintain support from China's growing middle class (Li, p. 5). To that end, and in a twist of irony, Xi had appointed fellow princeling and Hu Jintao protégé Li Keqiang (1955–2023) as premier (Cunningham, March 7, 2022, p. 25).

Like Xi, Li came from humble origins and as a youth was forced to work in rural areas. Over time, Li became known for supporting market-oriented reforms rather than highly centralized state economic intervention (Explained Desk, October 23, 2022). Despite the risk of rivalry, Xi seemed to have appointed Li premier due to Keqiang's penchant for economic policies in line with Xi's ambitions. Li had emphasized a policy that became known as "Likonomics" and involved "structural reform and debt reduction aimed to reduce China's dependency on debt-fuelled growth and steer the economy toward self-sustainability" (ibid.). Li also targeted poverty through "economic improvement and affordable housing," which again fed into Xi Jinping's appeal to poverty reduction (ibid.). Li's removal from the post of premier was announced in 2022 and interpreted as another power move by Xi to address a rivalry that perhaps he had not been able to fully take care of earlier (ibid.).

While Covid-19 challenged Beijing's economic ambitions and ability to fulfill a limited ruling bargain with citizens, Xi was also busy considering legal responses to the pandemic. Lockdown and related restrictive measures were announced through public notices that effectively served as emergency laws and allowed Xi to implement lockdown measures without effectively referring to them as such (Wang, May 12, 2021). For example, a notice issued by the Wuhan Command Centre restricted entry/exit points for any residential block to "only one entry/exit point, staffed with inspection personnel all hour round" and the implementation of this notice by district governments "effectively locked up some 11 million residents in their own apartments without any mobility allowed" (ibid.).

In addition to enforcing lockdown, such notices also encouraged citizens to share health information via a QR code to help control the spread of Covid. However, use of such QR codes was effectively mandatory, as "citizens without the app wouldn't be able to leave their residential compounds or enter most public places," and the sharing of data raised "concerns about privacy. The health codes rely on troves of data the authorities have collected from individuals—including their personal information, location, travel history, recent contacts and health status" (Culver, Gan, April 16, 2020).

Further, such public notices were merged with legal avenues traditionally designed to target civil disobedience. In other words, while these public notices did not mention legal consequences for noncompliance, existing laws already made it clear that there would be consequences. For example,

> article 50 of the Law of the PRC on Administrative Penalties for Social Order Administration imposed a fine of up to 500 Yuan RMB (in addition to detention

between five and ten days) in the case of non-compliance with government orders or decisions issued in times of emergency. For more serious cases, criminal sanctions are always available to the law enforcement authorities. (Wang, 2021)

By the end of May 2020, China was seeing a return of cases in Wuhan and experts began voicing concern about a second wave (British Foreign Policy Group, 2021). Amid further worry of Covid's economic impact on China (ibid.), it was in this context that Premier Li Keqiang addressed the third session of the thirteenth National People's Congress (NPC) (CGTN, May 22, 2020). The NPC can be regarded as "a 'ceremonial' legislature that functions as a 'rubber stamp' for the Chinese Communist Party" but as the legislature also stands as "the highest organ of the state" (Saich, November 2015, p. 1). Under its umbrella, "[d]elegates are elected for a term of five years and the NPC convenes once a year" (ibid.). The NPC often works closely with the Chinese People's Political Consultative Congress (CPPCC) as a "liaison with other political parties [that] promotes united front work, providing a discussion forum for some non-party intellectuals and prominent figures in other walks of life with no party affiliation" (ibid.). Membership of either congress "is highly prized, and those who are members of the latter body and can afford it pay a handsome voluntary contribution for the privilege" (ibid., p. 10). Of course, such contributions should not be a problem for most members, with over thirty billionaires in the NPC and up to fifty-two billionaires in the CPPCC in 2015 alone (ibid., p. 9).

On paper, the NPC has the authority to make laws, amend the constitution, and approve any national economic plan; however, in reality, these powers are held by the Chinese Communist Party (CCP) and its most senior leadership, with the NPC approving CCP decisions and appointments (ibid., pp. 1–2). Nonetheless, with a membership of roughly 3000 the NPC still remains a hub that brings together local and national governing officials and members of the armed forces annually (BBC, October 8, 2012). In addition, as this book attempts to consider public reactions to how leaderships responded to Covid and to what extent they justified restrictions through (nondemocratic) political factors such as Beneficial Consequences, it is worth mentioning that NPC sessions are broadcast live to households across China (The National People's Congress of the People's Republic of China, July 21, 2016).

Given the "rubber stamp" nature of the NPC, it is perhaps unsurprising that Li engages in proceduralism by asking "for [NPC] deliberation and approval. I also ask members of the national committee of the Chinese People's Political Consultative Conference (CPPCC) for their comments" (CGTN). Unlike speeches from Boris Johnson in the UK, there is no reference to Covid being an "invisible enemy," but it is acknowledged by Li as "the fastest spreading, most extensive, and most challenging public health emergency since the founding of the People's Republic" (ibid.). Immediately following discussion of Covid's health threat, Li turns to what can be considered strong leadership as a Beneficial Consequence by arguing that the government "have made major strategic achievements in our response to Covid-19" but that such achievements were successful under "the strong leadership of the Central Committee of the Communist Party of China with Comrade Xi Jinping at its core" (ibid.). The emphasis on the CCP and Xi himself is a reminder, perhaps, that the NPC ultimately answers to the CCP and its highest leadership: Xi Jinping, and that strong leadership under Xi has provided a Beneficial Consequence through security from the virus (ibid., Peter).

Just as previous pandemics in China saw a turn to patriotism and national unity through sacrifice, Li also credits strategic achievements against the novel coronavirus to "the hard work and sacrifice of our entire nation," drawing a parallel between the current restrictions under Covid and the SARS pandemic, during which CCP propaganda tried to emphasize the need for ordinary people to make sacrifices to combat SARS (Fewsmith, p. 7). It is interesting to note that Li seems to refer to Covid as an epidemic several times throughout the speech, while using the term "pandemic" only twice (CGTN). A pandemic is effectively the global spread of a virus, while an epidemic may be considered "an unexpected increase in the number of disease cases in a specific geographical area" (Columbia University Irving Medical Center, 2019).

That said, as Li uses both terms, it is likely he is simply differentiating between the effects of Covid domestically and the effects of Covid across the world (CGTN). In relation to Li's mention of the global effects from Covid, there is also an acknowledgment of Covid's economic damage, which attacked a key element of Xi's limited ruling bargain that has attempted to maintain the loyalty of the middle class and the rural poor (CGTN). Li admits that the government "must redouble our efforts to minimize the losses resulting from the virus and fulfill the targets and tasks for economic and social development this year" (ibid.).

To that end, Li engages in "a review of our work in 2019 and the first few months of 2020" (ibid.). To an extent, this review serves as what John Searle would call the preparatory condition, or providing the specific context of the current political (and economic) situation to justify actions or instructions, which ultimately seek to persuade listeners to accept the speaker's message or obey directions (Searle, p. 15). In particular, Li discusses China's challenges across 2019 to 2020 but links them to the international system as a way of emphasizing that these challenges are not unique to China (and that China's leadership is not fully to blame). Such challenging factors include the fact that "[w]orld economic growth was weak, international economic and trade frictions intensified, and downward pressure on the domestic economy grew" (CGTN).

Within such a context, Li can return to China's limited ruling bargain and the Beneficial Consequence of strong (centralized) leadership under Xi Jinping. Hence, the "Party Central Committee with Comrade Xi Jinping at its core rallied the Chinese people and led them in surmounting difficulties and accomplishing the year's main targets and tasks, thus laying the crucial foundation needed to reach the goal of building a *moderately* prosperous society in all respects" (CGTN, emphasis added). This section of Li's speech returns to notions of national unity that CCP propaganda has drawn on in previous pandemics. However, the preparatory condition of a weak global economy (due to Covid) sets up the mentioned goal of a moderate ruling bargain through limited economic growth, which acknowledges both the impact of Covid and links back to the CCP's original promise of limited economic opportunity in exchange for restricted political spaces for citizens (Feigenbaum).

However, even if such economic promises were intended to be modest, it is clear that Covid has threatened this pillar of nondemocratic legitimacy or Beneficial Consequence. This is seen both in Li's context of weak global economic growth (and subsequent pressure on domestic financial arrangements) but also through a subsequent list of accomplishments that remind audiences of the fact that the CCP is maintaining their social contract amid a pandemic. "The economy remained stable overall," Li asserts. "Around 13.52 million new urban jobs were added, and the surveyed unemployment rate was below 5.3 percent" (CGTN). It is clear that Li is outlining economic achievements such as "the economic structure [continuing] to improve" to reach out to rural citizens but also mentions certain economic reforms that mean "[e]merging industries continue to grow. Business startups and innovation continued to surge nationwide, with an average net increase of over 10,000 businesses per day" (ibid.). In addition, "[w]e cut taxes and fees by 2.36 trillion yuan, going well beyond our target of two trillion yuan, with manufacturing and micro and small businesses benefiting most" (ibid.). These latter elements of supporting entrepreneurs and tax cuts are no doubt meant to persuade China's growing middle class that the CCP is not leaving them behind amid the pandemic and maintaining economic promises to keep their support (Li, p. 2).

It is also worth noting that belligerent language is used to refer to economic "progress achieved in three critical battles" (CGTN). These battles encompass poverty alleviation, environmental improvements, and a stable financial sector. Again, emphasizing the economy through aggressive language can be interpreted as returning to a key buttress of Xi's legitimacy and persuading listeners that moderate prosperity is still a Beneficial Consequence of his rule (CGTN, Peter).

As discussed by Gilley and Hollbig, such performance legitimacy has often been merged under the CCP with nationalism (Gilley, Holbig, p. 395). Hence, it is no surprise that Li's list of aggressively phrased economic achievements is followed by a reminder that "[w]e celebrated the 70th anniversary of the founding of the People's Republic of China" (CGTN) and just as SARS saw an emphasis on national unity, the current crisis "has inspired a strong sense of patriotism among all Chinese people, creating a powerful force that will bring great victories for socialism with Chinese characteristics in the new era" (CGTN).

At the same time, there is also a turn to implying anti-corruption efforts. It is interesting that such an implication comes right after outlining economic achievements. Li elaborates on how the CCP

> worked to improve Party conduct and build a clean government, started an initiative to raise awareness of the need to stay true to the Party's founding mission, and strictly observed the central Party leadership's eight-point decision on improving work conduct. We continued to address the practice of formalities

for formalities' sake, bureaucracy, hedonism, and extravagance, and took steps to ensure that people working at the primary level are free from unnecessary restrictions and excessive burdens. (ibid.)

The mention of efforts to maintain a clean government can be understood twofold. First, it is a reminder that China's leadership (effectively Xi Jinping) is using anti-corruption probes as part of a continued policy that addresses economic woes. Indeed, an announcement in 2022 that "207,000 party officials in total had been handed some form of punishment in the 10 years since party leader Xi Jinping took power" seemed intended to remind citizens of Xi's fight against graft during a Covid-related economic downturn (AP News, October 17, 2022).

Second, the indirect mention of corruption acts not only as a reminder of Xi's Beneficial Consequences through limited economic benefits but also as a message to the CCP itself, officials, and others who may threaten Xi's authority. As previously discussed in Chapter 3, Xi used anti-corruption initiatives to purge rivals and centralize power (Rahn). As China and Xi in particular faced criticism over his handling of Covid-19, anti-corruption measures were leveraged to justify targeting dissidents and others who had publicly called out Xi (even if indirectly) during the pandemic. Such critics have faced arrest and worse. Ren Zhiqiang, "a well-connected and vocal member of the ruling party," went missing after publishing an article that denounced Xi's handling of the pandemic and called him a clown (Davidson, April 8, 2020). It was later revealed he'd been jailed for eighteen years (Guardian staff and agencies, September 22, 2020). No doubt Li's mention of a clean government was intended to also target potential critics of Xi's approach to Covid (including within state bodies) and warn them of consequences should they speak out of turn (CGTN).

Li eventually addresses Covid's impact on China at length. In this context, there is a return to belligerent language as Li insists containment of Covid remains a priority and that "[t]ogether, we have waged an all-out people's war against the virus" (ibid.). This "people's war" is linked to patriotism and national unity, with Li praising how "the sons and daughters of the Chinese nation, have stood together in the most trying of times and built a Great Wall of solidarity against the epidemic" (ibid.). While this language returns to similar national unity and martyrdom utilized by the government during SARS, there is also a turn to safety from the virus as a Beneficial Consequence and hence a justification for restrictions and lockdowns (Peter).

Regarding such justification, Li is very specific, arguing that "[w]e have achieved a decisive victory in the battle to defend Hubei Province and its capital city Wuhan by firmly implementing strict control measures, rallying the support of the entire country, dispatching over 40,000 doctors and nurses, rapidly increasing the number of hospital beds, and ensuring the availability of medical supplies" (ibid.). Just as Boris Johnson justified restrictions and responses through "following the science," Li augments the Beneficial Consequence of safety from the virus (at the expense of freedom of movement) by arguing that all "containment measures" and related restrictions "adopt a science-based approach" (ibid.).

It is clear, however, that Li must balance the Beneficial Consequence of security from the virus with the cost to the economy. For this reason, he acknowledges that "China has been able to contain Covid-19 in such a short time while also ensuring our people's basic needs" but "at a great price" (ibid.). Li reminds listeners that the financial cost of restrictions has been countered with socioeconomic packages that "stabilize employment, cut and exempted taxes and fees, exempted all tolls on highways, reduced the costs of energy use, and granted subsidized loans and continued the critical battle against poverty" (ibid.). Again, there is emphasis on maintaining moderate economic opportunities that were strengthened under Xi as a pillar of nondemocratic legitimacy. Indeed, by May 2020, Beijing had launched a $500 billion fiscal stimulus package for boosting business investment alone (Tang, May 22, 2020). And Li again emphasizes the Beneficial Consequence of strong leadership. "We owe what we have achieved," Li declares, "in economic and social development since last year and in Covid-19 control this year to the strong leadership of the Party Central Committee with Comrade Xi Jinping at its core" (CGTN).

Finally, although the speech's target audience is domestic, there seems to be an attempt at international legitimacy (or Peter's Political Cosmopolitanism) as well. Li praises "fruitful outcomes in pursuing China's major country diplomacy. We successfully hosted the second Belt and Road Forum for International Cooperation and other major diplomatic events" and Li connects this mention of the Belt and Road Initiative (BRI) with the fact that

> President Xi Jinping and other Party and state leaders visited many countries and attended major international events, including the G20 Leaders Summit, the BRICS Leaders Meeting, the Summit of the Conference on Interaction and Confidence Building Measures in Asia, the Shanghai Cooperation Organization Summit, the East Asian leaders' meetings on cooperation, the China-EU Leaders' Meeting, and the China–Japan–ROK Leaders' Meeting. (ibid.)

Both the BRI and listing China's international commitments are reminders that despite Covid, China remains globally active, ambitious, and recognized by other states in the international system (Peter). In particular, the mention of the G20 (also attended by Saudi Arabia's MBS) is a reminder of China's global influence (CGTN). The significance of Saudi Arabia's presence at the G20 will be explored further in Chapter 5.

Returning to discussions in Chapter 3, it would seem China still prioritizes the ambition of reforming global governance to reflect its own values. Indeed, Li even openly states that "[w]e played an active role in the development and reform of the global governance system, and promoted the building of a human community with a shared future. We successfully pursued economic diplomacy and cultural and people-to-people exchanges. China made important contributions to the advancement of world peace and development" (ibid.). Outlining China's self-declared role in the international system and drawing on the notion of international legitimacy and Political Cosmopolitanism serves as a preparatory condition that precedes the essential condition or instruction from China (or effectively Xi Jinping) to the global community:

> In the face of the public health crisis, severe economic recession, and other global challenges, all countries should work together. China stands ready to work with other countries to strengthen international cooperation on Covid-19 control, promote stability in the world economy, advance global governance, and uphold the international system with the United Nations at its core and an international order based on international law. (ibid.)

The emphasis on global cooperation can be linked to vaccine diplomacy and China's soft power and rehabilitation, as discussed in Chapter 2's section on vaccines. The notion of vaccine diplomacy and other forms of international legitimacy in China's public discourse will be further examined in Chapter 5.

An overview of Premier Li's speech reveals that, rather than providing a gleeful opportunity to increase authoritarianism, there was a need to justify security from the virus (one Beneficial Consequence) against the subsequent economic downturn that threatened a key pillar of Xi's nondemocratic legitimacy (economic growth, another Beneficial Consequence). While not explicitly stated, the preparatory condition of explaining how global economic weaknesses pressured China's own financial performance while justifying restrictions did frame an implied essential condition or instruction to citizens: they must continue to accept the CCP and Xi's rule, as the country's leadership has not only enforced restrictions that provide security from the virus but has outlined how economic benefits are still being addressed to ensure "moderate prosperity," the promised but limited ruling bargain offered by the CCP. Implying a "clean government" and indirectly bringing up anti-corruption measures serve both as a reminder that economic opportunity is through a social contract that forfeits citizens' political freedom and serve as a warning to critics within the party that there will be consequences for attacking the effectiveness of the government's Covid response.

As this speech was delivered amid a period when China saw a resurgence of cases, it is unsurprising that no reviewed media outlets mentioned any protests by citizens around March to May 2020. However, while Li's emphasis on economic recovery may have shown an understanding of one factor that could provoke protests in the long term, it did not seem to predict the factors that encouraged widespread protests in 2022. In addition to "anxieties about jobs and business [which are economic factors]," protests also expressed frustration over unequal access to healthcare (or none at all under lockdown), freedom of speech and the mental health effects of lockdown and restrictive measures (Davidson, November 28, 2022). "'Because they are so synchronised in terms of scope and the size of the crowds across these cities, it's a truly remarkable development,'" explains Professor Dali Yang from the University of Chicago" (ibid.).

Indeed, as Xi began his third term, such protests had grown threatening enough that he was forced to lift the strictest measures, "including forcing people into quarantine camps" (Mao). However, experts warned that easing of restrictions must be done slowly to ensure China's health system is not overwhelmed with an explosion of Covid cases. As previously discussed, it would seem that pandemics and politics are inextricable, and China was shifting from a WHO-praised response to Covid to an uncertain period in which protests and coronavirus were equally spreading threats for Xi Jinping (Mao).

Saudi Arabia's King Salman

As the novel coronavirus swept across the Saudi kingdom, Riyadh took swift action with a variety of restrictions and economic stimulus packages, as discussed in Chapter 3. Unlike China's issuance of public notices linked to penalties for civil disobedience, Saudi Arabia did not issue Covid-specific laws or any related emergency laws. As we will see in this chapter and as mentioned in Chapter 3, countries like the UK used Covid-specific laws to enforce restrictions and evade scrutiny of centralized government authority by democratic institutions (Ward, Ward, p. 14). However, Saudi Arabia relied on interpretations of *shariah* or Islamic law to address crises. Specifically, a state of emergency due to pandemics "was established by the saying of the Prophet Mohammed namely 'If you heard of a plague in a country do not enter it, and if you are in a country having plague do not leave it,'" which "opened the door for the main Sharia jurists to adopt the concepts of state of emergency in their teachings that were further adopted by the judges in [Saudi Arabia]" (AlDhabaan, Partners, 2020, p. 2). The implementation of restrictions and emergency measures under *shariah* and the need for Islamic scholars to interpret sayings in order to support state responses to Covid is a reminder that the religious elite are still required by MBS to legitimize sudden and controversial decisions by the House of Saud. Within the context of Covid, for example, Saudi Arabia's Grand Mufti issued a *fatwa* in 2021 confirming that getting vaccinated during the fasting hours of Ramadan "does not invalidate the fast of a fasting person, which is considered food and drink. The vaccine is administered intramuscularly, so it does not invalidate the fast" (Arab News, March 19, 2021).

As Saudi Arabia implemented restrictions and locked down the eastern region of Qatif, King Salman addressed the nation. While brief, the speech emphasized the importance of religion and economic Beneficial Consequences being maintained during or in response to Covid. Salman opens his address by confirming that "[w]e depend on the aid of God Almighty" to "deploy our full capabilities, supported by your strong determination to face adversaries with the steadfastness of believers at the forefront" (Khalid, May 20, 2020b). As discussed in Chapters 2 and 3, religion is almost inextricable from politics in Saudi Arabia and as keepers of the holy cities Mecca and Medina (officially referred to by the title Custodian of the Two Holy Mosques), the Saudi monarchy may draw on Islam and its practices as a utilitarian benefit to their rule (Due-Gundersen, 2022, pp. 13–14). Thus, reminding citizens of their role as believers is also a reminder of the House of Saud's holy status and hence religious legitimacy (ibid.).

Such religious language acts as a preparatory act, focused on both citizens and the monarchy being guided by God (and the monarchy having a divine right to rule) (ibid., p. 24). This context is followed by an indirect essential condition or instruction, similarly laced with religious imagery. Salman informs citizens that "your full cooperation with relevant government agencies are the most important contributing factors and pillars of the success of the state's efforts, which has prioritized safeguarding health and made it the state's top concern" (Khalid, May 20, 2020). In other words, it is expected that citizens obey restrictions in exchange for the Beneficial Consequence of security from the virus. However, this social contract draws on the mandatory pillars of Islam "which define the basic identity of Muslims—their faith, beliefs and practices—and bind together a worldwide community of believers into a fellowship of shared values and concerns" (Embassy of the Kingdom of Saudi Arabia, Washington, D.C., n.d.). As such pillars are mandatory, dubbing citizen cooperation as one of the required "pillars of success" implies that citizens must obey their monarchy as it would go against Islam to disobey (ibid.). Such disobedience has its own Islamic term—*fitnah*, with Islamic jurors regarding such disobedience against an Islamic ruler as unlawful as "it could threaten the integrity of the *umma* (community of believers)" (Ayoob, 2004, p. 9).

Salman expands on the Beneficial Consequences the state is providing during Covid. "Rest assured that we are very keen on providing the necessary medication, food, and living necessities for citizens and residents of this blessed land" (Khalid, May 20, 2020). In this context, there is a focus on the provision of a wide range of material benefits. Similar to China, Saudi Arabia practices a ruling bargain with citizens. However, while China offers "moderate prosperity," Saudi Arabia has traditionally drawn on oil wealth to provide a wider range of material rewards for political acquiescence, including "housing, subsidies, and jobs" and while the ruling bargain may be changing there is still some emphasis on material benefits (Brumberg). Hence, if anything, such material benefits will be strengthened during Covid (and include health and related provisions affected by the virus and restrictions) but in exchange for citizens obeying state-sanctioned measures, with a reminder that to not do so would be un-Islamic and perhaps *fitnah* (Ayoob, p. 9).

An overview of King Salman's speech in response to Covid reveals an emphasis on religion as a source of nondemocratic legitimacy but also a turn to security from the virus and provisions that tap into the greater ruling bargain in exchange for political acquiescence. As discussed in Chapter 3, Saudi Arabia responded to Covid with a relief fund of over $30 billion (Turak). As with China, there seems to be pressure to maintain economic performance or at least cushioning in the face of Covid as a benchmark of nondemocratic rule. While Saudi Arabia still draws on religion for such legitimacy, one wonders if Covid may entrench the ruling bargain if MBS's reforms are affected by the pandemic but also how the ruling bargain can cushion the effects of Covid during low oil prices (Guillo, March 27, 2020).

There was speculation in 2020 whether restrictions (along with later price hikes and spending cuts) may trigger protests against the monarchy (Fenton-Harvey, July 30, 2020). However, as discussed in Chapter 3, the lockdown in Qatif seemed more of a risk for provoking protest by stoking sectarian tensions (Agence-France Presse, March 9, 2020). Qatif was already seeing dissent between 2017 and 2020; however, such protests seemed related to existing political grievances rather than

Covid restrictions (Abouzzohour, March 8, 2021). As of 2022, there did not seem to have been sustained protests, and Saudi Arabia announced in January 2023 that *hajj* would return to pre-pandemic levels (Associated Press, January 10, 2023). According to Economist Intelligence, 2023 would see slow but still reasonably strong economic growth "following a stellar year of growth in 2022. The oil-rich state will retain large financial buffers and push ahead with ambitious investment programmes" (November 14, 2022). Indeed, early 2023 saw stronger oil prices. Saudi Arabia must be careful, however, to maintain true diversification into non-oil markets (ibid.).

Britain's Prime Minister Boris Johnson

> Good evening, The coronavirus is the biggest threat this country has faced for decades—and this country is not alone. All over the world we are seeing the devastating impact of this invisible killer. And so tonight I want to update you on the latest steps we are taking to fight the disease and what you can do to help. And I want to begin by reminding you why the UK has been taking the approach that we have. (Johnson, March 23, 2020)

On January 29, 2020, the UK reported its first Covid cases when two patients in York tested positive (British Foreign Policy Group). Less than a month later, the first British death from Covid was reported from a cruise liner (ibid.). By March 2020, Prime Minister Boris Johnson was urging for "everyone to stop non-essential contact and travel" (Institute for Government Analysis, December 9, 2022). Britain would soon enter lockdown, and such unprecedented restriction would be legally enforced by the Coronavirus Act (Cowie, March 2, 2022). This Act was a mix of temporary and permanent provisions, with all temporary provisions set to expire two years after the Act, in March 2022 (ibid.). At the same time, it would seem that when "legislating for emergency provisions, it's difficult to predict for how long they will be needed. The Coronavirus Act 2020 anticipated this, and allows ministers, by regulations, to:

- Temporarily suspend provisions
- Revive suspended provisions if they are needed again
- Permanently end provisions early
- Extend provisions before they expire (by up to six months at a time) (ibid.)"

As previously discussed in Chapter 3, the Coronavirus Act was used by Johnson to push through emergency powers without requiring parliamentary scrutiny and with claims of "following the science," his decisions regarding Covid could be presented as essential rather than political (Ward, Ward, p. 14, Flinders, p. 1). As the Act was being prepared, one socialist outlet claimed that Johnson was using it "to seize dictatorial powers" (Stevens, March 20, 2020). In addition to the bill being "rush[ed] through," World Socialist Website also explained that the Coronavirus

Act "provides for police state measures that are a grave threat," including through powers of police detention (ibid.). While perhaps using emotionally charged language, this criticism of the Coronavirus Act fed into the larger observation by outlets such as Foreign Policy that "emergency powers are chipping away at democracy—sometimes with public support" to risk what Professors Anwar Mhajne and Crystal Whetsone called "The Rise of the Covid Dictatorships" (October 16, 2020).

In their 2020 article, the pair argue that "[a]s the pandemic's death toll rose, many countries took aggressive measures to control the spread of Covid-19. Governments instituted national emergencies and travel bans and prohibited large gatherings. Such responses, however necessary they may have been from a health perspective, have allowed politicians to undermine democracy and human rights" (ibid.).

Returning to the notion of sweeping police powers, it would seem, however, that the UK's 2020 Coronavirus Act did not create the pervasive police state that the World Socialist Website feared. As outlined by Crown Prosecution Services, many offenses, for example, breaking screening and isolation procedures, were punishable with a limited fine (Crown Prosecution Service, July 18, 2022). There seems to be only one scenario where imprisonment may be imposed, if a person interferes with the closure of "an airport, seaport or an international rail terminal in the UK" (ibid.). If a person related to the management of such ports "fails without reasonable excuse to comply with a direction under the schedule [to cease port operations]" this offense is "punishable with a fine or 6 months' imprisonment or both" (ibid.). Over the course of 2020, no imprisonment seemed to have taken place and "breaches of coronavirus laws are mostly punished using fines rather than arrests and prosecutions—but fines that are not paid may result in a criminal charge" (Dearden, L., May 14, 2021). In addition, a 2021 report declared that "[e]very single prosecution brought using controversial powers introduced at the start of the coronavirus pandemic has been wrongful," forcing the Crown Prosecution Service to withdraw almost three hundred charges (ibid.).

It is worth mentioning that at the time of the 2021 report finding cases prosecuted under the Coronavirus Act unlawful, UK media had not yet reported Boris Johnson's breaking of his own Act through gatherings at Ten Down Street (known as Partygate) during lockdown (Crerar, November 30, 2021).

However, during March 2020, lockdown was only about to begin and as many citizens "felt panicked, afraid and unprepared as a result of the coronavirus pandemic," Johnson addressed the nation to announce restrictions (Mental Health Foundation, March 26, 2020, Johnson, March 23, 2020). No doubt such anxiety was not eased by Johnson's speech. As with China's Li Keqiang, Johnson opens his speech with belligerent language to refer to Covid-19 as "the biggest threat this country has faced for decades" and an "invisible killer" (Johnson, March 23, 2020). As with China, there is an emphasis on national unity, but, unlike Saudi Arabia, the UK is not a ruling bargain state with material benefits. Johnson's speech succinctly introduces a health-specific preparatory condition: the risk to the NHS (National Health Service) during the pandemic. There "will come a moment," he fears, "when no health service in the world could possibly cope; because there won't be enough ventilators, enough intensive care beds, enough doctors and nurses" and "that is the moment of real danger" (ibid.). Johnson provides a detailed preparatory condition or context that will lead up to his instructions, emphasizing this danger "simply" by explaining that "if too many people become seriously unwell at one time, the NHS will be unable to handle it—meaning more people are likely to die, not just from Coronavirus but from other illnesses as well" (ibid.).

While Saudi Arabia may be able to offer healthcare-related benefits under Covid, in Britain's democratic state the reverse was true. Britain's healthcare system had been facing staff shortages and underfunding since 2015 (British Medical Association, 2025). In addition, as discussed by Peter, although healthcare under the NHS is free of charge for UK residents, because Britain does not rule through Beneficial Consequences but rather has a political system of democratic legitimacy and popular participation, it is not obligated to maintain material benefits (Office for Health Improvements and Disparities, October 2, 2023, Peter). Hence, as the NHS is a free service but not a mandatory Beneficial Consequence, it is not offered as a measurement of political legitimacy when there is already popular participation, and Johnson can issue instructions that citizens must obey restrictions to "protect the NHS's ability to cope—and save more lives" (Johnson, March 23, 2020).

At the same time, Johnson also explains the lockdown as coming atop previous suggestions to "stay at home during this pandemic." Lockdown will now be enforced in order to "stop the disease spreading between households" (ibid.). The suggestion now shifts from previous pleas "asking people to stay at home" to the emphasized "instruction—you must stay at home" (ibid.). It is at this point in the speech that Johnson begins to dabble in what may be considered less democratic (or even nondemocratic) practices. While the NHS may not serve as a Beneficial Consequence typical of nondemocratic rule, he is now creating a new social contract under Covid that will mix Beneficial Consequences with threats as a "secondary, reinforcing motivation when the political order fails in its primary normative technique of authoritative guidance [through Beneficial Consequences]" (Peter).

First, his instruction that all "must stay at home" is followed by exceptions "for the following very limited purposes:

- shopping for basic necessities, as infrequently as possible
- one form of exercise a day—for example a run, walk, or cycle—alone or with members of your household;
- any medical need, to provide care or to help a vulnerable person; and
- travelling to and from work, but only where this is absolutely necessary and cannot be done from home" (Johnson, March 23, 2020).

Once the extent of instructions or essential conditions has been provided, Johnson turns to threats by declaring that if "you don't follow the rules, police will have the powers to enforce them, including through fines and dispersing gatherings" (ibid.).

At the same time, Johnson reminds listeners that in a democracy, no "Prime Minister wants to enact measures like this" and follows up threats of police powers and fines with Beneficial Consequences. Like China and Saudi Arabia, it would seem that economic protection has become a benchmark of legitimacy under Covid. That is why "we have produced a huge and unprecedented programme of support both for workers and for business" (ibid.). While this economic package is not elaborated on further, 2022 figures show that government spending across 2020 to 2021 was "about £167 billion higher than had been planned before the pandemic for that year" and that such "extra money was spent on public services (such as the NHS), support for businesses, and support for individuals. Some of the largest schemes include the Coronavirus Job Retention Scheme (CJRS, sometimes called the furlough scheme) and NHS Test and Trace" (Brien, Keep, March 29, 2022). In total, it seemed that "estimates of the cost of Government measures announced so far range from about £310 to £410 billion. This is the equivalent of about £4,600 to £6,100 per person in the UK" (ibid.).

The shift from suggesting people stay at home to mandatory lockdown, widening police powers but also promising unprecedented Beneficial Consequences (even if through borrowing), suggests a shift from the UK's regular social contract to one in which the political authority is obeyed in exchange for protection (from Covid), Beneficial Consequences through economic programs, and the threat of penalties for civil disobedience (Peter).

It is worth mentioning that such programs were not enough to prevent the UK from seeing a 20 percent fall in gross domestic product from April to June 2020 and a record 20 percent fall in spending for households (Office for National Statistics, 2021). Up to 20 percent of the UK working-age population was furloughed in April 2020 alone (McKinsey & Company, May 11, 2020).

It is impossible to know if Boris Johnson was fully aware that his "unprecedented programme of support both for workers and for business" would leave many behind (Johnson, March 23, 2020). However, while there does seem to be a shift in the social contract toward nondemocratic Beneficial Consequences (economic help, security from the virus) and threats, the speech is dotted with reminders that Johnson's government is a democratic system (ibid.). In addition to promising that no "Prime Minister wants to enact measures like this," Johnson recognizes the authoritative ring of his restrictions by promising that "we will keep these restrictions under constant review. We will look again in three weeks, and relax them if the evidence shows we are able to" (ibid.). Finally, one interesting note regarding Beneficial Consequences is the promise of a vaccine in the future. Johnson insists that as people obey lockdown, they will be rewarded from "the time you buy—by simply staying at home" with "accelerat[ed] search for treatments[,] pioneering work on a vaccine" and "millions of testing kits that will enable us to turn the tide on this invisible killer" (ibid.).

Hence, Johnson is presenting a social contract to citizens, which imposes nondemocratic restrictions in exchange for increasing safety from the virus through eventual treatments and testing kits and a future vaccine (ibid.). Such Beneficial Consequences are provided in detail before a concise repetition of

Johnson's essential condition: "I urge you at this moment of national emergency to stay at home, protect our NHS and save lives" (ibid.). The reminder that Covid in the UK is a national emergency indirectly ties back to the Coronavirus Act, which can be considered an attempt to legitimize government lockdown through legality as a source of political legitimacy that can be intrinsic rather than tied to democratic values (or scrutiny) (Peter, Ward, Ward, p. 14).

An overview of Johnson's 2020 speech announcing lockdown shows attempts to portray Covid as an invisible enemy and emphasize its threat through belligerent language. Much context is provided regarding the need to protect the NHS (a Beneficial Consequence that has seen defunding under democratic rule that is not obligated to provide material benefits). Such context is used to issue instructions that see a shift from asking people to stay home to imposing a lockdown that keeps people home and allows outside activity for very limited purposes. This shift in the social contract is indirectly admitted as uncharacteristic of a democratic state as no "Prime Minister wants to enact measures like this" (ibid.). Such a statement and other reminders that the UK remains a democracy do not change the fact that Johnson is now shifting the social contract toward nondemocratic factors such as security from the virus (a Beneficial Consequence) and making use of threats (such as police fines) in addition to economic aid as a Beneficial Consequence to bolster his political authority.

The recognition of this change in the social contract affecting so-called democratic freedom and the risk of veering into nondemocratic territory seems to influence the offer of (limited) material benefits. Like China, economic performance is emphasized and there is the promise of future Beneficial Consequences (a vaccine, testing kits) to enhance the Beneficial Consequence of security from the virus in exchange for citizens obeying lockdown. For a democratic state to offer Beneficial Consequences and use threats is not without irony, and perhaps it is for this reason that Johnson peppers the speech with reminders that his rule remains formally democratic (such as reviewing restrictions every three weeks), yet the emphasis on Beneficial Consequences and national unity (along with his attempt to centralize rule during his tenure) begs the question of how democratic Britain was leading up to Covid.

Responses to lockdown were mixed. Across 2020, London saw thousands participate in anti-lockdown protests, though it seems compliance with UK lockdowns was initially high (Gayle, October 24, 2020; Ganslmeier, Van Parys, Vlandas, March 9, 2022). In any event, the eventual lifting of restrictions and withdrawal of fines under the Coronavirus Act may imply that Johnson recognized the risk of having a less than democratic image and enforcement of such fines would be increasingly hard from a political standpoint after his own breaching of the rules during Partygate (Dearden, Crerar).

America's President Trump

> My fellow Americans, tonight I want to speak with you about our nation's unprecedented response to the coronavirus outbreak that started in China and is now spreading throughout the world. Today, the World Health Organization

officially announced that this is a global pandemic. We have been in frequent contact with our allies, and we are marshalling the full power of the federal government and the private sector to protect the American people. This is the most aggressive and comprehensive effort to confront a foreign virus in modern history. I am confident that by counting and continuing to take these tough measures, we will significantly reduce the threat to our citizens and we will ultimately and expeditiously defeat this virus. (Trump, March 11, 2020)

At the end of January 2020, the CDC announced the first detected case of Covid in the United States. The patient was a passenger who had recently returned from Wuhan, China. At the time, some authorities admitted they had "originally thought [Covid] to be spreading from animal-to-person, [but] there are growing indications that limited person-to-person spread is happening. It's unclear how easily this virus is spreading between people" (CDC, January 21, 2020). By February 3, the United States declared Covid a public emergency, following the WHO's confirmation of a global health emergency due to novel coronavirus (AJMC Staff, January 1, 2021).

While Boris Johnson pushed through a Coronavirus Act to legally formalize lockdowns, Trump declared a national emergency. Since Congress passed the 1976 National Emergencies Act, presidents have used national emergency declarations to tackle different crises and reroute national funding to other priorities (Sloane, 2019). Hence, Trump used this same tradition to enact various responses to Covid entering the United States. Such responses included banning entry of foreign nationals who have spent fourteen days in a country with a significant Covid outbreak (China, Iran, and Europe) and quarantine for citizens evacuated from foreign nations (Federal Register, March 18, 2020).

In addition, declaring Covid a national emergency was supposed to "accelerate the acquisition of personal protective equipment and streamline bringing new diagnostic capabilities to laboratories" (ibid.). As Chapter 3 discusses, personal protective equipment (PPE) distribution under Covid and Trump's assignment of PPE supply chain management to his son-in-law Jared Kushner would be heavily criticized in 2022. Other changes under the emergency declaration included the ability "to temporarily waive or modify certain requirements of the Medicare, Medicaid, and State Children's Health Insurance programs and of the Health Insurance Portability and Accountability Act Privacy Rule throughout the duration of the public health emergency declared in response to the Covid-19 outbreak" (ibid.). The declaration of a national emergency did not necessarily provide sweeping powers for nationwide lockdowns, and it would seem in any event that Trump's application (or understanding) of legal formalities to respond to the pandemic was inconsistent.

On the one hand, Trump did draw on the ability to declare a national emergency, which allowed for the implementation of some restrictive measures, and also claimed that the Cold-War-origin Defense Production Act (DPA) had been frequently drawn on to increase production of medical equipment (New York Times, January 20, 2021). The DPA originated during the Korean War and allows the executive branch to order production and distribution of any material deemed necessary for national defense. As NPR host Ayesha Rascoe put it, the government "can jump to the front of the line to buy goods from companies and ship them where needed" (March 25, 2020).

On the other hand, in the early months of 2020, Trump resisted calls to use the Act, "likening it to a government takeover of companies" and hence rejected calls from governors for a more centralized leadership approach (ibid.). Trump did, however, seem to give in and eventually "used the law to crack down on hoarding, limit exports of medical goods, and increase production of critical supplies" (Siripurapu, May 22, 2025).

However, when addressing the nation in a speech given to announce some of the first responses to Covid entering the United States, Trump did not invoke any production act but, inter alia, nationalism (as discussed in Chapter 3) and Sinophobia. Trump opens by discussing his administration's "response to the coronavirus outbreak that started in China and is now spreading throughout the world" (Trump, March 11, 2020). It goes without saying that emphasizing Covid-19's starting point in China and eventually using terms like "Chinese virus" led to accusations of racism, with Trump's tweets adopting such Sinophobic name-calling being linked to online anti-Asian hate across America (Kurtzman, March 18, 2021).

Some critics have linked Trump's use of the term to retaliation for a Chinese official implying that US army personnel "brought the epidemic to Wuhan" and spreading this misinformation by sharing articles from conspiracy sites that supported such an assertion (Molter, Webster, March 31, 2020).

However, there is also the possibility that Trump wants to begin his speech with a preparatory condition that taps into his platform of nationalism and anti-globalization. Recall that Trump campaigned on an exclusionary nationalism that emphasized the "backlash against increasing economic interdependence" of globalization, which for some Americans "generated deep-seated feelings of exclusion" if they are "unable to reap the benefits of globalization" (Regilme, p. 162). Within the context of Covid's infection of the United States, it seemed Trump may have taken the opportunity to frame Covid as a key danger of globalization and interdependence, to say that what happens in China "is now spreading throughout the world" because of globalization, thus validating his platform of populism and isolationism (with Trump to focus such isolationism on the US economy disconnecting from China in his 2020 reelection campaign) (Pisani, September 9, 2020).

It may also be for these reasons that Trump refers to Covid as "a foreign virus" and uses the redundant term "global pandemic"—a pandemic is, by definition, global, yet emphasizing the foreignness of the virus and its international threat may also serve to bolster Trump's anti-globalization (Trump, March 11, 2020). In a sense, Trump is indirectly drawing on Beneficial Consequences by succinctly implying that globalization allowed the virus to threaten "the American people (ibid.)," and that Trump's isolationism can offer security against such threats (Peter), perhaps in a second term, given that Trump had announced his bid for reelection as early as 2017 (Herbert, May 1, 2017).

Complementing blaming Covid on globalization is Trump's turn to exclusionary nationalism and American exceptionalism (Bonikowski, p. 113) as he insists "[o]ur team is the best anywhere in the world," continuing the theme of isolationism and exclusion by claiming that by "taking early intense action, we have seen dramatically fewer cases of the virus in the United States than are now present in Europe" (Trump, March 11, 2020). Trump would repeat this claim across 2020, ignoring the fact that some European states, such as Germany, Finland, and Denmark, seemed to be faring better under stronger leadership while the US's total deaths and cases per capita were considerably higher up until the end of the year (Edwards, Smith, November 9, 2020).

Trump continues his focus on Europe's mistakes by insisting that the "European Union failed to take the same precautions and restrict travel from China and other hot spots. As a result, a large number of new clusters in the United States were seeded by travelers from Europe" (Trump, March 11, 2020). While this extended attack on Europe may appear as blaming Europe as much as China, it would seem that Trump is also using Europe as a framework for attacking globalization. It is globalization that allowed Covid to spread from China to Europe and eventually the United States. Europe's interdependence rather than state-based nationalism or what Peter would term Political Nationalism has prevented individual states from imposing restrictions (Peter) and once again, America is being attacked by the forces of globalization (Regilme, p. 162). Indeed, Trump contrasts Europe's interdependence with strong state-based decision-making that emphasizes how "only the political institutions of nation states pose and can overcome the legitimacy problem and hence be a source of political legitimacy" (Peter). While Europe's interdependence prevented the imposition of necessary restrictions, Trump's America can "take several strong but necessary actions to protect the health and well being of all Americans" (Trump, March 11, 2020).

In discussing such strong steps in contrast to the European Union's (EU) failure, Trump is again attacking globalization and turning to security from the virus as a Beneficial Consequence that justifies such actions (Peter). Further, his belittling of the EU provides context for the announcement that, among other measures, "we will be suspending all travel from Europe to the United States for the next 30 days. Anything coming from Europe to the United States is what we are discussing" (Trump, March 11, 2020). Again, Trump is emphasizing a decoupling from globalization and a turn to isolationism, as promised to his supporters (McTague, Nicholas). However, it is interesting to note that such "restrictions will also not apply to the United Kingdom" (Trump, March 11, 2020).

Ironically, March 2020 saw a sudden increase in the UK's Covid cases (British Foreign Policy Group). However, Trump's decision to exclude the UK from the travel ban feeds back into Chapter 3's discussion of the parallels between Brexit and Trump's America First (even if Johnson did not take the comparison as a compliment) and implies that rather than following the science, Trump's Covid response was "driven by politics" (Wintour, March 12, 2020). While this exception may have served as a reminder that Trump's allies also embraced an exclusionary nationalism (Hirsch, June 27, 2016), such discourse did not necessarily match reality. "The White House," explains journalist Patrick Wintour, "said the US was closing its borders to foreign nationals who have been in the Schengen area in the last 14 days, which would apply to any British person who had recently been in the 26-nation visa-free area" (ibid.).

As with Boris Johnson, there is a pattern of imposing restrictions for the Beneficial Consequence of security from the virus while promising that "we will re-evaluate the restrictions and warnings that are currently in place for a possible early opening" (Trump, March 11, 2020). In the case of Johnson, however, such reevaluation pertained to domestic restrictions rather than travel bans and served as a reminder that the UK remained democratic. In Trump's case, such reevaluation pertains to travel bans rather than domestic restrictions, perhaps acting as a subtle cap on Trump's anti-globalization (ibid.).

However, Trump's overall attack on globalization is then followed by domestic Beneficial Consequences that target health but from a perspective that can be linked to what all the other case studies have in common: economics. Trump has "met with the leaders of [the] health insurance industry who have agreed to waive all co-payments for coronavirus treatments, extend insurance coverage to these treatments, and to prevent surprise medical billing" (ibid.). This promise of indirect financial support can be linked back to the powers Trump could exercise under a national emergency declaration (Federal Register). However, this move can also be seen as akin to providing material benefits similar to an economic package. Unlike Britain's NHS, which treats UK citizens and residents without cost, the United States does not have a public healthcare system but one in which citizens "shoulder [medical costs] directly—through co-payments, deductibles, and monthly coverage fees" (Wapner, August 14, 2020). Hence, Trump is indicating that during a period in which America has been attacked by the effects of globalization, he is providing healthcare-related assistance as a (limited) Beneficial Consequence, which includes "an $8.3 billion funding bill to help C.D.C. and other government agencies fight the virus and support vaccines, treatments and distribution of medical supplies" (Trump, March 11, 2020).

As with Boris Johnson, there is the promise made of a future Beneficial Consequence, namely a vaccine. However, while Trump may try to sell the image of healthcare cost relief as a benefit of his rule, as with UK exemptions from his EU travel ban, reality did not fully mirror his words. While Trump had promised financial relief and extended insurance coverage for Covid treatments, April 2020 saw some Americans hit with medical bills after seeking Covid treatment. Susan Adler, whose husband died of Covid-19 during treatment at a hospital in Oklahoma faced bills exceeding $20,000 (Wapner). Further, while testing is meant to be free of charge, loopholes in the existing legislation risked that "people may still have high out-of-pocket costs for tests done at an emergency room or other non-public site" (ibid.).

In any event, the context of Covid being the result of globalization and Trump's claim to provide security from the virus and health cost relief sets up his essential condition or instruction: "The highest risk is for [the] elderly population with underlying health conditions. The elderly population must be very, very careful.

In particular, we are strongly advising that nursing homes for the elderly suspend all medically unnecessary visits. In general, older Americans should avoid nonessential travel in crowded areas" (Trump, March 11, 2020). Curiously, Trump maintains an earlier stance that "[y]oung and healthy people can expect to recover fully and quickly if they should get the virus" and that for youth the "risk is very, very low" (ibid.).

Trump admitted in a fall 2020 interview that he had downplayed the danger of Covid-19. "I still like playing it down," he confirmed in the same interview, "because I don't want to create a panic" (Summers, October 2, 2020). It is true that early medical reports indicated that younger people were less likely to suffer severe Covid symptoms (Maragakis, April 9, 2020). However, Trump's emphasis that the virus was at highest risk for elderly persons with underlying health conditions "go against the guidance of most public health experts" (Summers).

In a notable coincidence, it is worth mentioning that the elderly (those aged sixty-five or over) were also in the age bracket most likely to vote for Trump. In the 2016 election that brought him to power, 53 percent of voters who chose Trump were sixty-five or older (Pew Research Center, August 9, 2018). In the 2020 elections that Trump lost, 52 percent of voters aged sixty-five or above still chose him (Bryant, November 5, 2020). Hence, while it may not have been intentional, by instructing the elderly to "be very, very careful," Trump was protecting his voter base (Trump, March 11, 2020).

However, despite authorizing health-related Beneficial Consequences and travel bans, Trump could not announce a lockdown in the manner of Boris Johnson. Instead, the executive could only "issue guidance on school closures, social distancing and reducing large gatherings" (ibid.). There is a sense of irony to Trump's guidelines after his attempts to centralize power under the executive branch. It would seem that President Trump, though asked by some governors to exercise stronger leadership, "has little to no power to act, because of states' sovereign rights" (Gostin, Wetter, March 31, 2020). In other words, Trump imposing "a large-scale quarantine would be legally murky, even if it's what the country needs to slow the spread of the coronavirus" (ibid.).

Just as Johnson's promise that domestic restrictions would be periodically reviewed acted as a "reminder" that his rule remained democratic, Trump's language eventually shifts from demonizing external countries and banning their citizens from the United States to coordinating with America's states on Covid guidelines, a reminder that, despite his Twitter tactics, he is still constrained by democratic institutions and federalism (ibid.). This notion is extended when Trump admits that "[e]very community faces different risks and it is critical for you to follow the guidelines of your local officials who are working closely with our federal health experts" (Trump, March 23, 2020).

That said, after providing a context of anti-globalization and protecting the elderly (and his voters), Trump does issue a wider essential condition: "For all Americans, it is essential that everyone take extra precautions and practice good hygiene. Each of us has a role to play in defeating this virus. Wash your hands, clean often-used surfaces, cover your face and mouth if you sneeze or cough, and most of all, if you are sick or not feeling well, stay home" (ibid.). It is important to note that these essential conditions are in contrast to Boris Johnson ordering a national lockdown that essentially forced everyone to stay home. While Trump may have provided a context of the virus being a global outbreak and requiring an aggressive response, unlike Johnson, Trump has not issued restrictions that could be considered mandatory and possibly undemocratic. For closures of public space, for example, Trump is "coordinating directly with communities" to "issue guidance" rather than mandatory instructions (ibid.). When issuing what may be considered mandatory instructions, these are limited to general cleanliness and staying home if unwell but there is no national lockdown and Trump, unlike Johnson, does not mention any police or related authority being able to enforce these instructions (ibid.).

However, one element of Trump's speech similar to Johnson's (and perhaps even China's and Saudi Arabia's) is an emergency economic package, "which is unprecedented, to provide financial relief. This will be targeted for workers who are ill, quarantined, or caring for others due to coronavirus" (ibid.). Such a package again presents a turn to Beneficial Consequences, albeit perhaps more limited than Saudi Arabia's but similar to Johnson's "unprecedented programme of support both for workers and for business" (Johnson, March 23, 2020). All four case study speeches have at some point turned to the economic damage of Covid-19. However, in another nod to limits on executive power, Trump admitted he needed to gain approval from "Congress to take legislative action to extend this relief" (Trump, March 11, 2020).

As with Trump's promise that UK nationals would not be affected by US-issued travel bans, promised economic aid was not available in March but only by December 2020, as Trump himself "previously refused to sign the bill," citing wasteful spending and items in the bill that should be removed for being fiscally unsound. As a result of his delay, "millions temporarily lost unemployment benefits" and Trump's eventual acquiescence came a month before he left office after losing the election (BBC, December 28, 2020).

As with Johnson, economic aid under Trump also included small businesses, with Trump ordering what was called the "Small Business Administration to provide capital and liquidity to firms affected by the coronavirus" and "low-interest loans [to] help small businesses overcome temporary economic disruptions caused by the virus" (Trump, March 11, 2020). Once again, Trump must admit the limits of executive reach by "asking Congress to increase funding for this program by an additional $50 billion" (ibid.).

Outlining such packages, Trump also turns to the notion of American exceptionalism within the context of the economy and Covid. He claims that because "of the economic policies that [I] have put into place over the last three years, we have the greatest economy in the world by far. Our unemployment is at a historic low. This vast economic prosperity gives us flexibility, reserves, and resources to handle any threat that comes our way" (Trump, March 11, 2020). Again, Trump's image is intended to feed into his America First policy and emphasize that a Beneficial Consequence of his isolationism and rule is economic prosperity (Peter). However, this claim is false. *USA Today* confirmed that Trump's tenure saw a "sharp drop in employment" and that "the economy lost just under 4 million employees during Trump's term" (Cox, 2020).

In addition, while Trump's Covid loans were taken up by millions of businesses (Qing, Price, December 2, 2020), a 2022 House Subcommittee report found that Trump mismanaged what was referred to as the Covid-19 Economic Injury Disaster Loan (EIDL) program and "failed to implement basic safeguards to prevent fraud, even directing loan reviewers to approve applications with serious fraud alerts without taking any steps to ensure that the applications were legitimate" (Select Subcommittee on the Coronavirus Crisis, June 14, 2022). Such findings come atop an earlier 2020 article that related loan programs benefited businesses associated with Trump and son-in-law Kushner (Lehren, Popken, December 2, 2020).

Other economic relief is briefly mentioned such as deferring tax payments. However, while such packages can be termed Beneficial Consequences, each one must be cleared by Congress, illustrating at each example of economic aid outlined by Trump the limits of executive power (and acting as a reminder that his rule remains democratic) (Trump, March 11, 2020).

Trump ends his speech by emphasizing how Covid is a platform to prove that his anti-globalization and exclusionary nationalism "will always put America first" by augmenting isolationism (through travel bans) from China and Europe and that security from the virus as a Beneficial Consequence is linked to his nationalism because "[n]o nation is more prepared or more resilient than the United States. We have the best economy, the most advanced healthcare, and the most talented doctors, scientists and researchers anywhere in the world" (ibid.).

An overview of Trump's speech in response to Covid illustrates his attempt to use Covid as a platform for his exclusionary nationalism and America First policy. Trump attacks Covid as a result of globalization and uses security against the virus as a reason to decouple from China and Europe, with a symbolic exception to fellow isolationist UK. Trump also presents economic relief as a further Beneficial Consequence, again illustrating how for democratic and nondemocratic regimes, economic performance became a pressure point that had to be acknowledged. However, unlike the UK's Boris Johnson, Trump cannot enforce a nationwide lockdown and can only issue instructions that serve as guidelines. Furthermore, many of Trump's economic actions require congressional approval, a reminder of his executive limits (despite his attempts to attack such limits during his tenure) and of the fact that he remains a democratic ruler.

There were lockdowns across different states and, subsequently, protests against these restrictions. However, as each state is responsible for such measures and not the executive, protests were directed against state governors and, in some cases, even supported by Trump himself (Gearan, Wagner, May 1, 2020). If anything, Trump's support of such protests may show that, even if forced to acknowledge congressional control and the independence of federalism in his speech, as with his use of Twitter, he could find a way to undermine democratic mechanisms (ibid.).

Economic Performance, Nationalism, and Isolationism

An overview of speeches given by leaders in China, Saudi Arabia, Britain, and America during the initial wave of Covid shows that both democratic and nondemocratic regimes were forced to respond economically to the effects of Covid, even if lockdowns were not enforced by the central government. The financial damage of the virus could not be ignored and there was hence mention of economic packages. Some were more generous than others, and certain financial programs that were outlined as Beneficial Consequences did not necessarily match such discourse in reality.

China and Saudi Arabia also drew on the notion of national unity and for Riyadh, the authority of religion as a Beneficial Consequence. In addition, most speeches did not specifically mention lockdown, with the exception being Boris Johnson's explicit instructions that all citizens "must stay at home," though the word "lockdown" was never used. Even China's Premier Li and Saudi Arabia's King Salman avoided using the term "lockdown," perhaps illustrating that Covid (and by extension pandemics in the past) did not defend dictatorships but challenged them and democracies, with all regimes forced to announce restrictions carefully, linking such decisions to democratic reluctance as Johnson insists that "[n]o Prime Minister wants to enact measures like this" or to religious obedience by presenting the need to obey government instructions as a pillar associated with Islamic customs, as King Salman did in his address. However, one anomaly to these speeches has been Trump's, which stood out by becoming a platform advocating isolationism and Trump's anti-global nationalism. Although Brexit Britain was also compared to Trump's America in Chapter 3, Johnson did not mention Brexit or his equivalent of American exceptionalism. On the theme of isolationism and anti-globalization, Trump is unique, but his references to Congress are a reminder of his democratic constraints, further showing that while he may draw on some Beneficial Consequences, he remains president of a democracy.

Chapter 4 has analyzed public discourse by leaderships across our case studies to examine how each leadership publicly responded to Covid, how they framed restrictions and allowed us to understand how such discourse presented restrictions. In addition, we have traced each case study's initial response to the arrival of Covid, the emphasis on economic performance, and the promise of vaccines in the future as a form of Beneficial Consequence outlined by Trump and Johnson. Analysis of speeches in Chapter 4 returns us to the key argument that during Covid, economic performance became a core concern for state political legitimacy. Chapter 5 will analyze discourse from each leadership as vaccines became available and understand to what extent each leadership advocated vaccine nationalism or vaccine diplomacy, which ties back to the wider debate on Political Nationalism versus Political Cosmopolitanism and globalization versus isolationism.

Chapter 5

PUBLIC DISCOURSE OF THE VACCINE RACE

Vaccine Nationalism or Vaccine Diplomacy?

After examining speeches given by democratic and nondemocratic leaderships in response to Covid, the current chapter will build on Chapter 2's discussion of vaccines by examining to what extent vaccine availability affected government discourse within the context of vaccine nationalism or vaccine diplomacy and to what extent such discourse connects with a turn toward Peter's Political Cosmopolitanism or the notion that states recognize global governance (Peter), and toward Ahram and Lust's international legitimacy, or the belief that states need international recognition of their sovereignty (Ahram, Lust, p. 8). It would be expected that discourse embracing vaccine diplomacy would connect with this notion of global legitimacy. On the other hand, discourse showing themes of vaccine nationalism connects with Peter's Political Nationalism or the notion that states are the highest authority in the international system (Peter). In addition, it is worth mentioning that while Saudi Arabia did not develop a vaccine, there still seemed to be an attempt to maintain global engagement, which can be analyzed through international legitimacy and Political Cosmopolitanism (Jalaby, Rashad, November 20, 2020). Such analysis of all four case studies will thus address to what extent Covid has seen an increase of isolationism or of global cooperation.

Vaccines, Nationalism, and Diplomacy

China's President Xi Jinping

As mentioned in Chapter 2's discussion of vaccines, China seemed to lean toward vaccine diplomacy as a form of soft power and shoring up allies as Biden replaced Trump in the United States. It is clear from Xi's opening that there is a tilt toward international legitimacy and Political Cosmopolitanism (ibid.). Indeed, the mention of Riyadh and the G20 meeting will be further analyzed in the following section on Saudi Arabia's Crown Prince Mohammed bin Salman (MBS). For Xi, there is consistent emphasis on "economic growth [as a] top priority for the international community" along with "global cooperation against the virus" (Xinhua, May 21, 2021).

To that end, Xi presents a five-point plan for international cooperation in a world where vaccines are key to countering Covid. An overview of these points makes it clear that Xi's speech is intended to attack vaccine nationalism and isolationism. He insists that "we must put people and their lives first" through "science-based policies and a coordinated and systemic response" (ibid.). While "following the science" was used by some leaders like Boris Johnson to avoid the appearance of pursuing political objectives during the pandemic, Xi seems to be implying that there should be global scientific cooperation rather than, for example, viral sovereignty and that "G20 members need to adopt responsible macro-economic policies and step up coordination to keep the global industrial and supply chains safe and smooth" (ibid.). No doubt emphasis on such cooperation tilts toward Political Cosmopolitanism, but Xi also mentions the need for all countries to "give continued support by such means as debt suspension and development aid to developing countries, especially vulnerable countries facing exceptional difficulties" (ibid.). This latter comment is interesting, as it partially reflects what some have identified as China's soft power strategy under the New Silk Road platform before Covid and part of China's "capability to reform the global governance system to reflect [its] priorities and values" (Council on Foreign Relations, 2025).

Linked to Political Cosmopolitanism is also Xi's insistence that states "must stick together and promote solidarity and cooperation" through "a global community of health for all, and firmly reject any attempt to politicize, label or stigmatize the virus. Political manipulation would not serve Covid-19 response on the domestic front. It would only disrupt international cooperation against the virus and bring greater harm to people around the world" (Xinhua). Xi has created a preparatory condition of the need for international cooperation in order to economically recover and to defeat the virus. In a sense, while his five-point plan can also be regarded as essential conditions or instructions, within each point a context is built to issue indirect instructions and possibly condemnation of isolationist actors across specific points of the plan.

When opening his third point that states we must stick together, Xi also issues an indirect instruction: Covid should not be politicized or used to blame. This is no doubt a response to comments from isolationist leaders like Trump that have labeled Covid the "China virus" and sought to blame China for the pandemic (Horsley, August 19, 2020). However, while Trump blamed China in order to attack globalization and promote isolationism, Xi argues that blaming China will hinder global cooperation. Hence, Xi is drawing on international legitimacy and the notion that "sovereignty is inextricable from international hierarchy" (Ahram, Lust, p. 8) by asserting China's role in global governance and the fact that only "international cooperation against the virus," rather than isolationism, will reduce harm to all (Xinhua). Again, such instructions feed into Political Cosmopolitanism by arguing that in exchange for no longer blaming China, states will benefit as China joins the international system as part of global governance and cooperation against Covid (ibid.).

It is in Xi's fourth point that the tension between vaccine nationalism and vaccine diplomacy is clearly discussed. For this point, Xi declares that the international system "must uphold fairness and equity as we strive to close the immunization gap" and addresses vaccine diplomacy (and China's leading role in this form of global health governance) by reminding other states that only one "year ago, I proposed that vaccines should be made a global public good. Today, the problem of uneven vaccination has become more acute" (ibid.). The contrast between vaccine inequality and China's vaccine diplomacy acts as a reminder that Beijing "increasingly asserts itself, seeking to regain its centrality in the international system and over global governance institutions" (Council on Foreign Relations, 2025). While this approach may be regarded as statism, China's emphasis on asserting its national sovereignty within the international system again connects with international legitimacy (Ahram, Lust, pp. 8, 11) and Political Cosmopolitanism (Peter).

Indeed, it is under this fourth point and within the context of China's vaccine diplomacy and international legitimacy that Xi calls on the global community to "reject vaccine nationalism and find solutions to issues concerning the production capacity and distribution of vaccines, in order to make vaccines more accessible and affordable in developing countries" (Xinhua, 2021). Xi's naming of vaccine nationalism (but not vaccine diplomacy) again feeds into China's assertion of global governance and a turn toward Political Cosmopolitanism rather than Political Nationalism (Peter).

Building on his attack on vaccine nationalism, Xi makes a sharper turn toward the international legitimacy of global governance in his fifth point to "improve the governance system" (Xinhua, 2021). In this context, Xi insists that "we strengthen and leverage the role of the UN and the WHO" (ibid.). Again, such elements feed into China's increasing role at the United Nations (UN) as part of their efforts to enhance their influence in global governance and health diplomacy (Jamali, Zhang, pp. 284, 283).

These five points may be regarded as essential conditions or instructions that also provide a context of international legitimacy and Political Cosmopolitanism. Xi indirectly implies that politicizing the virus and blaming China will do more harm than good and that (vaccine) nationalism must be replaced with international cooperation and Political Cosmopolitanism to address the economic and humanitarian damage caused by the virus (Xinhua). There are also hints that China is already leading in this role as part of a global governance system, with Xi's emphasis on international cooperation also juxtaposed against directly declaring that "China has mounted a massive global humanitarian operation to support global anti-pandemic cooperation" (ibid.).

It is in the context of leading global humanitarian cooperation that Xi mentions vaccine diplomacy and the fact that Beijing

> has honored its commitment by providing free vaccines to more than 80 developing countries in urgent need and exporting vaccines to 43 countries. We have provided 2 billion US dollars in assistance for the Covid-19 response and economic and social recovery in developing countries hit by the pandemic. We have sent medical supplies to more than 150 countries and 13 international

organizations, providing more than 280 billion masks, 3.4 billion protective suits and 4 billion testing kits to the world. A cooperation mechanism has been established for Chinese hospitals to pair up with 41 African hospitals, and construction for the China-assisted project of the Africa CDC headquarters officially started at the end of last year. Important progress has also been made in the China-UN joint project to set up in China a global humanitarian response depot and hub. China is fully implementing the G20 Debt Service Suspension Initiative for Poorest Countries and has so far put off debt repayment exceeding 1.3 billion US dollars, the highest deferral amount among G20 members (ibid.)

These extensive remarks again emphasize international legitimacy and Political Cosmopolitanism and by outlining China's engagement, it is clear that Beijing is billing itself as a leader of global governance under a system in which "sovereignty is inextricable from international hierarchy" (Ahram, Lust, p. 8).

Building on China's global activities, Xi ends his speech by outlining further promises of vaccine diplomacy, including financial aid and vaccine supply but also "waiving intellectual property rights on Covid-19 vaccines" (Xinhua). Such a move not only emphasizes global cooperation and international legitimacy but does so by attempting to use vaccine diplomacy to counter vaccine nationalism and viral sovereignty (Halabi, Rutschmann, p. 17). As discussed in Chapter 2, viral sovereignty, or the act of a state withholding virus samples from the international community to leverage vaccine access, is a practice often associated with developing nations that have felt left out by wealthier nations (and pharmaceutical companies) that produce or buy up vaccines that may be produced from samples provided by poorer nations (ibid.). By offering to waive China's intellectual property rights to their own vaccines, Xi is reaching out to such nations that often form a key strategy of China's soft power under initiatives such as the Belt and Road and New Silk Road forums (Jamali, Zhang, pp. 284, 283).

Finally, Xi ends his speech by proposing "setting up an international forum on vaccine cooperation for vaccine-developing and producing countries, companies and other stakeholders to explore ways of promoting fair and equitable distribution of vaccines around the world" (Xinhua). Again, this announcement can be regarded as Beijing expanding their international legitimacy through vaccine diplomacy and turning to a leadership role in global governance through Covid-19 (ibid.).

Within two months of Xi's address, such a forum was hosted (online) by China and included delegates representing "29 Chinese and foreign vaccine manufacturers" along with "Thailand, Uzbekistan, Malaysia, South Africa, Argentina, Brazil, Turkey, Chile, [the] Dominican Republic, Colombia, Egypt, Hungary, Indonesia, Kenya, Mexico, Morocco, Pakistan, the Philippines, Serbia, Sri Lanka, Ecuador, the UAE, and Russia," implying that through vaccine diplomacy, China was indeed gaining international legitimacy from developing countries (its soft power targets) but also US allies (the UAE) and US enemies (Russia) (Office of the Commissioner of the Ministry of Foreign Affairs of the People's Republic of China in Macao Special Administrative Region, August 5, 2021).

Saudi Arabia's Crown Prince Mohammed bin Salman

MBS's speech opens with an assertion of religious legitimacy, a reminder that the House of Saud is "the Custodian of the Two Holy Mosques" and that MBS speaks for "King Salman bin Abdulaziz Al Saud, King of the Kingdom of Saudi Arabia" (Khalid, November 22, 2020). However, as with China, the speech is ultimately focused on international legitimacy. In the case of Saudi Arabia, MBS's speech emphasizes the kingdom's role in hosting the G20. Indeed, there is a turn to Political Cosmopolitanism as MBS links "the Saudi G20 presidency" to the fact that the G20 stands as a platform for global governance by being "an essential link among our countries to deal with economic, financial, social and environmental issues" (ibid.).

Such a preparatory condition associates Saudi leadership with the G20 and global governance. As with China, Saudi Arabia is acknowledging that "sovereignty is inextricable from international hierarchy" and turning to the ability to use its sovereignty on the world stage (Ahram, Lust, p. 8).

Moreover, there is a parallel with China's use of Covid to turn to international legitimacy and Political Cosmopolitanism, as MBS emphasizes the need for international cooperation because "[t]his pandemic knows no borders. It has reached all countries and affected, directly and indirectly, every person living on this planet, which has necessitated the activation of the pivotal role played by the G20" (Khalid, November 22, 2020). While China seems to focus its international rehabilitation and global governance attempts on the UN and World Health Organization (WHO) (Jamali, Zhang, pp. 284, 283), Saudi Arabia is instead focused on its then leadership role under the G20 and how, as China advocates, international coordination rather than isolationism or Political Nationalism is required "to deal with the pandemic and its aftermath" (Khalid, November 22, 2020).

Although Saudi Arabia did not produce a vaccine, it is clear that they are using Covid as an opportunity to increase their soft power. As with China, Saudi Arabia has contributed significant economic aid. The G20 "injected over $11 trillion into the global economy to support businesses and protect individuals' livelihoods" and of this amount, "[t]he Kingdom contributed $500m to support these efforts" (ibid.). It is worth mentioning that Riyadh's generosity of half a billion dollars does not match the $61 billion spent on an initial Covid economic relief package domestically (Turak). Nonetheless, the economic contribution again indicates that under MBS, Saudi Arabia is pursuing international legitimacy and Political Cosmopolitanism, perhaps in response to Saudi dissident Khashoggi's murder and global repercussions for MBS's links to the assassination (Roberts). Indeed, the turn toward international legitimacy through "Covid diplomacy" and economic contribution "for the development of diagnostic tools, vaccines and effective therapeutics" (Khalid, November 22, 2020) may be pursued with generous resources, as MBS is no longer able to rely on Trump as "a steady source of domestic and international legitimacy and influence" (Harb, October 12, 2018).

Both China's Xi Jinping and Saudi Arabia's MBS also mention an element that health experts have warned of since long before Covid-19. The need to prepare for future pandemics. For Xi, a global governance system that streamlines cooperation with the UN and WHO will "improve the global disease prevention and control system to better prevent and respond to future pandemics" (Xinhua). For MBS, the need for "better protection from future pandemics" will be led by Saudi Arabia's "initiative to enhance access to pandemic tools" (Khalid, November 22, 2020). Elements of the Saudi initiative under "the G20 presidency" include:

- "Promote R&D, and distribution of diagnostic tools, therapeutics, and vaccines for all infectious diseases
- Encourage and facilitate international funding for global pandemic preparedness
- And support the training of epidemiologists from all over the world" (ibid.).

These outlined elements are partially similar to Xi's five points (Xinhua) and may indicate that Saudi Arabia is considering increasing its international legitimacy through Covid diplomacy and what some critics call "stethoscope diplomacy," which focuses on helping nations through the very initiatives outlined by MBS, such as financial and medical donations and relevant investment and training, considered by some analysts as "human capital investments proven to make populations better off and more trusting [of the donor actor]" (Jones, Kahwagl, February 9, 2021).

It would seem that China and Saudi Arabia wish to pursue global governance that is not centralized by the United States and are engaged in dialogue to "help build more strategic common understandings on major regional and international issues … and defend multilateralism" (Associated Press, December 7, 2022). However, the extent to which the two states would cooperate for Covid diplomacy is questionable. For China, such dialogue should increase access to much-needed oil and increase Xi's profile in the Middle East, while Riyadh gains access to Chinese companies "to upgrade its infrastructure, among them construction firms and the telecoms giant Huawei" (ibid.).

Overall, MBS's speech attempts to associate Saudi Arabia with the G20 through Riyadh's G20 presidency and hence turns toward international legitimacy and Political Cosmopolitanism through the G20 as a global governance institute, with this context framing the indirect essential condition advocated by China: global cooperation to confront Covid (although politicization of the virus and isolationism are not implied) (Khalid, November 22, 2020). However, it is also worth mentioning that within the international context of his speech, MBS does mention his domestic reforms and how G20 values and efforts are "aligned with Saudi Arabia undergoing major economic and social transformation, guided by our Vision 2030 which aims to ensure that all of our citizens, especially women and youth, can seize the opportunities of the twenty-first century" (ibid.). By associating Vision 2030 with G20 values and Saudi leadership of the G20, there certainly does seem to be an attempt to connect MBS's reforms with international legitimacy (ibid.). For Saudi Arabia, then, Covid has seen a turn toward global cooperation and diplomacy rather than isolationism and (vaccine) nationalism. As China seems to be using vaccine diplomacy to reverse the blame for Covid and enhance their international image, perhaps Saudi Arabia similarly seeks to counter the damage to MBS's global reputation by Khashoggi's murder (Pew Research Center, January 29, 2020).

Britain's Prime Minister Boris Johnson

"After exhaustive tests, so it has proved. That vaccine is safe and works extremely well, and now, only six months later, it is being made in multiple places from India to the US, as well as Britain, and it is being used around the world" (Johnson, March 16, 2021).

In early January 2021, the UK government announced that the National Health Service would give the first people the AstraZeneca jab (Department of Health and Social Care, January 7, 2021). A month later, Johnson released a statement on how the "Oxford vaccine shows why we and the world need Britain to be global" (Johnson, March 16, 2021). In it, Johnson emphasizes the vaccine's association with Oxford throughout, focusing on the vaccine's link to Britain while also adding that "it is being made in multiple places from India to the US, as well as Britain, and it is being used around the world" (ibid.). This latter aspect returns to Johnson's view of Brexit not meaning Trump's isolationism but the freedom for Britain to become global on its own terms (Swaine). Indeed, some of Johnson's remarks seem to be balancing (vaccine) nationalism and Political Nationalism with Political Cosmopolitanism. On the one hand, not only is the vaccine produced "around the world" but "the [UK] taxpayer has spent hundreds of millions of pounds to put jabs in the arms of other populations" (ibid.). On the other hand, Johnson boasts that the reasons for sharing the AstraZeneca vaccine are "blindingly obvious—the principle of enlightened self-interest" (ibid.).

Given the fact that Brexit has been associated with isolationism and that the primary definition of vaccine nationalism is the hoarding of vaccines for a state's own citizens, it is interesting that Johnson outlines such British self-interest as avoiding

> isolated national immunity. We need the whole world to be protected. We need the whole world to have the confidence to open up for trade and travel and holidays and business, all the things that drive jobs and improve our lives at home. The objective of Global Britain is not to swagger or strike attitudes on the world stage. It is to use the full spectrum of our abilities to engage with and help the rest of the world. That is how we serve the British interest, and I mean the economic interest of people up and down the country. And as the vaccine programme begins to inspire a new global hope, we want to use this moment to heal, both literally and figuratively (ibid.)

Again, Johnson's emphasis on Global Britain is a reminder that he distinguishes Brexit from Trump's exclusionary nationalism (Swaine). Further, it seems that

Johnson's emphasis on the AstraZeneca vaccine being British feeds into his image of Global Britain and global cooperation in vaccine uptake (Johnson, March 16, 2021). Hence, Johnson's preparatory condition or context is British pride in the AstraZeneca or Oxford vaccine but a recognition that global cooperation is needed (ibid.). Within such a context, Johnson's discourse fits the secondary rather than primary definition of vaccine nationalism: "attaching a national 'character' to vaccines, often expressed through nationalist metaphors of winning and achievement" (Douglas et al., p. 3). British achievement is certainly present across the speech. Labeling AstraZeneca as the "Oxford vaccine" and pointing to a "[s]uccessful UK vaccination programme" certainly implies winning and achievement, despite Johnson's insistence that the "objective of Global Britain is not to swagger" (Johnson, March 16, 2021).

However, Johnson's claim that the AstraZeneca vaccine should not be hoarded but available "for the whole world to be protected" tilts his speech toward Political Cosmopolitanism (Peter) and international legitimacy (Ahram, Lust, p. 8). It would seem that AstraZeneca has donated vaccine doses to lower income states, with the company claiming donations of up to two billion doses by 2021 (AstraZeneca, November 16, 2021). While such donations do not account for Britain's tensions with Europe regarding vaccine supply, as discussed in Chapter 2, such donations echo China's own vaccine diplomacy and a tilt toward international legitimacy, perhaps as Britain attempts to push its desired Global Britain image post-Brexit rather than one of isolationism (Swaine).

Indeed, as Saudi Arabia connected its international legitimacy to the G20, Johnson connects UK legitimacy to Britain's "G7 presidency" and efforts "to foster ideas for a new world treaty on pandemic preparedness so that the next time humanity avoids the [disorder and panicky] squabbling that has disfigured the last 12 months" (Johnson, March 16, 2021). It would seem that China, Saudi Arabia, and Britain all believe in global cooperation to address future pandemics, and by advocating a new world treaty to avoid fragmented responses, it seems Johnson is attacking vaccine nationalism by bringing up the very fragmentation that is associated with such nationalism and the subsequent "every state for itself" attitude it fostered during Covid (Crow, Milne, May 14, 2020). Johnson's indirect essential condition or instruction thus seems to be that states should accept a world treaty on pandemic preparedness (Johnson, March 16, 2021). The international pandemic treaty advocated by the WHO and attempts to ensure its formal creation and acceptance by states will be further discussed in Chapter 6.

Johnson's focus on such a treaty is similar to Xi's international forum on vaccine cooperation and seems to also be a way of reaching out to other nations. Indeed, two weeks after his statement on the Oxford vaccine, Johnson published a joint statement with other world leaders promoting said treaty (Johnson, March 30, 2021). The statement was authored by world leaders from over twenty countries, including France, Germany, Portugal, Kenya, Chile, South Africa, South Korea, and Tunisia (but not Saudi Arabia, China, or the United States), indicating that Johnson's essential condition brought together different states in agreement (ibid.).

Interestingly enough, as the WHO also garnered support for their International Treaty for Pandemic Prevention, Preparedness, and Response in December 2022, such a proposal was attacked by commentators in the United States "as an attempt by a biased World Health Organization to impose endless lockdowns and curtail Americans' rights" under a treaty that "could constrain American national sovereignty" (Imparato, Nagar, January 20, 2023). Perhaps Trump's nationalism has remained a concern for global health governance, as the WHO treaty advocates, inter alia, "clauses on ensuring an equitable global distribution of vaccines" (ibid.).

America's President Trump

> We're here to discuss a monumental national achievement. From the instant the coronavirus invaded our shores, we raced into action to develop a safe and effective vaccine at breakneck speed. It would normally take five years, six years, seven years, or even more. In order to achieve this goal, we harnessed the full power of government, the genius of American scientists, and the might of American industry to save millions and millions of lives all over the world. We're just days away from authorization from the FDA, and we're pushing them hard, at which point we will immediately begin mass distribution. (Trump, December 8, 2020)

Trump's speech to announce the efficacy of Pfizer and Moderna begins with an emphasis on American exceptionalism and associating "the genius of American scientists and the might of American industry" with the "gold standard vaccine," which, thanks to US vaccine procurement and development agreement Operation Warp Speed, "has been done in less than nine months" (ibid.). Just as Trump praised his administration's economic policies leading up to Covid, he reminded listeners that "my administration provided a total of $14 billion to accelerate vaccine development and to manufacture all of the top candidates in advance—long in advance" and it is because of Trump's "unprecedented investment" that "both Pfizer and Moderna have announced that their vaccines are approximately 95 percent effective" (ibid.).

It would seem that Trump is taking credit for the Pfizer vaccine's development as an American-funded project, conforming to the secondary definition of vaccine nationalism as "nationalist metaphors of winning and achievement" (Douglas et al., p. 3).

As discussed in Chapter 2, the primary definition of vaccine nationalism is "national control and ownership of vaccines" (ibid.) and a "my country first" approach to vaccine stockpiling and distribution (Bollyky, Bown, pp. 96-7). By associating vaccine efficacy with American investment and initiative, Trump's speech indirectly conforms to the primary definition of vaccine nationalism as well. However, the association with vaccine ownership and priority for national citizens is made more direct when Trump insists that "[e]very American who wants the vaccine will be able to get one" (ibid.), connecting more with the "my country first" definition of vaccine nationalism discussed by Bollyky and Bown (pp. 96-7). At the same time, Trump outlines that "the elderly and patients with underlying conditions, as well as healthcare workers and first responders," should be prioritized (ibid.). Trump's preparatory condition thus emphasizes vaccine efficacy as an American achievement under his administration, yet his essential condition or instruction is again linked to the constraints of executive power. He can only "hope [state] governors make wise decisions—who will decide where the vaccines go in their state and who will get them first," as "ultimate decision rests with the governors of the various states," and Trump can only "urge the governors to put America's seniors first, and also, I think those who work with seniors. And doctors, nurses, first responders, et cetera" (ibid.).

While Johnson discusses how the Oxford vaccine is part of a Global Britain and manufactured "in multiple places from India to the US, as well as Britain" (Johnson, March 16, 2021), Trump emphasizes how vaccine distribution is being fulfilled by "FedEx, UPS, and McKesson, those really, really great American companies" (ibid.). Throughout the speech, the emphasis is on American ownership and control (ibid.), feeding into vaccine nationalism and Political Nationalism rather than Political Cosmopolitanism and international legitimacy (Peter). While Trump does mention "working very closely with other nations also to get the vaccines out to other nations," he immediately after emphasizes "that the United States government prioritizes the getting out of the vaccine to American citizens before sending it out to other nations" (ibid.), connecting very directly with the primary definition of vaccine nationalism (Bollyky, Bown, pp. 96-7).

In typical Trump fashion, while leaning into vaccine nationalism, Trump once again attacks globalization. "And you look at other countries; they're having tremendous difficulties in Europe—tremendous. Beyond—relatively beyond what we're having," again drawing on his exclusionary nationalism and insisting "[t]hey're having [difficulties] all over the world" (Trump, December 8, 2020). As in his speech addressing the spread of Covid in the United States, Trump refers to "this horrible scourge" as "the 'China virus', because that's where it came from" (ibid.). Again, Trump draws on exclusionary nationalism and attacks globalization, implying that "this horrible scourge" is a result of globalization that would be avoided by isolationism (Regilme, p. 162).

There is an interesting moment where Trump seems to advocate global cooperation, which would imply international legitimacy and Political Cosmopolitanism. "The virus," he explains, "has really been looked at and studied all over the world, and our scientists, our industrial and economic mobilization has been like nobody else in the world could have done. And it's very important that we share that with others and other nations" (ibid.). Trump also claims, "we're making ventilators" and "sending them to countries all over the world" (ibid.). While these statements may imply global cooperation, it is paired once again with American exceptionalism and exclusionary nationalism, as any sharing of information will come from American scientists who are "like nobody else in the world" and within the context of competitive nationalism that demonizes China and boasts that American accomplishments during Covid have resulted in "more [innovative testing] than all the European Union combined" (ibid.).

With regard to ventilator donations, although Trump did spend "$200 million to send more than 8,700 ventilators to countries around the world," there was "no clear criteria for determining who should get them and no way to keep track of where many ended up" (Bernstein, Torbati, January 29, 2021). In addition, Trump's claims of America having tested more than other nations combined have been debunked as false by media outlets (Luthra, May 1, 2020).

However, as with Trump's speech in March 2020 when Covid attacked the United States, truth is not as important as asserting a nationalism that helped elect Donald Trump by insisting that "[w]e are the most exceptional nation in the history of the world" (ibid.) and repeatedly promoting American exceptionalism (Bonikowski, 2019, p. 110). Another claim that again asserts such exceptionalism and vaccine nationalism is Trump's succeeding statement that "American companies were the first to produce a verifiably safe and effective vaccine" (Trump, December 8, 2020). It is true that the vaccine by American company Pfizer was one of the first to receive approval anywhere in the West (Cyranoski, Ledford, Van Noorden, December 3, 2020). However, the Pfizer vaccine itself was created by Pfizer partner BioNTech and BioNTech's founders, Dr. Uğur Şahin and Dr. Özlem Türeci, a husband-and-wife team of Turkish-German origin, leading *Forbes* magazine to pen the headline "Trump Takes Credit For Vaccine Created By Others" days before Trump announced the Pfizer and Moderna efficacy rating (Anderson, December 1, 2020).

Ultimately, Trump's speech praising Operation Warp Speed and the efficacy of vaccines maintains the themes of his speech when Covid spread to America, asserting an anti-globalist nationalism that asserts vaccine nationalism and Political Nationalism. While there are some mentions of global cooperation and helping other states, such promises are buried under Trump's emphasis on American exceptionalism and maintaining his populist platform with sweeping statements rather than facts. Out of all the analyzed case studies, Trump's America has the strongest turn to vaccine nationalism and Political Nationalism rather than vaccine diplomacy, international legitimacy, or Political Cosmopolitanism.

International Cooperation against Pandemics

An overview of speeches given by democratic and nondemocratic regimes in response to the development of Covid vaccines reveals an overall tilt toward international legitimacy and Political Cosmopolitanism through advocating global cooperation to fight future pandemics and ensure equal vaccine access. For China, such an emphasis on international legitimacy and Political Cosmopolitanism echoes Beijing's vaccine diplomacy and opposition to vaccine nationalism and politicizing the virus as Xi Jinping seeks to use soft power to rehabilitate China's image. The rehabilitation of a state's global image through international legitimacy and medical or Covid diplomacy is also echoed by Saudi Arabia's MBS as he advocates global governance through the G20 to ensure international cooperation regarding future pandemic preparedness. Interestingly, for Brexit Britain, there seems to be a balance between vaccine nationalism through pride in the Oxford vaccine and an emphasis on global cooperation and the need for a treaty on pandemic preparedness. In addition, in his statement, Boris Johnson mentions the need for a world treaty for pandemic preparedness, and in the same month that he praised the Oxford or AstraZeneca vaccine, Johnson released a joint statement with various states again calling for a global treaty to address pandemics. Hence, these case studies seem to show greater emphasis on vaccine diplomacy or international legitimacy and Political Cosmopolitanism.

The exception to this pattern is Trump, who continues to promote American exceptionalism, anti-globalization, and a "my country first" definition of vaccine nationalism that minimizes the consideration of helping others. When help is mentioned, it is again framed within the context of American exceptionalism and exclusionary nationalism that helped Trump win his first term in the White House.

After analyzing how the aforementioned speeches consider vaccine nationalism or vaccine diplomacy and the need for global cooperation and international legitimacy, Chapter 6 will discuss the WHO-backed international pandemic treaty, its objectives, and the obstacles to its fulfillment by member states.

Chapter 6

WILL THERE BE AN INTERNATIONAL PANDEMIC TREATY?

In Chapter 5, we discussed the discourse of leaderships across China, Saudi Arabia, the UK, and the United States regarding the release and distribution of Covid vaccines. We found that most of the case studies publicly supported international legitimacy and vaccine or medical diplomacy, whether through making vaccines a global good (China's Xi Jinping), investing in Covid aid packages (Saudi Arabia's MBS), or ensuring vaccine manufacturing included the cooperation of diverse states (the UK's Boris Johnson). Out of our four case studies, the UK's Boris Johnson called for an international treaty for pandemic preparedness and later published a joint statement with several other state leaders advocating the very same. In Chapter 6, we examine further calls for a formal international pandemic treaty, its proposed objectives, and why the treaty faces obstacles that continue to highlight the tension between vaccine nationalism and vaccine diplomacy, the involvement and control of pharmaceutical companies, and the ongoing issues of health inequity and wealth inequality.

In November 2020, when Covid had been globally active for a year, European Council President Charles Michel proposed what would be the first global treaty to address pandemic preparation and coordination in response to emerging viral threats (European Council, April 24, 2024). In December 2021, a special session of the World Health Assembly agreed to the negotiation and drafting of a global pandemic treaty, and by March 2022, the Council of the European Union (EU) greenlit negotiations (ibid.). However, the May 2024 deadline for an agreed draft was missed by key WHO member states, despite health experts warning that another pandemic is "absolutely inevitable." Kat Lay, the Guardian's global health correspondent, explains that core disagreements remain "on finance; how much product pharmaceutical companies should be required to set aside for those countries most in need; intellectual property rights and sanctions" in addition to negotiations being targeted by widespread misinformation campaigns that echo similar campaigns that targeted Covid vaccines, "with false claims that the treaty represents a power grab by the World Health Organization, giving them the ability to impose lockdowns on countries" (May 29, 2024).

The aforementioned issues can return us to discussions of vaccine nationalism seen during Covid and during previous pandemics. However, before we examine the pandemic treaty's obstacles, let us outline its key objectives. An international pandemic treaty should address:

- "early detection and prevention of pandemics
- resilience to future pandemics
- response to any future pandemics, in particular by ensuring universal and equitable access to medical solutions, such as vaccines, medicines and diagnostics
- a stronger international health framework with the WHO as the coordinating authority on global matters
- the 'One Health' approach, connecting the health of humans, animals and our planet." (European Council, January 11, 2024)

These objectives can be united through a global treaty specifically, as such an approach should allow the WHO and member states (effectively the global community) to use a formal treaty to enhance global health cooperation. A treaty would formalize "higher, sustained and long-term political engagement at the level of world leaders of states or governments; define clear processes and tasks; enhance long-term public and private-sector support at all levels; [and] foster integration of health matters across all relevant policy areas" (ibid.). Within these objectives, we can obviously see an emphasis on international cooperation and Peter's Political Cosmopolitanism, but also the notion that health should be a public good. This notion connects with China's vaccine diplomacy on a larger scale, in which China argued during Covid that vaccines should be regarded as a public good to stem the pandemic, though it should be reiterated that China emphasized this stance within the context of promoting its own vaccines as safe and efficacious (Liu, Yan, Yang, 2024, p. 1).

There remain a variety of challenges in implementing a global pandemic treaty, ranging from the role of pharmaceutical companies to the competitive views of states. Returning to the theme of Peter's Political Nationalism versus Political Cosmopolitanism, a 2024 study by Ahmed Al-Jedal et al. outlined that there remain six key challenges to implementing a functioning global pandemic treaty, including:

- "global cooperation and political will
- equity in access to resources and treatments
- substantial financing
- compliance and enforcement mechanisms
- sovereignty concerns
- data sharing and transparency." (2024, p. 580)

These challenges can certainly return us to the tension between global governance and statism. Indeed, a sense of competing commitments remains across higher income countries and corporate stakeholders in any such treaty.

On the one hand, "[e]very member of the European Union has endorsed the pandemic treaty, which is also backed by the African Union, Asian, and South American governments." On the other hand,

> despite the large number of governments and agencies involved in the negotiations, it should be noted that several stakeholders advocating for the pandemic treaty negotiations, especially high-income countries (HICs) stockpiled vaccines and opposed an intellectual property (IP) waiver initiative introduced by India and South Africa in 2020 during the Covid-19 pandemic, a stance they maintained for two years. Numerous governments veered away from the WHO guidelines to contain Covid-19 spread, discarded the rhetoric of global unity, and restricted the export of medical resources.

This zero-sum approach to the treaty no doubt directly influenced the ineffectual zero draft, presenting a document criticized "for not including clear incentives and disincentives for political leaders, prompting them to alter their behavior in future outbreaks" (ibid., p. 582).

The ostensible concern for self-interest is further evident in the need for financing from states to ensure a successful treaty and pandemic preparedness. As previously discussed in Chapter 3, private sector investment, especially from the pharmaceutical industry, may be profit-oriented and limited. In addition, while such financing should be government-led, the long-term commitment the treaty would require of WHO member states appears to have clashed with their fears of "competing global priorities and economic uncertainties" (ibid.). It would seem that the requirement for all states to cooperate across financing, equitable viral and vaccine access, and data sharing is being blocked by statism and the related reluctance of corporate actors such as big pharma to share technology and research findings (ibid., p. 583).

It would thus appear that the ultimate threat to a successful international pandemic treaty is Political Nationalism and a competitive approach to international relations. Sadly, this reality was foreshadowed as early as 2005, as the SARS outbreak saw an attempt to "implement the International Health Regulations (IHR), a legally binding instrument of international law developed by the World Health Organization (WHO) as a neutral agency aiming to help the international community prevent and respond to acute public health risks" (ibid., p. 581). Similar to the current proposed international pandemic treaty, the IHR, which became active in 2007, involved:

- "core capacities, including surveillance and reporting systems, laboratory capabilities, and public health infrastructure
- notification and verification
- coordination and collaboration
- travel and trade measures
- monitoring and evaluation." (ibid.)

However, while the IHR system was designed to address global health unity and pandemic preparation, when put to the test by Covid, it saw key failures that would be echoed by ongoing debate regarding an international pandemic treaty in response to Covid. In particular (and perhaps unsurprisingly), critics who have evaluated the performance of IHR during Covid have identified a lack of compliance with IHR, poor cooperation between states, and funding as key gaps that became apparent during Covid (Kim et al., 2021, pp. 4, 5, 6). "Lack of compliance of State Parties with certain obligations under the IHR, particularly on preparedness, contributed to the Covid-19 pandemic becoming a protracted global health emergency," explains a 2021 study (ibid., p. 4).

> In the IHR each country was equipped with the ability to respond to the public health crisis, and the competency evaluation [for IHR implementation per country] was conducted annually. However, the average implementation rate of 174 countries submitted for the 2020 IHR implementation evaluation was only about 70 percent. Moreover, in the case of G20 countries, only 86 percent (ibid., p. 4)

Linked to the lack of implementation appears to be both state complacency in following IHR regulations and also "a lack of legal leadership in the face of an international health crisis" that has seen global bodies unable to clearly direct how IHR should be implemented (ibid., p. 5).

Returning to the issue of cooperation (or lack thereof), this includes not only between states but also domestically. The IHR's emphasis on notification and verification of an emerging disease saw, in reality, many countries unable to provide timely and open data on Covid due to fragmented domestic responses. The few "successfully managed countries sought scientific guidelines for new pathogens, cooperated with community health workers and community leaders, and involved marginalized people in decision-making. However, in countries that delay scientific knowledge, information, and notification" eventual responses to Covid were haphazard and confusing for citizens and also reflected a poor response in terms of those states cooperating with global institutes (ibid., p. 6). The involvement of marginalized people in decision-making for states successful in managing the pandemic versus their exclusion for states that saw haphazard responses returns us to the discussion in Chapters 1 and 2 that social and resistance movements can form in response to state exclusion of marginalized communities during a crisis but also that marginalized communities during Covid often saw disproportionately higher infection rates and medical neglect, and hence their inclusion in decision-making is essential for a successful pandemic response.

Finally, as with unsuccessful negotiations for an international pandemic treaty, funding has also been an issue for the IHR. For any legal framework addressing pandemics to be effective, there must be "predictable and sustainable financing at both national and international levels" (ibid.). In part, such an approach seeks to address the risk of inequality in global health governance and "ensure that poor countries could respond early" by stipulating that wealthier nations can plug the funding gap. The issue of funding continues to be an obstacle cited by states but also by pharmaceutical companies that are expected to produce vaccines for global distribution. Perhaps herein lies the problem: while international treaties and health regulation frameworks view the world as a universal community that should thus emphasize global health and universal and equitable human rights, the states and corporate actors that populate the international system remain driven by Political Nationalism or the notion that the state is the highest political authority on the (competitive) world stage, and from a realist perspective, that includes prioritizing profit for corporate actors that see a surge in influence during pandemics if they are in the health sector.

Indeed, global health inequality remains a core issue and impediment to global health governance and any successful international health regulation or international pandemic agreement. Scholars Anna Holzscheiter and Ilona Kickbusch argue that the inability of states to successfully negotiate a global pandemic treaty reveals a geopolitical reality of "the two big political divides in global health. The first is the scandalous health inequity that the global south is no longer willing to accept. The second is the intense state competition between big powers" (2021, p. 1). Expanding on this argument that geopolitics undermined a united response to Covid, it seems that the pandemic "came at a time when geopolitical rivalry and mistrust had picked up speed and resulted in a further weakening of support for the multilateral system," especially as "conflicts between China and the US became more pronounced, [which] not only affected and initially weakened the World Health Organization, but also made agreements at the G7 and G20 near impossible, rather than bringing competing countries together in a multilateral context. It also obstructed progress to achieve vaccine equity" (ibid.).

This competitive worldview is intensified by a shift in geopolitical power dynamics that directly clashes with the need for open data sharing, technological and knowledge sharing, and setting aside corporate interests. "Geopolitics is [now] about establishing a new technological order," explain Holzscheiter and Kickbusch,

> in which claims to power are inseparable from technology, science, ownership of data, and authority in the digital world—bringing with them new dimensions of inequality. Pandemic response is not only about health security and crisis governance, but also a field marked by innovation, technology, and multiple corporate interests, for which no international rules exist. Global health, with its strong base in science, technology, and data, is now part of a reassessment of how world politics should be organised, according to which principles and values it should proceed, which actors should be involved, and which hierarchy of institutions should apply. (ibid.)

It would seem that the restructuring of geopolitical governance across the globe is enhancing Political Nationalism, state rivalries, and conflict that are directly obstructing health equity. "For the global south to accept a binding [pandemic] treaty, it would need to address the concerns of low and middle income countries, such as equity and human rights, the sharing of knowledge, technology and innovation, and the financing of global public goods for health," elements that are precisely what the Global North-South divide is blocking from being achieved in an international system in which global health is at the mercy of Political Nationalism and a new geopolitical technological order in partial response to the pandemic (ibid.).

Returning to Porta's discussion of pandemics as emergency junctures, it is interesting to note that Porta's discussion of a global health crisis straining the capacity of existing institutes can certainly connect with Holzscheiter and Kickbusch's belief that the pandemic has invited a geopolitical response that is emphasizing statism over global governance. Porta argues that pandemics can provoke governments to centralize decision-making and emphasize economic and political solutions over liberty for citizens (pp. 5, 8, 6). This response on a national scale also impacts the international system, as it means governments prioritize a centralized national response over a coordinated international response (Holzscheiter, Kickbusch, p. 2). In addition, just as Porta discusses that governments may curb citizen rights and fail to acknowledge how a pandemic may impact domestic wealth inequality, the geopolitical backlash to the pandemic has seen a rise in state rivalries that exacerbates global wealth inequality and risks the vaccine hoarding we have seen practiced by wealthier states extending to increasing monopoly over technology, data, science, and digital ownership that is creating further inequality between states in the international system, which will undermine global health and more (ibid., p. 1).

To address the challenges of poor cooperation, health inequity, and sustainable financing, it will be necessary for all actors to agree to a treaty that clearly outlines the responsibilities during and before a pandemic for global actors, state actors, and corporate actors (Kim et al., p. 5). In addition, as previously discussed, any treaty must include a system of incentives and disincentives to prompt political leaders to respect the treaty and follow vaccine and health equity, which will also require government intervention in the development of vaccines and related technologies, ensuring that pharmaceutical companies that receive public funding do so on the condition that they ensure vaccine access that balances profit with universal health and agree to technology transfers that can be activated to address the increased need for vaccines during a pandemic (Al-Jedal et al., p. 582).

Further, to address sustainable financing, one suggestion from critics has been for states to create pandemic bonds. This approach allows for bonds to be purchased by investors as any other government-backed bond program. However, "the capital raised is earmarked for responding to pandemic outbreaks" and

> the repayment of their capital investment at maturity depends on whether a pandemic occurs. If there is no pandemic outbreak, then investors receive their initial investment on the maturity date. However, in the event of a pandemic, investors lose part or all their capital. That is otherwise used to finance the response to the outbreak in the eligible countries. (Shinh, March 2, 2021)

This approach predates the Covid pandemic, being launched by the World Bank in 2017 to "provide support to the Pandemic Emergency Financing Facility (PEF)" launched by the World Bank in 2016 "to help fund the fight against cross-border, large-scale outbreaks in the world's poorest countries" (ibid.).

However, it would appear that the World Bank's faith in pandemic bonds was shaken after the poor global response to Covid, which led to substantial financial losses by bond investors, and criticism over strict conditions governing payout of the bonds to pandemic-affected countries, including "that a certain number of deaths must have been officially recorded," prompting some critics to argue that the bonds can only address a pandemic rather than be used to prevent it and that the number of deaths becomes the key factor in receiving financial relief (Bris, Cantale, March 2020).

In addition to pandemic bonds, the World Bank also established a Pandemic Fund that saw a substantial increase in donations during Covid, exceeding $1.2 billion (Al-Jedal et al., p. 582). As of 2025, this amount has increased to almost $2 billion, with top donors including the United States, the EU, and Germany (World Bank Group, 2025). With the Fund devoted to pandemic prevention, preparedness, and response, it would seem that states have at least considered the impact of Covid and heeded the advice of health experts who have recommended increasing contributions (ibid., Al-Jedal et al., p. 583). Indeed, the Fund appears to have seen more success than pandemic bonds, with recent activity including the Pandemic Fund's ability to address the spread of mpox (formerly monkeypox) in 2024. Up to ten African Union member states benefitted from the $129 million package that the Africa Centres for Disease Control and Prevention (Africa CDC) confirmed "will bolster national and regional capacities in vital areas like disease surveillance, laboratory diagnostics, and networks, and workforce development. These efforts will be instrumental in implementing the Africa CDC-WHO Mpox Continental Preparedness and Response Plan for Africa, designed to strengthen health security across Africa while addressing the ongoing mpox outbreak" (September 21, 2024).

The Pandemic Fund's ability to quickly address mpox is a reminder that all pandemic prevention, preparedness, and response require sustainable financing in conjunction with multilateral cooperation that extends beyond state borders. In the case of African Union members addressing mpox, Pandemic Fund finances are combined with "a unified approach—ONE Team, ONE Plan, One Budget and ONE framework—aiming to improve surveillance, diagnostics, and workforce capacity while strengthening public health systems and engaging communities for a more effective and harmonized response across Africa" (ibid.).

The emphasis on sustainable funding to tackle and preempt pandemics returns us to the emphasis on economic performance as a source of legitimacy for global governance bodies and states during a pandemic, reminding us that a global health crisis can provoke political and economic challenges that may overshadow individual liberties (Porta, pp. 5, 8, 6). However, in addition to the tug-of-war between Political Nationalism and Political Cosmopolitanism, between every state for itself and calls for world cooperation, there is a further trend post-Covid regarding pandemic cooperation, which is the possibility of regional cooperation rather than global cooperation.

Already in 2020, as Covid spread, experts considered whether Covid would suspend globalization, possibly in favor of regionalization. In many cases, such predictions focused on trade and the economy. Peter Buckley and Peter Enderwick considered in 2020 that Covid had highlighted the risks and weaknesses of globalization and "that there is an opportunity to address some of the weaknesses of globalization through a more regionally-based world economy offering a better balance between national and international interests" (2020, p. 99). Taking this argument further is the notion that even before "the disruption caused by the pandemic, there were indications that the current globalization wave may have reached its peak" as countries like the United States prioritized competitive military superiority over global economic integration and cooperation, meaning that "institutions designed to bolster cross-border exchanges [and security] have been weakened through ongoing criticism, obstructions and the withholding of funding" (ibid., pp. 100–1).

We certainly saw an increase in statism during the pandemic, but also a trend of some states rejecting globalization more than others. As previously discussed, the United States under Trump attacked globalization as a threat to the US economy, while China seemed more willing to embrace globalization. The diverse response of states to Covid, such as embracing fully being part of the international community or considering (partial) withdrawal from it, may indicate a wider trend pushing "the world economy towards a more regionally-focused composition. This implies selective rather than wholesale de-globalization" that will see regional economies rather than a world economy (ibid., p. 103). Building on such economic regionalization is the notion that Covid will also influence a regional approach to future pandemics. During Covid, there were regional responses in Africa, Asia, and the Gulf to address diverse issues that Covid provoked, such as supply chain disruption, food security, and manufacturing. In response to the pandemic, the African Development Bank launched a $10 billion aid package to boost pandemic response and coordination for countries in the African Development Fund. Adding to this response, the Asian Development Bank provided members with a tripled assistance package of £20 billion (Oxford Business Group, May 28, 2020). When African states faced medicine shortages during the pandemic, in some cases due to pharmaceutical companies prioritizing orders from Western states, the African Union's CDC founded "a digital platform that pools orders from across the continent" and "coordinates efforts with Chinese counterparts to ensure an efficient medical equipment supply chain, along with negotiating set prices with Chinese suppliers" (ibid.).

Building on this regional approach, the recent agreement on an African Continental Free Trade Area (AfCFTA) emphasizes economic integration, envisioning

> the foundations for a single market between 54 states. This initiative foresees a significant seven percent increase in African GDP, equivalent to $450 billion,

and a thirty-four percent expansion of intra-African trade by 2045, with a potential of eighty-one percent if non-tariff barriers are lifted. Moreover, it aims to reduce poverty, lifting 30 million people out of extreme precariousness while improving the incomes of 68 million others. (Hzaine, January 15, 2025)

Regional economic growth under the AfCFTA will be driven by tariff elimination, integrated regional supply chains, and "the development of digital trade and cross-border services" in key areas including tourism, agriculture, communications, and financial services (ibid.).

The Gulf Cooperation Council, representing the Middle Eastern states of Qatar, Saudi Arabia, Bahrain, Oman, Kuwait, and the United Arab Emirates, responded to Covid by establishing a regional food supply network and, for some states, fortifying their already advanced digital capacities to enable work and study from home (Oxford Business Group). In addition, Covid seemed to accelerate diversification plans for Gulf States and prompted calls for regionwide coordination of economic diversification, especially in the further development of the knowledge and digital economies, which became strong focal points during Covid (Al Suwaidi, Due-Gundersen, 2024, p. 13).

The apparent turn to regionalization rather than globalization can be further seen in how some states are cooperating to address the fear of future health crises. In August 2024, a few months after WHO members failed to agree on a global pandemic treaty, Saudi Arabia and Morocco signed a memorandum of understanding (MoU) to strengthen cooperation in pandemic preparedness and the cross-regional health sector (Middle East Monitor, August 27, 2024). The MoU, signed by representatives from each respective country's health ministries, seeks to establish knowledge exchange and to develop "health services, therapeutic and preventive medicine, digital health and pandemic management" and appeared to be a regional response to the mpox epidemic that had spread across parts of Africa and Asia (ibid.).

As of writing, there are no further MoUs between other Arab states addressing pandemic preparation. Nonetheless, the overview of regional responses during Covid and in preparation for future pandemics feeds into calls during 2020 for greater regional cooperation to slow the spread of Covid and the use of regional fiscal packages to coordinate absorbing the financial shock of Covid across borders (Kalinina, May 1, 2020).

While regional cooperation may be regarded as an essential buttress to global governance, it would seem that, at least for now, the pandemic treaty remains in limbo. Just as during Covid, a wealth divide remains between the Global South and North, between pharmaceutical companies and poorer nations. Ultimately, wealthier states and corporate actors are not willing to share resources, prompting poorer nations to assert the need for clear stipulations over vaccine distribution, production, and related technology transfer—the very elements that force them to assert viral sovereignty and that capitalist actors refuse to give up.

In May 2025, world leaders finally seemed to agree on a global pandemic treaty. WHO Director Tedros Adhanom Ghebreyesus called it "a victory for public health, science, and multilateral action" (Lay, May 20, 2025). However, the agreement seemed to have been pushed through by delaying key areas of contention for later talks. Panel cochair and former New Zealand Prime Minister Helen Clark noted that "gaps remain in finance, equitable access to medical countermeasures and in understanding and evolving risks. Don't wait to get that started. Dangerous pathogens are looming, and they certainly will not wait" (ibid.). Despite such urgency, the United States was conspicuously absent and sent a recorded video message by Trump's US Health Secretary Robert F. Kennedy Jr. criticizing the new treaty. According to Kennedy, the treaty would "lock in all the dysfunctions of the WHO pandemic response" and the United States would maintain its withdrawal of WHO funding (ibid.). For now, the success of the new treaty remains to be seen.

Chapter 7

CONCLUSION

This book has analyzed public discourse from specific leaderships in response to the Covid-19 pandemic. The case studies of China and Saudi Arabia were chosen as examples of nondemocratic regimes that have both been affected by the novel coronavirus (and in China's case saw some of the very first infections), while the UK and America were chosen as ostensibly democratic case studies under isolationist and exclusionary nationalist leadership that emphasized narrow identity politics to break away from a regional political union or augment a narrow American exceptionalism. Discourse analysis of speeches across these case studies was used to answer the questions: How did leaders of democracies and dictatorships address the threat of Covid? How were speeches used to present Covid as a reason for restrictive measures, and what political factors (especially nondemocratic) were drawn on to justify restrictions and lockdowns in speeches to nations and the world?

From Chapter 3, it is clear that all four case studies reveal leaderships that focused on centralizing authority, whether they were sons of a communist elite, successors to an absolute monarch, or elected to office. Chapter 4 revealed that, contrary to earlier discussion in Chapter 1 that Covid may be empowering authoritarianism, the analyzed democratic and nondemocratic case studies do not draw heavily on diverse nondemocratic factors to justify restrictive measures such as lockdown. However, across all four case studies, economic performance is used as a Beneficial Consequence in response to Covid. Yet this does not necessarily mean that there is an increase in authoritarian factors of rule in public discourse. China's Premier Li is forced to defend the economic performance of the Chinese Communist Party (CCP) in the face of Covid amid a context of Xi Jinping's limited ruling bargain and history of supporting the middle-class and rural population through "moderate prosperity" and poverty alleviation, though there are references to strong leadership and security from the virus as a Beneficial Consequence. Saudi Arabia's King Salman promises essential (economic) provisions in exchange for citizen cooperation, which is linked to religious language that acts as a reminder of his religious legitimacy, a Beneficial Consequence unique to Saudi Arabia as a case study.

Britain's Boris Johnson is the only leader across all four case studies to directly address lockdown. As discussed in Chapter 4, Johnson outlines the lockdown extensively, listing exceptions for citizens to venture outside while also issuing threats through the mention of police powers in enforcing the lockdown and related restrictions. Johnson's speech, however, contrasts the lockdown with some democratic references and the promise of an economic package, again recognizing the financial damage of the virus and that economic performance will be scrutinized. Johnson thus draws on a Beneficial Consequence that can be seen as implying a change to Britain's social contract, but democratic language acts as a reminder that any such shift is temporary, in response to Covid, and should not indicate a (permanent) turn toward nondemocratic political legitimacy. Finally, Trump's speech in response to Covid spreading across America is characterized by attacking globalization and augmenting the exclusionary nationalism that got him elected in the first place. There is thus some discussion of how Trump's isolationism may offer a Beneficial Consequence through security from the virus. Trump does mention economic relief, a further turn to Beneficial Consequences but the risk of nondemocratic language is constrained by his admission of needing congressional approval and being able only to issue guidelines to states rather than enforce any centralized restrictions.

All four case studies discuss security from the virus as a Beneficial Consequence, however, it is clear that economic security is the strongest Beneficial Consequence in each analyzed speech, and in the case of Boris Johnson and Donald Trump, promises made in their speeches did not necessarily match reality. Within such a context, it can be said that pandemics challenge dictatorships and democracies, with an immediate and longer-term focus on economic damage but, as seen in China in 2022, eventual hostility to the very restrictions that are sold as security from the virus.

Chapter 5 analyzed public discourse from the same leaderships to address how the eventual introduction of vaccines influenced nationalism or global cooperation by leaderships, especially in the form of vaccine nationalism and Peter's Political Nationalism and vaccine diplomacy, more linked to Ahram and Lust's international legitimacy and Peter's Political Cosmopolitanism. Within such a context, analysis found that China and Saudi Arabia tilted more toward international legitimacy and Political Cosmopolitanism. For China, there was a strong link to vaccine diplomacy and an emphasis on leading global cooperation against the virus through, for example, their international forum for vaccine cooperation. This tilt toward Political Cosmopolitanism and attack on vaccine nationalism seems to be part of China's strategy to rehabilitate its international image after being blamed for the spread of Covid but also fits into their ambition to lead and influence global governance institutions. Saudi Arabia's MBS also seemed to tilt toward Political Cosmopolitanism and Covid diplomacy with similar ambitions to influence global governance via the G20. This emphasis on international legitimacy comes in the wake of the assassination of exiled Saudi journalist Jamal Khashoggi, and, like China, MBS seems to be seeking a rehabilitated image.

As discussed in Chapter 2, vaccine nationalism can be defined as a "my country first" strategy for vaccine ownership, stockpiling, and hoarding, a behavior pointed out by Bollyky and Bown as linked to Western nations as Covid began (pp. 96–7). However, a secondary definition of vaccine nationalism includes "attaching a national 'character' to vaccines, often expressed through nationalist metaphors of winning and achievement" (Douglas et al., 2021, p. 3). This secondary definition of vaccine nationalism is certainly seen in Johnson's statement on the Oxford (AstraZeneca) vaccine, which is linked to the notion of Global Britain and "enlightened self-interest," but also within the context of helping other countries rather than celebrating isolated immunity.

In perhaps an unexpected turn, Johnson's vaccine nationalism thus expresses national pride in the Oxford vaccine but connects with international legitimacy and Political Cosmopolitanism, a reminder that Johnson did not publicly regard Brexit as isolationist but rather as a model for Britain to expand its global agreements. Such a context is certainly augmented by his declaration that states should consider a world treaty for future pandemic preparation, an element that connects Johnson to China's Xi Jinping and Saudi Arabia's MBS. Perhaps this parallel shows that vaccine nationalism can coexist with international legitimacy and Political Cosmopolitanism, though Johnson's article leaves out how AstraZeneca was caught in EU-UK tensions within the context of Brexit. However, the reality of negotiations for a global pandemic treaty has revealed obstacles such as wealth inequity, health and vaccine inequity, and continued disagreement over sustainable financing and vaccine technology transfer.

Finally, it would seem that America's Trump provides the strongest example of vaccine nationalism, tying back into Trump's America First platform of exclusionary nationalism and Political Nationalism. Although Trump does mention helping other states, such help is diluted by the persistent image of American exceptionalism and vaccines being prioritized for US citizens. In this regard, Trump's speech conforms strongly to Bollyky and Bown's understanding of vaccine nationalism. Yet, it is interesting that within the context of all four case studies, Trump stands alone in such nationalism and this stubbornness is reflected in American fears of global cooperation undermining US sovereignty under the World Health Organization (WHO) International Treaty for Pandemic Prevention, Preparedness, and Response. Trump's second term as president has also seen him ordering US withdrawal from WHO membership in early 2025, which would see the United States stop all financial contributions by 2026. This move was met by China reiterating that the WHO should be strengthened rather than weakened and critics speculating that China may seek to fill the financial and political gap caused by Trump's withdrawal (Lay, January 21, 2025).

In addition to the issue of economic performance being a key concern for states vis-à-vis political legitimacy, we have also explored how many social movements arose during Covid to effectively plug state gaps in welfare and provide socioeconomic needs for their communities. The most effective of such social movements in the UK seemed to be those that were already established prior to Covid, with a focus on plugging gaps in provisions for the vulnerable. This focus was also seen in the United States and, to an extent, in China when local authorities could not meet provisional needs. Indeed, in China, protests during Covid seemed to occur in response to local authorities' inability to provide steady provisions during lockdown. That said, this did not mean that there was no protest regarding social justice especially, which may have been a stronger focus than individual rights.

In China, netizens carefully circumvented government censorship by using the deceased whistleblower Dr. Li Wenliang's social media account as a memorial, sharing their own experiences of Covid and mourning his loss as a hero who was attacked unfairly for trying to warn of the dangers Covid posed. This activity seemed to eventually pressure the state into censuring the police officers who had accused Wenliang of disturbing the public order and also saw the state issue an apology to Wenliang's family while declaring him a martyr. China later saw protests in 2022 against further lockdown. In the United States, systemic racism and the murder of George Floyd saw the rise of Black Lives Matter and the connection of diverse (sometimes transnational) social movements that shared discrimination as a commonality and the need for social justice. In other words, there were social movements that went far beyond economic issues (including socioeconomic disparities widened by Covid) and welfare gaps to protest against systemic discrimination.

Ultimately, Porta's discussion of pandemics as emergency junctures that provoke political and fiscal crises has provided an interesting framework to explore resistance and social movements during health crises. Discussions of social movements during Covid, however, have shown that many such movements addressed economic welfare gaps rather than keeping the state in check with regard to political, civic, and social rights, though again issues such as systemic racism and Black Lives Matter came to the fore during Covid. However, Black Lives Matter as a movement did not emerge as a direct result of Covid and addressed preexisting issues of social justice and, linking with other social movements, discrimination against non-Whites that Covid widened.

It is worth mentioning that this book has been limited in scope and thus has not considered in detail events related to Covid beyond 2021. First, the timeframe of the book's analysis is linked to the key question of understanding the language of political persuasion and factors of democratic and nondemocratic rule related to lockdown and similar restrictions, which were most prominent before vaccines became available (e.g., mainly across 2020). Second, analysis of public discourse in Chapter 5 sought to understand vaccine nationalism versus vaccine diplomacy and how these two respective reactions to vaccine development during Covid were expressed by leaderships across China, Saudi Arabia, Britain, and the United States.

Again, this meant analysis of public discourse around the time of nascent vaccine availability, which was across 2020 and 2021 (Klobucista, December 5, 2022). For this reason, the book has not analyzed Covid variants that emerged at the end of or after 2021, such as Omicron (World Health Organization, November 25, 2022) or its subvariant XBB.1.5 (Siddiqui, January 14, 2023). Finally, this book has not considered in detail the protests across China in 2022 against its zero-Covid policy, as, again, these events are beyond the timeframe of this book and beyond the scope of examining speeches given in response to Covid and lockdowns and

7. Conclusion 173

public discourse regarding initial vaccination, both of which happened before 2022. Perhaps future research can examine the context of such protests, to what extent Xi Jinping or China's leadership addressed them in public discourse, and whether or not such discourse engaged in political persuasion and drew on nondemocratic factors of political legitimacy to justify continued restrictions, though in 2022 it seemed the CCP was pressured into lifting many of them. Another prospect for research is to examine how new variants affect political leaderships and to what extent these variants are politicized. As this book has discussed, pandemics and politics are inextricable, and future pandemics (and variants) will come to prove this true time and again (Heymann, Ross, and Wallace, February 23, 2022).

APPENDICES

Appendix 1: Full Text: Premier Li's Speech at the Third Session of the 13th NPC

Fellow Deputies

On behalf of the State Council, I will now report to you on the work of the government. I ask for your deliberation and approval. I also ask members of the National Committee of the Chinese People's Political Consultative Conference (CPPCC) for their comments.

The Covid-19 epidemic is the fastest spreading, most extensive, and most challenging public health emergency China has encountered since the founding of the People's Republic. Under the strong leadership of the Central Committee of the Communist Party of China with Comrade Xi Jinping at its core, and through the hard work and sacrifice of our entire nation, we have made major strategic achievements in our response to Covid-19. At present, the epidemic has not yet come to an end, while the tasks we face in promoting development are immense. We must redouble our efforts to minimize the losses resulting from the virus and fulfill the targets and tasks for economic and social development this year.'

I A review of our work in 2019 and the first few months of 2020

In pursuing development last year, China faced many difficulties and challenges. World economic growth was weak, international economic and trade frictions intensified, and downward pressure on the domestic economy grew. The Party Central Committee with Comrade Xi Jinping at its core rallied the Chinese people and led them in surmounting difficulties and accomplishing the year's main targets and tasks, thus laying the crucial foundation needed to reach the goal of building a moderately prosperous society in all respects.

The economy remained stable overall. Gross domestic product (GDP) reached 99.1 trillion yuan, representing a 6.1 percent increase over the previous year. Around 13.52 million new urban jobs were added, and the surveyed unemployment rate was below 5.3 percent. Consumer prices rose by 2.9 percent. A basic equilibrium was maintained in the balance of payments.

The economic structure continued to improve, and the development priorities of regions are better aligned. Total retail sales of consumer goods exceeded 40 trillion yuan, and consumption continued to serve as the main engine driving growth. Advanced manufacturing and modern services registered rapid growth. Grain output was kept above 650 million metric tons. For the first time, permanent urban residents exceeded 60 percent of the population; progress was made in implementing major development strategies for regions.

New growth drivers became stronger. A number of major innovative achievements were made in science and technology. Emerging industries continued to grow; upgrading in traditional industries accelerated. Business startups and innovation continued to surge nationwide, with an average net increase of over 10,000 businesses per day.

Major headway was made in reform and opening up. Supply-side structural reform was further advanced, and breakthroughs in reform were made in key areas. We cut taxes and fees by 2.36 trillion yuan, going well beyond our target of two trillion yuan, with manufacturing and micro and small businesses benefiting most.

The reform of government bodies was completed. Reforms to streamline administration and delegate power, improve regulation, and upgrade services were steadily advanced. The Science and Technology Innovation Board, or STAR Market, was established. The joint efforts to pursue the Belt and Road Initiative (BRI) yielded fresh results. Regulations for the implementation of the Foreign Investment Law were adopted, and the China (Shanghai) Pilot Free Trade Zone Lin'gang New Area was established. Foreign trade and investment remained stable.

Pivotal progress was achieved in the three critical battles. Decisive achievements were made in poverty alleviation—the rural poor population was reduced by 11.09 million, and the poverty headcount ratio fell to 0.6 percent. Pollution prevention and control efforts continued, with further reductions in the discharge of major pollutants and overall improvements in the environment. The financial sector remained stable.

Living standards continued to improve. Per capita disposable personal income topped 30,000 yuan. Basic old-age insurance, health insurance, and subsistence allowance standards were raised. Further progress was made in the construction of urban government-subsidized housing and the rebuilding of dilapidated houses in rural areas. The number of students in compulsory education receiving living allowances increased by almost 40 percent, and enrollments at vocational colleges grew by one million.

We celebrated the seventieth anniversary of the founding of the People's Republic of China. This occasion has inspired a strong sense of patriotism among all Chinese people, creating a powerful force that will bring great victories for socialism with Chinese characteristics in the new era.

We worked to improve Party conduct and build a clean government, started an initiative to raise awareness of the need to stay true to the Party's founding mission, and strictly observed the central Party leadership's eight-point decision on improving work conduct. We continued to address the practice of formalities for formalities' sake, bureaucracy, hedonism, and extravagance, and took steps to ensure that people working at the primary level are free from unnecessary restrictions and excessive burdens.

We achieved fruitful outcomes in pursuing China's major country diplomacy. We successfully hosted the second Belt and Road Forum for International Cooperation and other major diplomatic events.

President Xi Jinping and other Party and state leaders visited many countries and attended major international events, including the G20 Leaders Summit, the BRICS Leaders Meeting, the Summit of the Conference on Interaction and Confidence Building Measures in Asia, the Shanghai Cooperation Organization Summit, the East Asian leaders' meetings on cooperation, the China-EU Leaders' Meeting, and the China–Japan–ROK Leaders' Meeting.

We played an active role in the development and reform of the global governance system, and promoted the building of a human community with a shared future. We successfully pursued economic diplomacy and cultural and people-to-people exchanges. China made important contributions to the advancement of world peace and development.

Fellow Deputies

Since the coronavirus first emerged, the Party Central Committee has made its containment the top priority. General Secretary Xi Jinping, putting the health and safety of our people before everything else, has personally taken charge and planned our response.

Under the leadership of the Party Central Committee, the central leading group for Covid-19 response has made timely decisions and plans; the central guidance group has provided effective guidance and supervision; the State Council interdepartmental task force has coordinated the response efforts; all local authorities and all government departments have fulfilled their respective duties, and people from every walk of life have given their full support. Together, we have waged an all-out people's war against the virus.

Our medical workers have fought with courage. Our servicemen and women have shouldered heavy responsibilities. Our scientists and researchers have joined forces in order to find a cure. Our community workers, policemen and women, officials working at the primary level, media personnel, and volunteers have stood fast at their posts.

Our deliverymen and women, our sanitation workers, and all who make and transport emergency supplies have continued their work with dedication. Hundreds of millions of other workers outside of the spotlight have also made their own contributions.

In Wuhan City and Hubei Province the people have carried on with fortitude and resilience, while people from all sectors of society and our fellow compatriots in Hong Kong, Macao, and Taiwan and overseas have made generous donations, both monetary and in-kind.

Through all these efforts, we, all the sons and daughters of the Chinese nation, have stood together in the most trying of times and built a Great Wall of solidarity against the epidemic.

Responding to the central Party leadership's call to stay confident, come together in solidarity, adopt a science-based approach, and take targeted measures, we have carried out all our work in a solid and meticulous manner. We promptly adopted containment measures, treating Covid-19 as a Class A infectious disease and activating a Level One public health emergency response in all localities.

We have achieved a decisive victory in the battle to defend Hubei Province and its capital city Wuhan by firmly implementing strict control measures, rallying the support of the entire country, dispatching over 40,000 doctors and nurses, rapidly increasing the number of hospital beds, and ensuring the availability of medical supplies. We continuously refined diagnostic and treatment plans, incorporated traditional Chinese medicine into treatment, and spared no effort in the treatment of patients, thus maximizing the cure rate and minimizing the mortality rate.

We extended the Spring Festival holiday nationwide, postponed the spring semester, facilitated flexible resumption of work, and staggered commute times. We have carried out a society-wide prevention and control effort, ensured early detection, reporting, quarantine, and treatment of cases, firmly controlled sources of infection, and effectively curbed the spread of the virus.

Intensive efforts have been made to develop drugs, vaccines, and testing reagents. We expanded production of medical supplies by a large margin within a short time, ensured supply and price stability of daily necessities, and maintained smooth transportation on trunk lines, as well as stable supplies of coal, electricity, oil, and gas. In response to changing Covid-19 dynamics, we have adopted regular prevention and control measures in a timely manner.

In the face of the global spread of Covid-19, we promptly set up a shield against possible imported cases, and we have provided increased care and support for Chinese citizens overseas. With an open, transparent, and responsible attitude, China has actively engaged in international cooperation, providing timely information, actively sharing prevention technologies and practices, and helping other countries with their response efforts.

As a developing country with 1.4 billion people, it is only by overcoming enormous difficulties that China has been able to contain Covid-19 in such a short time while also ensuring our people's basic needs. Our success has come at a great price. The economy posted negative growth in the first quarter of this year, and daily life and work have been greatly affected. However, life is invaluable. This is a price we must pay, and a price worth paying.

While continuing to advance epidemic control, we have also promoted economic and social development and lost no time in resuming work and production when appropriate. With ninety policy measures in eight categories, we have provided assistance to enterprises to stabilize employment, cut and exempted taxes and fees, exempted all tolls on highways, reduced the costs of energy use, and granted subsidized loans. We have approved the early issuance of special bonds by local governments according to due procedures. We kept up with the spring farming schedule, and continued the critical battle against poverty. We have provided assistance to people working on the front lines of Covid-19 control and to people in difficulty, and doubled temporary price subsidies.

These policies have benefited hundreds of millions of people, and ensured stable supplies and prices and the resumption of work and production in a timely and effective way. Indeed, the Chinese economy has shown great resilience and enormous potential.

Fellow Deputies

We owe what we have achieved in economic and social development since last year and in Covid-19 control this year to the strong leadership of the Party Central Committee with Comrade Xi Jinping at its core, the sound guidance of Xi Jinping Thought on Socialism with Chinese Characteristics for a New Era, and the concerted efforts of the Party, the armed forces, and the people of all ethnic groups in China.

On behalf of the State Council, I express sincere gratitude to the Chinese people of all ethnic groups, and to all other political parties, people's organizations, and public figures from all sectors of society. I express heartfelt appreciation to our fellow countrymen and women in the Hong Kong and Macao special administrative regions, in Taiwan, and overseas. I also express sincere thanks to the governments of other countries, international organizations, and friends from all over the world, who have shown understanding and support for China in its endeavor to achieve modernization and in its fight against Covid-19.

While recognizing our achievements, we are also keenly aware of the difficulties and problems we face. The shock of the Covid-19 pandemic has sent the world economy into severe recession, disrupted industrial and supply chains, and caused a contraction in international trade and investment and volatility in commodity markets.

Domestically, consumption, investment, and exports have declined. Pressure on employment has risen significantly. Enterprises, especially micro, small, and medium businesses, face growing difficulties. There are increasing risks in the financial sector and other areas. The budgetary imbalances of primary-level governments have intensified.

There is still room for improvement in the work of government. Pointless formalities and bureaucracy remain an acute issue. A small number of officials shirk their duties or are incapable of fulfilling them. Corruption is still a common problem in some fields. During the Covid-19 response, many weak links have been exposed in public health emergency management, and the people have expressed their views and suggestions, which deserve our attention. We must strive to improve our work and fulfill our responsibilities and make every effort to live up to the people's expectations.

II Main targets for development and the overall plan for the next stage of work

For the government to deliver this year, we must, under the strong leadership of the Party Central Committee with Comrade Xi Jinping at its core, do the following:

– follow the guidance of Xi Jinping Thought on Socialism with Chinese Characteristics for a New Era; implement the guiding principles of the Party's 19th National Congress and the second, third, and fourth plenary sessions of its 19th Central Committee in full; firmly act on the Party's basic theory, line, and policy;

– strengthen our consciousness of the need to maintain political integrity, think in big-picture terms, follow the leadership core, and keep in alignment with the central Party leadership; stay confident in the path, theory, system, and culture of socialism with Chinese characteristics; and uphold General Secretary Xi Jinping's core position on the Party Central Committee and in the Party as a whole, and uphold the Party Central Committee's authority and its centralized, unified leadership;

– carry out Covid-19 control and promote economic and social development to fulfill the targets and tasks for completing the building of a moderately prosperous society in all respects;

– while carrying out regular Covid-19 control, continue to follow the general principle of pursuing progress while ensuring stability, apply the new development philosophy, pursue supply-side structural reform as our main task, and draw momentum from reform and opening up to promote high-quality development;

– make progress in the three critical battles; step up efforts to ensure stability on six fronts and maintain security in six areas; steadfastly pursue the strategy of expanding domestic demand, ensure economic development and social stability, accomplish the targets and tasks for winning the battle against poverty, and bring to completion the building of a moderately prosperous society in all respects.

At present and for some time to come, China will face challenges like never before. However, we have unique political and institutional strengths, a strong economic foundation, enormous market potential, and hundreds of millions of intelligent and hardworking people. If we face challenges head-on, boost confidence in development, create strong impetus for growth, and preserve and make the most of this important period of strategic opportunity for our development, we will, without doubt, be able to make it through this challenging time. The horizons for China's development are full of promise.

On the basis of a comprehensive assessment of the current situation, we have made proper adjustments to the targets that we were considering before Covid-19 struck. This year, we must give priority to stabilizing employment and ensuring living standards, win the battle against poverty, and achieve the goal of building a moderately prosperous society in all aspects. Specifically, we have set the following targets:

- Over 9 million new urban jobs, a surveyed urban unemployment rate of around 6 percent, and a registered urban unemployment rate of around 5.5 percent;
- CPI increase of around 3.5 percent;
- More stable and higher-quality imports and exports, and a basic equilibrium in the balance of payments;
- Growth in personal income that is basically in step with economic growth;
- Elimination of poverty among all rural residents living below the current poverty line and in all poor counties;
- Effective prevention and control of major financial risks;
- A further drop in energy consumption per unit of GDP and the discharge of major pollutants;
- Accomplishment of the 13th Five-Year Plan.

I would like to point out that we have not set a specific target for economic growth this year. This is because our country will face some factors that are difficult to predict in its development due to the great uncertainty regarding the Covid-19 pandemic and the world economic and trade environment. Not setting a specific target for economic growth will enable all of us to concentrate on ensuring stability on the six fronts and security in the six areas. We must focus on maintaining security in the six areas in order to ensure stability on the six fronts. By doing so, we will be able to keep the fundamentals of the economy stable. Maintaining security will deliver the stability needed to pursue progress, thus laying a solid foundation for accomplishing our goal of building a moderately prosperous society in all respects.

We must be clear that efforts to stabilize employment, ensure living standards, eliminate poverty, and prevent and defuse risks must be underpinned by economic growth; so ensuring stable economic performance is of crucial significance. We need to pursue reform and opening up as a means to stabilize employment, ensure people's well-being, stimulate consumption, energize the market, and achieve stable growth. We need to blaze a new path that enables us to respond effectively to shocks and sustain a positive growth cycle.

We will pursue a more proactive and impactful fiscal policy

The deficit-to-GDP ratio this year is projected at more than 3.6 percent, with a deficit increase of one trillion yuan over last year. On top of this, one trillion yuan of government bonds for Covid-19 control will also be issued. These are extraordinary measures for an unusual time.

The aforementioned two trillion yuan will be transferred in full to local governments; a special transfer payment mechanism will be set up to ensure that funds go straight to prefecture and county governments and directly benefit businesses and people. These funds should be primarily used to ensure employment, meet basic living needs, and protect market entities. This includes giving support to cut taxes and fees, reduce rents and interest on loans, and increase consumption and investment. It is important to stress that government funds are public in nature and that no such funds are allowed to be withheld or diverted for non-designated uses.

We will work harder to improve the composition of fiscal spending. We will see that spending on people's basic well-being is only increased and not cut, ensure spending in key areas, and resolutely cut general expenditures. Construction of new government buildings and wasteful and excessive spending will be strictly prohibited.

Governments at all levels must truly tighten their belt. The central government will take the lead by committing to negative growth in its budgetary spending, with a more than 50 percent cut to outlays on non-essential and non-obligatory items. All types of surplus, idle and carryover funds that should be taken back will be withdrawn and reallocated. We will see that funds are put to better and more effective use; we will scrutinize all expenditure items and see that every cent is used where it is needed most and where market entities and the people will feel the greatest benefit from it.

We will pursue a prudent monetary policy in a more flexible and appropriate way

We will use a variety of tools such as required reserve ratio reductions, interest rate cuts, and re-lending to enable M_2 money supply and aggregate financing to grow at notably higher rates than last year. We will keep the RMB exchange rate generally stable at an adaptive, balanced level. As we work to develop new monetary policy instruments that can directly stimulate the real economy, it is crucial that we take steps to ensure enterprises can secure loans more easily, and promote steady reduction of interest rates.

We will strengthen the employment-first policy with comprehensive measures

We will create synergy to stabilize employment through the coordinated use of fiscal, monetary, and investment policies. We will strive to keep existing jobs secure, work actively to create new ones, and help unemployed people find work. All local governments need to overhaul or rescind excessive restrictions on employment, and adopt all possible measures to bolster employment.

Eliminating poverty is an obligatory task we must complete in order to build a moderately prosperous society in all respects. We will continue to apply the current poverty alleviation standards, take stronger steps to implement poverty reduction measures, and ensure that all remaining poor people are lifted out of poverty. We will improve and effectively utilize mechanisms for monitoring and assisting people who fall back into poverty and consolidate our gains in poverty alleviation. We will endeavor to protect our blue skies, clear waters, and clean lands, and meet the goals for the critical battle of pollution prevention and control. Strong prevention and control measures will be taken to forestall systemic risks.

Almost five months of this year have passed. In the next stage, we will not let up on any front of our long-term fight against Covid-19, nor will we lose any time in advancing China's economic and social development agenda. The policies we adopt should be both forceful and sustainable, and they may be adjusted as called for. We have both the resolve and ability to accomplish the targets and tasks set for this year.

III Forcefully implementing macro policies to keep businesses and employment stable

To ensure employment and people's well-being, we must instill confidence in over one hundred million market entities; and we must do our utmost to help enterprises, particularly micro, small, and medium businesses, and self-employed individuals get through this challenging time.

We will further cut taxes and fees

We will aggressively implement current policies in conjunction with institutional arrangements to create a more enabling environment and help market entities overcome difficulties and achieve development. We will continue implementing reductions of VAT rates and the share of employees' basic old-age insurance paid by enterprises, and we will make further tax and fee cuts of about 500 billion yuan. The policies introduced early this year that are due to expire by June will all be extended till the end of the year. They include the following: exempting micro, small, and medium businesses from contributions to basic old-age insurance, unemployment insurance, and work injury compensation insurance schemes; reducing or cancelling VAT for small-scale taxpayers; exempting VAT on services such as public transportation, restaurants and hotels, tourism and entertainment, and culture and sports; and reducing or cancelling civil aviation development fund contributions and port development fees. The payment of corporate income taxes by micro and small businesses and self-employed individuals will be postponed to next year. We expect that these measures will see additional savings of more than 2.5 trillion yuan for enterprises throughout the year. All tax and fee reduction policies must be fully implemented for our businesses, so that they can sustain themselves and assure success for the future.

We will reduce enterprises' production and operating costs

The policy of reducing electricity prices for general industrial and commercial businesses by five percent will be extended to the end of the year. The rates for broadband and dedicated internet access services will be cut by 15 percent on average. Rents for state-owned premises will be lowered or exempted, and all other types of property owners are encouraged to also reduce, waive, or defer rent payments, and they will receive policy support from the government in doing so. We will take firm steps to stop the unauthorized levy of fees on enterprises.

We will increase financial support to keep business operations stable

The policy allowing micro, small, and medium businesses to postpone principal and interest repayments on loans will be further extended till the end of March next year—payments on all inclusive loans of micro and small businesses eligible for this policy should also be deferred, and other businesses facing financial difficulties can discuss similar terms with their creditors. We will encourage banks to substantially increase credit loans, first-time loans, and loan renewals without repayment of principal for micro and small businesses. The scope of the government financing guaranty will be expanded and guaranty fees will be reduced significantly. Large commercial banks should increase inclusive finance lending to micro and small businesses by more than 40 percent. We will support enterprises in increasing bond financing.

We should tighten regulation and prevent funds from simply circulating in the financial sector for the sake of arbitrage. As financial institutions and the businesses that borrow from them share a common stake, we encourage banks to make appropriate interest concessions. To support market entities, we must ensure that micro, small, and medium businesses have significantly better access to loans and that overall financing costs drop markedly.

We will make every effort to stabilize and expand employment

We will increase employment support for key sectors and key groups. With 8.74 million college students graduating this year, we need to encourage market-based employment and ensure that colleges and the governments of localities where they are located provide employment services to these students on an ongoing basis.

We will ensure employment for demobilized military personnel. We will adopt a policy to see rural migrant workers have equal access to employment services in the cities where they work. We will help people with disabilities, zero-employment families, and other groups facing difficulty find jobs.

There are several hundred million workers, including casual laborers, in flexible employment in China. This year, low-income earners will be allowed to postpone the payment of their social insurance premiums, and all employment-related government charges will be cancelled.

We will finance skills training to stabilize employment. This year and next, more than 35 million vocational skills training opportunities will be provided, and enrollment in vocational colleges will grow by two million. This will help more people improve their skills and secure jobs.

IV Energizing market entities through reform and strengthening new drivers of growth

The greater the difficulties and challenges we face, the more important it is for us to go further in reform, get rid of institutional barriers, and boost internal forces driving development.

We will press ahead with reforms to streamline administration and delegate power, improve regulation, and upgrade services

While continuing to implement regular Covid-19 control measures, we will adjust relevant measures and simplify procedures to boost the resumption of work, production, and business activities. We will work to see our people are able to access more government services via a single website and complete all procedures for starting a business online. Location restrictions on business registration applying to micro and small enterprises and self-employed people will be relaxed, and entrepreneurs of all types will find it easier to register and start a business and access timely policy support. We will support enterprises of all sizes in pursuing development through collaboration with each other. We will conduct impartial regulation to ensure fair competition, and make sustained efforts to create a market-oriented, law-based, and internationalized business environment.

We will advance reforms to promote market-based allocation of production factors

We will encourage small and mid-sized banks to replenish capital and improve governance, so that they can better serve micro, small, and medium businesses. We will reform the ChiNext stock market and pilot a registration-based IPO system. The role of insurance in protecting against risks will be strengthened. Provincial-level government will be given more power to approve land use for construction projects. We will boost the flow of human resources, foster technology and data markets, and thus unleash the potential of all types of production factors.

We will improve the performance of state capital and SOE reforms

We will launch a three-year action plan for SOE reform. We will improve the system of state capital regulation and intensify mixed ownership reform of SOEs. We will basically complete the task of relieving SOEs of the obligations to operate social programs, and resolve their other longstanding problems. SOEs should focus on their main responsibilities and businesses, establish sound market-oriented operating mechanisms, and increase their core competitiveness.

We will foster an enabling environment for the development of the private sector

We will see that private businesses have equal access to production factors and policy support. We will review relevant regulations to abolish those that unfairly differentiate enterprises according to form of ownership. Deadlines will be set for government bodies to make overdue payments owed to private and small and medium businesses. We will foster a cordial and clean relationship between government and business and promote the healthy development of the non-public sector.

We will encourage the upgrading of manufacturing and the growth of emerging industries

We will markedly increase medium- and long-term loans to manufacturers. We will promote the industrial internet and boost smart manufacturing. New forms of business such as e-commerce, online shopping, and online services have played an important role during the Covid-19 response and more policies will be introduced in support of such businesses. We will advance Internet Plus initiatives across the board and create new competitive strengths in the digital economy.

We will boost our capacity to support technological innovation

We will provide stable support for basic research and application-oriented basic research, and encourage enterprises to increase investment in R&D. We will accelerate the development of national laboratories, restructure the system of key national laboratories, and develop private R&D institutions. We will intensify international cooperation on science and technology. Intellectual property protection will be strengthened. We will introduce an open competition mechanism to select the best candidates to lead key research projects.

We will continue to encourage business startups and innovation nationwide

We will support the growth of venture capital investment and increase guaranteed loans for startups. To further unleash the creativity of various sectors, we will launch a new round of pilot reforms for making innovations across the board, build more innovation and entrepreneurship demo centers, continue accommodating and prudential regulation, and develop the platform economy and the sharing economy.

V Implementing the strategy of expanding domestic demand and promoting accelerated transformation of the economic growth model

The potential of China's domestic demand is enormous. We will deepen supply-side structural reform, focus our efforts on improving the people's well-being, and boost consumption and expand investment in a mutually reinforcing way.

We will promote the recovery of consumption

We will stabilize employment, promote income growth and ensure people's basic needs are met to encourage and enable consumer spending. We will support the recovery and development of food and beverage, brick and mortar shopping, culture, tourism, domestic services, and other consumer services, and promote the integration of online and offline consumption. Elderly and child care services will be developed. Pedestrian streets will be upgraded. We will support the roll-out of e-commerce and express delivery services in rural areas to expand rural consumption. We will apply a combination of measures to boost consumption and meet diverse demand among consumers.

We will expand effective investment

This year, 3.75 trillion yuan of special local government bonds will be issued, a 1.6 trillion yuan increase over last year. The proportion of special bonds that can be used as project capital will be raised, and 600 billion yuan will be earmarked for investment in the central government budget.

Priority will be given to new infrastructure and new urbanization initiatives and major projects, which not only boost consumption and benefit the people, but also facilitate structural adjustments and enhance the sustainability of growth. Specifically, efforts will be made mainly in the following three areas:

First, we will step up the construction of new types of infrastructure. We will develop next-generation information networks and expand 5G applications. We will build more charging facilities and promote wider use of new-energy automobiles. We will stimulate new consumer demand and promote industrial upgrading.

Second, we will strengthen the development of a new type of urbanization. We will do more to improve public facilities and services in county seats, so as to meet the growing demand to work and settle in them among rural residents. We will begin the renovation of 39,000 old urban residential communities and support the installation of elevators in residential buildings and the development of meal, cleaning, and other community services.

Third, we will redouble efforts to develop major transportation and water conservancy projects, and increase national railway development capital by 100 billion yuan.

We will improve market-based investment and financing mechanisms to support private enterprises in participating in projects on an equal footing. We will ensure that projects are up to standard, so they do not create any undesired consequences and the investments made deliver long-term returns.

We will steadily advance new urbanization

We will leverage the role of leading cities and city clusters in driving the overall development of their surrounding areas, in an effort to foster new industries and increase employment. Acting on the principle that houses are for living in, not for speculation, we will implement city-specific policies to promote steady and healthy development of the real estate market. We will improve urban amenities, and make our cities places that people enjoy living and working in.

We will step up implementation of China's regional development strategies

We will continue to promote large-scale development in the western region, the full revitalization of the northeast, the rise of the central region, and the trailblazing development of the eastern region.

We will move forward with the coordinated development of the Beijing-Tianjin-Hebei region, the development of the Guangdong-Hong Kong-Macao Greater Bay Area, and the integrated development of the Yangtze River Delta.

We will advance well-coordinated environmental conservation in the Yangtze Economic Belt. An overall plan will be formulated for ecological protection and high-quality development in the Yellow River basin. Development of the Chengdu-Chongqing economic circle will be promoted.

We will encourage accelerated development in old revolutionary base areas, ethnic minority areas, border areas, and poor areas. We will develop the maritime economy.

We will implement a package of policies to support Hubei's development, helping it ensure employment, public well-being, and normal operations, and spurring the full recovery of economic and social activity there.

We will ensure more effective protection of ecosystems and the environment

Priority will be placed on curbing pollution in a law-based, scientific, and targeted way. We will intensify efforts to control air pollution in key areas. We will step up the construction of sewage and garbage treatment facilities. The relocation and transformation of producers of hazardous chemical products will be accelerated. We will boost the development of energy-saving and environmental protection industries. Illegal hunting and trading of wild animals will be severely punished. We will carry out major projects for protecting and restoring key ecosystems to promote ecological conservation.

We will safeguard energy security

We will promote cleaner and more efficient use of coal, develop renewable energy, improve systems for the production, supply, and sale of oil, natural gas, and electricity, and bolster our energy reserve capacity.

VI Achieving poverty reduction goals and working for good harvests and growth in rural income

We will implement poverty reduction and rural revitalization measures, ensure the supply of important agricultural products, and raise rural living standards.

We will win the fight against poverty

We will channel greater energy into eliminating poverty in all remaining poor counties and villages, and ensure rural migrant workers from these areas have stable jobs in places where they work. We will launch programs to boost the consumption of products from poor areas, and support businesses involved in poverty alleviation in resuming operations. Follow-up support will be provided to people relocated from inhospitable areas.

We will deepen collaboration on poverty alleviation between the eastern and western regions, and intensify assistance to targeted poor areas from central Party and government departments, offices of other political parties, as well as state-owned enterprises, public institutions, and universities under the central government.

We will work harder to ensure that the basic needs of the poor population are met. A poverty reduction survey will be conducted nationwide. We will continue to promote both poverty alleviation and rural revitalization in an all-out effort to help people who have risen out of poverty move toward prosperity.

We will work to bolster agricultural production

We will keep total crop acreage and grain output stable, raise the multiple cropping index, increase the minimum purchase price of rice, give more rewards to major grain-producing counties, and take effective measures to prevent and control major diseases and pests.

The acquisition of farmland for other purposes in violation of laws and regulations will be penalized. The area of high-standard cropland will be increased by 5.33 million hectares. We will further rural reform. We will promote a recovery in the production of hogs. We will fully implement the system of provincial governors assuming responsibility for the "rice bag" and city mayors for the "vegetable basket." It is imperative, and it is well within our ability, to ensure the food supply for 1.4 billion Chinese people through our own efforts.

We will create more channels for rural residents to find employment and increase their incomes

We will help rural residents seek employment or start businesses in places close to their homes, and expand work-relief programs to ensure that those who return to their homes have a job and income. We will support the development of appropriately scaled agricultural operations, and improve commercial services for farmers.

We will invest more funds raised through special bonds to support modern agricultural facilities, safe drinking water projects, and the improvement of living environments. This will promote steady improvements in rural living and working conditions.

VII Promoting higher-standard opening up and stabilizing the overall performance of foreign trade and foreign investment

Faced with changes in the external environment, we must stay committed to opening our door wider to the world, keep our industrial and supply chains stable, and make opening up a catalyst for reform and development.

We will stabilize the overall performance of foreign trade

To help businesses get more orders and keep their employees on, we will increase credit supply, extend the coverage of export credit insurance, lower compliance costs for imports and exports, and support the domestic sale of export products.

We will accelerate the growth of cross-border e-commerce and other new forms of business, and enhance our international shipping capacity. We will advance a new round of trials for innovative development of trade in services. We will make good preparations for the third China International Import Expo, work actively to expand imports, and foster a large globally oriented market of higher standards.

We will step up utilization of foreign capital

The negative list for foreign investment will be significantly shortened, while a negative list will also be drawn up for cross-border trade in services. We will grant greater autonomy in reform and opening up to pilot free trade zones, speed up the establishment of a free trade port in Hainan, open new pilot free trade zones and integrated bonded areas in the central and western regions, and launch further comprehensive trials on opening up the service sector. We will foster an enabling market environment in which all companies, Chinese and foreign, are treated as equals and engaged in fair competition.

We will focus on quality in the joint pursuit of the Belt and Road Initiative

Staying committed to achieving shared growth through consultation and collaboration, we will uphold market principles and international rules, give full scope to enterprises as the main actors, and work with our BRI partners for mutually beneficial outcomes. We will guide the healthy development of outbound investment.

We will promote liberalization and facilitation of trade and investment

We will firmly safeguard the multilateral trading regime, and actively participate in reform of the WTO. We will work for the signing of the Regional Comprehensive Economic Partnership, and advance free trade negotiations with Japan and the Republic of Korea as well as other countries. We will work with the United States to implement the phase one China-US economic and trade agreement. China will continue to boost economic and trade cooperation with other countries to deliver mutual benefits.

VIII Advancing the reform and development of social programs to safeguard and improve living standards

Despite the difficulties we face, we must unfailingly meet the basic living needs of our people and address issues of public concern.

We will enhance the public health system

We will always put life above everything else. We will reform the system for disease prevention and control, improve mechanisms for direct reporting and early warning of infectious diseases, and ensure prompt, open, and transparent release of epidemic information. We will make good use of Covid-19 bonds, increase inputs into the R&D of vaccines, medicines, and rapid testing technologies, build more medical facilities for epidemic control and treatment, set up more mobile laboratories, ensure emergency supplies, and strengthen public health and epidemic prevention at the primary level. We will launch extensive initiatives to improve public sanitation. We need to greatly enhance our prevention and control capability, resolutely prevent a resurgence of Covid-19, and protect the health of our people.

We will improve basic medical services

We will raise government subsidies for basic medical insurance for rural and non-working urban residents by an average of 30 yuan per person, and pilot inter-provincial on-the-spot settlement of outpatient bills through basic medical insurance accounts. We will provide support to medical institutions badly hit by the epidemic. We will promote the development of traditional Chinese medicine. Supervision over food and drugs will be tightened up to guarantee their safety.

We will develop more equitable and higher-quality education

We will see that teaching in primary and secondary schools and entrance examinations for senior high school and university are well-organized. We will strengthen the development of boarding schools in townships and towns and schools in county seats, provide quality special needs education and continuing education, support private schools and keep them well-regulated, and help private kindergartens overcome difficulties. We will step up efforts to develop world-class universities and world-class disciplines. We will expand the enrollment of students from rural and poor areas at colleges and universities. We will improve the mix of spending, making educational resources accessible to all our families and children and enabling them to embrace a brighter future.

We will make greater efforts to meet people's basic living needs

We will increase the basic pension for retirees and the minimum basic old-age pension for rural and non-working urban residents. Close to 300 million people in our country live on pensions, and we must ensure they receive their benefits on time and in full.

We will improve the systems of providing preferential treatment and employment services for demobilized military personnel, and ensure benefits for the families of people who have died in service of the public. We will extend the coverage of unemployment insurance and see that rural migrant workers and others out of work who are in the scheme less than a year are covered in the locality where they are living. Subsistence allowances will be expanded to cover all families in difficulty, and such allowances will be made promptly available to eligible urban unemployed people and migrant workers who have returned home. We will ensure assistance is provided to anyone who runs into temporary difficulty because of disaster or illness.

With these measures, we can ensure that all members of disadvantaged groups have their basic living needs met and that more unemployed people will have the support they need to secure their next job or start their own business.

We will organize rich intellectual and cultural activities for our people

We will foster and practice core socialist values, and continue to develop philosophy and social sciences, the press, publishing, radio, film, and television and to protect cultural relics. We will improve public cultural services, make preparations for the 2022 Winter Olympics and Paralympics in Beijing, and encourage people to exercise and keep fit. With these endeavors, our people will be full of vitality and striving to pursue excellence and moral integrity.

We will create new and better ways to conduct social governance

We will make sure that communities provide better services and support the sound development of social organizations, humanitarian assistance, volunteer service, and charity. We will protect the lawful rights and interests of women, children, the elderly, and people with disabilities. We will improve the system for handling public complaints, provide better legal aid, and ensure that justified public demands are addressed promptly. The seventh population census will be carried out. We will strengthen national security capacity building, punish crimes in accordance with law, and more effectively carry out the Peaceful China initiative.

We will strengthen accountability for workplace safety

We will intensify prevention efforts against flooding, fires, and earthquakes, deliver quality meteorological services, and enhance our capacity for emergency rescue and disaster prevention and mitigation. A campaign to enhance workplace safety will be launched. Strong steps will be taken to prevent major and extremely serious accidents.

Fellow Deputies

In the face of difficult and weighty tasks, governments at all levels must closely follow the Party Central Committee with Comrade Xi Jinping at its core in thinking, stance, and action and practice the people-centered development philosophy. We must enforce full, rigorous self-discipline of the Party, exercise law-based government administration, ensure transparency in all government affairs, and enhance our governance capacity.

We will accept, as required by law, the oversight of people's congresses and their standing committees at the same level, and readily subject ourselves to the democratic oversight of the CPPCC, public oversight, and oversight through public opinion. Auditing-based oversight will be stepped up. We will give full play to the role of trade unions, Communist Youth League organizations, women's federations, and other people's organizations. We in the government must readily accept the oversight of the law, supervisory bodies, and the people. We must redouble efforts to build a clean government and crack down on corruption.

We, in government at all levels, must take a fact-based approach to our work, and keep firmly in mind that we remain in the primary stage of socialism, which is the basic dimension of China's national context. We must abide by objective laws, base everything we do on actual conditions, and deliver in our work.

We will take strong steps to address the practice of formalities for formalities' sake, bureaucracy, hedonism, and extravagance, and release our primary-level officials from the fetters of pointless formalities so as to give full rein to their drive. We will stand behind officials who live up to their responsibilities, and we will work to see that they carry out their duties.

We must rely closely on the people, respect the pioneering spirit of those working at the primary level, advance reform and opening up with greater force, ignite the dynamism of our society, and bring together the energy and ingenuity of hundreds of millions of Chinese people. This is the source of inspiration that enables us to prevail over all difficulties and challenges.

We officials must not shy away in the face of difficulty; we must do solid work and make concerted efforts to pursue development and ensure the well-being of the people. As long as we stand together with the people through good times and bad and continue to forge ahead, we can surely fulfill the desires of the Chinese people for a better life.

This year, we will formulate the 14th Five-Year Plan, thus drawing the blueprint for us to embark on a new journey toward the second Centenary Goal.

Fellow Deputies

We will uphold and improve the system of regional ethnic autonomy, support ethnic minorities and ethnic minority areas in accelerating development, and forge a strong sense of community among the Chinese people.

We will fully implement the Party's fundamental policy on religious affairs and encourage religious leaders and believers to play an active part in promoting economic and social development.

China cares deeply about our overseas nationals, who serve as a crucial bridge linking China and the rest of the world. We will give play to the unique role of overseas Chinese nationals and their family members and relatives at home, and forge a stronger bond of attachment among all the sons and daughters of the Chinese nation. Together, we can create more remarkable achievements.

Since last year, we have achieved important progress in strengthening national defense and the armed forces. The people's armed forces demonstrated fine conduct by reacting swiftly to the Party's commands and shouldering heavy responsibilities in Covid-19 control.

We will thoroughly implement Xi Jinping's thinking on strengthening the armed forces and the military strategy for the new era. We will continue to enhance the political loyalty of the armed forces, strengthen them through reform, science and technology, and the training of capable personnel, and run the military in accordance with law.

We will uphold the Party's absolute leadership over the people's armed forces and strictly implement the system of ultimate responsibility resting with the chair of the Central Military Commission. We will firmly safeguard China's sovereignty, security, and development interests.

We will complete the crucial tasks laid down in the 13th Five-Year Plan for the development of the armed forces and draw up the 14th Five-Year Plan. We will deepen reforms in national defense and the military, increase our logistic and equipment support capacity, and promote innovative development of defense-related science and technology. We will improve the system of national defense mobilization and ensure that the unity between the military and the government and between the military and the people remains rock solid.

We will fully and faithfully implement the policy of "One Country, Two Systems," under which the people of Hong Kong govern Hong Kong and the people of Macao govern Macao, with a high degree of autonomy for both regions. We will establish sound legal systems and enforcement mechanisms for safeguarding national security in the two special administrative regions, and see that the governments of the two regions fulfill their constitutional responsibilities. We will support Hong Kong and Macao in growing their economies, improving living standards, and better integrating their development into China's overall development, and help them maintain long-term prosperity and stability.

We will adhere to the major principles and policies on work related to Taiwan and resolutely oppose and deter any separatist activities seeking "Taiwan independence." We will improve institutional arrangements, policies, and measures to encourage exchanges and cooperation between the two sides of the Taiwan Strait, further cross-Strait integrated development, and protect the well-being of our fellow compatriots in Taiwan. We will encourage them to join us in opposing "Taiwan independence" and promoting China's reunification. With these efforts, we can surely create a beautiful future for the rejuvenation of the Chinese nation.

In the face of the public health crisis, severe economic recession, and other global challenges, all countries should work together. China stands ready to work with other countries to strengthen international cooperation on Covid-19 control, promote stability in the world economy, advance global governance, and uphold the international system with the United Nations at its core and an international order based on international law. China is committed to building a human community with a shared future.

China will continue to pursue peaceful development, and advance friendship and cooperation with other countries as it opens up wider to the rest of the world. China will remain an important force promoting world peace, stability, development, and prosperity.

Fellow Deputies

The Chinese nation has never been daunted in the face of difficulties or obstacles. The Chinese people today have the ability and resolve to overcome all challenges before us. We must rally more closely around the Party Central Committee with Comrade Xi Jinping at its core, uphold socialism with Chinese characteristics, and follow the guidance of Xi Jinping Thought on Socialism with Chinese Characteristics for a New Era. Let us meet our challenges head-on, move determinedly forward in the fight against Covid-19 and in pursuit of economic and social development, and strive to fulfill the main targets and tasks for this year. Let all of us work together with perseverance to build China into a great modern socialist country that is prosperous, strong, democratic, culturally advanced, harmonious, and beautiful, and realize the Chinese Dream of national rejuvenation.

Source: "Full text: Premier Li's speech at the third session of the 13th NPC," available online at: https://news.cgtn.com/news/2020-05-22/Full-text-Premier-Li-s-speech-at-the-third-session-of-the-13th-NPC-QHaP1FpB8k/index.html (last accessed January 14, 2023)

Appendix 2: Full Text: Remarks by Chinese President Xi Jinping at the Global Health Summit

Your Excellency Prime Minister Mario Draghi,
Your Excellency President Ursula von der Leyen,
Dear Colleagues,

It gives me great pleasure to attend the Global Health Summit. Last year, the G20 successfully held an Extraordinary Leaders' Summit on Covid-19 and the Riyadh Summit. Many important common understandings were reached on promoting global solidarity against the virus and boosting world economic recovery.

The past year and more have seen repeated resurgence and frequent mutations of the coronavirus. The most serious pandemic in a century is still wreaking havoc. To clinch an early victory against Covid-19 and restore economic growth remains the top priority for the international community. G20 members need to shoulder responsibilities in global cooperation against the virus. In the meantime, we need to draw on experience both positive and otherwise, and lose no time in remedying deficiencies, closing loopholes and strengthening weak links in a bid to enhance preparedness and capacity for coping with major public health emergencies. Here, I want to make five points on what we need to do.

First, we must put people and their lives first. The battle with Covid-19 is one for the people and by the people. What has happened proves that to completely defeat the virus, we must put people's lives and health front and center, demonstrate a great sense of political responsibility and courage, and make extraordinary responses to an extraordinary challenge. No effort must be spared to attend every case, save every patient, and truly respect the value and dignity of every human life. Meanwhile, it is also important to minimize the potential impact on people's life and maintain general order in our society.

Second, we must follow science-based policies and ensure a coordinated and systemic response. Faced with this new infectious disease, we should advocate the spirit of science, adopt a science-based approach, and follow the law of science. The fight against Covid-19 is an all-out war that calls for a systemic response to coordinate pharmacological and non-pharmacological interventions, balance targeted routine Covid-19 protocols and emergency measures, and ensure both epidemic control and socio-economic development. G20 members need to adopt responsible macro-economic policies and step up coordination to keep the global industrial and supply chains safe and smooth. It is essential to give continued support by such means as debt suspension and development aid to developing countries, especially vulnerable countries facing exceptional difficulties.

Third, we must stick together and promote solidarity and cooperation. The pandemic is yet another reminder that we humanity rise and fall together with a shared future. Confronted by a pandemic like Covid-19, we must champion the vision of building a global community of health for all, tide over this trying time through solidarity and cooperation, and firmly reject any attempt to politicize, label or stigmatize the virus. Political manipulation would not serve Covid-19 response on the domestic front. It would only disrupt international cooperation against the virus and bring greater harm to people around the world.

Fourth, we must uphold fairness and equity as we strive to close the immunization gap. A year ago, I proposed that vaccines should be made a global public good. Today, the problem of uneven vaccination has become more acute. It is imperative for us to reject vaccine nationalism and find solutions to issues concerning the production capacity and distribution of vaccines, in order to make vaccines more accessible and affordable in developing countries. Major vaccine-developing and producing countries need to take up their responsibility to provide more vaccines to developing countries in urgent need, and they also need to support their businesses in joint research and authorized production with other countries having the relevant capacity. Multilateral financial institutions should provide inclusive financing support for vaccine procurement of developing countries. The World Health Organization (WHO) should speed up efforts under the Covid-19 Vaccine Global Access (COVAX) facility.

Fifth, we must address both the symptoms and root causes as we improve the governance system. The pandemic is an extensive test of the global health governance system. It is important that we strengthen and leverage the role of the UN and the WHO and improve the global disease prevention and control system to better prevent and respond to future pandemics. It is important that we uphold the spirit of extensive consultation, joint contribution and shared benefits, fully heed the views of developing countries, and better reflect their legitimate concerns. It is also important that we enhance our capacity of monitoring, early-warning and emergency response, our capacity of treatment of major pandemics, of contingency reserve and logistics, of fighting disinformation, and of providing support to developing countries.

Colleagues,
In this unprecedented battle against the pandemic, China has, while receiving support and help from many countries, mounted a massive global humanitarian operation. At the 73rd World Health Assembly held in May last year, I announced five measures that China would take to support global anti-pandemic cooperation. Implementation of those measures is well underway. Notwithstanding the limited production capacity and enormous demand at home, China has honored its commitment by providing free vaccines to more than eighty developing countries in urgent need and exporting vaccines to forty-three countries. We have provided 2 billion US dollars in assistance for the Covid-19 response and economic and social recovery in developing countries hit by the pandemic. We have sent medical supplies to more than 150 countries and 13 international organizations, providing more than 280 billion masks, 3.4 billion protective suits and 4 billion testing kits to the world. A cooperation mechanism has been established for Chinese hospitals to pair up with forty-one African hospitals, and construction for the China-assisted project of the Africa CDC headquarters officially started at the end of last year. Important progress has also been made in the China-UN joint project to set up in China a global humanitarian response depot and hub. China is fully implementing the G20 Debt Service Suspension Initiative for Poorest Countries and has so far put off debt repayment exceeding 1.3 billion US dollars, the highest deferral amount among G20 members.

In continued support for global solidarity against Covid-19, I wish to announce the following:

– China will provide an additional 3 billion US dollars in international aid over the next three years to support Covid-19 response and economic and social recovery in other developing countries.
– **Having already supplied 300 million doses of vaccines to the world, China will provide still more vaccines to the best of its ability.**
– **China supports its vaccine companies in transferring technologies to other developing countries and carrying out joint production with them.**
– **Having announced support for waiving intellectual property rights on Covid-19 vaccines, China also supports the World Trade Organization and other international institutions in making an early decision on this matter.**
– **China proposes setting up an international forum on vaccine cooperation for vaccine-developing and producing countries, companies and other**

stakeholders to explore ways of promoting fair and equitable distribution of vaccines around the world.

Colleagues,
The ancient Roman philosopher Seneca said, "We are all waves of the same sea." Let us join hands and stand shoulder to shoulder with each other to firmly advance international cooperation against Covid-19, build a global community of health for all, and work for a healthier and brighter future for humanity.

Source: "Full Text: Remarks by Chinese President Xi Jinping at the Global Health Summit," available online at: http://www.xinhuanet.com/english/2021-05/21/c_139961512.htm (last accessed January 19, 2023)

Appendix 3: Saudi King on Coronavirus: We Will Provide All Medicine, Food, Living Needs

Your nation, the Kingdom of Saudi Arabia, continues to take all precautionary measures to confront this pandemic and limit its effects. We depend on the aid of God Almighty, then on deploying our full capabilities, supported by your strong determination to face adversities with the steadfastness of believers at the forefront

The strength, steadfastness, determination that you have demonstrated during the honorable defiance of this difficult phase, and your full cooperation with relevant government agencies, are the most important contributing factors and pillars of the success of the state's efforts, which has prioritized safeguarding health and made it the state's top concern

Rest assured that we are very keen on providing the necessary medication, food, and living necessities for citizens and residents of this blessed land. All government sectors, led by the Ministry of Health, are doing all they can and taking all necessary measures to ensure the health of the nation's citizens and residents

We reaffirm that continuing this sincere and hard work at such a difficult time can't be achieved but with solidarity and collaboration, and by building on our positive spirits, further enhancing our individual and collective awareness, and strictly adhering to the instructions and guidelines provided to overcome this pandemic

You are well acquainted with my honesty in addressing public matters. That is why I started by saying that we are going through a difficult phase, as part of what the whole world is going through. I will tell you as well that the coming phase will be more difficult on a global level to confront the rapid spread of this pandemic

At the same time, I know that we will overcome hardships by believing in God, trusting His will, doing the deeds we have to do, and exerting and devoting all our efforts to protect the health and safety of humans and provide all the necessities required to ensure they lead decent lives, relying on your determination, the strength of your resolve, and your heightened sense of collective responsibility, may God preserve us and grant us all the best.

Source: "Saudi King on coronavirus: We will provide all medicine, food, living needs." Available online at: https://english.alarabiya.net/News/gulf/2020/03/19/Saudi-Arabia-s-King-Salman-to-address-nation-on-coronavirus (last accessed December 1, 2022)

Appendix 4: Full Transcript of Saudi Arabia's Mohammed bin Salman's Remarks at G20 Riyadh Summit

Peace be with you,

In the name of the Custodian of the Two Holy Mosques, King Salman bin Abdulaziz Al Saud, King of the Kingdom of Saudi Arabia, Chairman of the G20 Summit for the year 2020, I would like to express my heartfelt thanks to their Majesties, Excellencies and Highnesses, leaders of the G20 countries, and to everyone who has participated and contributed to our meetings from all countries and representatives of the international organizations, the business community and the civil society throughout the entire year of the Saudi G20 presidency.

The G20, since its foundation, has been an essential link among our countries. It has demonstrated the vitality of its role, over the years, to deal with economic, financial, social, and environmental issues.

In light of the outbreak of Covid-19 and its health, economic, and social repercussions, our cooperation has been important more than ever. Together we have addressed this challenge with seriousness necessitated by the responsibility to preserve human life, protect livelihoods, mitigate the ensuing damage of this pandemic, and raise readiness to face any future crises, God forbid.

This pandemic knows no borders. It has reached all countries and affected, directly and indirectly, every person living on this planet, which has necessitated the activation of the pivotal role played by the G20. To this end, the G20's leaders met twice during one presidency, a precedent since the foundation of the G20.

In order to confront this global threat facing all of humanity, the G20 took the initiative to adopt unprecedented measures and coordinated actions to deal with the pandemic and its aftermath.

We stand today at the end of an exceptional year in which we had the privilege and responsibility of the G20 presidency. Since the beginning of this year, we set one goal, "Realizing Opportunities of the 21st Century For All," which includes themes such as: empowering people, safeguarding the planet, and shaping new frontiers.

This year, the G20 adopted priorities that we worked on together to implement, on top of which is addressing the healthcare, economic, and social impacts of the pandemic. We also took all necessary measures to protect lives and livelihoods and support the most vulnerable groups. To achieve this, the G20 took the following actions:

First, we immediately provided the necessary resources to those at the frontline of the battle against Covid-19.

The G20 countries pledged, after the outbreak, more than $21 billion to support the immediate funding needs, notably for the development of diagnostic tools, vaccines and effective therapeutics. The Kingdom contributed $500 million to support these efforts.

In the G20 we agreed to spare no effort in creating the conditions for affordable and equitable access to Covid-19 vaccines, therapeutics, and diagnostic tools. We are still working on this.

Second, we took extraordinary measures to support our economies and peoples, as part of this year's G20 Action Plan.

We injected over $11 trillion into the global economy to support businesses and protect individuals' livelihoods. This is an unprecedented G20 economic stimulus.

We also extended the social safety nets to better protect those prone to losing their jobs or source of income.

Third, we provided emergency support to the most vulnerable countries in the world, where the pandemic risks jeopardizing decades of development progress already achieved.

With the Debt Service Suspension Initiative, we made available more than $14 billion in debt relief to the most vulnerable countries, whose collective population exceeds 1 billion. We have also extended this initiative and we will continue to assess the situation to see if another extension is needed.

In addition, over $300 billion has been mobilized via development banks, the IMF, and the World Bank which are working with the G20 to assist emerging and low-income countries.

We have demonstrated that, together, our strength lies in our unity. This is exactly what the G20 was created for—to bring countries from every continent together to address collectively the greatest challenges of the day and implement joint and effective solutions.

We fully realize the importance of better protection from future pandemics, and we must draw lessons from this crisis. To ensure that, the Saudi G20 Presidency proposed an initiative to enhance access to pandemic tools. This initiative works to achieve 3 goals:

Promote R&D, and distribution of diagnostic tools, therapeutics, and vaccines for all infectious diseases;

Encourage and facilitate international funding for global pandemic preparedness;

And support the training of epidemiologists from all over the world.

These crises remind us of our humanity, bringing about our sense of initiation and philanthropy. Despite the unexpected adversities that came with this pandemic globally, we persisted with the G20 Presidency themes, which are: Empowering People, Safeguarding the Planet, and Shaping New Frontiers.

These themes are now more relevant than ever for overcoming this global crisis, building an inclusive, resilient, and sustainable recovery, and shaping a better world for all.

The Saudi G20 Presidency has focused its efforts to build a stronger, more resilient and more sustainable world. This is aligned with Saudi Arabia undergoing major economic and social transformation, guided by our Vision 2030 which aims to ensure that all of our citizens, especially women and youth, can seize the opportunities of the twenty-first century.

Within the framework of the Saudi G20 presidency, the G20 members agreed on a number of vital initiatives that will act as a foundation for global recovery, which, we hope, will have positive impact for decades to come.

We have launched the Riyadh Initiative on the Future of the WTO to provide necessary support for WTO reforms, under WTO's own umbrella.

We continued our efforts to empower women and youth through quality education and financial inclusion.

The Saudi G20 Presidency greatly emphasized safeguarding the planet. Therefore, we, at the G20, endorsed the Circular Carbon Economy platform to better manage carbon emissions across all economy sectors and ensure access to cleaner, more sustainable, and affordable energy.

We launched the G20 Initiative to reduce land degradation and preserve coral reefs in order to protect our planet's essential ecosystems and biodiversity, both on land and in our oceans.

We stepped up our collective efforts to ensure that everyone on earth has access to safely-managed freshwater while addressing the key challenge of ensuring food security for everyone at a time when both demand and environmental pressures are growing.

It has been an exceptional challenge but an absolute honor to hold the G20 Presidency during this trying year. We wish we convened this summit in person in our capital, Riyadh, the city that tells the story of a nation proud of its old history, its genuine people, and its prosperous future thanks to its youths' resolve and determination.

We conclude this summit determined to take action and to continue working together until we overcome the pandemic, giving hope and reassurance to our nations and to the world. We are proud of what we have accomplished this year, and we know that plenty still needs to be done.

The Kingdom of Saudi Arabia will continue to support the international efforts related to providing equitable and affordable Covid-19 therapeutics and vaccines for all, once they become available. I know many join us in this commitment. We will work together with our international partners and the Italian G20 Presidency next year to achieve this.

The Kingdom will continue to answer the global call to address the challenges of the twenty-first century, together with the G20 members. We wish all the best for Italy.

Thank you very much

We hope to see you soon in the Kingdom of Saudi Arabia.

May peace be with you.

Source: "Full transcript of Saudi Arabia's Mohamed bin Salman's remarks at G20 Riyadh Summit," available online at: https://english.alarabiya.net/News/gulf/2020/11/22/Full-transcript-of-Saudi-Arabia-s-Mohammed-bin-Salman-s-remarks-at-G20-Riyadh-Summit (last accessed January 20, 2023)

Appendix 5: Prime Minister's Statement on Coronavirus (Covid-19): March 23, 2020

Good Evening,

The coronavirus is the biggest threat this country has faced for decades—and this country is not alone.

All over the world we are seeing the devastating impact of this invisible killer.

And so tonight I want to update you on the latest steps we are taking to fight the disease and what you can do to help.

And I want to begin by reminding you why the UK has been taking the approach that we have.

Without a huge national effort to halt the growth of this virus, there will come a moment when no health service in the world could possibly cope; because there won't be enough ventilators, enough intensive care beds, enough doctors and nurses.

And as we have seen elsewhere, in other countries that also have fantastic health care systems, that is the moment of real danger.

To put it simply, if too many people become seriously unwell at one time, the NHS will be unable to handle it—meaning more people are likely to die, not just from Coronavirus but from other illnesses as well.

So it's vital to slow the spread of the disease.

Because that is the way we reduce the number of people needing hospital treatment at any one time, so we can protect the NHS's ability to cope—and save more lives.

And that's why we have been asking people to stay at home during this pandemic.

And though huge numbers are complying—and I thank you all—the time has now come for us all to do more.

From this evening I must give the British people a very simple instruction—you must stay at home.

Because the critical thing we must do is stop the disease spreading between households.

That is why people will only be allowed to leave their home for the following very limited purposes:

- shopping for basic necessities, as infrequently as possible
- one form of exercise a day—for example a run, walk, or cycle—alone or with members of your household;
- any medical need, to provide care or to help a vulnerable person; and
- travelling to and from work, but only where this is absolutely necessary and cannot be done from home.

That's all—these are the only reasons you should leave your home.

You should not be meeting friends. If your friends ask you to meet, you should say No.

You should not be meeting family members who do not live in your home.

You should not be going shopping except for essentials like food and medicine—and you should do this as little as you can. And use food delivery services where you can.

If you don't follow the rules the police will have the powers to enforce them, including through fines and dispersing gatherings.

To ensure compliance with the Government's instruction to stay at home, we will immediately:

- close all shops selling non-essential goods, including clothing and electronic stores and other premises including libraries, playgrounds and outdoor gyms, and places of worship;
- we will stop all gatherings of more than two people in public—excluding people you live with;
- and we'll stop all social events, including weddings, baptisms and other ceremonies, but excluding funerals.

Parks will remain open for exercise but gatherings will be dispersed.

No Prime Minister wants to enact measures like this.

I know the damage that this disruption is doing and will do to people's lives, to their businesses and to their jobs.

And that's why we have produced a huge and unprecedented programme of support both for workers and for business.

And I can assure you that we will keep these restrictions under constant review. We will look again in three weeks, and relax them if the evidence shows we are able to.

But at present there are just no easy options. The way ahead is hard, and it is still true that many lives will sadly be lost.

And yet it is also true that there is a clear way through.

Day by day we are strengthening our amazing NHS with 7500 former clinicians now coming back to the service.

With the time you buy—by simply staying at home—we are increasing our stocks of equipment.

We are accelerating our search for treatments.

We are pioneering work on a vaccine.

And we are buying millions of testing kits that will enable us to turn the tide on this invisible killer.

I want to thank everyone who is working flat out to beat the virus.

Everyone from the supermarket staff to the transport workers to the carers to the nurses and doctors on the frontline.

But in this fight we can be in no doubt that each and every one of us is directly enlisted.

Each and every one of us is now obliged to join together.

To halt the spread of this disease.

To protect our NHS and to save many many thousands of lives.

And I know that as they have in the past so many times.
The people of this country will rise to that challenge.
And we will come through it stronger than ever.
We will beat the coronavirus and we will beat it together.
And therefore I urge you at this moment of national emergency to stay at home, protect our NHS and save lives.
Thank you.

Source: "Prime Minister's statement on coronavirus (Covid-19): March 23, 2020," available online at: https://www.gov.uk/government/speeches/pm-address-to-the-nation-on-coronavirus-23-march-2020 (last accessed January 17, 2023)

Appendix 6: PM Boris Johnson: The Oxford Vaccine Shows Why We and the World Need Britain to Be Global

It was in September last year that I felt the first stirrings of optimism about the coronavirus vaccine. I was at the Edward Jenner Institute in Oxford, standing behind a scientist as she looked at some magnified blood samples.

There were two sets of slides—one from subjects who had been given the vaccine prototype, and one from a control group. The slides from the control group were more or less blank, whereas the slides from the vaccinated group were full of dots—lots of dots. The dots were antibodies. I could tell from the excitement of the scientists that this was promising and that the Oxford-AstraZeneca vaccine looked as though it would work.

After exhaustive tests, so it has proved. That vaccine is safe and works extremely well, and now, only six months later, it is being made in multiple places from India to the US, as well as Britain, and it is being used around the world.

It is relatively easy to distribute, since it can be kept in an ordinary fridge, and under the terms of the deal struck between Oxford and the UK government it is being dispensed at cost. You may wonder why we have done it that way, or why the taxpayer has already spent hundreds of millions of pounds, through Covax and other schemes, to put jabs in the arms of other populations.

The answer is blindingly obvious—the principle of enlightened self-interest that underlies the integrated review of UK security, defence, development and foreign policy that is published today.

Successful as the UK vaccination programme may be, there is little point in achieving some isolated national immunity. We need the whole world to be protected. We need the whole world to have the confidence to open up for trade and travel and holidays and business, all the things that drive jobs and improve our lives at home.

The objective of Global Britain is not to swagger or strike attitudes on the world stage. It is to use the full spectrum of our abilities, now amplified by record spending on both defence and science, to engage with and help the rest of the world. That is how we serve the British interest, and I mean the economic interest of people up and down the country. And as the vaccine programme begins to inspire a new global hope, we want to use this moment to heal, both literally and figuratively.

The UK is using its G7 presidency to foster ideas for a new world treaty on pandemic preparedness so that next time humanity avoids the sauve qui peut squabbling that has disfigured the last 12 months. There is work to be done on the sharing of data, on the tracking of zoonotic diseases, on quarantine protocols and how to marshal drugs and personal protective equipment.

It is obvious from our experience that this would be good for Britain as much as the rest of the world. As we prepare to build back better, we are working with the World Trade Organization and its new director-general, Dr. Ngozi Okonjo-Iweala, not only to revive world trade but to address the stagnation that pre-dated the pandemic.

At the Cop26 summit in Glasgow the UK is leading the world in the campaign to reduce CO_2 emissions and arrest the overheating of the planet. Britain was the first major western country to commit to the goal of net zero by 2050 and it is wonderful—and moving—to see how other countries are now pledging themselves to the same goal.

Those pledges will be hollow, however, without serious commitments, mainly to the use of new technology, that will make those reductions happen. Again, we in the UK are taking those big and bold steps, not only because it is good for the world but because these green technologies, from wind to hydrogen to carbon capture, have the potential to create hundreds of thousands of high-wage, high-skill jobs in Britain.

It is thanks to our history and geography that the UK is already in many ways more global than our comparators. We have a vast diaspora of people, perhaps five or six million, living abroad, far more as a proportion than most others in the Organisation for Economic Co-operation and Development. We may have only 1 percent of the world's population, but we are the fifth biggest exporter of goods and services.

And we have a third invisible diaspora, far more important and more fruitful even than people or goods, and that is the vast dispersal of British ideas, and British values, puffed around the world like the seeds of some giant pollinating tree. I mean everything from habeas corpus and parliamentary democracy to freedom of speech and gender equality. Sometimes these ideas have flourished, and put forth great roots and branches. Sometimes, frankly, they still fall on stony ground.

So under this integrated review we will work ever harder, and give ourselves all the tools we need, to co-ordinate with like-minded democracies in the US, in Europe and around the world to protect and advance those ideas and beliefs against those who oppose them. These values are not uncontested. They are far from universal. That is why the world needs Global Britain more than ever and, to be truly prosperous and successful, Britain needs to be global.

Source: "PM Boris Johnson: The Oxford vaccine shows why we and the world need Britain to be global," available online at: https://www.gov.uk/government/speeches/pm-boris-johnson-the-oxford-vaccine-shows-why-we-and-the-world-need-britain-to-be-global (last accessed January 20, 2023)

Appendix 7: Read President Trump's Speech on Coronavirus Pandemic: Full Transcript

My fellow Americans, tonight I want to speak with you about our nation's unprecedented response to the coronavirus outbreak that started in China and is now spreading throughout the world.

Today, the World Health Organization officially announced that this is a global pandemic.

We have been in frequent contact with our allies, and we are marshaling the full power of the federal government and the private sector to protect the American people.

This is the most aggressive and comprehensive effort to confront a foreign virus in modern history. I am confident that by counting and continuing to take these tough measures, we will significantly reduce the threat to our citizens and we will ultimately and expeditiously defeat this virus.

From the beginning of time, nations and people have faced unforeseen challenges, including large-scale and very dangerous health threats. This is the way it always was and always will be. It only matters how you respond, and we are responding with great speed and professionalism.

Our team is the best anywhere in the world. At the very start of the outbreak, we instituted sweeping travel restrictions on China and put in place the first federally mandated quarantine in over fifty years. We declared a public health emergency and issued the highest level of travel warning on other countries as the virus spread its horrible infection.

And taking early intense action, we have seen dramatically fewer cases of the virus in the United States than are now present in Europe.

The European Union failed to take the same precautions and restrict travel from China and other hot spots. As a result, a large number of new clusters in the United States were seeded by travelers from Europe.

After consulting with our top government health professionals, I have decided to take several strong but necessary actions to protect the health and well being of all Americans.

To keep new cases from entering our shores, we will be suspending all travel from Europe to the United States for the next thirty days. The new rules will go into effect Friday at midnight. These restrictions will be adjusted subject to conditions on the ground.

There will be exemptions for Americans who have undergone appropriate screenings, and these prohibitions will not only apply to the tremendous amount of trade and cargo, but various other things as we get approval. Anything coming from Europe to the United States is what we are discussing. These restrictions will also not apply to the United Kingdom.

At the same time, we are monitoring the situation in China and in South Korea. And, as their situation improves, we will re-evaluate the restrictions and warnings that are currently in place for a possible early opening.

Earlier this week, I met with the leaders of the health insurance industry who have agreed to waive all co-payments for coronavirus treatments, extend insurance coverage to these treatments, and to prevent surprise medical billing.

We are cutting massive amounts of red tape to make antiviral therapies available in record time. These treatments will significantly reduce the impact and reach of the virus.

Additionally, last week, I signed into law an $8.3 billion funding bill to help C.D.C. and other government agencies fight the virus and support vaccines, treatments and distribution of medical supplies. Testing and testing capabilities are expanding rapidly, day by day. We are moving very quickly.

The vast majority of Americans: The risk is very, very low. Young and healthy people can expect to recover fully and quickly if they should get the virus. The highest risk is for the elderly population with underlying health conditions. The elderly population must be very, very careful.

In particular, we are strongly advising that nursing homes for the elderly suspend all medically unnecessary visits. In general, older Americans should also avoid nonessential travel in crowded areas.

My administration is coordinating directly with communities with the largest outbreaks, and we have issued guidance on school closures, social distancing and reducing large gatherings.

Smart action today will prevent the spread of the virus tomorrow.

Every community faces different risks and it is critical for you to follow the guidelines of your local officials who are working closely with our federal health experts—and they are the best.

For all Americans, it is essential that everyone take extra precautions and practice good hygiene. Each of us has a role to play in defeating this virus. Wash your hands, clean often-used surfaces, cover your face and mouth if you sneeze or cough, and most of all, if you are sick or not feeling well, stay home.

To ensure that working Americans impacted by the virus can stay home without fear of financial hardship, I will soon be taking emergency action, which is unprecedented, to provide financial relief. This will be targeted for workers who are ill, quarantined, or caring for others due to coronavirus.

I will be asking Congress to take legislative action to extend this relief.

Because of the economic policies that we have put into place over the last three years, we have the greatest economy anywhere in the world, by far.

Our banks and financial institutions are fully capitalized and incredibly strong. Our unemployment is at a historic low. This vast economic prosperity gives us flexibility, reserves, and resources to handle any threat that comes our way.

This is not a financial crisis, this is just a temporary moment of time that we will overcome together as a nation and as a world.

However, to provide extra support for American workers, families, and businesses, tonight I am announcing the following additional actions: I am instructing the Small Business Administration to exercise available authority to provide capital and liquidity to firms affected by the coronavirus.

Effective immediately, the S.B.A. will begin providing economic loans in affected states and territories. These low-interest loans will help small businesses overcome temporary economic disruptions caused by the virus. To this end, I am asking Congress to increase funding for this program by an additional $50 billion.

Using emergency authority, I will be instructing the Treasury Department to defer tax payments, without interest or penalties, for certain individuals and businesses negatively impacted. This action will provide more than $200 billion of additional liquidity to the economy.

Finally, I am calling on Congress to provide Americans with immediate payroll tax relief. Hopefully they will consider this very strongly.

We are at a critical time in the fight against the virus. We made a lifesaving move with early action on China. Now we must take the same action with Europe. We will not delay. I will never hesitate to take any necessary steps to protect the lives, health, and safety of the American people. I will always put the well-being of America first.

If we are vigilant—and we can reduce the chance of infection, which we will—we will significantly impede the transmission of the virus. The virus will not have a chance against us.

No nation is more prepared or more resilient than the United States. We have the best economy, the most advanced health care, and the most talented doctors, scientists and researchers anywhere in the world.

We are all in this together. We must put politics aside, stop the partisanship and unify together as one nation and one family.

As history has proven time and time again, Americans always rise to the challenge and overcome adversity.

Our future remains brighter than anyone can imagine. Acting with compassion and love, we will heal the sick, care for those in need, help our fellow citizens and emerge from this challenge stronger and more unified than ever before.

God bless you, and God bless America. Thank you.

Source: "Read President Trump's Speech on Coronavirus Pandemic: Full Transcript," available online at: https://www.nytimes.com/2020/03/11/us/politics/trump-coronavirus-speech.html (last accessed January 17, 2023)

Appendix 8: Remarks by President Trump at the Operation Warp Speed Vaccine Summit

THE PRESIDENT: Thank you very much. Please. (Applause).

Thank you very much. Appreciate it very much.

I'm honored to welcome doctors, scientists, industry executives, and state and local leaders to our historic Operation Warp Speed Vaccine Summit. It's been some journey for all of us. It's been an incredible success.

We're grateful to be joined by Vice President Mike Pence, who has done an absolutely incredible job on the Coronavirus Task Force. Mike, thank you. Stand up, Mike. (Applause.) Great job.

We're here to discuss a monumental national achievement. From the instant the coronavirus invaded our shores, we raced into action to develop a safe and effective vaccine at breakneck speed. It would normally take five years, six years, seven years, or even more. In order to achieve this goal, we harnessed the full power of government, the genius of American scientists, and the might of American industry to save millions and millions of lives all over the world. We're just days away from authorization from the FDA, and we're pushing them hard, at which point we will immediately begin mass distribution.

Before Operation Warp Speed, the typical timeframe for development and approval, as you know, could be infinity. And we were very, very happy that we were able to get things done at a level that nobody has ever seen before. The gold standard vaccine has been done in less than nine months.

On behalf of the entire nation, I want to thank everyone here today who has been involved in this extraordinary American initiative. I also want to recognize members of my administration who have worked tirelessly in this effort:

Alex Azar. Please, Alex. Where's Alex? Thank you, Alex. Great job. (Applause.)

Moncef Slaoui. Where are you, Moncef? Thank you very much. Great job. (Applause.)

A man who's now going to be very important, General Gus Perna. I have no doubt about it, right? (Applause.) Logistics.

Jared Kushner. He's worked so hard. Where's Jared? Jared, wherever you may be. Thank you. Thank you, Jared. (Applause.)

Dr. Deborah Birx. Deborah? Thank you very much, Deborah. (Applause.)

Admiral Brett Giroir. Where is Brett? (Applause.) Great job you've been doing, Brett.

Surgeon General Jerome Adams. (Applause.) Jerome, thank you very much. Terrific.

Dr. Robert Redfield. (Applause.) Robert, thank you very much. Appreciate it.

Administrator Seema Verma. Seema? Thank you. (Applause.)

Dr. Peter Marks. Peter? Where's Peter? Thank you. (Applause.)

Paul Mango, Adam Boehler, and Brad Smith—thank you very much. Great job. (Applause.) Thank you all very much. Incredible job. And many others, also. Many, many others.

We're also grateful to be joined by Governors Greg Abbott. Where's Greg? (Applause.) Bill Lee. Bill? (Applause.) Thank you. Thank you. Thank you, Bill. Ron DeSantis. Ron? (Applause.) Thank you, Ron. Thank you. Thank you very much. Great job, Ron. And John Bel Edwards. John Bel. Thank you. (Applause.) Thank you, John Bel. Thank you very much.

As well as Senator John Barrasso, who is a fantastic doctor, also, by the way, I have to say. (Applause.) When we—when I need info on that subject, I call up John. Thank you, John, very much.

Senator Steve Daines. Congratulations on a great win. Great win. (Applause.) That was easier than you thought, it turned out, right? It was a little easier than you thought. Great going. We're proud of you.

Congressman Greg Walden. Greg, thank you very much. (Applause.) Thank you very much.

And Congressman Brad Wenstrup. Thank you, Brad. (Applause.) Great job. And many, many others.

My administration provided a total of $14 billion to accelerate vaccine development and to manufacture all of the top candidates in advance—long in advance.

As a result of this unprecedented investment, we are exceedingly proud that both Pfizer and Moderna have announced that their vaccines are approximately 95 percent effective, which is a number that nobody expected to be able to get to, far exceeding anything that really we—that anybody thought. We went out and we said, "What do you think a maximum would be?" And I think doctors—we all came up to the conclusion that something like that would be really incredible.

And we have other candidates looking right now. We have some big ones that we're going to be announcing very soon. We have some companies—great, great companies out there you all know about: Johnson & Johnson and—and others. And they're all coming in, and they're coming in very quickly. We expect to have some news on that very shortly. And we have worked very well with the companies, but if for any reason we have any problems, we will be instituting the Defense Production Act, and we will make sure that we don't have any problems for very long. We've instituted it before.

Two additional companies, AstraZeneca and Johnson & Johnson—as you know, the Johnson & Johnson is a one-dose, one-shot vaccine, so we're going to see how that works. That would be very helpful if that all came out, and I think it probably will. Also, they're showing tremendous—tremendous promise, all of them. Tremendous prob-—

We're—we're very hopeful that the FDA will authorize the Pfizer vaccine within days. We got to get it moving. And Moderna vaccine almost immediately thereafter. Large numbers of tests and samples have been done, so hopefully that'll go very quickly.

If authorized, tens of millions of vaccine doses will be available this month. And we'll get it distributed very quickly. We have that all set. And hundreds of millions more will quickly follow.

Every American who wants the vaccine will be able to get the vaccine. And we think by spring we're going to be in a position that nobody would have believed possible just a few months ago. (Applause.) Yeah. Amazing. Really amazing. They say it's—they say it's somewhat of a miracle, and I think that's true.

The plan we put forward prioritizes the elderly and patients with underlying conditions, as well as healthcare workers and first responders.

The ultimate decision rests with the governors of the various states—and I hope the governors make wise decisions—who will decide where the vaccines will go in their state and who will get them first. We urge the governors to put America's seniors first, and also, I think those who work with seniors, which obviously you're going to have to do that. I think they have to go together. And doctors, nurses, first responders, et cetera.

This will quickly and dramatically reduce deaths and hospitalizations. And within a short period of time, I think we want to get back to normal. A very standard phrase. We want to just get back to normal, get back to where we were a little more than nine months ago. We were doing incredibly. And in many respects, we're still doing incredibly with our stock markets and everything else, which are hitting all new highs.

We've already finalized a partnership with Walgreens and CVS, whose executives join us today. Thank you very much for being here. Thank you very much. We appreciate it very much. (Applause.) And they will deliver vaccines directly to nursing homes as soon as the states request that they do so.

Later today, General Gus Perna will outline the detailed plan to rapidly distribute the vaccine to every state, territory, and tribe. States have designated over 50,000 sites that will receive the vaccine. We've worked very closely with the states. Actually, we've had very good relationships with the governors—I almost think all of the governors—at least in those conference calls that are somewhat secret, other than sometimes on occasion, Mike, the press will break in, which is fine too. (Laughter.)

It's amazing how you leave those rooms and about 10 seconds later—there wasn't even time for a leak—they were on the call. (Laughter.) But that's all right. So you assume that. You always assume that. But they'll be going through pharmacies, hospitals, healthcare providers.

Through our partnership with FedEx, UPS, and McKesson, we'll ship doses from warehouses directly to the designated sites. And we're thrilled to be joined by representatives of those, really, great American companies. Those companies have worked with us, and they've been incredible to work with. And I want to thank you all for being here. Please, thank you very much. (Applause.) Thank you. Thank you very much.

As I've stated all along—and I guess as you saw pretty vividly. I heard about the—I heard about what they—we're going to show prior to my coming. You saw that very few people thought that this was possible. Of course, they'll be saying now, "We always told you it was so." But we have them saying a little bit different.

But it has been incredible. And it will end the pandemic. It will end the pandemic. And we're working with other nations. As you see actually by looking at your screen today, we're working very closely with other nations also to get the vaccines out to other nations. And that's very important. We work with the world. We're working with the world. We have great companies, and we're working with the world.

In just a few minutes, I'll sign an executive order to ensure that the United States government prioritizes the getting out of the vaccine to American citizens before sending it to other nations.

Now, if necessary, I told you, we'll invoke the Defense Production Act, but we don't think it will be necessary. If it is—it's a very powerful act, as you know, because we've used it very, very successfully.

While we begin to swiftly deploy the vaccine, we'll continue to expand the availability of groundbreaking therapies. Since April, advances in treatments have already helped reduce the mortality rate by 85 percent. Think of that: 85 percent. (Applause.) It's an incredible number.

I've delivered on my solemn promise to make the antibody treatments—they're brilliant; they're highly successful—available to every American, and we're doing that free of cost—totally free of cost. So we're making them available, and they're available now. And if somebody gets sick, it works, where they go and they get treatment if that's what the doctors are prescribing. And it's been incredible, the success.

And when you hear 85 percent, that's some number. To me, that's a number that goes along with anything else, including the vaccines, when you think about it. As well as we've done with the vaccines, when you hear "85 percent," people—people find that one hard to believe. But you look at the stats, and you see what's happening.

And you look at other countries; they're having tremendous difficulties in Europe—tremendous. Beyond—relatively beyond what we're having. They're having them all over the world.

But this will vanquish the—the problem, this horrible scourge—as I call it, the "China virus," because that's where it came from.

The virus has really been looked at and studied all over the world, and our scientists, our industrial and economic mobilization has been like nobody else in the world could have done. And it's very important that we share that with others and other nations.

I've worked and invoked the Defense Production Act over 100 times to manufacture essential supplies in the United States. Despite the grim projections from the media eight months ago, where they said this was impossible—they actually said—and you saw that a little bit, but I could give you two hours' worth of it. But they said it will never happen; you could never do it; it was a pipe dream. But we—we did something that nobody thought was possible.

And we also did it where no American who has needed a ventilator has been denied a ventilator. When we—when this first came out, we weren't equipped for that. Nobody was equipped for that. And we're now making ventilators. And we have all we need in this country, but we're sending them to countries all over the world. We're making thousands and thousands of ventilators a month.

The United States has also created the largest, most advanced, and most innovative testing program in the world by far. We've conducted over 200 million tests. Think of that: 200 million tests—more than all of the European Union combined. It's not even close.

Just 10 months ago, none of these innovations even existed. The tremendous progress that we've made is a testament to what our nation is capable of. When America is faced with a challenge, we come through—and we always come through—to overcome every hardship and surmount every obstacle. And I think you'll be seeing that over the next few months; the numbers should skyrocket downward.

We are the most exceptional nation in the history of the world. Today, we're on the verge of another American medical miracle. And that's what people are saying. People that aren't necessarily big fans of Donald Trump are saying, "Whether you like him or not, this is one of the greatest miracles in the history of modern-day medicine" or any other medicine—any other age of medicine.

American companies were the first to produce a verifiably safe and effective vaccine. Together, we will defeat the virus, and we will soon end the pandemic, and we will save millions and millions of lives, both in our country and all over the world. And we've already started.

Thank you again to every person here today and for the incredible achievements that you've done. You're going to be very proud of this day, and you're going to be very proud of this period of time because nobody thought this was possible. Nobody thought it was even remotely possible to do what we've done in a period of less than nine months—something that—just not even thinkable.

And we took a lot of heat when we said this is our goal, and we, frankly, weren't even quite using the numbers that we used. We far exceeded what we thought. If we would have said "sometime next year," I think most people would have said, "That would be great. That would be a miracle." But we did it long before sometime next year.

So now I want to ask several leaders who have been crucial in this effort to join me on stage as I sign the executive order to ensure that American citizens have first priority to receive American vaccines. And then we're going to be working with other countries all over the world, and I think we'll be able to start doing that almost immediately also, because we have millions of doses coming in.

So thank you very much. Thank you. It's a great honor. (Applause.)

(The executive order is signed.)

So, let's see here. I guess we have to do our Vice President, right? (Applause.)

AUDIENCE MEMBER: Thank you, Mr. President.

THE PRESIDENT: Thank you very much. (Applause.)

Thank you very much, everybody. Thank you. (Applause.)

Any questions, please? (Applause.) Thank you. Thank you all. (Applause.)

Any questions, please? A question?

Yes, please.

Q Mr. President, it's clearly a success, this vaccine. I'm wondering, though, what your message is to the American people, given all of the increasing cases right now, about what they should do over Christmas and the hardship that they're all facing as this virus does get worse.

THE PRESIDENT: Yeah, well, CDC puts out their guidelines, and they're very important guidelines, but I think this: I think that the vaccine was our goal. That was number one because that was the way—that was the way it ends. Plus, you do have an immunity. You develop immunity over a period of time, and I hear we're close to 15 percent. I'm hearing that, and that is terrific. That's a very powerful vaccine in itself. And just tremendous progress has been made.

One of the reasons we do show so many—and I say this, and I've been saying it for a long time—so many cases is because of the fact that we have 200 million tests. And you take—I think India is actually in second place with just a fraction of that number. So we're many times greater than the second country, and India has 1.4 billion people where—our testing program has been incredible.

And we actually are also coming out with new tests very shortly that will make the process even easier, and you won't need doctors necessarily to do the test. So we have some incredible tests coming out in a very short period of time.

Yeah, please.

Q Mr. President, some of these scientific officials here in this room have encouraged Americans not to travel this holiday season, not to go to large gatherings. Across the street, you've been holding holiday parties with hundreds of people, many not wearing masks. Why are you modeling a different behavior to the American people than what your scientists tell?

THE PRESIDENT: Well, they're Christmas parties, and frankly, we've reduced the number very substantially, as you know. And I see a lot of people at the parties wearing masks. I mean, I would say that I look out at the audience at those parties, and we have a lot of people wearing masks, and I think that's a good thing.

Yeah, please. Over here. Go ahead.

Q The next administration will be the one, ultimately, that implements a lot of the distribution of this vaccine and will oversee much of the future of the way Operation Warp Speed goes forward. Why not include members of the Biden transition team as part of this summit that you're hosting today?

THE PRESIDENT: Well, we're going to have to see who the next administration is—because we won in those swing states, and there was terrible things that went on. So we're going to have to see who the next administration is. But whichever the next administration is will really benefit by what we've been able to do with this incredible science, the doctors—all of the people that came up—the lab technicians. The work that's been done is incredible, and it will be incredible for the next administration.

And hopefully the next administration will be the Trump administration, because you can't steal hundreds of thousands of votes. You can't have fraud and deception and all of the things that they did, and then slightly win a swing state. And you just have to look at the numbers. Look at what's been on tape. Look at all the corruption. And we'll see. You can't win an election like that.

So hopefully the next administration will be the Trump administration, a continuation—which has led us to the highest stock markets we've ever had, the best employment numbers we've ever had, a rebuilt military.

If you look at—the tax reductions are the greatest in history; the regulation reductions, the greatest in history. It leads us to Space Force, which nobody thought was possible. All of the things we've done. And we were rewarded with a victory.

Now, let's see whether or not somebody has the courage—whether it's a legislator or legislatures, or whether it's a justice of the Supreme Court or a number of justices of the Supreme Court. Let's see if they have the courage to do what everybody in this country knows is right.

I received almost 75 million votes, the highest number of votes in the history of our country for a sitting President—12 million more than the 63 million we received four years ago. President Obama received 3 million less in his second term, and he won easily. I received 12 million more, which, by the way, is a record. Twelve million more.

And they say that when the numbers came out—and the numbers came through machines. And all of those ballots were taken away and added. All you have to do is turn on your local television set and you'll see what happened with thousands of ballots coming out from under tables—with all of the terrible things you saw. All you have to do is take a look.

And if somebody has the courage, I know who the next administration will be. And I'll tell you what: Life will be much easier for this country because of what we've done right now and because of a lot of the people in this room. The job you've done on the vaccine, together with a lot of others, has been a modern-day miracle, and it's really been acknowledged as such.

And I want to thank you. I want to give you my love, and I want to give you my thanks because you're very special people.

And now, good luck. You distribute that, General, and really set records. Okay? Set records, just like we've been doing for four years.

Thank you very much. Thank you, everybody. Thank you. (Applause.)

END 2:28 P.M. EST

The White House

Source: "Remarks by President Trump at the Operation Warp Speed Vaccine Summit." Available online at: https://trumpwhitehouse.archives.gov/briefings-statements/remarks-president-trump-operation-warp-speed-vaccine-summit/ (last accessed December 2, 2022)

REFERENCES

Primary Data

Aita, F. 2025. "Email to author." May 25.

BBC. 2012. "Full text: China's new party chief Xi Jinping's speech." November 15. https://www.bbc.co.uk/news/world-asia-china-20338586 (last accessed May 21, 2025)

CGTN. 2020. "Full text: Premier Li's speech at the third session of the 13th NPC." May 22. https://news.cgtn.com/news/2020-05-22/Full-text-Premier-Li-s-speech-at-the-third-session-of-the-13th-NPC-QHaP1FpB8k/index.html (last accessed May 21, 2025)

EU Council Newsroom. 2025. "Email to author." May 16.

Johnson, B. 2020. "Prime minister's opening statement to the house of commons on the UK-EU deal: December 30, 2020." *GOV.UK*, December 30. https://www.gov.uk/government/speeches/prime-ministers-opening-statement-to-the-house-of-commons-on-the-uk-eu-deal-30-december-2020 (last accessed May 21, 2025)

Johnson, B. 2020. "Prime minister's statement on coronavirus (Covid-19): March 23, 2020." *GOV.UK*, March 23. https://www.gov.uk/government/speeches/pm-address-to-the-nation-on-coronavirus-23-march-2020 (last accessed May 21, 2025)

Johnson, B. 2021. "No government can address the threat of pandemics alone—we must come together." *GOV.UK*, March 30. https://www.gov.uk/government/speeches/no-government-can-address-the-threat-of-pandemics-alone-we-must-come-together (last accessed May 21, 2025)

Johnson, B. 2021. "PM Boris Johnson: The Oxford vaccine shows why we and the world need Britain to be global." *GOV.UK*, March 16. https://www.gov.uk/government/speeches/pm-boris-johnson-the-oxford-vaccine-shows-why-we-and-the-world-need-britain-to-be-global (last accessed May 21, 2025)

Khalid, T. 2020. "Full transcript of Saudi Arabia's Mohamed bin Salman's remarks at G20 Riyadh Summit." *Al Arabiya English*, November 22. https://english.alarabiya.net/News/gulf/2020/11/22/Full-transcript-of-Saudi-Arabia-s-Mohammed-bin-Salman-s-remarks-at-G20-Riyadh-Summit (last accessed May 21, 2025)

Khalid, T. 2020. "Saudi King on coronavirus: We will provide all medicine, food, living needs." *Al Arabiya English*, May 20. https://english.alarabiya.net/News/gulf/2020/03/19/Saudi-Arabia-s-King-Salman-to-address-nation-on-coronavirus (last accessed May 21, 2025)

The National People's Congress of the People's Republic of China. 2016. "The building and development of China's national people's congress website." July 21. http://www.npc.gov.cn/c191/c681/c1960/201905/t20190521_423200.html (last accessed May 21, 2025)

Trump, D. 2020. "Read President Trump's speech on coronavirus pandemic: Full transcript." *The New York Times*, March 11. https://www.nytimes.com/2020/03/11/us/politics/trump-coronavirus-speech.html (last accessed May 21, 2025)

Trump, D. 2020. "Remarks by President Trump at the Operation Warp Speed vaccine summit." *The White House*, December 8. https://trumpwhitehouse.archives.gov/

briefings-statements/remarks-president-trump-operation-warp-speed-vaccine-summit/ (last accessed May 21, 2025)

Xinhua. 2021. "Full text: Remarks by Chinese President Xi Jinping at the global health summit." *China Daily*, May 21. https://www.chinadaily.com.cn/a/202105/21/WS60a7bbcca31024ad0bac0b12.html (last accessed May 21, 2025)

Secondary Data

Academic Reports/Papers

Abousaleh, A., Alarabi, D., Al Zubaidi, K., Elsaid, M.F., Ghorab, O.K., Keshta, A.S., Keshta, M.S., Mallah, S.I., Salman, M.T., Taha, O.E., Tang, P., Zeidan, A.A. 2021. "Covid-19 versus SARS: A comparative review." *Journal of Infection and Public Health*, 14 (7), pp. 967–77

Africa Center for Strategic Studies. 2020. "Lessons from the 1918–1919 Spanish Flu Pandemic in Africa." May 13. https://africacenter.org/spotlight/lessons-1918-1919-spanish-flu-africa/ (last accessed May 27, 2025)

Ahmad, A., Krumkamp, R., Reintjes, R. 2009. "Controlling SARS: A review on China's response compared with other SARS-affected countries." *Tropical Medicine and International Health*, 14 (Suppl 1), pp. 36–45

Ahmed, Q.A., Assiri, A., Deming, M., Ebrahim, S.H., Memish, Z.A. 2010. "Letters: Pandemic H1N1 influenza at the 2009 Hajj: Understanding the unexpectedly low H1N1 burden." *J R Soc Med 2010*, 103 (10), p. 386.

Ahram, A.I., Lust, E. 2016. "The decline and fall of the Arab State." *Survival*, 58 (20), pp. 7–34

Al-Ali, S., Al-Abdel Latif, Z., Al-Abdely, H., Al Arbash, H., Al-Bakhit, H., Abdalla, M.O., Abdalla, O., Alshayeb, Z., Bin Saeed, A., Chahed, M., El Bushra, H.E., Lohiniva, A.L., Mohammed, M. 2016. "An outbreak of Middle East Respiratory Syndrome (MERS) due to coronavirus in Al-Ahssa Region, Saudi Arabia, 2015." *Eastern Mediterranean Health Journal*, 22 (7), pp. 467–74

Al-Dorzy, H.M., Alchin, J.D., Aldawood, A.S., Al Johany, S.M., Arabi, Y.M., Baharoon, S., Balkhy, H.H., Khan, R., Matroud, A.A. 2016. "The critical care response to a hospital outbreak of Middle East respiratory syndrome coronavirus (MERS-CoV) infection: An observational study." *Annals of Intensive Care*, 6 (101), pp. 1–11

Alexandre-Collier, A. 2022. "David Cameron, Boris Johnson and the 'populist hypothesis' in the British Conservative Party." *Comparative European Politics*, April 13, 20, pp. 527–43

Alhamid, S., Shujaa, A. 2015. "Health response to Hajj mass gathering from emergency perspective, narrative review." *Turkish Journal of Emergency Medicine*, 15 (4), pp. 172–6

Alhugbani, H.F. 2022. "Covid-19 compliance across societies: Testing health messaging models in the U.S. and the Kingdom of Saudi Arabia." *Advances in Applied Sociology*, 14 (8), pp. 387–403. https://www.scirp.org/journal/paperinformation?paperid=135138 (last accessed November 5, 2024)

Aljadeed, R., Alotaibi, A., Almohammed, O., Alrumaih, A.M., Alruthia, Y., Alwhaibi, M., Asiri, Y., Balkhi, B., Sales, I. 2021. "The impact of Covid-19 on essential medicines and personal protective equipment availability and prices in Saudi Arabia." *Healthcare (Basel)*, March, 9 (3), pp. 1–14. https://pubmed.ncbi.nlm.nih.gov/33800012/#:~:text=Approximately%2053%25%20of%20the%20participants,manageable%20in%20Saudi%20healthcare%20institutions (last accessed January 4, 2023), pp. 1–14

Al-Jedal, A., AlSalamah, S., Alzaaqi, S.M., Arafa, A., Llu, K., Muriungi, N.G., Sampaio, B.F.C., Sheerah, H.A., Shirai, K., Tromp, J., Withers, M. 2024. "Navigating hurdles: A review of the obstacles facing the development of the pandemic treaty." *Journal of Epidemiology and Global Health*, 14 (3), pp. 580–5

Alkhaldi, G. 2024. "An unprecedented experience: Personal and socio-political impacts of the Covid-19 lockdown in Saudi Arabia." *Cureus*, 16 (2), pp. 1–14

Almazroa, M.A., Alwadey, A.A., Memish, Z.A. 2010. "Pandemic influenza A (H1N1) in Saudi Arabia: Description of the first one hundred cases." *Annals of Saudi Medicine*, 30 (1), pp. 11–14

Alqahtani, A. 2022. "The influence of cultural and psychological factors on mental health status during Covid-19 in Saudi Arabia." *The Open Psychology Journal*, 15, pp. 1–6

Al-Qahtani, M., Al-Tawfiq, A., Bukamal, N., Seddiq, N. 2017. "Case report: First confirmed case of Middle East respiratory syndrome Coronavirus infection in the Kingdom of Bahrain: in a Saudi gentleman after Cardiac bypass surgery." *Case Reports in Infectious Diseases*, August 28, 2017, (1), pp. 1–4

Al-Rasheed, M. 2020. "Brute force and hollow reforms in Saudi Arabia." *Current History*, December, 119 (821), pp. 331–7

Al Suwaidi, K., Due-Gundersen, N. 2024. *Potential for the UAE as a Model for Coordinating GCC-Wide Economic Diversification*. Anwar Gargash Diplomatic Academy.

Arino, J., Calderon, F., Chabbra, A., Chan, A., Brownstein, J., Gardam, G., Heidebrecht, C., Hu, W., Janes, D.A., Khan, Kamran, Liauw, J., Macdonald, M., Memish, Z., Sears, J., Raposo, P., Wang, J. 2010. "Global public health implications of a mass gathering in Mecca, Saudi Arabia during the midst of an influenza pandemic." *Journal of Travel Medicine*, 17 (2), pp. 75–81

Armstrong, J.S., Downie, Gibbs, A.J. 2009. "From where did the 2009 'swine origin' influenza A virus (H1N1) emerge?" *Virology Journal*, 6 (207), pp. 1–11

Arzoz-Padrés, J., Córdova-Villalobos, J.A., Kuri-Morales, P., Manuell-Lee, G., Mendez, J.R. 2009. "The influenza A (H1N1) epidemic in Mexico. Lessons learned." *Health Research and Policy Systems*, 7 (21), pp. 1–7

Ayoob, M. 2004. "Political Islam: Image and reality." *World Policy Journal*, 21 (3), pp. 1–14

Bangerter, A., Clémence, A., Eicher, V., Gilles, I., Green, E.G. T., Mayor, E. 2012. "Dynamic social representations of the 2009 H1N1 pandemic: Shifting patterns of sense-making and blame." *Public Understanding of Science*, 22 (8), pp. 1011–24

Barber, R., Faust, J.S., Gisondi, M.A., Gottlieb, M., Raja, A., Strehlow, M.C., Westafar, L.M. 2022. "A deadly infodemic: Social media and the power of Covid-19 misinformation." *Journal of Medical Internet Research*, 24 (2), pp. 1–7

Barberis, I., Bragazzi, N.L., Gazzaniga, V., Martini, M. 2019. "The Spanish influenza pandemic: A lesson from history 100 years after 1918." *Journal of Preventive Medicine and Hygiene*, March 29, 60 (1), pp. 64–7. https://www.ncbi.nlm.nih.gov/pmc/articles/PMC6477554/ (last accessed December 4, 2022)

Barona, C.C., Mantilla, K.K. 2022. "Covid-19 vaccines as global public goods: Between life and profit." *Research Paper 154. South Centre*, May 9.

Barros, A.I., van Engers, T.M., Sloot, P.M., van der Zwet, K. 2022. "Emergence of protests during the Covid-19 pandemic: Quantitative models to explore the contributions of societal conditions." *Humanities and Social Sciences Communications*, 9 (68), pp. 1–11

Batool, M., Durai, P., Choi, S., Shah, M. 2015. "Middle East respiratory syndrome coronavirus: Transmission, virology and therepeutic targeting to aid in outbreak control." *Experimental & Molecular Medicine*, 47 (181), pp. 1–10

Bekheit, M.M., Blendon, R.J., Lubell, K., Steelfisher, G.K. 2010. "The public's response to the 2009 H1N1 influenza pandemic." *The New England Journal of Medicine*, 362 (65), pp. 1–6

Berger, C., Branje, S., Carlo, G., Carrizales, A., Cheng, T., De Moor, E.L., Garandeau, C.F., Gerbino, M., Hawk, S.T., Kaniušonyte, G., Kumru, A., Malonda, E., Rovella, A., Shen, Y., Spitzer, J.E., Taylor, L.K., Van der Graaff, J., van Zalk, M., Walker, L. P. 2022. "What should I do and Who's to blame? A cross-national study on youth's attitudes and beliefs in times of Covid-19." *PLOS One*, 17 (12), pp. 1–20

Bi, Y., Gao, G.F., Li, S., Liu, Y., Su, S., Wong, G. 2015. "MERS in South Korea and China: A potential outbreak threat?" *The Lancet*, June 13, 385 (9985), pp. 2349–50

Boddington, N., Parry-Ford, F., Pebody, R., Phin, N. 2015. "Public health response to two incidents of confirmed MERS-CoV cases travelling on flights through London Heathrow Airport in 2014-lessons learnt." *Euro Surveillance*, May 7, 20 (18), pp. 1–7

Bollyky, T.J., Bown, C.P. 2020. "The tragedy of vaccine nationalism: Only cooperation can end the pandemic." *Foreign Affairs*, 99 (5), pp. 96–108

Bootsma, M.C.J., Ferguson, N.M. 2007. "The effect of public health measures on the 1918 influenza pandemic in the US cities." *Proceedings of the National Academy of Sciences of the United States of America*, April 6, 104 (18), pp. 7588–93. https://pubmed.ncbi.nlm.nih.gov/17416677/ (last accessed December 9, 2022)

Bradley, T., Malki, I., Ghalib, A., Ziniel, C. 2021. "The case of the United Kingdom: Mapping localism, resilience, and civic activism in response to the Covid-19 pandemic." *International Journal of Social Quality*, 11 (1&2), pp. 145–75

Bryan, P., Davies, C., Seabroke, S. 2010. "H1N1 vaccine safety: Real-time surveillance in the UK." *The Lancet*, 376 (9739), pp. 417–18

Buckley, P., Enderwick, P. 2020. "Rising regionalization: Will the post-Covid-19 world see a retreat from globalization?" *Transnational Corporations*, 27 (2), pp. 99–112

Bunga, S., Dunville, R.L., Erdman, D.D., Gerber, S.I., Haynes, L., Kuhar, D., Mason, K.A., Pallansch, M.A., Pesik, N., Poser, S., Rotz, L., St. Pierre, J., Swerdlow, D.L., Williams, H.A. 2015. "CDC's early response to a novel viral disease, Middle East Respiratory Syndrome Coronavirus (MERS-CoV), September 2012–May 2014." *Public Health Reports*, 130 (4), pp. 307–17

Caliendo, G. 2022. "Vaccine nationalism or 'Brexit Dividend'? Strategies of legitimation in the EU-UK post-Brexit debate on Covid-19 vaccination campaigns." *Societies*, 12 (37), pp. 1–15

Cao, X., Evans, R., Zeng, R. 2022. "Digital activism and collective mourning by Chinese netizens during Covid-19." *China Information*, 36 (2), pp. 159–79

Carter, J. 2014. "WHO's virus is it anyway? How the World Health Organization can protect against claims of 'Viral Sovereignty.'" *Georgia Journal of International & Comparative Law*, 38 (3), pp. 718–40

Cetron, M., Foster, J.A., Misrahi, J.J., Shaw, F.E. 2004. "HHS/CDC legal response to SARS outbreak." *Emerging Infectious Diseases*, 10 (2), pp. 353–5

Chakrabarti, C., De Leon, J., Homan, P., Mehta, J.M., Skipton, T., Sparkman, R. 2022. "Assessing the role of collectivism and individualism on Covid-19 beliefs and behaviors in the Southeastern United States." *PLOS One*, 18 (1), pp. 1–17

Chan, M.C.H., Hui, D.S.C., Ng, P.C., Wu, A.K. 2004. "Severe acute respiratory syndrome (SARS): Epidemiology and clinical features." *Postgraduate Medical Journal*, 80 (945). https://academic.oup.com/pmj/article/80/945/373/7033890 (last accessed May 18, 2025)

Chan, R.K.H. 2021. "Tackling Covid-19 risk in Hong Kong: Examining distrust, compliance and risk management." *Current Sociology*, 69 (4), pp. 547–65

Cheng, K.F., Leung, P.C. 2007. "What happened in China during the 1918 influenza pandemic?" *International Journal of Infectious Diseases*, 11 (4), pp. 360–4

Chi, W., Ferrall, L., Hung, C., Li, Y., Su, J., Wu, T. 2020. "Coronavirus vaccine development: From SARS and MERS to Covid-19." *Journal of Biomedical Science*, 27 (104), pp. 1–23

Cowling, B.J., Ip, D.K.M., Lau, E.H.Y., Nishiura, H., Wu, J.T., Wu, P. 2013. "The epidemiological and public health research response to 2009 pandemic influenza A (H1N1): Experiences from Hong Kong." *Influenza and Other Respiratory Viruses Journal*, 7 (3), pp. 367–81

Cunningham, M. 2022. *Looking Ahead to China's 20th Party Congress*. Asian Studies Center, March 7.

Daphi, P., Fominaya, C.F., Romanos, E. 2024. "Introduction: Mobilizing during Covid-19: Social movements in times of crisis." *Social Movement Studies*, 23 (6), pp. 667–75

Delpech, V.C., Goddard, N.L., Nicoll, A., Regan, M., Watson, J.M. 2006. "Lessons learned from SARS: The experience of the Health Protection Agency, England." *Journal of the Royal Institute of Public Health*, 120 (1), pp. 27–32

DeSisto, C., Moore, C.W., Moser, K., Rodriguez-Lainz, A., Waterman, S., Wiedemann, M.S., Williams, W.W. 2019. "Influenza vaccination coverage among US-Mexico land border crossers: 2009 H1N1 pandemic and 2011–2012 influenza season." *Travel Med Infect Dis.*, 27, pp. 1–12

Douglas, N., Emary, K., English, M., Henry, J., Hodgson, S.H., Moore, M., Naude, R., Patrick-Smith, M., Pollard, A.J., Stuart, A., Thomas, T., Vanderslott, S. 2021. "Vaccine nationalism and internationalism: Perspectives of Covid-19 vaccine trial participants in the United Kingdom." *BMJ Global Health*, 6 (10), pp. 1–11

Elbe, S. 2022. "Who owns a deadly virus? Viral sovereignty, global health emergencies, and the matrix of the international." *International Political Sociology*, 16 (1–18), pp. 1–18

Fera, D., Gupta, R.K., Kosakovsky-Pond, S.L., Nouhin, J., de Oliveira, T., Tao, K., Tzou, P.L., Shafer, R.W. 2021. "The biological and clinical significance of emerging SARS-CoV-2 variants." *Nature Reviews Genetics*, September 17, 22.

Fewsmith, J. 2003. "China's response to SARS." *China Leadership Monitor*, 7, pp. 1–10

Flinders, M. 2020. "Democracy and the politics of coronavirus." *Parliamentary Affairs*, June 23, 74 (2), pp. 1–20. April 2021. https://www.ncbi.nlm.nih.gov/pmc/articles/PMC7337828/ (last accessed January 10, 2025), pp. 1–20

Ganslmeier, M., Van Parys, J., Vlandas, T. 2022. "Compliance with the first UK Covid-19 lockdown and the compounding effects of weather." *Scientific Reports*, 12, March 9. https://www.nature.com/articles/s41598-022-07857-2 (last accessed May 22, 2025)

Geng, W., Lai, D., Li, X., Tian, H. 2013. "Was mandatory quarantine necessary in China for controlling the 2009 H1N1 pandemic?" *International Journal of Environmental Research and Public Health*, 10 (10), pp. 4690–700

Gilley, B., Hollbig, H. 2010. "Reclaiming legitimacy." *Politics & Policy*, 38 (3), pp. 395–422

Guo, H., Hu, B., Shi, Z., Zhou, P. 2020. "Characteristics of SARS-CoV-2 and Covid-19." *Nature Reviews Microbiology*, October 6, 19 (2021), pp. 141–54. https://www.nature.com/articles/s41579-020-00459-7 (last accessed December 4, 2024)

Halabi, S.F., Rutschmann, A.S. 2022. "Viral sovereignty, vaccine diplomacy, and vaccine nationalism: The institutions of global vaccine access." *Emory International Law Review*, 36 (1), pp. 1–32

Hayton, R. 2021. "Conservative party statecraft and the Johnson government." *The Political Quarterly*, 92 (3), pp. 412–19

Hilton, S., Smith, E. 2010. "Public views of the UK media and government reaction to the 2009 swine flu pandemic." *BMC Public Health*, 10 (697), pp. 1–10

Holzscheiter, A., Kickbusch, I. 2021. "Can geopolitics derail the pandemic treaty?" *BMJ*, 375, pp. 1–4

Honigsbaum, M. 2013. "Regulating the 1918–19 pandemic: Flu, Stoicism and the Northcliffe Press." *Medical History*, April, 57 (2), 165–85

Hung, L.S. 2003. "The SARS epidemic in Hong Kong: What lessons have we learned?" *Journal of the Royal Society of Medicine*, 96 (8), pp. 374–8

Jamali, A.B., Zhang, D. 2022. "China's 'Weaponized' vaccine: Intertwining between international and domestic politics." *East Asia*, 39 (3), pp. 279–86

Ji, J.S. 2020. "Origins of MERS-CoV, and lessons for 2019-nCoV." *The Lancet*, January 30, 4 (3)

Jiang, S., Wei, Q., Zhang, L. 2022. "Individualism versus collectivism and the early-stage transmission of Covid-19." *Social Indicators Research*, 164 (2), pp. 791–821

Johnson, R., Korkut, U., Sahin, O. 2021. "Policy-making by tweets: Discursive governance, populism, and Trump Presidency." *Contemporary Politics*, 27 (5), pp. 591–610

Kazuko, K. 2020. "Politics under Xi Jinping: Centralization and its implications." *Public Policy Review*, September, 16 (3), pp. 1–21

Kim, S.Y., Koh, D.H., Lee, S., Ro, D., Sohn, M. 2021. "The problems of International Health Regulations (IHR) in the process of responding to Covid-19 and improvement measures to improve its effectiveness." *Journal of Global Health Science*, 3 (2), pp. 1–7

Kirgizov-Barskii, A.V., Morozov, V.M. 2022. "Vaccine diplomacy and vaccine nationalism." *Russia in Global Affairs*, 20 (3), pp. 162–81

Kraut, A.M. 2010. "Immigration, ethnicity, and the pandemic." *Public Health Reports*, 125 (Supplement 3), pp. 123–33

Lavizzari, A., Porta, D., Reiter, H. 2022. "The spreading of the Black Lives Matter movement campaign: The Italian case in cross-national perspective." *Sociological Forum*, 37 (3), pp. 700–21

Lee, S.H. 2003. "The SARS epidemic in Hong Kong." *Journal of Epidemiol Community Health*, 57 (2), pp. 652–54

Li, C. 2019. *Xi Jinping's "Proregress": Domestic Moves toward a Global China*. Brookings, September. https://www.brookings.edu/research/xi-jinpings-proregress-domestic-moves-toward-a-global-china/ (last accessed May 22, 2025)

Liu, H., Yan, Y., Yan, g. Y. 2024. "Media debates about China's role as a global public goods supplier: Frame contestation in reporting on the Chinese COVID-19 vaccine." *Humanities and Social Science Communications*, 11 (1341), pp. 1–13

Madani, T.A.A. 2004. "Preventive strategies to keep Saudi Arabia SARS-free." *American Journal of Infection Control*, 32 (2), pp. 120–2

Markel, H., Navarro, J.A. 2021. "Politics, pushback, and pandemics: Challenges to public health orders in the 1918 influenza pandemic." *AJPH: Covid-19 and History*, 111 (3), pp. 416–22

McCauley, M., Minsky, S., Viswanath, K. 2013. "The H1N1 pandemic: Media frames, stigmatization and coping." *BMI Public Health*, 13 (1116), pp. 1–16

Meyer, D.S., Rohlinger, D.A. 2024. "Protest during a pandemic: How Covid-19 affected social movements in the United States." *American Behavioural Scientist*, 68 (6), pp. 810–28

Morens, D.D., Taubenberger, J.K. 2006. "1918 Influenza: The mother of all pandemics." *Emerging Infectious Diseases*, 12 (1), pp. 15–22

Nevo, J. 1998. "Religion and national identity in Saudi Arabia." *Middle Eastern Studies*, 34 (3), pp. 34–53

Nuzzo, J., Rambhia, K. 2009. *2009 H1N1: International Progress in Vaccine Development and Distribution*. Center for Biosecurity of University of Pittsburgh Medical Center, December 17.

Peter, F. 2010. *Political Legitimacy. Stanford University*, April 29. https://plato.stanford.edu/entries/legitimacy/#PolLegDem (last accessed May 21, 2025)

Pitlik, S.D. 2020. "Covid-19 compared to other pandemic diseases." *Rambam Maimonides Medical Journal*, 11 (3), pp. 1–17

Regilme, Jr. S.S.F. 2019. "The decline of American power and Donald Trump: Reflections on human rights, neoliberalism, and the world order." *Geoforum*, 102, pp. 157–66

Rieger, M.O., Wang, M. 2022. "Trust in Government actions during the Covid-19 crisis." *Social Indicators Research*, 159, pp. 967–89

Rolland, N. 2020. "China's pandemic power play." *Journal of Democracy*, July, 31 (3). https://www.journalofdemocracy.org/articles/chinas-pandemic-power-play-2/ (last accessed May 22, 2025)

Saich, T. 2015. *The National People's Congress*. Harvard Kennedy School, November.

Santiago, A.M., Smith, R.J. 2020. "Community practice, social action, and the politics of pandemics." *Journal of Community Practice*, 28 (2), pp. 89–99

Sheline, A., Ulrichsen, K.C. 2019. "Mohammed bin Salman and religious authority and reform in Saudi Arabia." *Baker Institute for Public Policy*, September 19. https://www.bakerinstitute.org/research/mbs-political-religious-authority-saudi-arabia (last accessed May 21, 2025)

Vowles, J. 2022. "Authoritarianism and mass political preferences in times of Covid-19: The 2020 New Zealand general election." *Frontiers in Political Science*, May 18, 4, pp. 1–14. https://www.frontiersin.org/articles/10.3389/fpos.2022.885299/full (last accessed May 22, 2025)

Wang, Z. 2023. *State and Territorial Mobilisation: The Case of Socio-Territorial Movements during the Covid-19 Pandemic Lockdown in Shanghai, China*. Elsevier. https://papers.ssrn.com/sol3/papers.cfm?abstract_id=4679368 (last accessed May 21, 2025)

Ward, B., Ward, J. 2021. "From Brexit to Covid-19: The Johnson government, executive centralisation and authoritarian populism." *Political Studies*, December 28, 00 (0), pp. 1–19

Zevnik, A. 2023. "Anxiety and political action in times of the Covid-19 pandemic." *International Relations*, 37 (1), pp. 164–71

Zhang, L. 2018. "Britain, the United States and isolationism." *Camden Conference*, May 24. https://www.camdenconference.org/wp-content/uploads/2018/06/zhangzhenyanglareina_1533789_63613132_Lareina-New-World-Disorder-FINAL-1.pdf (last accessed May 19, 2025)

Zhou, Y.R. 2022. "Vaccine nationalism: Contested relationships between Covid-19 and globalization." *Globalizations*, 19 (3), pp. 450–65

Media Sources and Blog Reports

ABC News. 2016. "How a Donald Trump victory is similar to Brexit." November 9. https://abcnews.go.com/Politics/donald-trump-victory-similar-brexit/story?id=43420714 (last accessed May 21, 2025)

Abouzzohour, Y. 2021. "Heavy lies the crown: The survival of Arab monarchies, 10 years after the Arab Spring." *Brookings*, March 8. https://www.brookings.edu/blog/order-from-chaos/2021/03/08/heavy-lies-the-crown-the-survival-of-arab-monarchies-10-years-after-the-arab-spring/ (last accessed January 16, 2025)

AFP 2022. "Covid-19: China orders millions in Hebei Province around Beijing into lockdown." *Hong Kong Free Press*, August 30. https://hongkongfp.com/2022/08/30/Covid-19-china-orders-millions-in-hebei-province-around-beijing-into-lockdown/ (last accessed May 21, 2025)

Africa Centres for Disease Control and Prevention. 2024. "Africa CDC statement on the pandemic fund's fast-track allocation of US$128.9 Million to address Mpox in 10 Countries." September 21. https://africacdc.org/news-item/africa-cdc-statement-on-the-pandemic-funds-fast-track-allocation-of-us128-89-million-to-address-mpox-in-10-countries/ (last accessed May 21, 2025)

Agence-France Presse. 2020. "Saudi Arabia seals off Shia Qatif region over coronavirus fears." *The Guardian*, March 9. https://www.theguardian.com/global/2020/mar/09/saudi-arabia-seals-off-shia-qatif-region-over-coronavirus-fears (last accessed January 10, 2025)

Agoda. 2022. "The Ritz-Carlton, Riyadh." https://www.agoda.com/the-ritz-carlton-riyadh/hotel/riyadh-sa.html?cid=-217 (last accessed January 10, 2025)

Ailoaiei, A. 2024. "Is Covid-19 paving the way for authoritarianism and mass surveillance?" *Cyber Ghost*, December 15. https://www.cyberghostvpn.com/en_US/privacyhub/Covid19-authoritarianism/ (last accessed January 30, 2025)

AJMC Staff. 2021. "A timeline of Covid-19 developments in 2020." *AJMC*, January 1. https://www.ajmc.com/view/a-timeline-of-Covid19-developments-in-2020 (last accessed January 17, 2025)

Al-Mutairi, D. 2023. "How Saudi identity is shaped by the values, principles and traditions of the nation's ancestors." *Arab News*, September 23. https://www.arabnews.com/node/2376036/saudi-arabia (last accessed May 21, 2025)

Al-Rasheed, M. 2020. "Brute force and hollow reforms in Saudi Arabia." *Current History*, December, 119 (821), pp. 331–7

Alshammari, H. 2020. "'We're all responsible' slogan reflects unified Saudi efforts to defeat Covid-19." *Arab News*, May 11. https://www.arabnews.com/node/1672821/saudi-arabia (last accessed May 21, 2025)

Al Shrebini, R. 2020. "Covid-19: Qatif lockdown eased in Saudi Arabia." *Gulf News*, April 30. https://gulfnews.com/world/gulf/saudi/Covid-19-qatif-lockdown-eased-in-saudi-arabia-1.1588254421142 (last accessed January 10, 2025)

Amnesty International. 2020. "Pho noodles and pandas: How China's social media users created a new language to beat government censorship on Covid-19." *Amnesty International*, March 6. https://www.amnesty.org/en/latest/news/2020/03/china-social-media-language-government-censorship-Covid/ (last accessed May 21, 2025)

Amusa, K., Monkam, N., Viegi, N. 2016. "How and why China became Africa's biggest aid donor." *The Conversation*, April 26. https://theconversation.com/how-and-why-china-became-africas-biggest-aid-donor-57992 (last accessed January 6, 2025)

Anderson, S. 2020. "Trump takes credit for vaccine created by others, including immigrants." *Forbes*, December 1. https://www.forbes.com/sites/stuartanderson/2020/12/01/trump-takes-credit-for-vaccine-created-by-others-including-immigrants/?sh=27d98bb5374c (last accessed January 20, 2025)

AP. 2021. "Timeline: China's Covid-19 outbreak and lockdown of Wuhan." January 22. https://apnews.com/article/pandemics-wuhan-china-coronavirus-pandemic-e6147ec0ff88affb99c811149424239d (last accessed May 21, 2025)

AP News. 2022. "China party says nearly 5 million members probed for graft." October 17. https://apnews.com/article/health-china-business-Covid-economy-6618e65ef6148e0c75fce4dc2a28011f (last accessed January 16, 2025)

Arab News. 2021. "Saudi Arabia's grand mufti ahead of Ramadan: COVID-19 vaccine does not invalidate fast." *Arab News*, March 19. https://www.arabnews.com/node/1827816/saudi-arabia (last accessed May 20, 2025)

Aratani, L. 2020. "How did face masks become a political issue in America?" *The Guardian*, June 29. https://www.theguardian.com/world/2020/jun/29/face-masks-us-politics-coronavirus (last accessed November 4, 2025)

Associated Press in San Angelo, Texas. 2021. "Texas man who led anti-mask protests in name of 'freedom' dies of Covid-19." *The Guardian*, August 29. https://www.theguardian.com/us-news/2021/aug/29/texas-caleb-wallace-anti-mask-protests-freedom-dies-Covid-19 (last accessed May 21, 2025)

Associated Press. 2022. "China's Xi visiting Saudi Arabia to boost economy." *The Independent*, December 7. https://abcnews.go.com/International/wireStory/chinas-xi-visiting-saudi-arabia-amid-bid-boost-94644710 (last accessed January 21, 2023)

Associated Press. 2023. "Saudi Arabia says this year's hajj pilgrimage will return to pre-Covid levels." *NPR*, January 10. https://www.npr.org/2023/01/10/1148063709/saudi-arabia-says-this-years-hajj-pilgrimage-will-return-to-pre-Covid-levels (last accessed January 16, 2025)

AstraZeneca. 2021. "Two billion doses of AstraZeneca's Covid-19 vaccine supplied to countries across the world less than 12 months after first approval." November 16. https://www.astrazeneca.com/media-centre/press-releases/2021/two-billion-doses-of-astrazenecas-Covid-19-vaccine-supplied-to-countries-across-the-world-less-than-12-months-after-first-approval.html (last accessed January 20, 2025)

Baker, G. 2022. "Boris Johnson and Trump's populism is still alive." *The Sunday Times*, July 7. https://www.thetimes.co.uk/article/boris-johnson-and-donald-trumps-populism-is-still-alive-jfw8w3k7g (last accessed January 11, 2025)

Bartlett, N., Glaze, B. 2020. "Trump aide warns UK to dump Iran nuclear pact to get a better Brexit trade deal." *The Mirror*, January 15. https://www.mirror.co.uk/news/politics/trump-aide-warns-uk-dump-21283122 (last accessed January 13, 2025)

Batchelor, T. 2020. "Impromptu cricket game on London street draws crowd after 10pm crowd curfew." *The Independent*, October 11. https://www.independent.co.uk/news/uk/home-news/coronavirus-curfew-cricket-game-london-peckham-street-video-b960527.html (last accessed May 21, 2025)

Bayly, M. 2020. "Fatalism and an absence of public grief: How British society dealt with the 1918 flu." *LSE*, October 28. https://blogs.lse.ac.uk/politicsandpolicy/public-memory-1918-flu/

BBC. n.d. "Swine flu: Country by Country." http://news.bbc.co.uk/1/hi/uk/8083179.stm (last accessed December 27, 2024)

BBC. 2012. "Full text: China's new party chief Xi Jinping's speech." November 15. https://www.bbc.co.uk/news/world-asia-china-20338586 (last accessed January 6, 2025)

BBC. 2012. "How China is ruled: National People's Congress." October 8. https://www.bbc.co.uk/news/world-asia-pacific-13908155 (last accessed January 14, 2025)

BBC. 2015. "Mers virus: China tracking nearly 200 for possible infections." May 29. https://www.bbc.co.uk/news/world-asia-china-32926170 (last accessed January 4, 2025)

BBC. 2019. "Hong Kong protests: What is the 'Umbrella Movement'?" September 28. https://www.bbc.co.uk/newsround/49862757 (last accessed May 21, 2025)

BBC. 2020."Coronavirus: Amazon workers strike over virus protection." March 31. https://www.bbc.co.uk/news/business-52096273 (last accessed 21, May 2025)

BBC. 2020. "Coronavirus: How they tried to curb Spanish flu pandemic in 1918." May 10. https://www.bbc.co.uk/news/in-pictures-52564371 (last accessed May 21, 2025)

BBC. 2020. "Covid: Trump signs relief and spending package into law." December 28. https://www.bbc.co.uk/news/world-us-canada-55463276 (last accessed May 21, 2025)

BBC. 2020. "Trump declares national emergency over coronavirus." March 13. https://www.bbc.co.uk/news/world-us-canada-51882381 (last accessed May 21, 2025)

Beck with, R.T. 2016. "Real Donald Trump's 'America first' foreign policy speech." *Time USA*, April 27. https://time.com/4309786/read-donald-trumps-america-first-foreign-policy-speech/ (last accessed May 21, 2025)

Bekiempis, V. 2020. "Keep on digging: Team holds press conference at suburban garden centre." *The Guardian*, November 8. https://www.theguardian.com/us-news/2020/nov/08/the-other-four-seasons-trump-team-holds-press-conference-at-suburban-garden-centre (last accessed May 21, 2025)

Ben Gassem, L. 2020. "Spanish flu: How the deadly pandemic affected the Arab world." *Arab News*, March 29. https://www.arabnews.com/node/1649051/saudi-arabia (last accessed May 21, 2025)

Ben-Ghiat, R. 2020. "Trump, the coronavirus, and what happens when strongmen fall Ill." *The New Yorker*, October 13. https://www.newyorker.com/culture/cultural-comment/trump-the-coronavirus-and-what-happens-when-strongmen-fall-ill (last accessed May 21, 2025)

Bernal, N. 2021. "Amazon took a chunk of Deliveroo. Then things got interesting." *Wired*, February 11. https://www.wired.com/story/deliveroo-pandemic-amazon/ (last accessed December 6, 2024)

Bernstein, L., Torbati, Y. 2021. "Trump White House donated 8,700 ventilators to other nations. Officials now don't know where many of them are, watchdog finds." *The Washington Post*, January 29. https://www.washingtonpost.com/national-security/2021/01/29/usaid-trump-ventilators-watchdog/ (last accessed May 21, 2025)

Bienkov, A. 2019. "'The Brexit Party rebadged': Boris Johnson expels 21 Conservative moderate MPs, including 2 former chancellors and Winston Churchill's grandson." *Business Insider*, September 4. https://www.businessinsider.com/boris-johnson-list-21-conservative-rebels-winston-churchill-ken-clarke-2019-9?r=US&IR=T (last accessed May 21, 2025)

Bill of Health. n.d. "Covid-19, social movements, and health." https://petrieflom.law.harvard.edu/2021/07/27/symposium-Covid-19-social-movements-and-health/ (last accessed May 21, 2025)

Blackpast. 2024. "The Black Lives Matter movement (2013–)." Available online at: https://www.blackpast.org/black-lives-matter-movement-2013/ (last accessed May 21, 2025)

Blake, M. 2020. "A Netflix series predicted a global pandemic. It was dismissed as 'a show about the flu.'" *Los Angeles Times*, April 1. https://www.latimes.com/entertainment-arts/tv/story/2020-04-01/pandemic-netflix-documentary-coronavirus (last accessed May 21, 2025)

Bloomberg News. 2020. "WHO says China actions blunted virus spread, leading to drop." Bloomberg UK, February 24. https://www.bloomberg.com/news/articles/2020-02-24/who-says-china-lockdown-blunted-new-epidemic-leading-to-decline?leadSource=uverify%20wall (last accessed May 21, 2025)

Boseley, S. 2021. "How the AstraZeneca vaccine became a political football-and a PR disaster." *The Guardian*, March 26. https://www.theguardian.com/business/2021/mar/26/how-the-astrazeneca-vaccine-became-a-political-football-and-a-pr-disaster (last accessed January 10, 2023)

Branswell, H. 2021. "Covid-19 overtakes 1918 Spanish Flu as deadliest disease in American history." *STAT*, September 20. https://www.statnews.com/2021/09/20/Covid-19-set-to-overtake-1918-spanish-flu-as-deadliest-disease-in-american-history/ (last accessed May 21, 2025)

Brien, P., Keep, M. 2022. "Public spending during the Covid-19 pandemic." *UK Parliament*, March 29. https://commonslibrary.parliament.uk/research-briefings/cbp-9309/ (last accessed May 11, 2025)

Brimelow, B. 2018. "Saudi Arabia's powerful crown prince met with everyone from Trump and Mattis to The Rock and Oprah on a crazy US tour." *Business Insider*, April 5. https://www.businessinsider.com/saudi-arabia-crown-prince-mohammed-bin-salman-us-trip-meetings-2018-3?r=US&IR=T (last accessed May 21, 2025)

Bris, A., Cantale, S. 2020. "Pandemic bonds in coronavirus times: 'Financial goofiness' or fiscal genius?" *IMD*, March. https://www.imd.org/research-knowledge/finance/articles/pandemic-bonds-in-coronavirus-times/ (last accessed May 21, 2025)

British Foreign Policy Group. 2021. "Covid-19 timeline." https://bfpg.co.uk/2020/04/Covid-19-timeline/ (last accessed May 21, 2025)

British Medical Association. 2025. "An NHS under pressure." https://www.bma.org.uk/advice-and-support/nhs-delivery-and-workforce/pressures/an-nhs-under-pressure (last accessed May 21, 2025)

British Red Cross. 2021. "'Spanish Flu': The British Red Cross' work in the face of a global pandemic." January 27. https://www.redcross.org.uk/stories/health-and-social-care/health/coronavirus-how-the-red-cross-helped-in-the-spanish-flu-pandemic (last accessed May 21, 2025)

Brumberg, D. 2018. "Mapping Saudi Arabia's new ruling bargain." July 3. Available online at: https://arabcenterdc.org/resource/mapping-saudi-arabias-new-ruling-bargain/ (last accessed May 21, 2025)

Bryant, M. 2020. "US voter demographics: Election 2020 ended up looking a lot like 2016." *The Guardian*, November 5. https://www.theguardian.com/us-news/2020/nov/05/us-election-demographics-race-gender-age-biden-trump (last accessed May 21, 2025)

Burgess, S. 2022. "Undeleted posts on social media site Weibo expose the extent of China's Covid protest crackdown." *Sky News*, December 15. https://news.sky.com/story/weibo-the-Covid-19-posts-banned-by-one-of-chinas-biggest-social-media-platforms-12766970 (last accessed May 21, 2025)

Business Insider. 2020. "How Covid-19 made Amazon's Jeff Bezos the richest person in history, adjusted for inflation – now worth double Elon Musk." *Style*, August 29. https://www.scmp.com/magazines/style/tech-design/article/3099297/how-Covid-19-made-amazons-jeff-bezos-richest-person (last accessed May 21, 2025)

Butler, S. 2020. "Just eat takeaway sales soar 54% in 2020 as pandemic shifts eating habits." *The Guardian*, March 10. https://www.theguardian.com/business/2021/mar/10/just-eat-takeaway-sales-soar-54-in-2020-as-pandemic-shifts-eating-habits (last accessed May 21, 2025)

Camacho, A.E., Glicksman, R.L. 2020. "The Trump administration's pandemic response is structured to fail." *The Regulatory Review*, May 19. https://www.theregreview.org/2020/05/19/camacho-glicksman-trump-administration-pandemic-response-structured-fail/ (last accessed May 21, 2025)

Carroll, R., Tuckman, J. 2009. "Swine flu: Mexico braces for unprecedented lockdown." *The Guardian*, April 30. https://www.theguardian.com/world/2009/apr/30/swine-flu-mexico-government-lockdown (last accessed May 21, 2025)

CDC. 2020. "First travel-related case of 2019 Novel Coronavirus Detected in the United States." January 21. https://archive.cdc.gov/#/details?url=https://www.cdc.gov/media/releases/2020/p0121-novel-coronavirus-travel-case.html (last accessed May 21, 2025)

CDC. 2023. "2009 H1N1 pandemic timeline." August 31. https://archive.cdc.gov/#/details?url=https://www.cdc.gov/flu/pandemic-resources/2009-pandemic-timeline.html (last accessed May 21, 2025)

Centers for Disease Control and Prevention. 2010. "The 2009 H1N1 pandemic: Summary highlights, April 2009–April 2010." June 16. https://archive.cdc.gov/#/details?url=https://www.cdc.gov/h1n1flu/cdcresponse.htm (last accessed May 21, 2025)

Centers for Disease Control and Prevention. 2018. "Partner key messages on the 1918 influenza pandemic commemoration." August 10. https://archive.cdc.gov/#/details?url=https://www.cdc.gov/flu/pandemic-resources/1918-commemoration/key-messages.htm (last accessed May 21, 2025)

Centers for Disease Control and Prevention. 2019."1919 pandemic (H1N1 virus)." March 20. https://archive.cdc.gov/#/details?url=https://www.cdc.gov/flu/pandemic-resources/1918-pandemic-h1n1.html (last accessed May 21, 2025)

Centers for Disease Control and Prevention. 2019. "MERS in the U.S." August 2. https://www.cdc.gov/coronavirus/mers/us.html (last accessed January 5, 2023)

Champine, R.D., Strochlic, N. 2020. "How some cities 'flattened the curve' during the 1918 flu pandemic." *National Geographic*, March 27. https://www.nationalgeographic.com/history/article/how-cities-flattened-curve-1918-spanish-flu-pandemic-coronavirus (last accessed May 21, 2025)

Chan, C.H., Fu, K., Fung, I.C., Hao, Y., Schaible, B., Tse, Z.T., Ying, Y. 2013. "Chinese social media reaction to the MERS-CoV and avian influenza A (H7N9) outbreaks." *Infectious Diseases of Poverty*, 2 (31), pp. 1–11.

Chan, H. 2020. "Hong Kong's coronavirus panic reminds me of the dark days of Sars." *The Telegraph*, January 28. https://www.telegraph.co.uk/global-health/science-and-disease/hong-kong-virus-lockdown-reminds-dark-days-sars/ (last accessed May 21, 2025)

Chee, F.Y. 2024. "Exclusive: Amazon likely to face investigation under EU tech rules next year, sources say." *Reuters*, November 21. https://www.reuters.com/technology/amazon-likely-face-investigation-under-eu-tech-rules-next-year-sources-say-2024-11-21/ (last accessed May 21, 2025)

Cheung, E., Gan, N., Wang, S. 2022. "Beijing to distribute Pfizer antiviral drug as Covid wave strains health system." *CNN*, December 26. https://edition.cnn.com/2022/12/26/china/china-Covid-beijing-paxlovid-distribution-intl-hnk/index.html (last accessed May 21, 2025)

Chiappa, C., Eccles, M. 2024. "European commission fights vaccine transparency court ruling." *Politico*, October 8. https://www.politico.eu/article/european-commission-vaccine-transparency-court-ruling-pfizer-Covid19-pfizergate/ (last accessed May 21, 2025)

Chulov, M. 2020. "'Night of the Beating': details emerge of Riyadh Ritz-Carlton purge." *The Guardian*, November 19. https://www.theguardian.com/world/2020/nov/19/saudi-accounts-emerge-of-ritz-carlton-night-of-the-beating (last accessed May 21, 2025)

Collier, I. 2020. "Coronavirus: China apologises to family of doctor who died after warning about Covid-19." *Sky News*, March 20. https://news.sky.com/story/coronavirus-china-apologises-to-family-of-doctor-who-died-after-warning-about-Covid-19-11960679 (last accessed May 21, 2025)

Columbia University Irving Medical Center. 2019. "Epidemic, endemic, pandemic: What are the differences?" https://www.publichealth.columbia.edu/public-health-now/news/epidemic-endemic-pandemic-what-are-differences (last accessed May 21, 2025)

Council of Europe. 2022. "Emergency powers-what standards?" https://www.coe.int/en/web/human-rights-rule-of-law/venice-commission-Covid19 (last accessed December 26, 2022)

Council on Foreign Relations. 2025. "China's approach to global governance." https://www.cfr.org/china-global-governance/ (last accessed January 6, 2025)

Cowie, G. 2022. "Expiry of the Coronavirus Act's temporary provisions." *UK Parliament*, March 2. https://commonslibrary.parliament.uk/expiry-of-the-coronavirus-acts-temporary-provisions/ (last accessed May 21, 2025)

Cox, C. 2020. "Fact check: Chart of job growth by president shows historic unemployment under Trump." *USA Today*. https://eu.usatoday.com/story/news/factcheck/2020/11/06/fact-check-pandemic-unaccounted-presidential-job-growth-chart/6177339002/ (last accessed May 21, 2025)

Crerar, P. 2021. "Boris Johnson 'broke Covid lockdown rules' with Downing Street parties at Xmas." *The Mirror*, November 30. https://www.mirror.co.uk/news/politics/boris-johnson-broke-Covid-lockdown-25585238 (last accessed May 21, 2025)

Crisis24. 2020. "Saudi Arabia: Nationwide curfew implemented March 23/update 17." March 23. https://crisis24.garda.com/alerts/2020/03/saudi-arabia-nationwide-curfew-implemented-march-23-update-17 (last accessed December 1, 2022)

Crow, D., Milne, R. 2020. "Why vaccine 'nationalism' could slow coronavirus fight." *Financial Times*, May 14. https://www.ft.com/content/6d542894-6483-446c-87b0-96c65e89bb2c (last accessed May 21, 2025)

Crown Prosecution Service. 2022. "Coronavirus Act 2020." July 18. https://www.cps.gov.uk/legal-guidance/coronavirus-act-2020 (last accessed January 17, 2023)

Culbertson, A. 2019. "Ex-chancellors and Churchill's grandson: The 21 Tories sacked for defying Boris Johnson over Brexit." *Sky News*, September 4. https://news.sky.com/story/ex-chancellors-and-churchills-grandson-the-21-tories-sacked-for-defying-boris-johnson-over-brexit-11801765 (last accessed May 21, 2025)

Culver, D., Gan, N. 2020. "China is fighting the coronavirus with a digital QR code. Here's how it works." *CNN*, April 16. https://edition.cnn.com/2020/04/15/asia/china-coronavirus-qr-code-intl-hnk/index.html (last accessed May 21, 2025)

Cyranoski, D., Ledford, H., Van Noorden, R. 2020. "The UK has approved a Covid vaccine—here's what scientists need to know." *Nature*, December 3. https://www.nature.com/articles/d41586-020-03441-8 (last accessed January 20, 2023)

Davidson, H. 2020. "China puts city of Shulan under Wuhan-style lockdown after fresh Covid-19 cases." *The Guardian*, May 19. https://www.theguardian.com/world/2020/may/19/china-puts-city-of-shulan-under-wuhan-style-lockdown-after-fresh-Covid-19-cases (last accessed May 21, 2025)

Davidson, H. 2020. "Critic who called Xi a 'clown' over Covid-19 crisis investigated for 'serious violations.'" *The Guardian*, April 8. https://www.theguardian.com/world/2020/

apr/08/critic-xi-jinping-clown-ren-zhiqiang-Covid-19-outbreak-investigated-china (last accessed May 21, 2025)

Davidson, H. 2022. "China brings in 'emergency' level censorship over zero-Covid protests." *The Guardian*, December 2. https://www.theguardian.com/world/2022/dec/02/china-brings-in-emergency-level-censorship-over-zero-Covid-protests (last accessed May 21, 2025)

Davidson, H. 2022. "China Covid protests explained: Why are people demonstrating and what will happen next?" *The Guardian*, November 28. https://www.theguardian.com/world/2022/nov/28/china-protests-explained-why-are-people-demonstrating-blank-piece-white-paper-a4-what-will-happen-next-zero-covid-policy-protest (last accessed May 20, 2025)

Davis, N. 2024. "Cost of private Covid jabs risks widening health inequalities, experts warn." *The Guardian*, March 28. https://www.theguardian.com/society/2024/mar/28/cost-of-private-Covid-jabs-risks-widening-health-inequalities-experts-warn (last accessed May 21, 2025)

Dayan, M., McCarey, M. 2022. "Has Brexit affected the UK's medical workforce?" *Nuffield Health*, November 27. https://www.nuffieldtrust.org.uk/news-item/has-brexit-affected-the-uk-s-medical-workforce (last accessed May 21, 2025)

Dearden, L. 2021. "All 270 charges brought under Coronavirus Act wrongful, official review finds." *The Independent*, May 14. https://www.independent.co.uk/news/uk/home-news/coronavirus-act-prosecutions-wrongful-cps-review-b1847194.html (last accessed May 20, 2025)

de Haan, E. 2023. "Big Pharma raked in USD 90 billion in profits with Covid-19 vaccines." SOMO, February 27. https://www.somo.nl/big-pharma-raked-in-usd-90-billion-in-profits-with-Covid-19-vaccines/ (last accessed May 21, 2025)

De La, O., Gasparian, A., Sakthivel, T., Siamdoust, V., Szucs, N., Zhang, A., T. 2020. "Democracy and rise of authoritarianism in Covid-19 world." *Macmillan Center for International and Area Studies at Yale*, April 24. https://macmillan.yale.edu/stories/democracy-and-rise-authoritarianism-Covid-19-world (last accessed May 21, 2025)

De Loera-Brust, A. 2020. "As the U.S. Exports coronavirus, Trump is blaming Mexicans." *Foreign Policy*, July 14. https://foreignpolicy.com/2020/07/14/as-the-u-s-exports-coronavirus-trump-is-blaming-mexicans/ (last accessed May 21, 2025)

Deloitte. 2023. "Tackling Brexit and Covid-19 together." https://www2.deloitte.com/uk/en/pages/global-markets/articles/tackling-brexit-and-Covid-19-together.html (last accessed February 10, 2023)

Department of Health and Social Care. 2021. "First people to receive Oxford University/AstraZeneca Covid-19 vaccine today." *GOV.UK*, January 7. https://www.gov.uk/government/news/first-people-to-receive-oxford-universityastrazeneca-Covid-19-vaccine-today-4-january-2021 (last accessed May 21, 2025)

Di-Miceli, A. 2021. "Social rhetoric in the time of Covid-19: The art of compliance." LSE, February 7. https://blogs.lse.ac.uk/psychologylse/2021/02/07/social-rhetoric-in-the-time-of-Covid-19-the-art-of-compliance/ (last accessed May 21, 2025)

Dimock, M., Gramlich, J. 2021. "How America changed during Donald Trump's presidency." *Pew Research Center*, January 29. https://www.pewresearch.org/2021/01/29/how-america-changed-during-donald-trumps-presidency/ (last accessed May 21, 2025)

Doucleff, M. 2022. "Fact check: The theory that SARS-CoV-2 is becoming milder." *NPR*, January 14. https://www.npr.org/sections/goatsandsoda/2022/01/14/1072504127/fact-check-the-theory-that-sars-cov-2-is-becoming-milder (last accessed May 21, 2025)

Due-Gundersen, N. 2020. "Playing tourist: Impressions of Riyadh, Saudi Arabia during the coronavirus." *International Policy Digest*, June 15. https://intpolicydigest.org/playing-tourist-impressions-of-riyadh-saudi-arabia-during-the-coronavirus/ (last accessed May 21, 2025)

Economist Intelligence. 2022. "Things to watch in Saudi Arabia in 2023." November 14. https://country.eiu.com/article.aspx?articleid=2022563985&Country=Saudi+Arabia&topic=Economy&subtopic=Outlook (last accessed May 21, 2025)

Edwards, E., Smith, A. 2020. "Trump tried to justify rising Covid cases by pointing to Europe. Experts say he's wrong." *NBC News*, November 9. https://www.nbcnews.com/health/health-news/trump-tried-justify-rising-Covid-cases-pointing-europe-experts-say-n1246786 (last accessed May 21, 2025)

Embassy of the Kingdom of Saudi Arabia, Washington, D.C. n.d. "The five pillars of Islam." https://www.saudiembassy.net/five-pillars-islam (last accessed January 16, 2025)

Engler, M., Engler, P. 2024. "A new wave of movements against Trumpism is coming." *Resilience*, November 12. https://www.resilience.org/stories/2024-11-12/a-new-wave-of-movements-against-trumpism-is-coming/ (last accessed February 5, 2025)

European Council. 2024. "The global agreement on pandemics in a nutshell." April 24. https://www.consilium.europa.eu/en/infographics/towards-an-international-treaty-on-pandemics/ (last accessed January 7, 2025)

European Council. 2024. "An international agreement on pandemic prevention and preparedness." January 11. https://www.consilium.europa.eu/en/policies/coronavirus-pandemic/pandemic-treaty/ (last accessed January 7, 2025)

European Council. 2025. "G20 summit, 21-22 November 2020." January 9. https://www.consilium.europa.eu/en/meetings/international-summit/2020/11/21-22/ (last accessed January 23, 2025)

Explained Desk. 2022. "China's premier Li Keqiang removed from post: What is happening and why?" October 23. https://indianexpress.com/article/explained/chinas-premier-li-keqiang-removed-from-post-what-is-happening-and-why-8225165/ (last accessed May 21, 2025)

Farley, R. 2020. "Remembering the Spanish Flu in Asia." *The Diplomat*, March 25. https://thediplomat.com/2020/03/remembering-the-spanish-flu-in-asia/ (last accessed May 21, 2025)

Federal Register. 2020. "Declaring a national emergency concerning the Novel Coronavirus Disease (Covid-19) outbreak." March 18. https://www.federalregister.gov/documents/2020/03/18/2020-05794/declaring-a-national-emergency-concerning-the-novel-coronavirus-disease-Covid-19-outbreak (last accessed May 21, 2025)

Feigenbaum, E.A. 2017. "The big bet at the heart of Xi Jinping's 'New Deal.'" *Carnegie Endowment*, November 27. https://carnegieendowment.org/2017/11/27/big-bet-at-heart-of-xi-jinping-s-new-deal-pub-74847 (last accessed May 22, 2025)

Fenton-Harvey, J. 2020. "Will Saudi Arabia's Covid-19 cutbacks trigger anti-regime protests?" *TRT World*, July 30. https://www.trtworld.com/magazine/will-saudi-arabia-s-Covid-19-cutbacks-trigger-anti-regime-protests-38520 (last accessed May 21, 2025)

Fieschi, C. 2022. "Culture notes: The EU and Britain can still be friends." *Chatham House*, December 2. https://www.chathamhouse.org/publications/the-world-today/2022-12/culture-notes-eu-and-britain-can-still-be-friends (last accessed May 21, 2025)

Firth, S. 2022. "House subcommittee report details pandemic failures, lessons learned." *Medpage Today*, December 15. https://www.medpagetoday.com/infectiousdisease/Covid19/102268 (last accessed May 21, 2025)

France24. 2022. "Study confirms AstraZeneca jab's higher risk of very rare clot." October 27. https://www.france24.com/en/live-news/20221027-study-confirms-astrazeneca-jab-s-higher-risk-of-very-rare-clot (last accessed May 21, 2025)

Gabbatt, A. 2020. "Thousands of Americans backed by rightwing donors gear up for protests". *The Guardian*, April 18. https://www.theguardian.com/us-news/2020/apr/18/coronavirus-americans-protest-stay-at-home (last accessed May 22, 2025)

Gannon, S. 2010. "H1N1 influenza and the U.S. response: Looking back at 2009." *Center for Strategic and International Studies*, January 12. https://www.csis.org/blogs/smart-global-health/h1n1-influenza-and-us-response-looking-back-2009 (last accessed May 22, 2025)

Gause, F.G. 2018. "After the Killing of Jamal Khashoggi: Muhammad bin Salman and the future of Saudi-U.S. relations." *Center for Strategic and International Studies*, December 12. https://www.csis.org/analysis/after-killing-jamal-khashoggi-muhammad-bin-salman-and-future-saudi-us-relations (last accessed online May 22, 2025)

Gayle, D. 2020. "Thousands march in London in fourth anti-lockdown protest." *The Guardian*, October 24. https://www.theguardian.com/world/2020/oct/24/london-braces-for-fourth-protest-against-Covid-19-restrictions (last accessed May 22, 2025)

Gearan, A., Wagner, J. 2020. "Trump expresses support for angry anti-shutdown protestors as more states lift coronavirus lockdowns." *The Washington Post*, May 1. https://www.washingtonpost.com/politics/trump-expresses-support-for-angry-anti-shutdown-protesters-as-more-states-lift-coronavirus-lockdowns/2020/05/01/25570dbe-8b9f-11ea-8ac1-bfb250876b7a_story.html (last accessed May 21, 2025)

Gerstein, J., Hesson, T. 2018. "Supreme Court upholds Trump's travel ban." *Politico*, June 26. https://www.politico.com/story/2018/06/26/supreme-court-upholds-trumps-travel-ban-673181 (last accessed May 22, 2025)

Global Data. 2024. "How Covid-19 M&A performed in the pharmaceutical industry in Q3 2024." *Pharmaceutical Technology*, December 2. https://www.pharmaceutical-technology.com/dashboards/deals-dashboards/ma-activity-Covid-19-pharmaceutical-industry/?cf-view&cf-closed (last accessed May 22, 2025)

Gostin, L., Wetter, S. 2020. "Why there's no national lockdown." *The Atlantic*, March 31. https://www.theatlantic.com/ideas/archive/2020/03/why-theres-no-national-lockdown/609127/ (last accessed May 22, 2025)

Gov.uk. 2013. "Health protection agency." https://www.gov.uk/government/organisations/health-protection-agency (last accessed May 22, 2025)

Gov.uk. 2018. "MERS-CoV case in England." October 4. https://www.gov.uk/government/news/mers-cov-case-in-england (last accessed January 5, 2023)

Gov.uk. n.d. "Public health England." https://www.gov.uk/government/organisations/public-health-england (last accessed May 22, 2025)

Greenwood, S., Keegan, M., Mordecai, M., Schumacher, S., Silver, L. 2020. "In U.S. and UK, globalization leaves some feeling 'Left Behind' or 'Swept Up'." *Pew Research Center*, October 5. https://www.pewresearch.org/global/2020/10/05/in-u-s-and-uk-globalization-leaves-some-feeling-left-behind-or-swept-up/ (last accessed May 22, 2025)

Greig, J. 2020. "'It's collective punishment'-people in the North on their tier 3 lockdown." *Vice*, November 26. https://www.vice.com/en/article/93wk37/the-north-reacts-tier-3-lockdownmeasures (last accessed May 22, 2025)

The Guardian Editorial. 2020. "The Guardian view on a Covid-19 parliament: Unable to do its job." June 2. https://www.theguardian.com/commentisfree/2020/jun/02/the-guardian-view-on-a-Covid-19-parliament-unable-to-do-its-job (last accessed May 22, 2025)

Guardian reporter in Hong Kong. 2020. "'Hero who told the truth': Chinese rage over coronavirus death of whistleblower doctor." February 7. https://www.theguardian.com/global-development/2020/feb/07/coronavirus-chinese-rage-death-whistleblower-doctor-li-wenliang (last accessed May 22, 2025)

Guardian staff and agencies. 2020. "Ren Zhiquang-who called Chinese president a 'clown'- jailed for 18 years." September 22. https://www.theguardian.com/world/2020/sep/22/ren-zhiqiang-who-called-chinese-president-a-clown-jailed-for-18-years (last accessed May 22, 2025)

Guillo, N. 2020. "Covid-19 and low oil prices risk setbacks to MBS's reforms, but Riyadh will be prepared to continue price war over coming months." *Torchlight*, March 27. https://www.torchlight.ai/reports/Covid-19-and-low-oil-prices-risk-setbacks-to-mbss-reforms-but-riyadh-will-be-prepared-to-continue-price-war-over-coming-months/ (last accessed January 16, 2023)

Hajj Reporters. 2020. "Thermal cameras, electric walkways install at Jedda Airport as Flight Resume in Saudi Arabia." May 31. http://www.hajjreporters.com/thermal-cameras-electric-walkways-install-at-jedda-airport-as-flight-resume-in-saudi-arabia/ (last accessed May 22, 2025)

Harb, I.K. 2018. "The Khashoggi affair and the future of Saudi Arabia." *Arab Center Washington DC*, October 12. https://arabcenterdc.org/resource/the-khashoggi-affair-and-the-future-of-saudi-arabia/ (last accessed May 22, 2025)

Harris, J. 2020. "How Amazon became a pandemic giant – and why that could be a threat to us all." *The Guardian*, November 18. https://www.theguardian.com/technology/2020/nov/18/how-amazon-became-a-pandemic-giant-and-why-that-could-be-a-threat-to-us-all (last accessed May 22, 2025)

Hauser, C. 2020. "The mask slackers of 1918." *The New York Times*, August 3. https://www.nytimes.com/2020/08/03/us/mask-protests-1918.html (last accessed May 22, 2025)

Hawkins, D., Wagner, J. 2020. "Coronavirus: Trump's 'inconsistent and incoherent' response slammed by The Lancet." *The Independent*, May 16. https://www.independent.co.uk/news/world/americas/coronavirus-trump-response-vaccine-deaths-test-lancet-cdc-a9518026.html (last accessed May 22, 2025)

Haynes, D. 2020. "Boris Johnson tells Xi Jinping he 'loves China' and will 'work together' to fight coronavirus." *Sky News*, February 19. https://news.sky.com/story/boris-johnson-tells-xi-jinping-he-loves-china-and-will-work-together-to-fight-coronavirus-11937167 (last accessed May 22, 2025)

Henderson, S. 2022. "Saudi Arabia adjusts its history, diminishing the role of Wahhabism." *The Washington Institute for Near East Policy*, February 11. https://www.washingtoninstitute.org/policy-analysis/saudi-arabia-adjusts-its-history-diminishing-role-wahhabism (last accessed May 22 2025)

Herbert, G. 2017. "President Trump launches first campaign ad for 2020 election – 1282 days away." *Syracuse.com*, May 1. https://www.syracuse.com/politics/2017/05/trump_2020_election_campaign_ad.html (last accessed May 22, 2025)

Heymann, D., Ross, E., Wallace, J. 2022. "The next pandemic-when could it be?" Chatham House, May 1. https://www.chathamhouse.org/2022/02/next-pandemic-when-could-it-be (last accessed May 22, 2025)

Hirsch, M. 2016. "Why the new nationalists are taking over." *Politico*, June 26. https://www.politico.com/magazine/story/2016/06/nationalism-donald-trump-boris-johnson-brexit-foreign-policy-xenophobia-isolationism-213995/ (last accessed May 22, 2025)

Hong, A. 2018. "Viral sovereignty: Equity and global health risk controversy." Global Health Institute, May 1. https://globalhealth.georgetown.edu/posts/viral-sovereignty-equity-and-global-health-risk-controversy (last accessed May 22, 2025)

Horsley, J.P. 2020. "Let's end the Covid-19 blame game: Reconsidering China's role in the pandemic." *Brookings*, August 19. https://www.brookings.edu/blog/order-from-chaos/2020/08/19/lets-end-the-Covid-19-blame-game-reconsidering-chinas-role-in-the-pandemic/ (last accessed May 22, 2025)

Horton, R. 2020. "Coronavirus is the greatest global science policy failure in a generation." *The Guardian*, April 9. https://www.theguardian.com/commentisfree/2020/apr/09/deadly-virus-britain-failed-prepare-mers-sars-ebola-coronavirus (last accessed May 22, 2025)

Hsing, Y. 2011. "Territoriality and space production in China." *Cross-Currents: East-Asian History and Culture Review*, 1 (1), pp. 1–11

Huang, Y. 2004. "The SARS epidemic and its aftermath in China: A political perspective." https://www.ncbi.nlm.nih.gov/books/NBK92479/ (last accessed May 22, 2025)

Human Rights Watch. 2020. "Covid-19 fueling Anti-Asian racism and Xenophobia worldwide." May 12. https://www.hrw.org/news/2020/05/12/Covid-19-fueling-anti-asian-racism-and-xenophobia-worldwide (last accessed May 22, 2025)

Hzaine, E.H. 2025. "The AfCFTA challenge: Advanced integration and unity as Africa's path to prosperity." *Morocco World News*, January 15. https://www.moroccoworldnews.com/2025/01/367688/the-afcfta-challenge-advanced-integration-and-unity-as-africas-path-to-prosperity (last accessed January 16, 2025)

Imparato, S., Nagar, S. 2023. "The WHO's new pandemic treaty is good for the world—and the U.S." *STAT*, January 20. https://www.statnews.com/2023/01/20/new-pandemic-treaty-good-for-world-and-america/ (last accessed May 22, 2025)

The Independent. 2018. "Mohammed bin Salman US visit: Leaked itinerary shows Saudi crown prince to meet with Oprah, politicians and media bosses." March 28. https://www.independent.co.uk/news/world/middle-east/mohammad-bin-salman-us-visit-itinerary-oprah-saudi-arabia-prince-google-trump-washington-dc-a8276751.html (last accessed May 22, 2025)

Institute for Government Analysis. 2022. "Timeline of UK government coronavirus lockdowns and restrictions." December 9. https://www.instituteforgovernment.org.uk/data-visualisation/timeline-coronavirus-lockdowns (last accessed May 22, 2025)

Ioffe, J. 2020. "Your rugged American individualism is making you dangerous." GQ, March 14. https://www.gq.com/story/american-individualism-in-the-age-of-coronavirus (last accessed May 22, 2025)

Jalaby, R., Rashad, M. 2020. "Covid deals blow to Saudi Arabia's G20 summit ambitions." *Reuters*, November 20. https://www.reuters.com/article/us-g20-saudi-idUSKBN2800YI (last accessed May 22, 2025)

Jazeera, Al. 2018. "Saudi Arabia admits Jamal Khashoggi killed in Istanbul consulate." October 20. https://www.aljazeera.com/news/2018/10/20/saudi-arabia-admits-jamal-khashoggi-killed-in-istanbul-consulate (January 9, 2025)

John Hopkins Medicine. n.d. "What is coronavirus?" https://www.hopkinsmedicine.org/health/conditions-and-diseases/coronavirus (last accessed May 22, 2025)

Jones, K., Kahwagl, M. 2021. "Health care initiatives could be the key to rebuilding U.S. influence in the region—and healthier economies and societies for the region's citizens." *Foreign Policy*, February 9. https://foreignpolicy.com/2021/02/09/united-states-middle-east-health-care-stethoscope-diplomacy/ (last accessed May 22, 2025)

Jong, H.N., Ompusunggu, M. 2017. "Indonesia steps up fight against biopiracy." *The Jakarta Post*, March 20. https://www.thejakartapost.com/news/2017/03/20/ri-steps-up-fight-against-biopiracy.html (last accessed May 22, 2025)

Kalinina, A. 2020. "What the world can learn from regional responses to Covid-19." *World Economic Forum*, May 1. https://www.weforum.org/stories/2020/05/Covid-19-what-the-world-can-learn-from-regional-responses/ (last accessed January 17, 2025)

Kalra, A., Stecklow, S. 2021. "A Reuters special report: Amazon copied products and rigged search results to promote its own brands, documents show." *Reuters*, October 13. https://www.reuters.com/investigates/special-report/amazon-india-rigging/ (last accessed May 22, 2025)

Kane, P.L. 2020. "The anti-mask league: Lockdown protests draw parallels to 1918 pandemic." *The Guardian*, April 29. https://www.theguardian.com/world/2020/apr/29/coronavirus-pandemic-1918-protests-california (last accessed May 22, 2025)

Kansas State University. 2009. "1918 Flu resulted in current lineage of H1N1 swine influenza virus." May 1. https://www.sciencedaily.com/releases/2009/04/090430111640.htm (last accessed May 22, 2025)

Kazuko, K. 2020. "Politics under Xi Jinping: Centralization and its implications." *Public Policy Review*, September, 16 (3), pp. 1–21

Kelland, K., McDowell, A. 2014. "Saudi Arabia sacks minister criticized over handling of MERS." *Reuters*, June 3. https://www.reuters.com/article/us-health-mers-saudi-idUSKBN0EE1I420140603 (last accessed January 4, 2025)

Kelland, K., McDowell, A. 2014. "Saudi MERS response hobbled by institutional failings." *Reuters*, June 12. https://www.reuters.com/article/us-saudi-mers-failings-insight-idUSKBN0EN1I520140612 (last accessed May 22, 2025)

Kimball, S. 2023. "The Covid pandemic drives Pfizer's 2022 revenue to a record $100 billion." *CNBC*, January 31. https://www.cnbc.com/2023/01/31/the-Covid-pandemic-drives-pfizers-2022-revenue-to-a-record-100-billion.html (last accessed May 22, 2025)

Kinder, M., Stateler, L. 2020. "Amazon and Walmart have raked in billions in additional profits during the pandemic, and shared almost none of it with their workers." *Brookings*, December 22. https://www.brookings.edu/articles/amazon-and-walmart-have-raked-in-billions-in-additional-profits-during-the-pandemic-and-shared-almost-none-of-it-with-their-workers/ (last accessed May 22, 2025)

Kliem, F. 2020. "Opinion-realism and the coronavirus crisis." *E-International Relations*, April 11. https://www.e-ir.info/2020/04/11/opinion-realism-and-the-coronavirus-crisis/ (last accessed May 22, 2025)

Klobucista, C. 2022. "A guide to global Covid-19 vaccine efforts." *Council on Foreign Relations*, December 5. https://www.cfr.org/backgrounder/guide-global-Covid-19-vaccine-efforts (last accessed May 22, 2025)

Knobler, S., Lemon, S., Mahmoud, A. 2004. "Overview of the SARS epidemic." *National Academy of Sciences*. https://www.ncbi.nlm.nih.gov/books/NBK92478/ (last accessed May 22, 2025)

Krelle, H., Tallack, C. 2021. "One year on: Three myths about Covid-19 that the data proved wrong." *The Health Foundation*, March 23. https://www.health.org.uk/publications/long-reads/one-year-on-three-myths-about-Covid-19-that-the-data-proved-wrong (last accessed May 22, 2025)

Kurtzman, L. 2021. "Trump's 'Chinese Virus' tweet linked to rise of anti-Asian hashtags on Twitter." *University of California San Francisco*, March 18. https://www.ucsf.edu/news/2021/03/420081/trumps-chinese-virus-tweet-linked-rise-anti-asian-hashtags-twitter (last accessed May 22, 2025)

Kushner, J. 2019. "China is leading the next step in fighting malaria in Africa." *The Atlantic*, July 4. https://www.theatlantic.com/international/archive/2019/07/china-tackles-malaria-kenya/592414/ (last accessed May 22, 2025)

Law, E. 2021. "Timeline: Covid-19 in China." *Straits Times*, December 18. https://www.straitstimes.com/asia/east-asia/chinas-Covid-19-outbreak-timeline (last accessed May 22, 2025)

Lay, K. 2024. "Global pandemic treaty could be more than a year away after deadline missed." *The Guardian*, May 29. https://www.theguardian.com/global-development/article/2024/may/29/global-pandemic-treaty-could-be-more-than-a-year-away-after-deadline-missed (last accessed May 21, 2025)

Lay, K. 2025. "'Sowing seeds for next pandemic': Trump order for US to exit WHO prompts alarm." *The Guardian*, January 21. https://www.theguardian.com/us-news/2025/jan/20/trump-executive-order-who-withdrawal (last accessed May 22, 2025)

Lay, K. 2025. "World agrees pandemic accord for tackling outbreaks of disease." *The Guardian*, May 20. https://www.theguardian.com/global-development/2025/may/20/world-agrees-pandemic-accord-for-tackling-outbreaks-of-disease-who-covid (last accessed May 21, 2025)

Lehren, A. W., Popken, B. 2020. "Release of PPP loan recipients' data reveals troubling patterns." *NBC News*, December 2. https://www.nbcnews.com/business/business-news/release-ppp-loan-recipients-data-reveals-troubling-patterns-n1249629 (last accessed May 22, 2025)

Levi, J. 2009. "The swine flu response." *Health Affairs*, May 1. https://www.healthaffairs.org/do/10.1377/forefront.20090501.001058 (last accessed May 22, 2025)

Lin, K. 2022. "A new chapter for Hong Kong's labour movement?" *Made in China Journal*, March 8. https://madeinchinajournal.com/2022/03/08/a-new-chapter-for-hong-kongs-labour-movement/ (last accessed May 22, 2025)

List, C. 2019. "Is Brexit the will of the people?" *LSE*, April 16. https://www.lse.ac.uk/philosophy/blog/2019/04/16/is-brexit-the-will-of-the-people/ (last accessed May 22, 2025)

Lo, K. 2021. "China calls on rich nations to give more to UN, with apparent dig at US as 'major' defaulter." *South China Morning Post*, October 5. https://www.scmp.com/news/china/diplomacy/article/3151263/china-calls-rich-nations-give-more-un-apparent-dig-us-major (last accessed May 22, 2025)

Lobo, F. 2024. "The vaccine industry after the Covid-19 pandemic: An international perspective." *Research Paper 203*. South Centre, July 11

London, D. 2022. "Saudi Arabia's political trajectory." *Middle East Institute*, July 7. https://www.mei.edu/publications/saudi-arabias-political-trajectory (last accessed May 22, 2025)

Long, K.A. 2021. "In the 15 years since its launch, Amazon Web Services transformed how companies do business." *Seattle Times*, March 13. https://www.seattletimes.com/business/amazon/in-the-15-years-since-its-launch-amazon-web-services-has-transformed-how-companies-do-business/ (last accessed May 22, 2025)

Lopez, G. 2016. "Polls show many-even most-Trump supporters really are deeply hostile to Muslims and nonwhites." *Vox*, September 12. Polls show many — even most — Trump supporters really are deeply hostile to Muslims and nonwhites - Vox (last accessed May 22, 2025)

Lowry, R. 2020. "Trump's coronavirus response Isn't the work of a dictator." *National Review*, March 17. https://www.nationalreview.com/2020/03/coronavirus-outbreak-president-trump-response-not-work-of-dictator/ (last accessed May 22, 2025)

Luthra, S. 2020. "Trump's claim that U.S. tested more than all countries combined is 'Pants On Fire' wrong." *KFF Health News*, May 1. https://khn.org/news/trumps-claim-that-u-s-tested-more-than-all-countries-combined-is-pants-on-fire-wrong/ (last accessed May 22, 2025)

MacFarquhar, N. 2011. "In Saudi Arabia, royal funds buy peace for now." *The New York Times*, June 8. https://www.nytimes.com/2011/06/09/world/middleeast/09saudi.html (last accessed May 22, 2025)

Madhani, A. 2020. "Trump turns coronavirus conversation into 'US vs. THEM' debate." *AP News*, June 19. https://apnews.com/article/donald-trump-ap-top-news-elections-oklahoma-virus-outbreak-fe8d83b196f703520495ab7a92ba4dcc (last accessed May 22, 2025)

Mankikar, K.A. 2022. "The Xi Plan: The political factors driving China's Covid-19 strategy." *Observer Reach Foundation*, December 19. https://www.orfonline.org/research/the-xi-plan-the-political-factors-driving-china-s-covid-19-strategy (last accessed May 22, 2025)

Mao, F. 2022."China abandons key parts of zero-Covid strategy after protests." *BBC*, December 7. https://www.bbc.co.uk/news/world-asia-china-63855508 (last accessed May 22, 2025)

Maragakis, L.L. 2020."Coronavirus and Covid-19: Younger adults are at risk, too." Broadcast Med, April 9. https://www.broadcastmed.com/infectiousdiseases/5225/news/coronavirus-and-covid-19-younger-adults-are-at-risk-too (last accessed January 18, 2023)

Marquez, A., Traylor, J., Frankel, J. 2024. "Trump talks shooting at press, ramps up election fraud claims at Pa. rally." NBC News, November 3. https://www.nbcnews.com/politics/donald-trump/trump-wouldnt-mind-if-someone-shot-media-pa-rally-rcna178573 (last accessed May 22, 2025)

Maxmen, A. 2022. "Wuhan market was epicentre of pandemic's start, studies suggest." *Nature*, February 27. https://www.nature.com/articles/d41586-022-00584-8 (last accessed May 22, 2025)

McKenna, M. 2018. "Big pharma has the flu." *Wired*, February 1. https://www.wired.com/story/flu-vaccine-big-pharma/ (last accessed May 22, 2025)

McKinsey & Company. 2020. "Covid-19 in the United Kingdom: Assessing jobs at risk and the impact on people and places." May 11. https://www.mckinsey.com/industries/public-and-social-sector/our-insights/Covid-19-in-the-united-kingdom-assessing-jobs-at-risk-and-the-impact-on-people-and-places (last accessed May 22, 2025)

McTague, T., Nicholas, P. 2020. "How 'America First' became America alone." *The Atlantic*, October 29. https://www.theatlantic.com/international/archive/2020/10/donald-trump-foreign-policy-america-first/616872/ (last accessed May 22, 2025)

MEED Editorial. 2020. "Covid-19 disrupts Riyadh's Vision 2030." April 14. https://www.meed.com/Covid-19-disrupts-riyadhs-vision-2030 (last accessed May 22, 2025)

Mental Health Foundation. 2020. "Millions of UK adults have felt panicked, afraid and unprepared as a result of the coronavirus pandemic-new poll data reveal impact on mental health." March 26. https://www.mentalhealth.org.uk/about-us/news/millions-uk-adults-have-felt-panicked-afraid-and-unprepared-result-coronavirus-pandemic-new-poll (last accessed May 22, 2025)

Merrick, R. 2021. "UK 'dangerously close to elected dictatorship' under Boris Johnson, Ken Clarke warns." *The Independent*, November 19. https://www.independent.co.uk/news/uk/politics/johnson-ken-clarke-elected-dictatorship-b1964326.html (last accessed May 22, 2025)

Metcalfe, T. 2022. "1919 flu mutated to become deadlier in later waves, century-old lungs reveal." *Live Science*, July 15. https://www.livescience.com/1918-flu-variant-deadlier-later-waves-lung-tissue.html (last accessed May 22, 2025)

Mhajne, A., Whetstone, C. 2020. "The rise of the Covid dictatorships." *Foreign Policy*, October 16. https://foreignpolicy.com/2020/10/16/the-rise-of-the-Covid-dictatorships/ (last accessed May 22, 2025)

Middle East Monitor. 2024. "Saudi Arabia, Morocco sign MoU to strengthen health sectors, pandemic preparedness." August 27. https://www.middleeastmonitor.com/20240827-saudi-arabia-morocco-sign-mou-to-strengthen-health-sectors-pandemic-preparedness/ (last accessed May 22, 2025)

Mironova, V. 2020. "The world's most dangerous coronavirus lockdowns." *Foreign Policy*, April 1. https://foreignpolicy.com/2020/04/01/prisons-coronavirus-lockdown-incarcerated-pandemic/ (last accessed May 22, 2025)

Molter, V., Webster, G. 2020. "Virality project (China): Coronavirus conspiracy claims." *Freeman Spogli Institute for International Studies*, March 31. https://fsi.stanford.edu/news/china-Covid19-origin-narrative (last accessed May 22, 2025)

Mullin, L. 2022. "How zero Covid protests broke through China's internet censorship." *The Diplomat*, December 6. https://thediplomat.com/2022/12/how-zero-Covid-protests-broke-through-chinas-internet-censorship/ (last accessed May 22, 2025)

NBC News. 2015. "Analysis: China's Xi Jinping amasses power in huge corruption crackdown." January 1. https://www.nbcnews.com/storyline/2014-year-in-review/analysis-chinas-xi-jinping-amasses-power-huge-corruption-crackdown-n270001 (last accessed May 22, 2025)

Netflix. 2020. *Pandemic: How to Prevent an Outbreak*. Episode 6. https://www.netflix.com/gb/title/81026143?trackId=14170289&tctx=1%2C0%2Ceae41428-ce7f-49a1-9136-7342ae072f17-43976236%2CNES_3DB9C1689DAED6D5A12F2277E9826F-994911DC4F528C-DD619CB78E_p_1746720529191%2CNES_3DB9C1689DAED6D5A12F2277E9826F_p_1746720529191%2C%2C%2C%2C81026143%2CVideo%3A81048763%2CdetailsPageEpisodePlayButton (last accessed May 8, 2025)

New York Times. 2021. "Despite claims, Trump rarely uses wartime law in battle against Covid." 20 January. https://www.nytimes.com/2020/09/22/health/Covid-Trump-Defense-Production-Act.html (last accessed May 22, 2025)

Nunn, J. 2021. "Covid should have been a boon for Deliveroo – but it still hasn't turned a profit." *The Guardian*, March 31. https://www.theguardian.com/commentisfree/2021/mar/31/Covid-boon-deliveroo-still-hasnt-turned-a-profit (last accessed May 22, 2025)

Office for Health Improvements and Disparities. 2023. "NHS entitlements: Migrant health." *GOV.UK*, October 2. https://www.gov.uk/guidance/nhs-entitlements-migrant-health-guide (last accessed May 17, 2025)

Office for National Statistics. 2021. "GP and events in history: How the Covid-19 pandemic shocked the UK economy." https://www.ons.gov.uk/economy/grossdomesticproductgdp/articles/gdpandeventsinhistoryhowtheCovid19pandemicshockedtheukeconomy/2022-05-24 (last accessed May 22, 2025)

Office of the Commissioner of the Ministry of Foreign Affairs of the People's Republic of China in Macao Special Administrative. 2021. "Wang Yi hosts the first meeting of the international forum on Covid-19 vaccine cooperation." August 5. http://mo.ocmfa.gov.cn/eng/zxxw/szyw/202108/t20210806_8902522.htm (last accessed May 22, 2025)

Oppermann, K. 2017. "'Brexit' and the politics of resilience in the US-UK special relationship." June. https://www.ippapublicpolicy.org/file/paper/5941755d543af.pdf (last accessed May 22, 2025)

Oxford Business Group. 2020. "Covid-19: A win for regionalisation?" May 28. https://oxfordbusinessgroup.com/articles-interviews/Covid-19-a-win-for-regionalisation (last accessed January 16, 2025)

Parry, J. 2003. "United Kingdom has its first confirmed case of SARS." *BMJ*, May 24. https://www.ncbi.nlm.nih.gov/pmc/articles/PMC514033/ (last accessed May 22, 2025)

Pekosz, A. 2020. "No, Covid-19 is not the Flu." *John Hopkins Bloomberg School of Public Health*, October 20. https://publichealth.jhu.edu/2020/no-Covid-19-is-not-the-flu (last accessed May 22, 2025)

Pelcastre, I.F. 2020. "The success and failures of Trump's Twitter diplomacy." *Fair Observer*, May 25. https://www.fairobserver.com/region/north_america/ivan-farias-pelcastre-donald-trump-twitter-diplomacy-us-foreign-policy-news-14771/ (last accessed May 22, 2025)

Petriat, P. 2020. "The painful history of epidemics in Saudi Arabia." *Orient XXI*, May 21. https://orientxxi.info/magazine/the-painful-history-of-epidemics-in-saudi-arabia,3895 (last accessed May 22, 2025)

Pew Research Center. 2018. "An examination of the 2016 electorate, based on validated voters." August 9. https://www.pewresearch.org/politics/2018/08/09/an-examination-of-the-2016-electorate-based-on-validated-voters/ (last accessed May 22, 2025)

Pew Research Center. 2020. "Saudi Arabia's Mohammed bin Salman garners little trust from people in the region and the U.S." January 29. https://www.pewresearch.org/fact-tank/2020/01/29/saudi-arabias-mohammed-bin-salman-garners-little-trust-from-people-in-the-region-and-the-u-s/ (last accessed May 22, 2025)

Phillips, M. 2020. "Trump lashes out at Woodward book as a 'political hit job' as McEnany defends president over coronavirus comments." *Fox News*, September 9. https://www.foxnews.com/politics/mcenany-trump-woodward-coronavirus (last accessed May 22, 2025)

Pisani, N. 2020. "Trump's China 'decoupling' and coronavirus: Why 2020 upheaval won't kill globalization." *The Conversation*, September 9. https://theconversation.com/trumps-china-decoupling-and-coronavirus-why-2020-upheaval-wont-kill-globalisation-145814 (last accessed May 22, 2025)

Pondo, A. 2020. "How Covid-19 is different from other coronaviruses." *Tampa General Hospital*, April 23. https://www.tgh.org/news/tgh-health-news/2020/april/how-Covid-19-is-different-from-other-coronaviruses (last accessed May 22, 2025)

Prabhu, M. 2021. "A deadly alliance-war and the pandemic influenza of 1918." *Gavi*, July 30. https://www.gavi.org/vaccineswork/deadly-alliance-war-and-pandemic-influenza-1918 (last accessed May 22, 2025)

Prater, E. 2022. "Will Covid ever end? A forgotten pandemic from the late 1800s might offer some clues." *Fortune*, April 23. https://fortune.com/2022/04/23/when-will-Covid-end-meet-the-russian-flu-forgotten-pandemic-coronavirus-Covid-19-sars-cov-2-omicron-fauci/ (last accessed May 22, 2025)

Price, P.J. 2020. "How a fragmented Country fights a pandemic." *The Atlantic*, March 19. https://www.theatlantic.com/ideas/archive/2020/03/how-fragmented-country-fights-pandemic/608284/ (last accessed May 22, 2025)

Prisie, M.Y.N. 2024. "Indonesia advocates for national interests in Pandemic Treaty talks." *Antara*, June 5. https://en.antaranews.com/news/315237/indonesia-advocates-for-national-interests-in-pandemic-treaty-talks (last accessed May 22, 2025)

Public Health England. 2015. "Risk assessment of Middle East Respiratory Syndrome Coronavirus (MERS-CoV)." https://assets.publishing.service.gov.uk/government/uploads/system/uploads/attachment_data/file/461192/MERS-COV_RA_sep_2015_final.pdf (last accessed May 22, 2025)

Qing, K.G., Price, M. 2020. "U.S. government releases more data on millions of businesses that took pandemic aid." *Reuters*, December 2. https://www.reuters.com/article/us-health-coronavirus-usa-aid-idUKKBN28C0AC (last accessed May 22, 2025)

Rahn, W. 2017. "A political weapon for Xi Jinping?" *DW*, October 17. https://www.dw.com/en/chinas-corruption-tiger-hunt-a-political-weapon-for-xi-jinping/a-40939473 (last accessed May 22, 2025)

Rascoe, A. 2020. "Trump resists using wartime law to get, distribute coronavirus supplies." *NPR*, March 25. https://www.npr.org/2020/03/25/821285204/trump-sends-mixed-messages-about-invoking-defense-production-act (last accessed May 22, 2025)

Reuters. 2020. "Saudi Arabia announces first case of coronavirus." March 2. https://www.reuters.com/article/us-health-coronavirus-saudi-idUSKBN20P2FK (last accessed May 22, 2025)

Reuters. 2024. "Global pandemic treaty to be concluded by 2025, WHO says." June 1. https://www.reuters.com/business/healthcare-pharmaceuticals/global-pandemic-treaty-be-concluded-by-2025-who-says-2024-06-01/ (last accessed May 22, 2025)

Roberts, W. 2021. "MBS approved to capture or kill Khashoggi: US report." *Al Jazeera*, February 26. https://www.aljazeera.com/news/2021/2/26/mbs-oversaw-saudi-killers-of-khashoggi-us-intel-report (last accessed May 22, 2025)

Roos, R. 2003. "SARS cases reach 115 in US, but most patients have recovered." *CIDRAP*, April 4. https://www.cidrap.umn.edu/sars/sars-cases-reach-115-us-most-patients-have-recovered (last accessed May 22, 2025)

Roos, R. 2008. "Indonesia details reasons for withholding H5N1 viruses." *CIDRAP*, July 15. https://www.cidrap.umn.edu/avian-influenza-bird-flu/indonesia-details-reasons-withholding-h5n1-viruses (last accessed May 22, 2025)

Roos, R. 2013. "Saudis to send animal samples to US in MERS-CoV probe." *CIDRAP*, May 24. https://www.cidrap.umn.edu/mers-cov/saudis-send-animal-samples-us-mers-cov-probe (last accessed May 22, 2025)

Rosenbaum, M. 2017. "Local voting figures shed new light on EU referendum." BBC, February 6. https://www.bbc.co.uk/news/uk-politics-38762034 (last accessed May 22, 2025)

Rudd, K. 2018. "Kevin Rudd speaks to the Lee Kuan Yew school of public policy: Xi Jinping, China and the global order – The significance of China's 2018 central foreign policy work conference." June 26. https://www.kevinrudd.com/archive/2018-06-26-kevin-rudd-speaks-to-the-lee-kuan-yew-school-of-public-policy-xi-jinping-china-and-the-global-order-the-significance-of-chinas-2018-central-foreign-policy-work-conference (last accessed January 6, 2023)

Sala, I.M. 2020. "Hong Kong's coronavirus panic buying isn't hysteria, it's unresolved trauma." *Quartz*, February 12. https://qz.com/1798974/how-sars-trauma-made-hong-kong-distrust-beijing (last accessed May 27, 2025)

Salmon, D., Sharfstein, J.M. 2020. "Lessons for monitoring Covid-19 vaccine safety from the H1N1 pandemic." *STAT*, October 29. https://www.statnews.com/2020/10/29/lessons-h1n1-monitoring-Covid-19-vaccine-safety/ (last accessed May 22, 2025)

Schaer, C. 2021. "Saudi Arabia reforms: Royal power play or meaningful change?" *DW*, June 27. https://www.dw.com/en/saudi-arabia-reform-royal-family/a-58017860 (last accessed May 22, 2025)

Scott, E. 2021. "Lockdown 1.0 and the pandemic one year on: What do we know about the impacts?" *UK Parliament*, March 5. https://lordslibrary.parliament.uk/lockdown-1-0-and-the-pandemic-one-year-on-what-do-we-know-about-the-impacts/ (last accessed May 22, 2025)

Scroll Staff. 2020. "'It's just a flu that you need to get over': British tourists in Spain continue to party." *Scroll.in*, March 18. https://scroll.in/video/956509/its-just-a-flu-that-you-need-to-get-over-british-tourists-in-spain-continue-to-party (last accessed May 22, 2025)

Select Subcommittee on the Coronavirus Crisis. 2022. "Select subcommittee report details Trump administration's failure to prevent fraud In economic injury disaster loan program." June 14. https://coronavirus.house.gov/news/press-releases/select-subcommittee-report-details-trump-administration-s-failure-prevent-fraud (last accessed May 22, 2025)

Serrieh, J. 2020. "Coronavirus: Saudi Arabia activates thermal cameras in Medina's Prophet's Mosque." *Al Arabiya English*, April 17. https://english.alarabiya.net/coronavirus/2020/04/17/Coronavirus-Saudi-Arabia-activates-thermal-cameras-in-Medina-s-Prophet-s-Mosque (last accessed May 22, 2025)

Serwer, A. 2020. "Birtherism of a nation." *The Atlantic*, May 14. https://www.theatlantic.com/ideas/archive/2020/05/birtherism-and-trump/610978/ (last accessed May 22, 2025)

Settle, M. 2022. "Boris Johnson accused of 'appalling authoritarianism' after large swathes of England placed under tough Covid restrictions." *The Herald Scotland*, November 26. https://www.heraldscotland.com/news/18900686.boris-johnson-accused-appalling-authoritarianism-large-swathes-england-placed-tough-Covid-restrictions/ (last accessed May 22, 2025)

Shapiro, J. 2020. "Britain voted for independence, but it has achieved isolation." *European Council on Foreign Relations*, January 20. https://ecfr.eu/article/commentary_britain_voted_for_independence_but_it_has_achieved_isolation/ (last accessed January 13, 2023)

Shinh, R. 2021. "Pandemic bonds: What are they and how do they work?" *GOV.UK*, March 2. https://actuaries.blog.gov.uk/2021/03/02/pandemic-bonds-what-are-they-and-how-do-they-work/ (last accessed May 22, 2025)

Siddiqui, U. 2023. "What do we know about new Covid variant XBB.1.5?" *Al Jazeera*, January 14. https://www.aljazeera.com/news/2023/1/14/what-is-the-new-Covid-variant-xbb-1-5 (last accessed May 22, 2025)

Siripurapu, A. 2025 "What is the defense production act?" *Council on Foreign Relations*, May 22. https://www.cfr.org/in-brief/what-defense-production-act (last accessed May 20, 2025)

Sky News. 2022. "Lifting of lockdowns in major Chinese cities signals shift in Covid stance after wave of protests." December 1. https://news.sky.com/story/lifting-of-lockdowns-in-major-chinese-cities-signals-shift-in-Covid-stance-after-wave-of-protests-12759167 (last accessed May 22, 2025)

Sloane, R. 2019. "Is Trump's declaration of a National Emergency Constitutional?" *The Record*. https://www.bu.edu/law/record/articles/2019/is-trumps-declaration-of-a-national-emergency-constitutional/ (last accessed May 22, 2025)

Solly, M. 2020. "What we can learn from 1918 influenza diaries." *Smithsonian Magazine*, April 13. https://www.smithsonianmag.com/history/what-we-can-learn-1918-influenza-diaries-180974614/ (last accessed May 22, 2025)

Soussi, A. 2018. "The Spanish flu epidemic and its impact on the Middle East." *The National*, February 10. https://www.thenationalnews.com/lifestyle/the-spanish-flu-pandemic-and-its-impact-on-the-middle-east-1.703289 (last accessed May 22, 2025)

Sparrow, A. 2021. "The Chinese government's cover-up killed health care workers worldwide." *Foreign Policy*, March 18. https://foreignpolicy.com/2021/03/18/china-Covid-19-killed-health-care-workers-worldwide/ (last accessed May 22, 2025)

Stevens, R. 2020. "UK: Johnson government uses coronavirus crisis to seize dictatorial powers." *World Socialist Website*, March 20. https://www.wsws.org/en/articles/2020/03/20/emer-m20.html (last accessed May 22, 2025)

Storey, H. 2019. "After Khashoggi: A Saudi pivot to Russia and China?" *Foreign Brief*, February 8. https://www.foreignbrief.com/middle-east/after-khashoggi-a-saudi-pivot-to-russia-and-china/ (last accessed May 22, 2025)

Strickler, L. 2021. "Trump gave an agency $100 million to fight Covid. Here's what happened." *NBC News*, November 17. https://www.nbcnews.com/health/trump-gave-agency-100-million-fight-Covid-s-happened-rcna5692 (last accessed May 22, 2025)

Stronski, P. 2021. "What went wrong with Russia's Sputnik V vaccine rollout?" *Carnegie Endowment*, November 15. https://carnegieendowment.org/2021/11/15/what-went-wrong-with-russia-s-sputnik-v-vaccine-rollout-pub-85783 (last accessed May 22, 2025)

Summers, J. 2020. "Timeline: How Trump has downplayed the coronavirus pandemic." *NPR*, October 2. https://www.npr.org/sections/latest-updates-trump-Covid-19-results/2020/10/02/919432383/how-trump-has-downplayed-the-coronavirus-pandemic (last accessed May 22, 2025)

Swaine, J. 2016. "Boris Johnson distinguishes Brexit from Donald Trump's 'America First' policy." *The Guardian*, July 22. https://www.theguardian.com/politics/2016/jul/22/boris-johnson-distances-brexit-donald-trump-isolationism (last accessed May 22, 2025)

Sweney, M. 2020. "Streaming services add 4.6m new subscribers during UK lockdown." *The Guardian*, May 15. https://www.theguardian.com/media/2020/may/15/streaming-services-uk-netflix-amazon-prime-video-disney-subscribers-coronavirus (last accessed May 22, 2025)

Tang, F. 2020. "Coronavirus: China unveils $500 billion fiscal stimulus, but refrains from going all-in." *South China Morning Post*, May 22. https://www.scmp.com/economy/china-economy/article/3085654/coronavirus-china-unveils-us500-billion-fiscal-stimulus (last accessed May 21, 2025)

Tanne, J.H. 2005. "Royalty payments to staff researchers cause new NIH troubles." *BMJ*. https://pmc.ncbi.nlm.nih.gov/articles/PMC545012/ (last accessed May 22, 2025)

Time. 2018. "Saudi Arabian Crown Prince Mohammed bin Salman talks to time about the middle East, Saudi Arabia's plans and president Trump." April 5. https://time.com/5228006/mohammed-bin-salman-interview-transcript-full/ (last accessed May 22, 2025)

Together TV n.d. "Together for good – mutual aid Covid-19." https://www.togethertv.com/together-good-mutual-aid-Covid19 (last accessed May 22, 2025)

Travers, T. 2020. "Persuading fearful Britons to venture out again is the government's next challenge." *LSE*, May 1. https://blogs.lse.ac.uk/Covid19/2020/05/01/persuading-fearful-britons-to-venture-out-again-is-the-governments-next-challenge/ (last accessed May 22, 2025)

Trump, D. 2020. "Read President Trump's speech on coronavirus pandemic: Full transcript." *The New York Times*, March 11. https://www.nytimes.com/2020/03/11/us/politics/trump-coronavirus-speech.html (last accessed May 21, 2025)

Trust for America's Health. 2015. *Top Actions the United States Should Take to Prepare for MERS-CoV and Other Emerging Infections.* June. https://www.tfah.org/report-details/issue-brief-top-actions-the-united-states-should-take-to-prepare-for-mers-cov-and-other-emerging-infections/ (last accessed May 22, 2025)

Turak, N. 2020. "Saudi Arabia announces $32 billion in emergency funds to mitigate oil, coronavirus impact." *CNBC*, March 20. https://www.cnbc.com/2020/03/20/coronavirus-and-oil-saudi-arabia-announces-32-billion-stimulus.html (last accessed May 22, 2025)

UK Research and Innovation Council. 2020. "What is coronavirus? The different types of coronaviruses." March 25. https://coronavirusexplained.ukri.org/en/article/cad0003/ (last accessed May 22, 2025)

Waldersee, V. 2020. "Could the new coronavirus weaken 'anti-vaxxers'?" *Reuters*, April 11. https://www.reuters.com/article/us-health-coronavirus-antivax-idUSKCN21T089 (last accessed May 22, 2025)

Walker, S. 2020. "Authoritarian leaders may use Covid-19 crisis to tighten grip." *The Guardian*, March 31. https://www.theguardian.com/world/2020/mar/31/coronavirus-is-a-chance-for-authoritarian-leaders-to-tighten-their-grip (last accessed May 22, 2025)

Walsh, F. 2022. "AstraZeneca vaccine: Did nationalism spoil UK's 'gift to the world'?" BBC, February 7. https://www.bbc.co.uk/news/health-60259302 (last accessed May 22, 2025)

Wang, J. 2021. "China's legal response to Covid-19." *Lex Atlas*, May 12. https://lexatlas-c19.org/chinas-legal-response-to-Covid-19/ (last accessed May 22, 2025)

Wapner, J. 2020. "Covid-19: Medical expenses leave many Americans deep in debt." *BMJ*, August 14. https://www.bmj.com/content/370/bmj.m3097 (last accessed May 22, 2025)

Webber, E. 2022. "UK's Liz Truss admits US trade deal out of reach." *Politico*, September 20. https://www.politico.eu/article/liz-truss-admits-us-trade-deal-out-of-reach/ (last accessed May 22, 2025)

Weinberg, A. 2020. "During the 1918 Flu's second spike, Americans resisted social distancing. Could that happen again?" *Mother Jones*, June 11. https://www.motherjones.com/coronavirus-updates/2020/06/coronavirus-flu-pandemic-mask-protests/ (last accessed May 22, 2025)

Wheaton, S. 2020. "Chinese vaccine would be 'global public good', Xi says." *Politico*, May 18. https://www.politico.com/news/2020/05/18/chinese-vaccine-would-be-global-public-good-xi-says-265039 (last accessed May 22, 2025)

WHO. 2021. "The true death toll of Covid-19." May 20. https://www.who.int/data/stories/the-true-death-toll-of-Covid-19-estimating-global-excess-mortality (last accessed May 22, 2025)

Wintour, P. 2020. "Why did Donald Trump exclude the UK from his coronavirus travel ban?" *The Guardian*, March 12. https://www.theguardian.com/us-news/2020/mar/12/donald-trumps-eu-travel-ban-is-driven-by-politics-not-science-coronavirus (last accessed May 22, 2025)

Wolffe, R. 2019. "Johnson and Trump: Two leaders afraid to do the hard work of running a country." *The Guardian*, September 6. https://www.theguardian.com/commentisfree/2019/sep/06/boris-and-donald-two-leaders-afraid-to-do-the-hard-work-of-running-a-country (last accessed May 22, 2025)

World Health Organization. 2022. "One year since the emergence of Covid-19 virus variant Omicron." November 25. https://www.who.int/news-room/feature-stories/detail/one-year-since-the-emergence-of-omicron (last accessed May 22, 2025)

Zampano, G. 2019. "China's Qu Dongyu elected as new FAO general director." *US News*, June 23. https://www.usnews.com/news/world/articles/2019-06-23/un-food-agency-members-vote-to-elect-new-director-general (last accessed January 6, 2025)

Zhai, Z. 2016. "Referendums and policy decision making: The Brexit example." *Policy Perspectives*, November 20. https://policy-perspectives.org/2016/11/20/referendums-and-policy-decision-making-the-brexit-example/ (last accessed May 22, 2025)

Printed/Online Books and Book Chapters

Bonikowski, B. 2019. "Trump's Populism: The Mobilization of Nationalist Cleavages and the Future of US Democracy." In *When Democracy Trumps Populism*, edited by Madrid R.L., Weyland, K. Cambridge University Press, pp. 110–31

Chan, C., Tsui, A. 2022. "26: Hong Kong: From Democratic Protests to Medical Workers' Strikes in a Pandemic." In *Social Movements and Politics during Covid-19: Crisis, Solidarity and Change in a Global Pandemic*, edited by Bringel, B., Pleyers, G. Bristol University Press, pp. 202–8

Christakis, N.A. 2020. *Apollo's Arrow: The Profound and Enduring Impact of Coronavirus on the Way We Live*. Little, Brown Spark

Due-Gundersen, N. 2022. *Non-Democratic Legitimacy during the Arab Spring: Defending Dictatorship*. Palgrave Macmillan

Gravante, T., Poma, A. 2022. "20: 'Solidarity Not Charity': Emotions as Cultural Challenge for Grassroots Activism." In *Social Movements and Politics during Covid-19: Crisis, Solidarity and Change in a Global Pandemic*, edited by Bringel, B., Pleyers, G. Bristol University Press, pp. 155–62

Kavada, A. 2022. "19: Creating a Hyperlocal Infrastructure of Care: Covid-19 Mutual Aid Groups in the UK." In *Social Movements and Politics during Covid-19: Crisis, Solidarity and Change in a Global Pandemic*, edited by Bringel, B., Pleyers, G. Bristol University Press, pp. 147–54

Kim, J., Sangubotla, R. 2021. "Chapter 19 – Covid-19 and Its Effects on Neurological Expressions." In *Pandemic Outbreaks in the 21st Century: Epidemiology, Pathogenesis, Prevention, and Treatment*, edited by Viswanath, B. Academic Press, pp. 287–92

Porta, D. 2022. *Contentious Politics in Emergency Critical Junctures*. Cambridge University Press

Searle, J. 1965. "What Is a Speech Act?" In *Philosophy in America*, edited by Black, M. Allen and Unwin, pp. 221–39

International Organization and Government Reports

AlDhabaan & Partners. 2020. *Coronavirus (Covid-19) in Saudi Arabia*

Congressional Budget Office. 2021. *Research and Development in the Pharmaceutical Industry*, April

de Haan, E., Kate, A. 2023. *Pharma's Pandemic Profits: Pharma Profits from Covid-19 vaccines*. SOMO, February

Human Rights Watch. 2019. *The High Cost of Change: Repression under Saudi Crown Prince Tarnishes Reforms*.

Lobo, F. 2024. "The vaccine industry after the Covid-19 pandemic: An international perspective." *Research Paper 203*, South Centre, July 11

Oxfam. 2021. "Pfizer, BioNTech and Moderna making $1,000 profit every second while world's poorest countries remain largely unvaccinated." *Reliefweb*, November 16 https://reliefweb.int/report/world/pfizer-biontech-and-moderna-making-1000-profit-every-second-while-world-s-poorest (last accessed May 22, 2025)

UNI Global Union. 2020. *Amazon and the Covid-19 Crisis: Essentially Irresponsible*

United Nations Saudi Arabia. 2020. *Socio-Economic Impact of Covid-19 in the Kingdom of Saudi Arabia and How to Build Back Better*, November

World Bank Group. 2025. "The pandemic fund." https://fiftrustee.worldbank.org/en/about/unit/dfi/fiftrustee/fund-detail/pppr (last accessed January 14, 2025)

World Health Organization. 2013. *Evolution of a Pandemic: A (H1N1) 2009, April 2009-August 2010* (2nd edition). World Health Organization

World Health Organization. 2022. "COVAX calls for urgent action to close vaccine equity gap." May 20. https://www.who.int/news/item/20-05-2022-covax-calls-for-urgent-action-to-close-vaccine-equity-gap (last accessed May 22, 2025)

World Health Organization. 2022. Global Vaccine Market Report

World Health Organization. 2024. "Vaccine equity." https://www.who.int/campaigns/vaccine-equity (last accessed May 22, 2025)

INDEX

A
Advanced Purchase Agreements (APAs): 112–14, 116–17, 120
African Continental Free Trade Area (AfCFTA): 166–7
African Development Bank: 166
African Union: 161, 165–6
Amazon: 117–22
America First: 6, 20, 82, 103, 109, 141, 144–5, 171, 207
Amoy Gardens residential estate: 36, 61
Anti-Extradition Bill Movement (AEBM): 63
Anti-Mask League: 34, 73, 77
anti-vaxxer movements: 51, 53
Arab Spring: 58, 95, 98
Arabian Peninsula: 28–9, 35, 93
Asian Development Bank: 166
AstraZeneca: 6, 81–2, 99, 114, 153–4, 158, 171, 203, 209

B
Beijing: 28, 36–8, 41, 45, 47, 61, 66, 80–1, 90–2, 97, 103, 125, 130, 149–50, 157, 186, 191
Bezos, Jeff: 117, 122
big pharma: 6–7, 82–4, 86–7, 111–15, 122, 150, 159–61, 163–4, 167
Bin Salman, Mohammed (MBS): 1, 4, 20, 22–3, 92–8, 100, 121, 130, 132–3, 147, 151–3, 157, 159, 170–1, 198
Black Lives Matter (BLM): 69–71, 76, 86–7, 172
blood clots: 6
Brexit: 3, 6, 10, 20–1, 23, 81–2, 87, 99–105, 108–10, 120, 141, 146, 153–4, 158, 171

C
Centers for Disease Control and Prevention (CDC): 42–3, 48, 52–3, 59, 139, 142, 150, 165–6, 196, 206, 212

Clinton, Hillary: 105, 109
collectivism versus individualism: 6, 15, 66–8, 71–7
Coronavirus Act: 101–2, 134–5, 138–9
corporate actors: 6, 69–71, 82–3, 98, 111–14, 115–23, 160–1, 163–4, 167, 184
Covid-19 variants: 14, 25, 172–3
curfew: 2, 32, 98

D
Defense Production Act (DPA): 139–40, 209–11
Deliveroo: 119–21
democratic legitimacy: 20–2, 136
disinformation and misinformation: 3, 6, 32, 53, 74, 105, 140, 159, 196

E
economic performance: 5–6, 8, 10, 15–17, 19, 21–3, 44–5, 47, 69–71, 76–8, 86–7, 89–90, 92, 94–5, 97–8, 116, 120–3, 125–34, 137–8, 140, 142, 144–7, 151, 164–5, 169–71, 174, 177–92, 194, 199, 206–7, 213
emergency laws: 3, 36, 42, 51, 101, 125–6, 132, 134–5, 138–9, 143
emergency relief fund: 2, 98
European Union (EU): 7, 20, 81–2, 88, 99–100, 104, 109, 112–13, 121, 130, 141–2, 157, 159, 161, 165, 171, 176, 205, 211

F
fake news: 32, 73, 105
fatalism: 30–1
fear: 4, 6, 9, 12, 17, 19, 31, 33, 35, 49–50, 68, 72–4, 76, 131, 135, 171
First World War: 26, 29–32, 35, 72
Floyd, George: 69–70, 172
"Four Seasons Total Landscaping": 103

G

GCC (Gulf Cooperation Council): 167
Ghebreyesus, Tedros Adhanom: 167
Gillen, Charles P.: 73
Giuliani, Rudy: 103
global governance: 4, 8, 23, 80–2, 91, 103–4, 107, 109–10, 115, 130–1, 140–1, 147–52, 155, 160, 162, 164–5, 167, 170, 176, 193, 195

H

hajj: 39, 48–9, 57–8, 97, 134
Health Protection Agency (HPA): 41–3
Hong Kong: 28, 35–6, 41, 46–7, 49–50, 54, 56, 58, 61–3, 66, 176, 178, 186, 193
Hong Kong SARS Expert Committee Report: 41

I

International Health Regulations (IHR): 161–2

J

Jiabao, Wen: 37, 90
Jinping, Xi: 4, 22, 81, 88–91, 93, 95–7, 100, 103, 106, 110, 121, 125–32, 147–50, 152, 154, 157, 159, 169, 171, 173–4, 176, 178–9, 191, 193–4
Jintao, Hu: 37, 89–90, 125
Johnson, Boris: 2–5, 31, 99–105, 108–10, 121, 126, 129, 134–9, 141–6, 148, 153–4, 156, 158–9, 169–71, 203

K

Kennedy Jr., Robert F.: 168
Keqiang, Li: 4, 92, 123, 125–31, 135, 146, 169, 174
King Salman: 4, 22, 92, 94–5, 97, 132–3, 146, 151, 169, 198
Kushner, Jared: 52–3, 139, 145, 208

L

lockdown: 1–3, 9, 12, 14–17, 24, 28, 32, 38, 44, 55, 63, 66, 75, 92, 98, 101–3, 116–17, 121, 123, 125, 129, 131, 133–9, 143–6, 155, 159, 169–70, 172, 201
London: 1–2, 32, 41, 52, 58, 97, 120

M

Mecca: 29–30, 35, 39–40, 48–9, 57–8, 132
Mexico: 44–5, 52–3, 72, 74, 105, 107, 109
Moderna: 6, 82, 110–11, 113–16, 155, 157, 209
mutual aid groups: 10–13, 16, 69, 74, 76

N

national emergency: 2, 138–9, 142, 203
National Preparedness and Response Plan: 45
New York: 1, 103, 109, 116
NHS (National Health Service): 2–5, 11, 31–2, 41–2, 99, 135–8, 142, 201–3
nondemocratic legitimacy: 20, 128, 130–1, 133

O

Obama administration: 51, 104–5, 107, 214
Omicron: 14, 25, 172
"One Country, Two Systems": 61–2, 193
One Health approach: 160
online activism: 15–16, 55–6, 64–6, 77
Operation Warp Speed: 82, 155, 157, 207–8, 213–14

P

Pandemic: How to Prevent an Outbreak: 1
pandemic bonds: 164–5
Pandemic Fund: 165
Partygate: 135, 138
Personal Protective Equipment (PPE): 25, 38, 42–3, 52–3, 57, 97, 139, 204
Pfizer: 6, 19, 82, 110–16, 155, 157, 209
Political Cosmopolitanism and Political Nationalism: 23, 79–80, 82, 86, 130, 141, 146–54, 156–8, 160–1, 163–5, 170–1
political legitimacy: 4–5, 10, 15, 17, 20–3, 34, 38, 63, 66–7, 78–9, 86–7, 89, 103, 121–3, 125–9, 131–3, 136–8, 140–1, 149, 171, 173
political persuasion: 4, 17, 127, 130–1, 172–3
populism: 6, 10, 23, 71–4, 77–8, 89, 99–105, 108–9, 121, 140, 157

Porta, Donatella della: 5–6, 8, 17, 60, 66, 68–9, 71, 78, 85, 108, 121, 164, 172
protest: 5, 8–9, 12, 15, 25, 34, 38, 43, 58, 61–3, 70, 74, 76, 92, 95, 98, 105, 108, 121, 131, 133–4, 138, 171–3

R
regionalization: 166–7
restrictions: 4–5, 8–9, 17, 27, 32–3, 36, 39–40, 42–6, 63, 67–8, 72–3, 75, 86–7, 98, 102–3, 121–3, 125–6, 129, 131–6, 141–4, 146, 169–70, 172–3, 176–7, 183, 205
Riyadh: 1, 47, 94, 96–8, 121, 132, 146–7, 151–2, 194, 198, 200
Ritz-Carlton purge: 96
Russia: 7, 27, 51, 97, 110, 150

S
Saudi Arabia: 1, 9, 22, 28–9, 35, 39–40, 43, 47–9, 54, 56–8, 66–7, 76–7, 80, 86, 92–8, 102, 108, 121–3, 130, 132–7, 144, 146–7, 151–4, 157, 159, 167, 169–72, 197–200
Searle, John: 4–5, 17, 127
Shanghai: 14–16, 28, 61, 63, 66, 90, 175
Sinophobia: 72, 140
Sinovac: 111, 113
social distancing: 1, 5–6, 34, 46, 51, 57, 68, 71, 77, 101, 117, 121, 206
social inequality: 9, 16, 19, 63, 68–71, 73–4, 76–7, 85–7, 98, 116, 123, 131, 159, 162–4, 171–2
social media: 3, 6, 16, 55, 64–7, 74, 77, 105–8, 145, 172
social movements: 5, 8–9, 13–15, 17, 60, 64, 66, 71, 74, 76–8, 85–7, 109, 121, 162, 171–2
social spaces: 1, 13–14, 27, 32, 44, 61, 63–8, 71–3, 76–7, 98, 201
soft power: 8, 20, 80–1, 86, 91, 93, 121, 131, 147–8, 150–1, 157
Speech Acts: 4–5, 127, 133, 136, 140, 142–4, 148–9, 151–4, 156
Sputnik vaccine: 7
statism: 4, 7, 13, 17, 23, 82, 91, 123, 141, 149, 155–6, 160–1, 164–6
Sunak, Rishi: 119
super spreaders: 35
Sykes, Mark: 29
Sykes-Picot Agreement: 29

T
Territorialization, De-territorialization and Re-territorialization (TDR): 14, 63–4, 76–7
Together TV: 11–12
travel ban: 2–3, 22, 36, 38–40, 43, 52, 62, 98, 105–6, 135, 141–5, 205
Trump, Donald J.: 2, 4, 6, 19–20, 22, 52–3, 69, 71–4, 80–2, 91, 93, 103–10, 121, 138–46, 148, 151, 153, 155–8, 166–8, 170–1, 205, 211, 213

U
UK SARS Task Force: 41–3
umbrella movement: 61, 63

V
vaccine diplomacy: 8, 20, 22–3, 80–2, 86, 115, 121, 123, 131, 146–50, 153–4, 157–60, 170, 172
vaccine nationalism: 7, 17, 19–20, 23, 45, 48–50, 52, 58, 78–82, 86–7, 99, 111, 113, 115, 123, 146–50, 153–9, 161, 164, 170–2, 195
vaccine royalty system: 83–4
vaccine safety: 50–2
viral sovereignty: 8, 17, 19, 23, 52, 78–80, 82–7, 91, 113, 121, 148, 150, 167
Vision 2030: 1, 20, 94–7, 152, 200

W
war: 3, 26, 32, 35, 107, 129, 176, 195
Weibo: 55, 64–5, 77
welfare: 10, 15–17, 61, 63, 66, 76, 81, 86–7, 98, 117, 133, 171–2, 190, 197
Wenliang, Li: 64–6, 77, 172
Whitty, Chris: 102
World Bank: 97, 165, 199
World Health Organization (WHO): 3, 8, 10, 23, 27, 36, 41, 43–6, 48–9, 52, 54, 56, 59, 79–80, 82–5, 91–2, 111, 113, 115, 117, 132, 138–9, 149, 151–2, 154–5, 158–61, 163, 167–8, 171, 195–6, 205
Wuhan: 2, 14, 20, 24, 64, 88, 92, 123, 125–6, 129, 139–40, 176–7

Z
zero-Covid policy: 14, 38, 47, 55, 92, 131, 172–3